10672498

To

Your

Ac-

mit.

EFF

LONG

Fo

CHRIST,

books create confusion when leaders of other cultures read them. The aim of this book is to discover and spotlight those 'constant' principles as far as leadership is concerned,'' says Dr. Haggai.

This book brims with scriptural principles, anecdotes from the lives of great world leaders (and biblical characters), and Dr. Haggai's own interaction with Third World and Western leaders. Its principles apply in all areas of leadership, with special usefulness in church leadership training classes. The book is designed to spur the leader's personal growth and equip him or her for greater service.

Dr. John Haggai is founder and director of the Haggai Institute for Advanced Leadership Training. Born to a Syrian father and an American mother, Dr. Haggai speaks throughout the world in leadership conferences for business, civic, and church organizations. His previous books include *How to Win Over Worry* and *New Hope for Planet Earth*. Graduates of the Haggai Institute serve in leadership posts in some eighty-two nations of the world.

Author photo by Gittings

Jacket design by Tom Williams

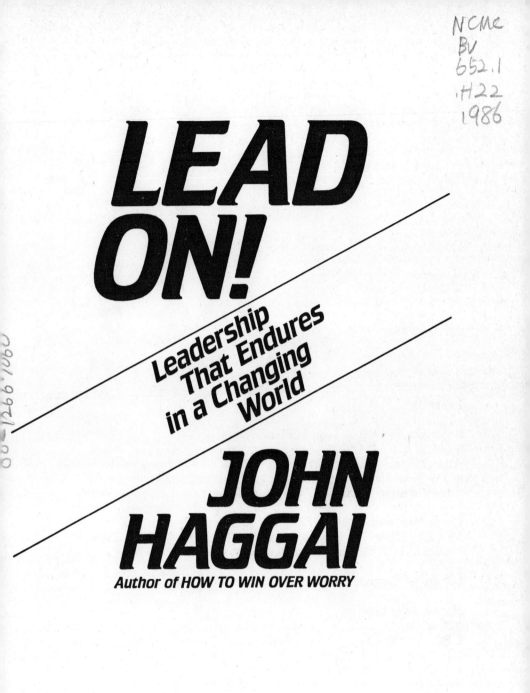

LEAD ON!

Leadership That Endures in a Changing World

JOHN HAGGAI

Author of *HOW TO WIN OVER WORRY*

WORD BOOKS
PUBLISHER
WACO, TEXAS

A DIVISION OF
WORD, INCORPORATED

Library of Congress Cataloging-in-Publication Data

Haggai, John Edmund.
  Lead On!
  Bibliography: p.
  Includes index.
  1. Christian leadership.   I. Title.
BV652.1.H22   1986   262'.1   85–22793
ISBN 0-8499-0544-3

567898 F6 987654321

Printed in the United States of America

To
Dr. Kyung Chik Han (*Han Kyung Chik*)
of Korea, whom I consider to be
the outstanding leader of my lifetime.

Contents

Foreword

Too often "attempts to analyze leadership tend to fail because the would-be analyst misconceives his task. He usually does not study leadership at all. Instead, he studies popularity, power, showmanship, or wisdom in long-range planning." So said W. C. H. Prentice, writing for the *Harvard Business Review* twenty-five years ago.[1] Prentice was right then; he's still right.

To Prentice's list of misconceptions, I could add many more from present-day analysts of Christian leadership: the servant spirit, organizational acumen, administrative expertise, and fervency in prayer. All of these, important as they are, fail to address the subject of leadership.

It is the identification of twelve principles of leadership that sets this book apart from others. These principles are not skills—although skills may be used to enhance them—but they are characteristics. They are those factors that make a leader different from other people. Developing these principles will help you to fulfill the responsibilities of your leadership position in the most effective way possible.

You will notice that this book centers on leaders, not simply on achievers. We thank God for those achievers who enrich our culture and who inspire by their example. However, I make a distinction between achievers and leaders. Not all achievers are leaders, although the kind of leader I'm talking about is also an achiever.

For more than twenty years I have been observing leaders from Asia, Africa, Latin America, and Oceania. I have been with heads of state and heads of corporations, with international bankers and South

Sea islanders. It was this observation that began my concentrated study of what constituted leadership.

Sixteen years ago, the Haggai Institute for Advanced Leadership Training began in Singapore. This Institute has presented the principles of leadership found in this book to influential Third World leaders. They have examined the characteristics of a true leader. They have seen how the skills they sometimes practiced by intuition could be sharpened and made more effective. These highly credentialed leaders equal and in some cases excel my Western colleagues in leadership skill. I've learned from them. This volume encompasses the principles I've heard discussed and seen expressed in the lives of these leaders.

Among the nearly 4,000 people who have been through this training are the Arab world's premier Christian author, a pastor of one of the two largest churches in the world (60,000 members and growing!), a general of the second largest army in Asia, university presidents, a former secretary of state, a former strategy chief for the Mau Maus, archbishops, celebrated doctors, media leaders, and others.

I have written this book because our world needs leaders and because I believe the cultivation of the twelve principles discussed here will make better leaders. I have also written this because of the need for such a book that bypasses Western ethnocentricity—the prejudices of race and culture.

Cultural differences do exist. What would a Westerner think if, in response to a request for directions to a certain town, a man responded in total silence . . . only pursing his lips and pointing with his chin in a certain direction? If you're from a certain area in Africa, you'd understand that your request had been answered politely.

In many areas of Asia, crossing the legs in public is rude and insulting. When I mentioned this in an address a few years ago, my father, who was born in Damascus, Syria, said, "I had a flashback while you were speaking.

"As I prepared to flee Damascus in 1912, a godly Syrian told me to watch out for modernists in some American churches. 'Modernists deny the inspiration of Scriptures and the great Bible truths like Christ's virgin birth, atoning death and resurrection from the dead.' I determined to avoid these heretics and stay true to the Bible."

Shortly after his arrival in America, my father attended the First Presbyterian Church in Bridgeport, Ohio. To his great astonishment, he saw the pastor cross his legs . . . and on the platform of all places! *Oh, oh,* he thought, *the minister must be a modernist; he has his legs crossed!* Later my father learned that crossing the legs in American society carried no stigma.

In parts of the Third World, presenting a gift with the left hand is the pinnacle of rudeness, an insult as monstrous as spitting in someone's face in the West. Why? Because the left hand is the profane hand—the one which takes care of toiletries, for example.

In the West, there's an unwritten rule that you put your face no closer than eighteen inches (4.57 centimeters) to another person. In some areas of Latin America, friends will talk almost nose to nose.

In parts of India, the leader shows his importance by tardiness. You go to a government office. They open the door and invite you in. The top man may go to his desk, take thirty minutes to read a paper while you wait; he's showing his importance.

Biblical truths span *all* cultures; however, their specific application must be tailored to each culture. Because this is not done, many good books create confusion when leaders of other cultures read them. Still, certain principles remain constant. Laws are constant. The law of gravity never changes. The laws of physics remain the same. And since God is the lawmaker, He is the architect of these constants. The aim of this book is to discover and spotlight these constants as far as leadership is concerned.

My major sources have been the Bible and the analysis of men and women who have deliberately and successfully exerted a special influence of beneficial permanence on the many whom they have led toward goals of fulfilled needs. I have asked myself, "What has worked, where, and under what conditions?"

In addition to the Bible, I have read biographies, memoirs, news stories, and journals. During my 61 trips around the world and 145 intercontinental journeys, I've visited schools, farms, businesses, government headquarters, churches, publication houses, and athletic events. I've met, studied, and worked with leaders such as Dr. Han Kyung Chik of Korea—a leader whom I consider to be without peer in our world today.

Keep in mind that in this book I deal with principles, not with detailed action steps. For instance, while I discuss the principle of vision, I cannot delineate the vision God gives you. Nor can I define your personal mission. While I discuss goals, I can't spell out the steps that you must take to accomplish them. This you must do. And while I deal with the principle of love, you will have to determine how to express love. While I discuss the principle of communication, I can't put words in your mouth or at the end of your pen.

The twelve principles in this book are important not only for those who lead thousands but for those who lead small groups as well. The size of the group does not reflect the quality of the leadership.

The family is the small group that most needs leadership. The Western press screams out the news of today's revolt against leadership in the home. Worse still, in many homes there's no leadership against which to revolt!

Where normal conditions prevail, fathers, leading by love, will find in the principles of this book the insight and inspiration for leading their wives and children to undreamed of heights of abundant living.

Thomas Dixon, a self-taught and powerful clergyman, gave such leadership to his family that each of his five children matured into world Christians. Theirs is the only family in which all five children were listed in "Who's Who in America" at the same time. Each one made an impact because of the leadership of the father.

The ultimate example of leadership is Jesus. His group consisted of twelve, including one who doubted, one who denied knowing Him, and one who betrayed Him to murderers. Yet, with this small group, He changed the world.

May this book, while making clear the essential principles of leadership, help to demystify the practice of leadership. I hope it will encourage those who should be leading to overcome the fear of risk. I pray that it will help you to rise to your full potential.

Look over the table of contents. Then read the book through at a relaxed pace. After that, I suggest you study it, principle by principle. Determine which principles you need to master. Underline what you consider important to you. Note in the margin what you think should be added to, altered, or eliminated. Disagree, and write out why you disagree. Think! Then reread; rethink! Through repetition, internalize the parts of this book you deem important.

Leadership is an awesome responsibility. Develop these principles of leadership and you will see your effectiveness soar. God wants you to develop the potential He has given you. The extent to which your performance fails to live up to your potential is the extent to which you are failing God. The extent to which you are fulfilling your potential is the extent to which you are serving God.

As many writers have done, I have struggled with the shortcoming of the English language that requires a choice of "he" or "she" when referring to a word such as *leader* that has no gender. Leaders can, of course, be male or female. For expediency's sake, I have taken the traditional approach and used "he," "his," and "him" to refer to all people. I trust this will not be a stumblingblock to women leaders reading this book.

Acknowledgments

Because of her interest in my writing from my prenatal days, my mother must head the list of those I wish to acknowledge. She had been told that an unborn child is influenced by the dominating thoughts of its mother's mind during pregnancy. While she wasn't sure it was a fact, she was certain that positive, productive thoughts would have no damaging effect, and so she concentrated on my being a person of words, of letters.

Because I was a sickly child, I spent most of my boyhood days in the house. My mother used many of these hours to discuss her favorite authors and play games that revolved around famous writers. She encouraged me to keep a written diary. Aware of the great need for good writers of Christian fiction and nonfiction, she gave me books that she thought represented good writing; some of them related to leadership. One book she highly regarded was *The Investment of Influence* by Newell Dwight Hillis. Not once did she belittle my dreams.

My father, from whom I developed a great love for the Bible.

My brother Tom, with whom I have interacted for more than thirty years on the subject of leadership.

Three missionaries, all deceased, who made a profound impact on my early days, from four years of age to eighteen years of age: Paul Metzler, Carl Tanis, and Paul Fleming.

Ernest H. Watson of Australia, of whom you will read in this book.

Sir Cyril Black of Wimbledon, England.

Paul M. Cell, who first opened my eyes to the importance and teaching of the stewardship of money.

Two speech professors who taught me communications: Professor J. Manley Phelps of DePaul University and T. J. Bittikofer of Moody Bible Institute.

Matthijs Van den Heuvel of the Netherlands, Portugal, and now Switzerland, who, in the 1960s and 1970, demonstrated a leadership in Portugal that God used to bring blessings of beneficial permanence to thousands of Portugese, both Catholics and Protestants.

J. C. Massee, who influenced my life from 1928 until he passed away a few years ago at the age of 94.

Paul J. Meyer, progenitor of Success Motivation Institute of Waco, Texas. The elements of the SMART goals which I mention in chapter 3 I learned from him. Leaders in seventy-five nations concur he has produced the best motivation materials available. I have meticulously gone through more than twenty of his fifty courses during the past twenty-five years, and I recommend them without reservation. What makes them especially valuable is that Paul is a supernaturalist rather than a humanist, and everything he writes and says is predicated on his personal commitment to the Lord Jesus Christ. He understands "beneficial permanence."

Anthony D'Souza of Francis Xavier University in Bombay and faculty member of Haggai Institute in Singapore.

My younger colleague Michael Youssef, much of whose Ph.D. work focused on the father of contemporary leadership studies, Max Weber of Germany.

Benjamin Moraes of Brazil.

The late Chandu Ray of Pakistan and Australia.

George Samuel of India.

The men and women who have served on the various Haggai Institute boards of directors and trustees around the world.

Larry Stone, whose superb editing and counsel brought this book to a final conclusion and publication. Larry is one of those rare persons who can accept candor as well as express it. This made for a good relationship and an immeasurable improvement of the manuscript.

Norma Byrd, my research and literary assistant, whose expertise in checking out syntax, grammar, and structure made for greater clarity. She demonstrated dedication and attention to detail in typing and retyping the manuscript, from its inception, through its metamorphic stages, to completion.

Harold Keown, Jr., who reviewed the manuscript carefully.

S. H. Adamson, a young man who, in his twenties, presented me with a copy of *Leaders and Leadership* by Henry S. Bogardus. In the flyleaf he wrote, "To a Christian leader with the prayer that he might become an even greater leader for Christ. S. H. Adamson, 2/24/53."

Won Sul Lee of Korea, who urged me for ten years to write a book on leadership.

Paul Hiebert, who kept pressuring me to finish it as quickly as possible.

A special thanks to my wife, Christine, for patiently enduring my long stretches of preoccupation during the writing of the book.

And to a host of others whose contribution to my life and understanding have influenced this volume.

1

A Call to

LEADERSHIP

God is calling leaders. Not power holders. Not Madison Avenue hype artists. Not mutual congratulation experts. Not influence peddlers. Not crowd-manipulating, exhibitionistic demagogues. God is calling leaders!

THE LEADERSHIP CRISIS

The call for leaders is necessary because we are experiencing a crisis of leadership in our world. It is similar to the crisis of spiritual leadership eighteenth-century Europe experienced. Agnostics had been on a rampage. The books of Morgan and Hume, with their denials of all that was spiritually right and noble, were published and distributed with reckless abandon. The populace in general regarded Christianity as a pipe dream and its teachings as fit only for ridicule. Voltaire, who criticized supernaturalism, religion, and Christianity, was Europe's most popular writer. Frederick the Great of Prussia was a practical atheist. Across Europe, men were hailing the disappearance of Christianity. The deterministic, fatalistic, and materialistic teachings of these agnostics saturated the thinking of the people and snapped the fetters of moral restraint.

Revolution was raging in France. In England, every sixth house became a grog shop. In the streets of London, gin shops offered to sell "enough gin for one pence to make one drunk, or enough for two pence

1

to give a dead drunk." Free-thinking clubs were everywhere. Europe needed spiritual leaders.

A few young men knew that the only way to save the world from impending doom was a return to the message of the Bible. Men like John and Charles Wesley and George Whitfield became flaming evangels and carried the message of the Bible throughout Britain and America.

This evangelical leadership made a positive impact worldwide. John Howard instituted prison reforms in Europe. In the next century, J. Hudson Taylor founded the China Inland Mission, which by 1910 had sent out 968 missionaries. John Barnardo began his mission work in London which rescued and trained 70,000 homeless children. William Booth organized the Salvation Army which was to encircle the globe.

God used these leaders to save a civilization and to give it spiritual direction.

Just as eighteenth-century Europe needed leaders, our changing world needs leaders today. By next year at this time, there will be ninety million more people on this planet than there are today. Who will lead them? Will their leaders develop them or destroy them? Will these leaders improve our world or imperil our global village? India's annual net increase (births over deaths) exceeds the total population of Australia. What kind of leadership will these millions of people have?

Will the leaders of these new citizens of the world be honorable or corrupt? Self-sacrificing or self-aggrandizing? Humble or haughty? Will the new leaders be like Adolph Hitler, the dictator of Germany, or like Han Kyung Chik, the Christian statesman of Korea? Will they be like Al Capone, the gangster of Chicago, or John Calvin, the theologian of Geneva? Will they be like Nero, the oppressor, or Paul, the apostle?

The population explosion is frightening and real and is one cause of the crisis of leadership. Another cause of this crisis is that many in leadership positions have abdicated their responsibility.

Recently a highly placed woman educator told me, "My husband and I are weary of going to our church every Sunday and hearing our minister air his own personal problems and apprehensions. We want a word of authority, a word from God, a word to help us with our problems." Such a minister forfeits leadership and thus compounds the problems of the people in the pews. This minister demonstrates the crisis in leadership.

A top multinational executive friend of mine, who had massive personal problems, sought the help of a psychologist. Before the third session, the psychologist was seeking counsel from my friend, the patient. The psychologist demonstrated the crisis in leadership.

One celebrated head of state is known to leave his country when an emergency arises he cannot handle. On the one hand, that might be the wisdom of benign neglect; on the other hand, that may be a demonstration of the crisis in leadership.

The editor of one of the world's most prestigious multinational business journals wrote sometime ago, "What we hear in the pulpit on Sunday is what we ourselves wrote during the week. What we want to hear is a new voice, a voice from beyond . . . the voice of God." What an indictment of leaderlessness—at least in one pulpit!

This crisis of leadership trickles down from the presidency of corporations, the governorship of states, and the pulpits of churches to local leaders. There is today a crisis of leadership in the family. This is more pronounced in the West, but evidence of increased family breakdown mounts in the Third World as well. Divorce, with its growing threat, is frequently the ultimate abdication of leadership in the family. In the West, self-centeredness prevents parents from taking the time and effort to lead—not just manage—their children.

At all levels, our world's societies plead for leadership—in our educational system, in international politics, in our Christian churches. The masses look for true leadership. The world does not need a coterie of elitists who talk love and compassion while isolating themselves from *real* people. It does not need a retinue of cliché-spouting, self-avowed "quick fix" magicians. The world is looking for men and women—leaders—committed to God and compassionately concerned for people. The world needs leaders who will exert that special influence over aching people looking for a way to resolve their personal crises. This influence carries the stamp of beneficial permanence.

Through the prophet Ezekiel, God described the crisis in leadership in Ezekiel's day: "So I sought for a man among them who would make a wall, and stand in the gap before Me on behalf of the land, that I should not destroy it; but I found no one" (Ezekiel 22:30).

There are examples today of strong leadership, but they are rare. On 26 June 1983, for instance, I read William Pfaff's editorial in the *International Herald Tribune* in tribute to Pope John Paul II:

The pope has undertaken the liberation of Eastern Europe.

His program involves serious risks, but it also displays an intelligence, an understanding of history, and a power of will that is all but invisible among Western statesmen, and certainly nonexistent in today's Washington. . . .

The pope obviously does not expect a retreat of armies, collapse of alliances, unbarring of the Iron Curtain. He nonetheless means to change the terms on which the Poles and others in Eastern Europe are ruled, and to force concessions from the Communist authorities.

He seems largely indifferent to what Western governments . . . may think of this. . . . He simply does not think that Soviet Russia is all powerful and unchallengeable.[2]

We are glad when we see the kind of leadership Pope John Paul II displayed. But the crisis in leadership still exists. Who will stem the tide? Perhaps you will be the one. Will you face up to the danger and act upon the opportunity?

WHAT IS LEADERSHIP?

Before discussing leadership further, let's define the word *leadership*. If those who attempt to analyze leadership misconceive their task, as W. C. H. Prentice said, it is in part caused by a misunderstanding of what leadership is.

Leadership is the discipline of deliberately exerting special influence within a group to move it toward goals of beneficial permanence that fulfill the group's real needs.

Each word in this definition is important. *Discipline* was chosen to indicate that leaders are made, not born. There are some who intuitively exercise some of the characteristics of a leader, but true leadership is a discipline.

Deliberately indicates a commitment on the part of the leader to his calling as a leader. For all leaders, and for the Christlike leader especially, this should be a spiritual commitment. I believe that spiritual commitment strengthens the so-called secular enterprise rather than weakens it. Godly leadership carries the stamp of unique superiority anywhere in the world. In times of painful reverses, strength and wisdom are found. In times of enormous achievement, gratitude and humility are revealed.

Around the world an increasing number of leaders in all vocations unashamedly display a personal Bible on their desks, begin board meetings with prayer, and relate their activities to the principles of Scripture. I have encountered this in Japan and Fiji, in Germany and Lebanon, in Brazil and Canada, on the subcontinent of India, and the great continent of Africa.

The true leader exerts *special influence.* That influence is not forced on others. Many who think of themselves as leaders are really power-holders, exerting force on people. People follow them out of fear. A true leader's power, however, is the result of a profound trust among his followers. They are convinced that through him and with him they can realize self-enriching, humanitarian, ennobling, and God-glorifying results which would otherwise seem unlikely or impossible. True leaders are followed out of respect and love because they display love, humility, and self-control. Jesus Christ, of course, was our greatest example in this regard. He told His disciples, "If you love Me, keep My commandments" (John 14:15).

People who are in some way homogeneous are usually thought of as a *group.* In some way they are similar. Perhaps they are members of the same family or tribe with the same grandparents or ancestors. Perhaps they are members of the same church. Perhaps they are all alumni of the same school and, therefore, have all experienced a similar educational background. Or perhaps they are citizens of the same country. It is essential that the leader understand the group's sameness and all its implications.

More important than the sameness of origin, education, or nationality, however, is sameness of purpose. People feel most like a group when they are unified in purpose. Perhaps the purpose is to increase the membership of a church or to stop a law from being passed. An example of unity of purpose was President Roosevelt's mobilization of the United States to fight World War II while just a few months earlier it had been an isolationist country. An example of unity of purpose for evil was Hitler's unification of the Nazis with the purpose of exterminating the Jews and the establishment of world control.

The most important factor in forming a cohesive group is a unity of purpose. The leader's ability at fostering such unity is an important factor in his success as a leader.

The word *goals* has two meanings. Broadly, it refers to the leader's vision, his dream of what he sees his group being or doing. This concept is developed in chapter 2. It is the leader's vision that sets him apart and makes him a leader. The commitment to act upon the leader's vision becomes his mission. *Goals* also refers to a set of specific, measurable achievements designed to implement the mission. The development of effective goals is discussed in chapter 3.

Permanence refers to the fact that the vision of a leader should be for changes that are continuing, enduring, and lasting—for time and eternity. The term *beneficial permanence* contrasts with *malevolent permanence.* There have been many who have exhibited all of the characteristics or principles of a leader but who have sought goals detrimental to the group rather than for the group's benefit.

The twelve principles of leadership found in this book can be used for good or for evil. Amin, Hitler, and Nero all demonstrated powerful leadership characteristics, but their leadership corrupted, destroyed, and damned. Their leadership resulted in malevolent permanence. When parents shut off children from all access to the knowledge of God, they create a malevolent permanence.

I have written this book for those who desire to develop leadership with the dimension of beneficial permanence. The ultimate criterion is Christlike leadership. This is the leadership that most honors God and benefits all humankind.

The leader must have an understanding of the *real needs* of others. He maintains a sensitivity, a keen awareness, to the people for whom God has given him responsibility. He is attuned to his surroundings, thoroughly assesses the situation, and prepares to take action. But his sensitivity to others is always focused through the vision God has given him. He seeks to move the group toward goals that will fulfill the group's real needs—whether the group understands those needs or not. Such leadership demands foresight, wisdom, determination, and knowledge of God's will. History is full of instances when the group wanted what was *not* in its best interest. Samuel, for instance, was given permission by God to let the children of Israel choose a king so that they could be like their ungodly neighbors—even though it was not meeting their real needs. On the other hand, Abraham Lincoln moved the United States toward goals that fulfilled the real needs of the people—unity with freedom for all citizens—even though many people did not understand the beneficial permanence that would result.

Leadership, then, is the discipline of deliberately exerting special influence within a group to move it toward goals of beneficial permanence that fulfill the group's real needs.

LEADERSHIP AND CHANGE

Is this discussion of a "leadership crisis" a bit alarmist? Surely we would also have crises where there are shortages of doctors and teachers and scientists. The difference is that the leader induces and directs the change that most benefits the group. Change will occur whether there is effective leadership or not. But without positive leadership, the change will tend to be that of deterioration and destruction rather than improvement.

The crisis of leadership, therefore, occurs because constant change will not wait for a leader to appear. Our world is not like an automobile in a driveway waiting for a driver. It is rather like an automobile moving down a highway at fifty-five miles per hour. Without a driver, it will surely crash. With a driver, it will go where we want it to go.

Everything changes. There is no living thing that does not change and move. Constant change is the essence of all existence. The present becomes the past, and both determine the future. The future becomes the present. New life arises from the old.

Oscar Wilde said in his book *Soul of Man Under Socialism,* "The only thing that one really knows about human nature is that it changes. Change is the one quality we can predicate of it. The systems that fail are those that rely on the permanency of human nature, and not its growth and development." The only changeless thing about human nature is change itself! The Greek philosopher Heraclitus said that you cannot step into the same stream twice.

Financier John Templeton once told me that "a leader must encourage change." He must not simply tolerate or accept it, but a leader must actually *encourage* it. The ultraconservative thought pattern that insists on a 1950 mindset would find no ally in this seventy-year-old man's philosophy. I found it refreshing to spend time with a person who acts rather than reacts and who uses the past only to give insight into the present and direction for planning the future.

The current crisis requires millions of leaders now. The need grows every day. You can make a difference, but you will have to face up to the dangers, seize the opportunity, and pay the price.

ARE LEADERS BORN OR MADE?

Surely there are some who constitutionally will be better leaders than others. They will be better in their ability to utilize that combination of gifts that secures willing and intelligent "followership." However, through training, anyone who guides the action of others in a purposeful way can be made more influential and effective.

All things being equal, it would appear that those who lead effectively have a generous endowment of physical and emotional energy. They have a compelling drive toward a specific purpose or goal. They have a mastery of the methods of achieving the aim they profess. They are capable of sustaining the confidence, loyalty, and frequently the affection of those whom they lead. They are persuasive in enlisting followers to support the cause that demonstrably leads to the followers' own best interests.

In 1980, the *Harvard Business Review* collected fifteen articles on leadership under the title *Paths Toward Personal Progress: Leaders Are Made, Not Born.* These articles explain that like a surgeon, an astronaut, or a pulpit orator, a leader is made, not born. God may give special gifts, but these gifts will never surface if no effort is made to develop and exercise them.

A leader works toward a goal through the cooperation of people. The process of gaining their cooperation can be learned and developed. The leader motivates people's participation by insuring their personal fulfillment through involvement in the common venture.

Aptitude for leadership cannot be dismissed. Aptitude is inherited potential ability in a special field. It possesses driving power, but it is dependent upon personal discipline and social environment for ultimate expression and development.

On the other hand, since leaders are made, not born, lack of aptitude does not disqualify one from being a leader. God designed leadership roles for Moses, Jeremiah, and Paul the apostle, but they had to learn leadership skills just as a man called to the gospel ministry must learn how to preach.

A vocal teacher once told Mary Martin that she should abandon her goal to become a singer; she had an inferior voice and would never make it in the field of music. Mary Martin determined otherwise and for half a century reigned as one of America's most respected and popular singers. She overcame her aptitude deficiency by determination and exacting self-discipline.

My late brother, Ted, decided to become an electrical engineer, but his college aptitude tests put him at the bottom of the class in math. His teachers told him to forget his chosen field and select another. He refused. Day after day he worked on developing skill in math. He lost thirty pounds, and his adviser feared for his health; but by his third year in college, Ted was tutoring in math and graduated with honors. Later, he was given the L. A. Hyland award for scientific achievement.

Demosthenes suffered such speech impediments that he was embarrassed to speak to a group. He shaved one side of his head so he wouldn't be tempted to waste time by seeing anybody. He then invested agonizing hours by the sea in his unrelenting practice to overcome his speech problems. Demosthenes became the most famous orator of all time.

Just as attitude can overcome lack of aptitude in other areas of life, it can overcome lack of aptitude for leadership. In *You Can Be a Powerful Leader,* Ivan W. Fitzwater says leadership is neither an inborn trait nor an inherited tendency. He says the real difference between leaders and nonleaders is attitude.

You may not have the aptitude for leadership, yet, under God, you can develop into a leader. Think now of those God has given you to lead. If you're a child of God, and if you have a burning desire to be a leader, the very desire is His guarantee that you *can* be a leader. It will take unrelenting discipline to develop the skills needed. But you can rise above aptitude.

WHAT KIND OF LEADERSHIP?

A frightened world is looking for leadership. It is looking for those who have a vision and can deliberately exert special influence to move a group or a country toward goals of beneficial permanence that will fulfill the real needs of the people.

For the Christian, a position of leadership must lead to the pursuit of world evangelism. World evangelism is not to be a hobby with Christians, but an all-consuming priority. Thus, if the Christian is in a position of leadership over non-Christians, the foremost beneficial permanence that the leader would want for his followers is their salvation through Jesus Christ. If the Christian is in a position of leadership over other Christians, he should be motivating them to pursue world evangelism themselves. The true Christian never coerces.

Christ explicitly commanded every believer to put world evangelism in a place of priority in his life. He said, for instance, "Go therefore and make disciples of all the nations, baptizing them in the name of the Father and of the Son and of the Holy Spirit" (Matthew 28:19; see also Mark 16:15 and Acts 1:8).

There are many ways to carry out Christ's command for world evangelism. On the one hand, every attitude and action of the believer should focus on this objective. But evangelism does not just mean being a missionary or pastor. I think of late leaders such as Dr. Helen Kim, a premier educator in Korea, of Thomas F. Staley, an investment banker from Wall Street, of Eliseo Pajaro, a prominent musician from the Philippines, of John Bolten, Sr., a German-American industrialist, and of Benjamin Moraes, a jurist, linguist, professor, and pastor from Brazil. Although these were all leaders in their fields, they were all also carrying out Christ's command for world evangelism.

In this day of crisis and change, who will lead? Only the leader who recognizes the authority of Jesus Christ can point the way to true values. Only such a leader can defuse the ticking time bomb of angry people in the world. The world longs for a leader with the skill and courage to enlighten with the truth that "one's life does not consist in the abundance of the things he possesses" (Luke 12:15).

If it is your desire to be that leader with the dimension of beneficial permanence, this book can help you. The twelve principles of leadership—

vision, goalsetting, love, humility, self-control, communication, investment, opportunity, energy, staying power, authority, and awareness—
will help you understand and practice effective leadership.

SUMMARY

God is calling leaders. This call is necessary because of the crisis
of leadership, a crisis brought about by the population explosion and
the fact that our so-called leaders do not want to lead. Our world's
society pleads for leadership.

What is leadership? It is the discipline of deliberately exerting special
influence within a group to move it toward goals of beneficial permanence
that fulfill the real needs of the group.

Leadership is no option. The leadership crisis is not like a crisis
of a lack of plumbers. Our society is moving quickly and changing rapidly,
and we must be directed and led.

Leaders are made, not born. Admittedly, some people have more
aptitude for leadership than others, but aptitude alone will not make a
leader. Conversely, someone with no aptitude for leadership but with a
burning desire to lead can attain leadership success.

What kind of leadership does our world need? Bible-based, Christ-
centered leadership is the only kind that will defuse the ticking time
bomb of angry people on the earth. Such a leadership will have world
evangelism as its primary concern.

2

The Principle of

VISION

In 1863, Abraham Lincoln signed the Emancipation Proclamation that freed the slaves in America. And yet 100 years later black people in America were still the victims of segregation. In 1963, in a speech at the Lincoln Memorial, Martin Luther King, Jr., expressed his vision for America. He wanted "the riches of freedom and the security of justice" for *all* people. "*Now* is the time to open the doors of opportunity to all of God's children," he said. "*Now* is the time to lift our nation from the quicksand of racial injustice to the solid rock of brotherhood. . . .

"I say to you today, my friends, that in spite of the difficulties and frustrations of the moment I still have a dream. . . . I have a dream that one day in the red hills of Georgia the sons of former slaves and the sons of former slave owners will be able to sit down together at the table of brotherhood. I have a dream that one day even the state of Mississippi, a desert state sweltering with the heat of injustice and oppression, will be transformed into an oasis of freedom and justice. I have a dream that my four little children will one day live in a nation where they will not be judged by the color of their skin but by the content of their character. I have a dream . . . of that day when all of God's children, black men and white men, Jews and Gentiles, Protestants and Catholics, will be able to join hands and sing in the words of the old Negro spiritual, 'Free at last! Free at last! Thank God almighty, we are free at last!' "[3]

Regardless of how King's critics assess his personal character and conduct, no one can deny he had a vision and deliberately exerted special influence to move the country in which he lived toward the goals that permanently fulfilled the real needs of that country. He expressed that vision in a clearer and more moving way than most leaders. A vision such as Martin Luther King had sets a leader apart.

● Leadership begins when a vision emerges. Proverbs 29:18 says, "Where there is no vision, the people perish" (KJV). The true meaning of these words is "Without a vision, the people cast off restraint." When a group is under the direction of a person who has no vision, the result is confusion, disorder, rebellion, uncontrolled license, and—at worst—anarchy. ●

The principle of vision is the key to understanding leadership. With a clear-cut vision to which he is wholeheartedly committed, a person has taken the first step toward leadership. Without such a commitment to a vision, a person cannot be a leader but will be an imitation, playing at what he wishes he could be.

UNDERSTAND WHAT A VISION IS

A vision is a clear picture of what the leader sees his group being or doing. A vision could be of health where there is sickness—such as Albert Schweitzer had for Africa; of knowledge where there is ignorance—which motivated Gilbert Tennent to found what is now Princeton University; of freedom where there is oppression; or of love where there is hatred. From that clear picture, the leader then plans how that vision will become a reality.

When John Sung returned to his native China in 1929, after having received his Ph.D. from Ohio State University, his preacher father said, "Good, John. Now, with your education, you can get an important teaching post and provide an education for your six brothers." Chinese children always obey the direct commands of their fathers. It was unusual, therefore, for John to tell his father that he could not take a teaching post because God had called him to evangelize China and southeast Asia. John had a vision of Chinese people becoming followers of Jesus Christ, and he felt he had only fifteen years to fulfill that vision.

Over the next fifteen years, John Sung did the work of a dozen men. And, in fact, he died at the end of those fifteen years, in 1944! John Sung was committed to the fulfillment of his vision. That explains his feverish pace in carrying it out. Asia and the South Pacific are different today because of the ministry of John Sung. It all began with a vision translated into a mission and implemented by well-defined goals.

Mahatma Gandhi had a vision of a free and independent India at a time when it was governed by the British. Henry Ford had a vision of every family in America owning its own automobile at a time when most people were frightened of the new invention. William Wilberforce had a vision of the abolition of slavery at a time when slaves were a very profitable trade item for the British. Daniel K. Ludwig had a vision for a self-supporting industrial region in the heart of the Brazilian jungle at a time when there was no industry, no electricity, and no cities of any kind for hundreds of miles. Mahatma Gandhi, Henry Ford, William Wilberforce, and Daniel Ludwig committed themselves to the clear picture they had of what their group would become or do as a result of the special influence they would exert.

The vision of the leader is different from the vision of the scientist who works alone. The solitary scientist's success will benefit others, but it doesn't require the direct involvement of others. The leader, however, works through other people.

•Having a vision is not enough. There must be a commitment to act on the vision. That is called a mission. There must also be a set of specific, measurable steps to achieve the mission. Those steps are called goals. Goals design the program for achieving the mission and thus fulfilling the vision. A leader will have one vision and one mission but many goals. •

God blessed me by giving me my life's vision—the evangelization of the world—when I was only ten years old. I saw clearly people in freedom and peace under the lordship of Jesus Christ, people who had formerly lived in slavery to their sin and hatred. I committed myself to the fulfillment of that vision, and I had a mission. To pursue that life mission has required a program of many goals, including finding and maintaining buildings in Singapore to house the Haggai Institute (physical goals), reading three books a week to be aware of the cultures of the world (mental goals), building friendships with people who could share my vision and mission (social goals), raising an endowment to carry on the work of the Lord through the Institute (financial goals).

A mission is simply a vision acted upon. This is clearly illustrated by America's Apollo program.

In 1960, President John Kennedy challenged the American people with his dream of an American on the moon by 1970. That was a vision. Almost immediately, the government launched a program designed to accomplish that vision—the Apollo mission. The president communicated his vision to the American people. The people, through the government, then committed to the fulfillment of that vision with a mission. The mission required an elaborate goals program consisting of millions of individual goals.

The biblical story of Nehemiah reveals that he had a vision of a rebuilt wall around Jerusalem. Nehemiah was in captivity 1500 kilometers from Jerusalem. He was a servant, a cupbearer to King Artaxerxes of Persia. The holy city of Jerusalem had been captured and much of it destroyed. But Nehemiah had a vision of a rebuilt Jerusalem with strong walls for the glory of God. His mission was to realize the vision. Then came an elaborate system of goals to carry out the mission. His first step was prayer. Next Nehemiah presented his case to King Artaxerxes. And then he set out a plan for rebuilding the walls and overcoming opposition. Nehemiah is one of history's greatest examples of leadership.

It's one thing to be consumed by a vision for world evangelism—the picture of every person on our planet hearing the gospel in an understandable, culturally relevant way. It's even a greater thing to create a mission designed to realize the vision. And it is yet a greater undertaking to create, under God, the goals program necessary to carry out the mission and fulfill the vision.

The leader cherishes his vision. He thinks on it by day and dreams of it by night. He transfers the vision to the group. He then motivates the group to commit to the mission that will realize the vision and meet their real needs.

Continuously thinking about the vision induces action. It sounds the death knell to complacency. As the psalmist said, "My heart was hot within me; while I was musing, the fire burned" (Psalm 39:3).

UNDERSTAND WHERE A VISION COMES FROM

Any worthy vision comes from God, whether it deals with so-called "spiritual" matters or not—and whether the person with the vision is a Christian and realizes the source of the vision or not. Worthy visions are a gift of God. James said, "Every good gift and every perfect gift is from above, and comes down from the Father of lights, with whom there is no variation or shadow of turning" (James 1:17).

Our tendency is to compartmentalize our lives so that God is seen as having influence on and relevance to "spiritual" visions, missions, and goals, but little relationship to "secular" visions, missions, and goals. But St. Augustine said, "Let every Christian understand that wherever truth is found, it belongs to his Master." God is the God of *all* truth. And God is the source of *all* worthy visions.

In 1774 and 1775, the American colonies were contemplating

breaking away from England. Confusion, disagreement, and rancor threatened to undermine the purpose of the Continental Convention. Yet many of the participants had a clear vision and credited it to God. Benjamin Franklin told the Convention, "I believe that Providence guides the affairs of men, and never a sparrow falls to the ground that God does not attend its funeral, and that all the hairs of our heads are numbered. I don't believe that an empire or a republic can be launched without His help, and I move you, Mr. President, that this convention open with prayer and that we petition Divine guidance and help in the step we are about to take."

America's founders shared a vision of freedom for the colonies. To actualize that vision required a mission, implemented by a full goals program. They knew that their vision came from God.

A vision for the kind of change that will yield beneficial permanence for the group comes from God whether the leader acknowledges it or not. More than five hundred years ago, God gave King Sejong a vision of an improved language for his Korean people. King Sejong actualized his vision through a mission implemented by a goals program that gave the Koreans the first alphabet in the Orient. He did not know the God of the Bible and His Son Jesus Christ, but he successfully fulfilled the vision God had nevertheless given him.

God rules over the affairs of men. He gives vision and understanding.

Sometimes a vision may result in great wealth, and sometimes it results in relative poverty. But if it is a worthy vision, it originates with God. Paul J. Meyer started out without a dollar. At the age of twenty-five he was a millionaire. He had built the largest insurance agency in the world. His young pastor, Dr. Bill Hinson, challenged him: "Paul, you're happiest when you're helping others reach their full potential." Paul caught the vision of motivating others to achieve their full potential and left the insurance business. It didn't seem as if he would make as much money as he had done selling insurance, but he couldn't stifle the vision God had given him.

Today, Paul Meyer's Success Motivation Institute has helped thousands. Leaders in seventy-five countries point to the SMI program as the instrument that opened a new world of possibility to them. The SMI program has transformed some welfare recipients into corporate heads and university scholars.

It's tragic that so many times God's people seem impervious to the opportunities all about them. They settle for less when God wants them to master the highest echelons of achievement.

For the Christian, a vision of any kind must start with an

understanding of God. God is perfect, immutable, and eternal. Christlike leaders see God and recognize their dependence upon Him. No one can fully understand himself or his environment until his vision of God is clear.

After gaining an understanding of God, the Christian leader must understand himself. A proper self-evaluation precedes any achievement of beneficial permanence. The person who would be a leader God can use sees his potential as God sees it.

As the leader catches a vision of himself, he may be tempted, like Isaiah, to mourn, "Woe is me, for I am undone! Because I am a man of unclean lips. And I dwell in the midst of a people of unclean lips." He may feel, like Moses, that inadequacy disqualifies him for the job. But God will work through the sinner, through the inadequate person, if that person has faith not in his own power but in the power of God— the God who provided the vision to begin with. It requires faith to cherish the vision, convert the vision into a mission, implement it with a proper goals program, and mobilize others to fulfill their own real needs. The Christlike leader must not only have an understanding of God and of himself, but he must also have an understanding of the real needs of others. His sensitivity to others is always focused through the vision God has given him. Without a vision, awareness and sensitivity to the needs of others leads only to corrosion of the spirit and confusion of the mind.

UNDERSTAND WHY A VISION IS IMPORTANT

Without a wholehearted commitment to a vision, you cannot be a leader. You may be in a leadership position, you may be a manager, but what separates the true leaders from others is vision. A vision is important because it is a key factor in successful leadership.

Vision underlies and underpins all leadership. Without a vision, there will not be an adequate mission. Without a mission, there is no possibility of a productive goals program. Without a goals program, there is no leadership. Without leadership, the world will languish in sin and sorrow. Leadership begins with a vision.

A manager can preside over the status quo, but it takes a leader to motivate people to accomplish those changes that meet their real needs. While the world needs managers today, the world's most desperate need is for leaders. And what sets a leader apart from a manager is that a manager does not encourage change, whereas a leader demands change because he is moving a group toward goals of beneficial permanence. A leader has a vision.

A vision is important because it is the foundation of all true leadership. The significance of a person's leadership depends on the "bigness" of his vision. Prime Minister Lee Kuan Yew of Singapore had a significant vision that affected not only his own nation, but all of southeast Asia. His influence has rippled across the world. A father may have a vision for the educational or spiritual goals of his family that is less significant because it affects fewer people. For those people, however, the vision is no less important. While the significance of a leader's vision depends on the bigness, the effectiveness of a person's leadership depends on how well he moves the group toward the fulfillment of his vision—and their real needs.

UNDERSTAND WHO MUST GRASP THE VISION

Both the leader and the followers must grasp the vision. Leadership starts with a vision on the part of the leader, but for the followers to give credence to the leader's direction, they must understand the vision too. A major responsibility of the leader, therefore, is to accurately communicate his vision to his group. He must make the definition and dimension of the vision clear to the followers. How to do this is more fully developed in chapter 7 on the principle of communication.

The leader's grasp of the vision begins with a clear understanding not only of his own vision, but of his potential under God. He must know that God created him to be somebody, and then he is to fulfill the vision God gave him. Paul the apostle said, "Not that I have already attained, or am already perfected; but I press on, that I may lay hold of that for which Christ Jesus has also laid hold of me" (Philippians 3:12). Paul knew his shortcomings, yet he kept moving toward the accomplishment of his mission, for he knew "I can do all things through Christ who strengthens me" (Philippians 4:13).

Peter Daniels of Adelaide, Australia, helps people realize their potential under God. He has demonstrated himself the potential that is in a person. When he became a follower of Jesus Christ at the age of twenty-six, he could neither read nor write. He was profane, broke, and belligerent. He had been tossed from one broken home to another. God saved him, and Peter grasped a vision of his possibilities and keeps growing with unabated consistency.

Today, Peter Daniels is wealthy, literate, influential, and is one of Australia's outstanding speakers. He has committed his wealth to the expansion of God's kingdom. He has invested his influence in service through four international boards. Peter Daniels asks four questions of those who yearn for meaning in their lives:[4]

1. What is the age you have set as your goal for reaching your full potential that God might maximize your life?

2. Tell me in fifty pages or more what your full potential is in every area of your life. (Daniels requires at least fifty pages. Otherwise, a person could put down a few words which, Daniels says, would be "frivolous." Forcing people to write at least fifty pages drives them to assess the sincerity of their concern.)

3. Accepting your potential as 100 percent, what percentage rating do you give yourself right now?

4. Accepting the deficiency between the two scores, what plan have you made to make up the difference and when will you accomplish that plan?

Responding to these four questions could take the better part of a day. But when a person responds fully and honestly, a clear picture of the situation emerges. Peter Daniels' four questions are designed to develop what I call "inspirational dissatisfaction." These questions are designed to point out the difference between where you could be if you were living at your full potential and where you are now—and what you should do to get to your full potential. Without inspirational dissatisfaction, a person would make peace with the status quo, he would not see a need for change, could not grasp a vision of growth, and could not step out in faith. Inspirational dissatisfaction is an essential step to grasping a vision.

Inspirational dissatisfaction is different from a morose, brooding, cynical dissatisfaction that impels one to withdraw into a shell or, on the other hand, aggressively criticize the alleged reasons for his dissatisfaction. Inspirational dissatisfaction inspires a person to high attainment. Despondent dissatisfaction paralyzes the action nerve, corrodes the spirit, and wrecks the life.

Look again at Nehemiah. Inspirational dissatisfaction preceded his vision and leadership. The wall of Jerusalem was broken down. The gates had been burned. Travelers told of the affliction and reproach of God's people. Nehemiah sat down and wept; he fasted and prayed. He confessed his own sin and the sin of his people. He reviewed the promises of God. He requested from the king a leave of absence and letters of reference in preparation for his return to Jerusalem to rebuild the wall.

For three nights Nehemiah circled the ruins of Jerusalem. He observed, but kept his counsel. A study of Nehemiah's work in rebuilding the wall provides an ideal biography of a leader with vision who sees the need, commits to a mission to realize the vision, and moves toward his potential.

The leader must have an understanding of his potential. He must see clearly the vision he has for his group. Then the followers must catch the vision God has given the leader regarding some great project. Nehemiah didn't rebuild the wall of Jerusalem by himself. Others grasped the vision too.

In a vision given by God, the apostle Peter learned that the gospel was for the Gentiles as well as for the Jews. Under the leadership of the Holy Spirit, he then had to "sell" that vision to his colleagues.

Dwight L. Moody had a vision of building a Bible Institute that would train laypeople to become effective in evangelism. It was a new concept. God gave Moody, the businessman turned evangelist, the vision. Then Moody had to light the flame so that others could see the vision and commit to the mission.

God gave Dr. Han Kyung Chik a vision of a church in Seoul, Korea, at the end of World War II. Initially, only twenty-seven people— refugees all—shared his vision. Today, the church stands 60,000 strong, built not by one person, but by many followers who caught the vision of Dr. Han.

A vision generates direction, order, devotion. It overcomes aimlessness, chaos, lawlessness. Leadership grasps God's will, clarifies it to the group, then motivates the group to act on it. The greatest vision a leader can have is one that participates in God's will for world evangelism and explains to the group how it is to be accomplished.

UNDERSTAND WHAT TO DO WITH THE VISION

You now understand what a vision is, where a vision comes from, why a vision is important to a leader, and who it is that must grasp a vision. What do you do with a vision? The obvious answer is, you commit to act on the vision (that commitment is called a mission) and then design a goals program to achieve the mission and thus fulfill the vision. That commitment includes a determination to overcome difficulties and eliminate obstacles.

A leader dishonors God when he professes a vision and then, when difficulties arise and enemies assault, he complains, "God must not want this, or we would not be having so much trouble." Instead, a leader is committed to his vision.

The importance of that commitment can be seen most dramatically when the vision seems least logical. In 1929, Will H. Houghton, pastor of the 4,000-member Baptist Tabernacle in Atlanta, Georgia, was visiting Europe with his wife and her mother. Halfway through the scheduled itinerary, Houghton felt a compulsion to return to America at once. He didn't know why, but he knew God was directing him to return.

He left his wife and mother-in-law to finish the trip, while he took a fast ship to New York. He arrived on a Wednesday in time to attend the midweek prayer service at Calvary Baptist Church across the street from world-famous Carnegie Hall.

The pastor, John Roach Straton, had just become seriously ill, and Houghton was asked if he would fill the pulpit temporarily. He returned to Calvary Baptist Church in January, 1930, preaching in the city often dubbed "the graveyard of preachers." Straton died in October, 1930, and Houghton accepted the invitation to the pastorate. He was one of the few who thrived as a preacher in New York City.

From Calvary's highly visible pulpit, Houghton came to the attention of James M. Gray, the 88-year-old president of Moody Bible Institute. Gray became convinced that Houghton should follow him as president and reported his conviction to the Board of Trustees. Houghton served as president of Moody Bible Institute until 1946. Had Houghton ignored the vision, it is unlikely he would have fulfilled his leadership potential. However, because of his sensitivity, he was put in a position of leadership where he had a world-changing impact on the lives of millions for the glory of God.[5]

Leaders used by God respond to the vision He gives them.

God gave Noah the vision of an ark, and he built it.

God gave Abraham a vision of a city, and he looked for it.

God gave Nehemiah a vision of a wall, and he built it.

God gave Paul the apostle a vision of evangelizing the whole world, and he covered the earth with the message of Christ.

God gave David Livingstone a vision of Africa, and he opened the way for thousands of missionaries to preach the gospel.

God gave John Sung the vision of evangelism in east Asia, and he changed the spiritual complexion of every nation he visited.

If God has put a desire in your heart, accept the presence of the desire as His oath that it can be realized and commit yourself to the fulfillment of the vision. Failure to act on your vision can lead to personal stagnation, a troubled spirit, and a critical attitude. A God-given vision is an awesome responsibility. Fulfillment can lead you to the heights of tremendous service to God and your fellow-man. Failure to follow the vision will deprive others of the leadership they need.

THE IMPORTANCE OF SOLITUDE

You can't see a vision when the artificial lights of the Broadways, the Rialtos, and the commercial offices of the world blind your eyes, any more than you can see the stars at night when you're standing in New York's Times Square, Tokyo's Ginza, or London's Picadilly Circus.

You're more likely to discern a vision in the cloistered halls of solitude than in the screaming jostle of the metropolitan concrete jungle. Perhaps in the cathedral of the trees, under the silence of the stars, or by the moaning sea, you'll be most likely to see the true light and hear "the still, small voice."

In 1964, I made a visit to West Asia. It brought me into contact with Christian leaders who jolted me with the statement that the traditional mission approach was coming to an end in many Third World nations. I thank God for traditional Western-dominated missions because it was through one such missionary that my father came to faith in Christ Jesus. However, just as colonialism brought many blessings but is no longer viable, so, too, the old mission approach is no longer realistic in most Third World nations.

Shortly after that visit, on the island of Bali in Indonesia, a fire began to burn in my soul. I told my three traveling companions that I would be "out of circulation" for a while. They understood and cooperated. I didn't leave my room. In absolute solitude, the vision of Third World Christian leaders, clergy and laity alike, evangelizing their own people came on the screen before my inner eyes like a technicolor movie. I wrote as fast as I could, my thoughts often tumbling ahead of my words. The informal creed I scribbled that day still remains the basic philosophy of world evangelism on which the Haggai Institute functions.

Within the next twelve months, Jerry Beavan and Tom Haggai made incisive, specific suggestions for the best way to implement the vision. Ernest Watson of Australia, Max Atienza of the Philippines, Han Kyung Chik of Korea, Chandu Ray of Pakistan and Singapore, Ah Tua Teo of Singapore, George Samuel of India, and many others all contributed to the fulfillment of the vision.

But it all started in the sanctuary of solitude! Had I spent all my days in crowded socializing, there would be no Haggai Institute. The vision came from God. It was delineated in solitude.

A famous anthropologist said years ago, "The Western mind says, 'Don't just stand there; do something.' So we in the West are action oriented. The Eastern mind says, 'Don't do anything; stand there.' So the Eastern mentality is more attuned to contemplation than action."

These differences between East and West are being modified somewhat as the East becomes more action-oriented and the West sees the value of contemplation. You must prepare for effective action by clear thinking. And the best thinking is done in solitude.

The late Cecil B. Day, Sr., the creator and founder of Day's Inn budget-luxury motels, liked to find his solitude in his "shack" at Tybee Beach in Savannah, Georgia. Sometimes he went there to fast and pray. When the incoming tides at the Day Companies headquarters became crashing breakers, Cecil would go to Tybee. He would walk along the beach to think and pray, the gentle waves cleansing his mind of the tension that clouded clear thinking. He loved the bustle of the headquarters building in Atlanta, but he couldn't do his best creative thinking in the atmosphere of roaring commerce. After walking the deserted beaches, he returned to the city energetic and creative.

Day's vision for his motel chain came in solitude. At two o'clock one morning in 1970, he awakened, grabbed a yellow legal pad, and began writing. For fourteen hours he penned the thoughts brimming over in his mind. When it was done, he had the core idea for the Day's Inn budget-luxury motel. "The ideas were beyond my capacity," reported Cecil later. "It was God's leadership for an idea that has been called the 'Volkswagen of motels.' "

It is possible to create one's own environment of solitude, even in a crowd. But one must not fall into the trap of eliminating occasional solitude in quiet, undisturbed surroundings just because he may have the ability to create his own quiet environment in the midst of noise.

Many times a leader is forced to make an immediate decision without the benefit of prior reflection and deliberation. It is at this point that the power of voluntary solitude enables him to do his thinking, set his course, and determine his plan of action . . . to the benefit of the group.

In Panama, where I was conducting an evangelistic crusade many years ago, a lady called my name as I was crossing a busy thoroughfare. She said, "Suppose at three o'clock this afternoon you were to face an unavoidable decision which would involve thousands of innocent lives and millions of dollars of other people's money, and you had only two minutes to decide, what would you do?"

"I would follow my best judgment."

Aghast, she said, "You mean you wouldn't pray about it?"

"Dear lady, you have given me two minutes. It will consume every second of those two minutes to grasp as much of the relevant data as possible."

"But, I thought you would pray."

"I have. You see, this morning, I had my quiet time with the Lord. I committed the day to Him. And He, who knows the end from the beginning and with whom there is no past, present, or future, has already prepared me. I therefore have full confidence that in this situation, my best judgment would be the expression of His will."

It is in a situation like that, posed by the lady in Panama, that solitude in the midst of the bustling arena is required.

But whether the leader grasps a vision in a beautiful solitary expanse or in a mental seclusion of his own making, he must commit to fulfilling the vision or his influence will go nowhere.

The Christlike leader needs to continually ask himself: (1) Will the vision produce results of beneficial permanence? and (2) Will the vision move the people toward goals that fulfill their real needs?

For the Christlike leader, a vision is a revelation of God's will. A leader grasps the challenge of the vision, commits to the mission, and implements the goals that will accomplish the mission and fulfill the vision.

But it all starts with a vision—the foundation of leadership.

SUMMARY

Leadership begins with a vision. A vision is a clear picture of what the leader sees his group being or doing. A vision could be of health where there is sickness, of knowledge where there is ignorance, of freedom where there is oppression, or of love where there is hatred. The leader is wholeheartedly committed to his vision, which involves beneficial change for his group.

The leader is aware of the importance of his vision and makes it the driving force behind his leadership. The leader's commitment to act on the vision is called a mission. There must also be a set of specific, measurable steps to achieve the mission. Those steps are called goals. A leader will have one vision and one mission but many goals.

Any worthy vision comes from God, whether it deals with so-called "spiritual matters" or not and whether the person with the vision is a Christian and realizes the source of the vision or not. For the Christian, a vision must start with an understanding of God. The leader must then understand himself and also understand the real needs of others.

A vision is important because it is the foundation of all true leadership. A vision must be grasped not only by the leader, but by the followers as well. Therefore, a major responsibility of the leader is to accurately and effectively communicate his vision to the group. Both the leader and the followers then commit to act on the vision, and proceed to design a goals program to achieve the mission and thus fulfill the vision. The commitment includes a determination to overcome difficulties and eliminate obstacles.

Because solitude is necessary to hear the voice of God most clearly and understand the vision He has given, the leader should set aside times when he can be apart by himself. This will prepare him for those times when he must act in a situation when quiet communion with God is not possible.

A vision is the revelation of God's will. A vision is the foundation of leadership.

3

The Principle of

GOALSETTING

You have the vision. Now sharpen the focus of your vision. Are you setting goals to achieve your mission or do you get sidetracked with nonessentials?

The late Cecil B. Day, Sr., had a vision of developing a business to generate funds for God's work worldwide. The most visible part of his business was the motel chain he founded, Day's Inns. In four years he built 40,000 rooms. That achievement has not been even remotely approximated before or since.

In less than five years after Cecil Day founded the motel chain, the oil embargo threatened to bring American traffic to a halt. The scarcity of gasoline lowered highway traffic dramatically. This cut into his revenue dangerously. Furthermore, the hike in oil prices froze liquidity across the country. When the motels under construction at the time of the oil crisis were completed, the lending institutions had no money to fulfill their commitment for conventional loans. As a result, Cecil was saddled with high-interest construction loans.

He never lost his vision. He visited three bankers a day, five days a week for twenty-one months. He not only maintained his vision, but he continually kept refining and executing his well-thought-out action steps for the goals required to make the vision a reality. When he died in 1978, the entire business was intact, and his vision had been carried out.

A leader must have a vision, but that vision must be fulfilled by goals that work toward the achievement of the vision. He cannot waste time with nonessentials. There's no question that Napoleon had a vision. He saw himself as emperor of all Europe. He motivated those who fought for him. But he failed because his egomaniacal plan could never fulfill his vision for European conquest.

A vision is the foundation of all leadership. The leader's vision requires a commitment to act. That commitment is called a mission. But where the rubber meets the road is with a set of specific, measurable steps designed to achieve the mission. Those steps are called goals. A leader without goals is like a ship's captain without reference points or a cross-country motorist without location signs and mileposts.

In the early seventies, sociologist Daniel Yankelovich said that young people were disillusioned. He said that a number of the best-educated and most promising young adults had lost enthusiasm for their business careers. There was a "crisis of purpose."

After having traveled, worked, and fellowshipped on all six continents, I sadly conclude that a high percentage of people in Christian leadership positions also suffer a "crisis of purpose." They are good, sincere, dedicated people for whom the dilemma of finding purpose through the pursuit of traditional Christian activities remains achingly unsolved. With one breath, they say their life's mission is to "serve the Lord." With the next breath, they lament their tragic inability to specify how or in what way.

To be effective, a leader must constantly sharpen the focus of his vision. He does this with effective goalsetting. The clearer the leader's goals, the sharper his focus and vice versa. Effective goalsetting focuses the leader's vision by spelling out what steps he will take to accomplish that vision.

For a leader to lack goals would be as absurd as for a university physics professor to come into class and ask, "What subject shall we consider today?" The students would suffer. In short order, the university would fire the professor. Unfortunately, there are "leaders" in Christian work who, like that professor, lack goals and therefore lack direction. No wonder their influence dwindles, and God's work is slandered.

Henry Kaiser said, "Determine what you want more than anything else in life, write down the means by which you intend to attain it, and permit nothing to deter you from pursuing it."

Setting goals is like programming a computer. Both tasks take skill because nothing can be assumed or left out. For instance, when one of the Haggai Institute graduates sets up a seminar, the objective may sound simple, but to write a program explaining every step could be very complex.

First, he must determine the objective of the seminar in precise detail. Second, he must determine the faculty. Third, he must determine the participants. Fourth, he must determine the facility to be used. Fifth, he must determine the time, both the length of the sessions and the length of the entire seminar. Sixth, he must determine the funding required. Seventh, he must then enlist the faculty. Eighth, he must secure the facilities. Ninth, he must secure the appropriate materials and equipment. Tenth, he must produce the necessary funding. Eleventh, he must recruit the participants. And there are many other steps.

The vision is important, but the vision will never be realized unless a goals program is put in place and followed faithfully. The vision will stay the same over a long period of time and the mission will correspond to the vision. But the goals should be reviewed frequently in order to adjust them to changing situations so that the vision can be realized.

Perhaps your vision is for the development of a secondary school that will be the finest in the city. You realistically expect that it will take eight years to accomplish this mission. You will need to establish a series of goals for the faculty, student body, curriculum, physical facilities, public relations, and other areas each year. The first year, for instance, one of your goals might be to have three teachers with masters degrees, a student-teacher ratio of 30:1 or lower, and 20 percent of the faculty participating in continuing education. The fourth year, however, might include goals of having ten teachers with masters' degrees, a student-teacher ratio of 22:1 or lower, and 35 percent of the faculty participating in continuing education.

Goalsetting is not easy, and it takes constant review and change. The leader who rises above the others, however, will do so not because of his vision, as important as vision is, but because of the successful implementation of an effective goals program. Without a goals program, the vision is merely wishful thinking.

If goalsetting is so important, the leader needs to be able to do it as if it were second nature. Therefore, we need to look at it carefully. First, we will look at the basis of goalsetting—how to do it and the characteristics of good goals. Then we will examine some problem areas in goalsetting that need your careful attention. Finally, we will show the benefits of goalsetting and show how it will help you to be a better, more effective leader. But before ending the chapter, we also need to see why it is that some people object to goalsetting.

S–M–A–R–T GOALS

Setting goals simply involves writing out the steps it will take to accomplish your vision. It may take five years, it may take twenty years, but the vision must be broken down into steps so that you know what you are to accomplish in each area every month.

A good goal-setting program will be S-M-A-R-T: *S*pecific, *M*easurable, *A*ttainable, *R*ealistic, and *T*angible.

Make Your Goals Specific.

It is not a satisfactory goal to say, "I want to honor the Lord." That's a valid desire, but it does not describe a step that will move you toward the accomplishment of your vision. That would be like Noah saying, "I want to survive the flood" or Nehemiah saying, "I want to protect Jerusalem."

Each goal must be a specific step rather than a vague desire.

Make Your Goals Measurable.

"If you can't measure it, you can't monitor it," says Paul J. Meyer of Success Motivation Institute. And since the purpose of goalsetting is to establish a set of steps for the accomplishment of your vision, it is important to know whether each step has been accomplished or not.

A goal of "increasing efficiency in world evangelism" is not measurable. A goal of training 100 credentialed leaders within a year in the "how" of evangelism is measurable. If 98 went through the training, you know you came close to your goal, even though you fell a little short.

Goals should be measurable, not only in terms of *what* is accomplished but *when* it is accomplished. Every goal should specify when the result will be achieved. You shouldn't just have a goal of increasing the average attendance in your church to 300. You should state when it will be accomplished. The reason for this is that each goal is part of an entire goal system designed to fulfill your vision. The accomplishment of one goal is frequently necessary before other goals can be started.

God drove me to set a goal to assist in world evangelism. This was more than half a century ago. One of the action steps arising from this long and continuing overall goal, this mission, is the writing of this book. It has taken four years of my time. It has taken more of my time than the other six books I have written combined. It required me to work with a publisher so that I knew when the manuscript must be completed if the book were to be in the hands of world leaders by early 1986.

I had an intermediary goal of having the manuscript done by May, 1985. I then set goals for myself of when each chapter should be done:

one per month for twelve months, with one month at the end for review and rewrite. Each of these smaller goals was specific, measurable, attainable, realistic, and tangible.

Some of these smaller goals were only for a month. I had broken down my major goal of writing this book into sub-goals. If my goal were just to write this book, I would have faced an overwhelming task. The tendency would have been not to start. But by breaking it down into chapter goals of one month each, I could tell quickly whether I was accomplishing this task.

Make Your Goals Attainable.

A man with a bass voice should not expect to become a soprano soloist. A seventy-year-old woman should not expect to bear a child. An illiterate should not expect to become a famous author within a three-month period. Don't waste your time trying to teach a horse to fly or a snake to sing "The Hallelujah Chorus."

> Although there is much to be said in behalf of courage, enthusiasm, and "the old school try," these attributes may cause more harm than good if they permit emotion to overrule common sense or encourage the commitment of time, effort, and money to objectives that are unattainable.[6]

Set high goals, but not unattainable ones. The Holy Spirit will give you wisdom in setting goals. He will direct you to commit to goals you could never attain in your own strength but which you can attain with His power.

This is an admittedly difficult subject for the Christian. What is attainable? We are to have faith in God. And we are told that with His power all things are possible. However, some Christians are presumptuous, thinking that God should help them do anything. God's help and power come only with those things that are in His will. But He can and does make the impossible possible.

Moses sent twelve spies into Kadesh Barnea to spy out the land. They reported a land flowing with milk and honey and abounding in incomparable fruit. They all agreed it was a desirable land, but ten of the spies soured the report and terrified the Israelites by their description of the "giants" in the land. "We are not able to go up against the people," they said.

However, two of the spies, Caleb and Joshua, brought the minority report. They, too, saw the giants, but they insisted the land was God's provision and He would see them through to victory. The goals of Joshua and Caleb were unattainable in terms of human ability. But they were attainable to those who moved ahead by faith in the wisdom and strength of God. Caleb and Joshua were the only spies permitted to enter the promised land forty years later.

Make your goals attainable, but also remember that as a Christian you have the power of the Holy Spirit inside you, and you do not have to look only to your human strength.

Make Your Goals Realistic.

State what results can be realistically achieved, given your available resources. For a college senior to say, "My goal is to be the president of the university within twelve months" is unrealistic. If he says, "My goal is to be college or university president in twenty years," that will be more realistic, especially if he sets down the intermediate goals: What further training must he get? Where should he take this further training? What steps should he take vocationally in preparation for the presidency? If a man who has barely enough to pay his survival costs today sets his goal to be a millionaire tomorrow, he is unrealistic. To set a goal to be a millionaire in twenty years may be realistic. Here again, concrete and precise measures must be determined and taken.

If a person wants to evangelize an entire nation within a period of five years, he is unrealistic. One reason is that the population keeps exploding. To set a goal to train one evangelist for every 1500 people in the country over the next twenty years may be realistic. This goal is concrete. It is precise. The measures determined and taken must be realistic.

Make Your Goals Tangible.

As you think about your goals, there will be some accomplishments that are intangible. You can achieve these intangible goals by achieving related tangible ones. The goals you set before yourself should always be tangible.

For instance, if you're impatient, you can't achieve the intangible goal of "developing patience" by affirming it or by will power, although both are fine in their place. How will you know when you have enough patience? Set some specific, tangible goals that breed patience. For instance, you could say,

"I won't complain for the next ten days when my wife is late."

"I won't blow my horn for the next ten days when the driver in front of me ignores the traffic light that has changed to green."

"I will smile when my plane is delayed and I may miss an important engagement."

"When an employee repeats a mistake, I will quietly and kindly repeat the correct instructions."

A goal such as "I want to be spiritually minded" doesn't tell you much because it is not tangible, and it is open to a great deal of interpretation. But you can set such tangible goals as:

"I will devote the first thirty minutes of each day to a quiet time of Bible reading and prayer."

"I will not only give the first part of each day to spiritual matters, but I will also devote the first day of each week and the first tenth of every dollar to the Lord and His work."

"I will tell someone what the Lord has done for me at least five days out of every week."

"At least once a week I'll inconvenience myself, if need be, to visit someone in need, for the purpose of encouraging and helping that person in Jesus' name."

Making your goals tangible is the only realistic way of achieving intangible goals.

In addition to making your goals SMART, there are a number of other principles that are useful.

Predicate your goals on your own behavior rather than hoped-for behavior from others. I can list a score of hospitals, churches, Christian organizations and universities that based their goals on hoped-for money from wealthy people, only to be doomed to disappointment at the death of the anticipated philanthropist.

Many leaders have been seriously detained in the pursuit of worthwhile goals because they had a Pollyanna confidence in an employee's performance that did not materialize. In some instances it was the fault of the leader for failing to provide sufficient training, or provide proper supervision, or for not insisting on performance reviews twice a year or quarterly.

Ideally, your goals should be based on things that are under your control—things you and the people who work with you can do. But this is one area that is a unique problem for Christian and nonprofit organizations who depend on volunteer help. You cannot always get the same cooperation from volunteer workers that you can get from those who are employed. This is why in most businesses a manager can direct people's work, but in many Christian organizations, excellence in leadership reveals itself by the motivation of people to serve.

Let your mind soar. Don't limit God or the wonderful things He has in store for you by permitting your own previous experience or the observation of other people's performance to stifle your vision.

Evangelist D. L. Moody asked a pathetically small audience, "How many of you believe God can fill the chairs in this hall with people?" Every hand went up.

"How many of you believe God *will* fill the chairs in this hall with people?" Fewer than thirty hands went up.

"You see," he chided, "it takes no faith to say God *can* do it; it takes great faith to say God *will* do it."

Let your mind soar and have your goals be the expression of your noblest qualities—a desire to be and to do your maximum for God.

Write out your goals in detail. Lord Bacon said, "Writing maketh an exact man." Writing crystallizes your thoughts and makes your ideas specific. Writing also brings the senses into play and sensory-rich images are photographed on the brain.

State your goals positively. The mind cannot picture a vacuum. To say, "My goal is that I'll stop procrastinating" is ineffective. Goals need the motivational force of a positive mental image of yourself doing what you want to do or being what you want to become. How do you visualize "stopping procrastination"?

Make sure your goals include behavioral changes. You must set goals of becoming, of developing whatever characteristics you lack. Working toward internal changes is an essential factor in goalsetting. Your behavior patterns must be compatible with your goals.

You can't expect to lose weight (if that is your goal) when your habit impels you to eat fats and sugars throughout the day. You must change your behavior. You can't launch a new program or enterprise if you permit fear of risk to paralyze you. You must have a behavioral change by developing courage before you can proceed.

Make your goals personal. To set your own personal goals requires a robust character, especially when the goals are different from the norm in your society. It's still impossible for a David to fight in Saul's armor. And it's equally impossible for you to lead with goals handed to you by someone else.

This principle is true throughout an organization. Each person in the organization should set his own goals. The manager may provide guidance for goalsetting, and the goals of each person should certainly contribute to the overall goals and objectives of the organization; but if each person sets his own goals, he will be more likely to achieve his goals and less likely to blame others if his goals are not met.

A young black boy named Carver discerned his vision early in life, and that vision governed his goalsetting, no matter what others thought.

Since he did not know his family, he picked the name George Washington Carver because he liked it. While wandering about the southern part of the United States as a boy, he shuddered to witness a mob beat out the brains of a black man and burn his body in the public square.

Little George had no residence. He slept in barns until one day a laundry lady asked him to help her. He taught himself between school sessions. Finally Highland University, after reviewing his high school grades, accepted him. When the president saw him, he heartlessly barked, "We don't take niggers." George Washington Carver went to Simpson College where he led his class scholastically.

Carver's paintings of flowers won prizes at the World's Fair Colombian Exposition. His musical genius won him a scholarship to the Boston Conservatory of Music. But he chose to specialize in agricultural chemistry in graduate school.

"I can be of more service to my race in agriculture," he said. "I want to help the man furthest down—the Negro—by teaching him how to help himself." That was his lifelong mission. Everything else he achieved was simply the fulfillment of goals toward the accomplishment of this mission.

Declining a prestigious teaching position at Iowa College, he packed his shabby suitcases and proceeded to Tuskegee Institute where he gave his people new goals by showing them the possibility of success. Working incredibly long hours in a shanty-type laboratory, he discovered ways to make plastics from soybeans, rubber from peanuts, flour from sweet potatoes. Thomas Edison offered him a salary in six figures. A rubber company and a chemical firm offered him blank-check retainers to work for them. But he stuck to his mission. He pursued his goals. He stayed at Tuskegee for $1,500 a year.

George Washington Carver could have been a multimillionaire, but he *never* deviated from his goals. He has been called the "Wizard of Farm Chemistry" and is one of the few Americans ever chosen to a fellowship by the London Royal Society for the Encouragement of Arts, Manufactures, and Commerce.

What is your vision? Whatever it is, do you know how you will get there? Write out each goal step by step. Leave no assumptions unstated. This will force you to analyze the resources you need—money, time, personnel—and adjust your plan so that it is a realistic one that reveals potential problem areas.

As you make goalsetting a practice, there are several specific problems you need to watch for.

GOAL CONFLICTS

Writing down your goals forces you to establish priorities, for often two very desirable goals will come into conflict. Buying a new home may conflict with sending your child to university. Prioritize your values to determine which is the most important. Your value system will determine whether to delay the purchase of the new home or postpone the sending of your child to a university.

Sometimes the conflict can be resolved by time. In 1912, my father fled from persecution in the Mideast, arriving in the United States when he was fifteen. Five years later, he wanted to leave for school to prepare for the ministry. His mother said, "You are the only Christian in the family. Your brothers are lost and going to hell. How can you leave to study about how to bring other people to Christ when you neglect your own brothers?"

Because it was an old-world family, the mother had the last word, the father having died previously. There was no recourse but for my father to accede to her suggestion. Furthermore, what she said made sense to him. He delayed his schooling for three more years, during which time his brothers and his brother-in-law came to the Lord.

Conflicts of goals can occur not just between two very desirable goals, but between the goals of different people involved in fulfilling the vision. Your vision may be for a great university that educates many young people in a Christian context. The faculty and staff members may all share the same vision, but their own personal goals of professional advancement or financial security may conflict with the goals that will accomplish the vision for the university. It is the leader who resolves these conflicts.

Harold Geneen, former chief executive officer of ITT, points out that "leadership is the ability to inspire other people to work together as a team under your direction in order to attain a common objective, whether in business, in politics, in war, or on the football field. No one can possibly do it all alone. Others in the organization must want to follow your lead." The leader challenges people to work at those goals that fulfill a vision. Geneen says, "I wanted to get people to reach for goals that they might have thought were beyond them. I wanted them to accomplish more than they thought possible. And I wanted them to do it not only for the company and their careers, but for the *fun* of it."[7]

STATED AND UNSTATED GOALS

In a perfect world, everyone would be candid and straightforward. But we don't live in a perfect world, and sometimes we deceive even ourselves. Thus, as you seek to fulfill your vision, you will write down a series of goals, but you may have other goals toward which you work. You may not express them, even to yourself. In addition to causing confusion, such unstated goals frequently hinder the accomplishment of the stated goals.

Perhaps your stated goals are the steps needed to build an evangelistic church. And yet one of your unstated goals is to provide employment for the members of your family. You wouldn't tell anyone that, but if you're not careful, the unstated goal will cause you to make decisions that are not in the best interest of accomplishing your stated goals. For instance, you may decide to develop an elaborate brochure not because the church really needs it, but because your sister owns a printing company and needs the business.

As more and more people follow your vision, each person with his or her own unstated goals, it becomes increasingly important to keep the stated goals in front of everyone involved and be aware of the possibility of unstated goals conflicting with stated ones.

HOW TO GET STARTED

Here's the way I did it. You might find it helpful. I knew my life mission. Now, what goals were necessary to accomplish that mission?

Every day I would take a yellow, lined pad and write down every conceivable step I felt must be taken to move toward the accomplishment of the mission. There was no particular logic or sequence. I wrote as fast as the ideas came to my head.

Prior to each of these sessions, which lasted anywhere from fifteen minutes to an hour and a half, I had my quiet time and earnestly asked God to guide me. I took great comfort in the words of James: "If any of you lacks wisdom, let him ask of God, who gives to all liberally and without reproach, and it will be given to him" (James 1:5). And I kept reminding the Lord that I qualified for that wisdom because I lacked it.

Every week or so I would review the items I had written down. I would eliminate some, combine some, and alter some. In reviewing, I would come up with other ideas. This continued for the better part of a year.

In addition to the items I had writen down, I made a list of my assets and a list of liabilities. I wrote down every quality or performance I could think of that indicated a personal liability. I also wrote down every criticism I could remember. On the other side of the sheet, I wrote down every asset as I perceived it. In addition, I listed every commendation I had received. This helped me to understand myself as never before, and it helped me to delineate the life mission to which I felt God had called me.

I blush with embarrassment when I confess that it was not until I was in my thirties that I finalized my crystallized expression of my life mission and the goals to attain it. Oh, yes, I had been called to preach when I was six years old. I knew from the time I was ten I wanted to be involved in a worldwide ministry. In that sense, my vision has remained unchanged. But I was nearly thirty-five before I finally worked out my life program under what I believed to be divine direction.

I specified the achievements I felt were necessary—both personal achievements and achievements of others who would be working with me—if the life mission were to be accomplished. This involved every conceivable area of life and activity, including place of residence, personal lifestyle, travel requirements, mental development, social activities, financial goals, family goals, organizational goals, and, of course, spiritual goals. Some items I found to be mutually exclusive. It was then I had to determine my value system and make a decision with regard to priorities.

A leader has one life-dominating vision which he converts to a life-compelling mission. But his goals are many. A vision must be broad enough to be permanent. Goals will change and develop.

Goals change because conditions change. Your life vision and mission remain constant. You alter goals as the changing times require. John Naisbitt gives an illustration in *Megatrends* that Christians should ponder.

In America in the early 1900s, the most successful business was considered to be the Pennsylvania Railroad. When a widow was left with some money, often she was advised to invest it in Pennsylvania Railroad stock, with the encouraging words, "You can always count on the old Pennsy."

In 1905, industrial analysts hailed the Pennsylvania Railroad as the largest and best-managed company in the U.S. Meanwhile, the railroad business moved into almost the same obsolescence as the buggy whip. Why? Naisbitt points out that if the executives of the Pennsylvania Railroad had been asked, "What is your business?" they would have answered, "Railroads." They should have realized they were in the transportation business rather than railroading. They then could have expanded their business to include heavy trucking, highways, jumbo jets, buses, helicopters; but these railroad men remained, as Harvard professor Theodore Levitt has written, "imperturbably self-confident."[8]

The evangelization of the young people of London is an important vision. It is a vision that will be permanent because the need for such a ministry will always be there. But the goals will change. Today, one set of goals might have to do with the development of a drug rehabilitation program—a need that didn't exist as strongly thirty years ago. In the 1960s and 1970s, the development of a coffee house ministry might have been a valid goal, but no longer.

The danger is that instead of making your vision permanent and your goals changing, you will make the vision changing and the goals permanent. This is what happens when an institution—such as a church— outlives its usefulness and yet people want it preserved. Perhaps a neighborhood has changed its character and the church refuses to adapt to the new neighborhood. The institution is preserved because of "the great things God has done here in the past." The vision has changed, but the goals have remained the same. How tragic that is.

I cannot insist too strongly that setting goals is not a one-time exercise. It is an ongoing discipline. Life is not static; it is dynamic. Your goals must be constantly modified. Therefore, you need to stay on top of your goals so that a changing environment will not catch you by surprise. And while you are working on your immediate goals, be sure to keep your eyes on your long-range goals, too.

BENEFITS OF GOALSETTING

I said that it is only through the establishment of a goals program that you can hope to accomplish your mission and thus fulfill your vision. Without a goals program, a vision is merely wishful thinking. The fulfillment of the vision is the primary benefit of goalsetting, but there are many other benefits as well.

Goals simplify the decision-making process. If the decision to be made relates positively to the leader's particular goal, the answer can be "yes." If it does not relate positively to his goal, the answer is "no." If the answer is yes, but he hasn't time for both the new activity and current activities, he must determine which of the two good decisions must be acted on, consistent with his value system and priorities. In this way, the leader conserves energy by concentrating on well-defined goals.

Goals tone up mental and physical health. Most stress comes from confusion and fear. Goals tend to eliminate confusion and override fear. Psychiatrist Dr. Ari Kiev says,

> I have repeatedly found that helping people to develop personal goals has proved to be the most effective way to help them to cope with problems and maximize their satisfaction. . . . With goals, people can overcome confusion and conflict over incompatible values, contradictory desires, and frustrated relationships . . . all of which often result from the absence of rational life strategies.
>
> Without a central goal [a mission], your thoughts may become worrisome; your confidence and morale may be undermined, and you may be led to the feared circumstances. Without a goal, you will focus on your weaknesses, and the possibilities of errors and criticism. This will foster indecision, procrastination, and inadequacy and will impede the development of your potential.[9]

John Wesley was assaulted, beaten, maligned, and yet he remained calm and cheerful. Goals kept him stress-free. He could say, "For I consider that the sufferings of this present time are not worthy to be compared with the glory which shall be revealed in us" (Romans 8:18).

Some of the world's leading medical personalities now emphasize the importance of goals as a deterrent to sickness and as a stabilizer of health. A recent book, *Getting Well Again,* written by Dr. O. Carl Simonton and his wife, Dr. Stephanie Matthews Simonton, and James Creighton, makes a case that goalsetting and striving constitute one of the most important and successful therapies in combating cancer. They say the most effective tool for getting patients well is to ask them to set new life goals. In so doing, they conceptualize and visualize their reasons for living. It is a way by which they reinvest themselves in life.[10]

Goals generate respect. Almost universally, people who know where they're going attract a following. Goals inspire willing followership.

Goals provide a system of measure so one may enjoy the feeling of accomplishment. It is absolutely necessary for the psychological satisfaction of each individual that he or she have a feeling of being worthwhile—usually through accomplishment. The achievement of goals will do this.

Goals produce persistence. The late Bob Pierce, founder of World Vision, told me a story that changed the course of my own life and work. When Pierce was a young man, a respected clergyman told him, "I have studied leaders and organizations. I have devoured biographies and autobiographies. I have immersed myself in history. I have carefully observed the contemporary leadership of my day. I've come to the conclusion that one factor distinguishes the organization that wins. It's staying power.

"In many cases," Pierce said this clergyman told him, "organizations headed by leaders more qualified by virtue of educational achievement, name recognition, natural gifts, and powerful relationships withered and died, while those of seemingly lesser advantages went on to spectacular achievement. The latter simply exercised staying power. When they were hanging on the ledge, ready to crash into the abyss, fingers bleeding as their nails were pulled off from their fingers, the people who won were those who just kept clinging. Somehow, some way, God intervened; He honored their staying power and gave them deliverance." Their goals produced persistence.

Goals, under God, deliver the leader from bondage to the plaudits of people. Conceivably, no greater peril threatens leadership effectiveness than slavery to the plaudits of the crowd. Such slavery borders on idolatry. Shortly before his death, Dr. J. C. Massee, whose Sunday sermons were reported each week in the Boston papers during his seven-year ministry from 1922–1929, said, "The most virulent disease threatening American evangelicalism is the mad passion for applause." He then quoted John 5:44, "How can you believe, who receive honor from one another, and do not seek the honor that comes from the only God?"

Just before his retirement in the early 1960s, the editor of the *Boston Herald* told me, "Massee was the most quotable preacher in Boston during my forty years in the newspaper business, but he seemed impervious to acclaim." Massee preached to 2,600 morning and night throughout his Boston ministry. A higher calling than fame, implemented by clearly defined goals, kept him free from bondage to the fickle response of the crowds.

THE FEAR OF GOALSETTING

If goalsetting is so wonderful, why don't more people do it? I must admit that the primary reason is probably that effective goalsetting is hard work. It takes determination. It takes commitment. But there are at least four reasons why people are afraid of goalsetting.

(1) *The fear of imperfect goals.* Some do not set goals because they are afraid their goals will not be perfect. Actually, a penchant for perfection is perilously close to an irreverent assumption of personal omniscience. Of course your goals will not be perfect. And it's true you may not perfectly reach a given goal. Nevertheless, you have an obligation, under God, to know precisely what you ought to do.

(2) *The fear of defeat.* The fear of defeat is first cousin to the fear your goals may not be perfect. Of course you may suffer defeat. But in the defeat, most probably you will learn some great lessons that will make your ultimate success all the greater. Usually the soundest Christian character is created through temporary defeats.

Defeat is a destructive force only when it is accepted as failure. When you accept it as a needed lesson, it is always a blessing. Defeats are God's great crucible in which He burns the dross from the human heart and purifies the spiritual mettle so that it can withstand the harder tests. In my study of history, I have concluded that the achievements of each man and woman seem to be in ratio to the intensity of the obstructing forces he or she had to surmount.

(3) *The fear of ridicule.* When I was twenty-two years old, I bought a little book, *Thirty Days to a More Powerful Vocabulary,* [11] by William Funk and Norman Lewis, and I started working on my vocabulary. I had realized that the larger a person's vocabulary, the wider the scope and the deeper the penetration of his thinking. Doubtlessly, I was a bit too free in using these new "double-jointed" words. A man whom I considered to be like an older brother quipped, "To understand John Haggai preach today, you must take along a volume of systematic theology and Webster's Unabridged Dictionary." That hurt!

Just as I was about to abandon my vocabulary-building discipline, a country preacher said to me, "John, you are working on vocabulary." I winced. He noticed and said, "Don't be embarrassed. I admire you. At first you will possibly seem a little stilted, but I want to encourage you not only to proceed, but to maintain the discipline as long as you live. It will widen your capacity for knowledge and understanding."

What a blessing that man was to me. I proceeded to enlarge my vocabulary, but my friend's criticism moderated my enthusiasm for displaying the newly acquired words.

Prior to the pastor's encouragement, I had abandoned the idea of pursuing speed-reading and memory courses. But, after overcoming the fear of ridicule, I proceeded with both.

The moment you set a goal, you can anticipate opposition and possibly some ridicule. For one thing, those who know they should be doing the same thing are condemned within their own hearts if they are shirking personal development. They have an alternative: either do what they know they should do or ridicule you. So look on this kind of ridicule as a disguised compliment.

(4) *The fear of considering goalsetting presumptuous.* Some may not set goals because of the verse which says, "Keep back your servant

also from presumptuous sins" (Psalm 19:13). But goalsetting meshes perfectly with the sovereignty of God.

Several years ago, I was lecturing to a group of Brazilian Christian leaders. The editor of a large denominational publishing house queried, "Dr. Haggai, how do you reconcile goalsetting with the sovereignty of God? Is not goalsetting a presumption on God's will?"

We had been discussing goals as they related to the number of people we wanted to see evangelized in the Third World. I asked him, "How many children do you have?"

"Three."

"May I assume your great passion is that they might give their lives to the Lord and live God-honoring, Christ-centered lives?"

"Of course."

"May I also assume that you and your dear wife are praying fervently, instructing the children, and creating the atmosphere in your home most conducive to leading them to such a spiritual commitment, while at the same time maintaining care not to pressure them? In other words, you want the decisions to be their own decisions. Am I correct in this?"

"Yes. Our great desire is that they may know the Lord."

"May it not be said, then, that you and your wife have set a goal, and that this goal relates to the salvation of your children? If that be true, do you think you are profaning the sovereignty of God? Within the parameters of God's sovereignty, He gives freedom for our choice."

We do not profane God's sovereignty by setting goals. Rather, we are to set our goals with reference to His will as we understand it. The goals then are the steps we take in carrying out the will of God!

The Living Bible paraphrases Proverbs 24:3–4, "Any enterprise is built by wise planning, becomes strong through common sense, and profits wonderfully by keeping abreast of the facts."

AN ONGOING DISCIPLINE

Goalsetting is an ongoing discipline of the true leader. Failure at this point destroys the confidence of the followers because it destroys the credibility of the leader.

If you lack a goals program, outside conditions and other people will take over the control of your life, whether you like it or not. If you are not in charge of you, somebody else will be—or some other thing. Specific goals with measurable standards will keep you on target toward the accomplishment of your life mission.

Let me give you an illustration. Hundreds of world leaders participate in the Haggai Institute program each year. Prior to their being
accepted, they agree to conduct training sessions for fellow countrymen
when they return to their homes. They agree to attempt the training
of at least 100 people. Now that can be a goal within the framework
of their life mission.

One might state the goal in this way, "My goal is to train twenty
credentialed Christian leaders for effective evangelism within the next
twelve months." To achieve that goal, one must put down supplementary
goals:

1. Determine how to contact and recruit the leaders.
2. Determine who will help do the training.
3. Determine the curriculum (in many cases, he will feel he can
adapt much of the material discussed at the Haggai Institute training
session).
4. Determine how to schedule the sessions so as not to cripple
the regular work.
5. Determine the cost and set a procedure for raising the funds
(Haggai Institute does not fund any activity of its graduates).

Each of these steps must be accompanied by time targets.

On occasion, some have had to alter their initial plans because of
an unusually destructive monsoon or unexpected interruptions in their
civic life or in their church programs. To keep their activities up to
date, however, they don't hesitate, in such situations, to change their
intermediate goals, but they refuse to change their large goal.

Today's persistent acceleration of change in people, places, and
things demands nothing less than a clearly defined goals program. What
is brand new today becomes obsolete tomorrow. *And the leader must
always know what day it is! His followers are counting on it.*

SUMMARY

A vision is the foundation of all leadership. The leader's vision
requires a commitment to act, which is called a mission. But the
vision and mission are put into practice with a set of specific, measurable steps designed to achieve the mission. Those steps are called
goals. The vision and mission will remain constant, but the goals should
be reviewed monthly or more often. At that review you should assess
what goals have been accomplished, examine those that are not completed, determine what corrective measures should be taken, and set
new goals.

A good goalsetting program is a S-M-A-R-T one. The goals are *S*pecific, *M*easurable, *A*ttainable, *R*ealistic, and *T*angible. Each goal must be a specific step rather than a vague desire. Goals should be measurable not only in terms of *what* is to be accomplished, but *when* it is to be accomplished. Goals should be high ones but attainable, recognizing that the Holy Spirit can help you attain the "impossible." Evaluate your available resources so that the goals are realistic. Achieve intangible goals by stating and achieving related tangible ones.

In addition to making goals SMART, you should predicate your goals on your own behavior rather than hoped-for behavior of others. You should let your mind soar. Don't limit God. Write out your goals in detail. State your goals positively. Make sure your goals include behavioral changes. Make your goals personal.

As you make goalsetting a practice, there are several specific problems you need to watch for. Sometimes two very desirable goals will come into conflict with each other. Prioritize your goals. Be aware of unstated goals and the influence they can have on your own and other's effectiveness at carrying out the stated goals. Be aggressive about modifying your goals to changing situations.

Goalsetting brings many benefits. Goals simplify the decision-making process. Goals tone up mental and physical health. Goals generate respect. Goals provide a system of measure so you may enjoy the feeling of accomplishment. Goals produce persistence. And goals, under God, deliver the leader from bondage to the plaudits of people.

In spite of the many benefits of goalsetting, many people do not do it. Some fail to set goals because it is hard work. Others have a fear of imperfect goals or a fear of defeat or a fear of ridicule—or a fear of goalsetting being considered presumptuous. All of these fears can keep a person from practicing goalsetting.

Goalsetting is an ongoing discipline. You cannot do it once and ignore it. Today's persistent acceleration of change in people, places, and things demands nothing less than a clearly defined goals program.

4

The Principle of

LOVE

J. R. Ewing, the star of "Dallas," the most popular television series in television history, failed at being a leader because he does not move people toward goals of beneficial permanence. He destroys people. He may have vision. He may have a mission. He may even have a goals program, but he lacks a basic ingredient for leadership—love.

Christ makes leaders both fearless and strong as well as loving and self-giving. "For God has not given us a spirit of fear, but of power and of love and of a sound mind" (2 Timothy 1:7). The strongest power in leadership is love.

Napoleon Bonaparte's intellectual greatness and his own intense egotism make his alleged tribute to the supremacy of leadership by love particularly striking. He said, "Alexander, Caesar, Charlemagne, and myself founded great empires; but upon what did the creations of our genius depend? Upon force. Jesus alone founded His empire upon love, and to this very day millions would die for Him."

In his book *Managing,* Harold Geneen makes an important distinction between a leader and a commander. The leader leads his people; the commander tells his people, "I want this done by this date, and if it is not done, then heads will roll!"[12] The commander rules by fear; the leader guides by love.

Vision sets a leader apart from a manager. And love sets a true leader apart from a power-holder. W. C. H. Prentice said that too often we confuse leadership with popularity, power, showmanship, or wisdom in long-range planning. Most so-called leaders today—both within and without the church—are not true leaders but power-holders. And maintaining one's position by popularity or power not only fails to emphasize love, but it sees demonstrating love as a definite weakness because one can't love without making oneself vulnerable. One can't love while keeping one's options open. To truly love—whether it is one's spouse, children, or the people one leads—one must give himself unreservedly in such a way that he can be hurt, that he can be rejected. But the fundamental principle on which a power-holder operates is to protect himself—*not* to be vulnerable.

Love as a characteristic of leadership seems to be out of place. Yet there cannot be true leadership without love. This is a reality in all true leaders, whether Christian or not. But its highest example is found in the person of Jesus Christ. And since Christians are to imitate Christ, they should be in a better position to exhibit love as leaders.

WHAT IS LOVE?

The love of which I speak is not a sentimental emotion. It is the outgoing of the totality of one's being to another in beneficence and help. *Love* as used here refers to a mind-set, an *act of the will.* It is not the exercise of emotions.

A world leader sitting across the table from me in my office said, "You must have great love for the Third World."

I stunned him by saying, "If by that you mean that right now my veins are pulsating with the rich, excitement-charged blood of deep emotion, no. At this very moment, I have no more emotional warmth toward the Third World than I do toward this table. But I have great love for the Third World; you're right.

"I have great love for my son who died in his twenty-fifth year. As I talk with you, I may feel no great emotion about him. However, if I talk about him for a few minutes, reflecting on our experiences together as a family, I shall be nearly overcome emotionally—which, of itself, indicates no greater love. My love doesn't increase with emotion and decrease without it!"

My friend looked at me wide-eyed. He finally grasped what I was saying. Few seem to understand the meaning of true love—the kind of love that is described by the Greek word *agape.*

Agape love is Godlike love. The word *agape* is essentially a Christian word, haloed with a glory given it by God. He used it to express His own attitude toward *all* men and women.

A continuous emotional "high," like that experienced at the birth of a child, the commitment to a marriage relationship, or a victory on the athletic field would destroy us. The psyche, as well as the body, could not handle it. True love, while often including this kind of emotion, far exceeds a temporary ecstasy.

True love involves the totality of one's being. God, and only He, expresses it perfectly. He gave His all. The Man on the middle cross was God. In life, Jesus expressed it when He said, "I am among you as the One who serves." In death, He expressed it when He said, "No one takes [My life] from Me, but I lay it down of Myself."

The love of which I speak includes unconquerable consideration, charitableness, benevolence. It means no matter what anyone does by way of humiliation, abuse, or injury, the Christlike leader works toward that person's highest good. Indeed, without this kind of love, leadership fails the ultimate test—permanence.

Love relates to real needs. Love will not pander to perceived needs that are not real needs. The leader knows what the real needs of the group are because he loves the people in his group. And his love is real, not a self-serving imitation.

When a man who was crippled cried to Peter and John for money, they did not give him money; they healed him. They met his real needs, not his perceived needs.

The child who is never disciplined, whose parents do not love him enough to impose restrictions (to meet his real needs) feels rootless and does outlandish things in order to get attention and appreciation. Even though a child may be angry with the parents for some discipline imposed, studies have proved that the disciplined child feels a sense of belonging. Eventually, he may come to realize that the truly loving parents have the child's highest good at heart.

The same is true with adults. The leader, expressing genuine love, seeks to lead his followers toward those things that meet their real needs, even though the measures taken at the time may not seem palatable.

Love is *active*. It demands expression. It is never passive. Love is *transitive*. It demands an object. Love is *serving*. Love is *sacrificing*.

True love is under the control of one's will rather than a fortuitous flash outside one's control. So there is no excuse for a loveless leadership.

The Christlike leader loves God, himself, and his neighbor. He is emotionally whole because he is spiritually healthy.

The leader sustains a winning attitude by faithfully obeying Christ's two commandments, which mark the starting point for superior leadership. A lawyer cross-examined Jesus: " 'Teacher, which is the great commandment in the law?' Jesus said to him, 'You shall love the Lord your God with all your heart, with all your soul, and with all your mind. This is the first and great commandment. And the second is like it: You shall love your neighbor as yourself' " (Matthew 22:36–39).

In our Lord's two commandments, three areas of love surface: first, love of God; second, love of neighbor; and third, love of self. The love God has demonstrated toward us furnishes us the ultimate illustration of what our love is to be like. His love is the communication of His being to us in beneficence and help. The word *beneficence* means the practice of doing good: active goodness, kindness, or charity—literally, well-doing. Loving God, as commanded here by Christ, means the communication back to God of that which He has given to us. This is demonstrated by our love of our neighbor—which is to be modeled after God's love for us. Jesus talks about it as giving a cup of cold water or visiting someone in jail "in My name." And our love of ourselves arises from the fact that God loves us. It is by understanding and believing that God loves, forgives, and accepts us as we are that we can have a healthy self-esteem.

LOVE GOD

Christ says you must love "your God." You, as a leader, must so live as never to leave a question in anyone's mind as to who your God is. God says, "You shall have no other gods before Me" (Exodus 20:3). Anything or anyone that has a greater formative influence in your life than God is an idol. An idol can be a habit, a person, a thing, just as much as a graven image. Loveless leadership is idolatrous leadership because it replaces God with an idol. The Christlike leader despises idolatry.

Isaiah said, "In the year that King Uzziah died, I saw the Lord sitting on a throne, high and lifted up" (Isaiah 6:1). Uzziah had to die before Isaiah saw the Lord. Uzziah had been an idol to Isaiah. Isaiah had transgressed God's commandment "You shall have no other gods before Me." Uzziah had been a god to him. Other gods are helpless. They only succeed in blurring the leader's necessary focus.

Loveless, self-centered idolatry had stifled Isaiah's leadership. Idolatrous leadership, no matter how brilliant and disciplined, ultimately fails. But poor, egomaniacal man spurns the lessons of history and thinks he will achieve where others failed. Leader after leader has thought that he could make himself like God and has demanded worship and reverence. In fairness, sometimes the idolatry comes from the people with little encouragement on the part of the leader. For instance, Sukarno's fall in Indonesia in the 1960s paralyzed some Indonesian Christians with fear because they had idolized him. Some courageous men lovingly denounced their idolatry. God, who "raises up kings," raised up President Suharto, and the nation entered upon a period of tranquillity and stability.

Love for God must be exclusive, "with all your heart, with all your soul, with all your strength, and with all your mind." Jesus is saying, "Your love for God is to be concentrated and exclusive, surpassing, and all-consuming. You are to love God with your intelligence, your emotions, and your volition—with the totality of your personality."

Love Yourself

Loving God with the totality of your personality and accepting the love God has for you is the foundation for loving yourself. A proper understanding of self-love is a teaching that has not been emphasized among Christians because of a reaction to a Greek emphasis on "high-mindedness." Aristotle had promoted a concept that fostered pride and regarded those who were humble as contemptible, mean-spirited, and without energy and goals. He exaggerated the importance of an air of loftiness.

In response to this, many Christians taught that we should be humble, but they taught humility in the sense of downgrading ourselves or running ourselves into the ground. We will discuss a correct understanding of humility in the next chapter. Being truly humble, however, is *not* inconsistent with loving yourself. God wants us to have a healthy self-esteem. He wants us to love ourselves. A healthy self-love is essential to good leadership.

In his book *Seeds of Greatness,* Denis Waitley, who served as a consulting psychologist to the American astronauts, says, "The first best-kept secret of total success is that we must feel love inside ourselves before we can give it to others." He then explains, "If there is no deep, internalized feeling of value inside of us, then we have nothing to give or to share with others."[13]

Loving yourself means that you are contributing to your highest needs with beneficence and help. This is not narcissism. It is not putting yourself ahead of everyone else. Rather, it is putting God first. For instance, when you take proper nutrition, sleep, and exercise, you are fortifying your body, which is the temple of God. When you are contributing to your intellectual development with proper knowledge, you are loving yourself. When you exercise your will to avoid engagements that dishonor Christ, you are engaged in the highest form of self-love.

The fad of loving yourself that floods the airwaves and the bookshelves today is too often a preoccupation with self, rather than a preoccupation with God and with your neighbors.

Because the Spirit of God lives in us, He gives confidence and a proper self-esteem. True self-confidence issues from the domination of the Holy Spirit and a subsequent confidence in His leadership.

LOVE YOUR NEIGHBOR

Loving God and accepting God's love for you is the foundation for loving yourself. And loving yourself is the foundation for loving your neighbor, for a healthy self-esteem releases you from spending your energy building up your own self-confidence through power games and putting down others. It lets you give of yourself freely. It lets you experience the outgiving of the totality of your being to another in beneficence and help.

Often we want to love our neighbor, but we don't know how to express it. Ted Engstrom, president of World Vision International, gives ten very practical and powerful principles of expressing love in his book *The Fine Art of Friendship.* [14] These ten principles tell us how to express love to our neighbor.

1. "We must decide to develop friendships in which we demand nothing in return." Love is unconditional. If it's not unconditional, it's not love, but self-serving manipulation. Sadly, manipulation is more common among so-called leaders than is true love.

2. "It takes a conscious effort to nurture an authentic interest in others." Our natural tendency is to be self-centered (which is *not* the same as having a healthy self-esteem). It therefore takes a conscious effort to love.

3. "Each of us is a one-of-a-kind creation. Therefore, it will always take time—often a long time—to understand one another." Leaders are usually busy people, and yet love takes time. There is no substitute.

4. "Commit yourself to learning how to listen." Do you *really* listen to people, trying to understand what they're saying, or do you listen to give an answer—letting another talk while you plan what you will say next? The one who loves listens with understanding.

5. "Simply be there to care, whether you know exactly what to do or not." Loving one's neighbor involves fulfilling, in a visible way, Christ's promise, "I will never leave you nor forsake you." Be available.

6. "Always treat others as equals." Just because God has put you in a position of leadership does not mean He has made you "better"

than others. It is the leader most of all who needs to heed the words of Paul "not to think of himself more highly than he ought to think" (Romans 12:3).

7. "Be generous with legitimate praise and encouragement." Such words build up the self-esteem of others. Words of criticism and discouragement, however, kill enthusiasm and love in others.

8. "Make your friends Number One, preferring them above yourself." This is another point at which we see a clear difference between the leader who loves and the power-holder who manipulates. The leader puts others first. The power-holder "looks out for Number One" (himself!) by "pulling his own strings" and "winning through intimidation."

9. "Learn to love God with all your heart, soul, mind, and strength. Then love your neighbor as yourself."

10. "Emphasize the strengths and virtues of others, not their sins and weaknesses." To illustrate this point, Ted Engstrom tells the following story:

It seemed that Joe had just about had it with his wife of three years. He no longer thought of her as attractive or interesting; he considered her to be a poor housekeeper who was overweight, someone he no longer wanted to live with. Joe was so upset that he finally decided on divorce. But before he served her the papers, he made an appointment with a psychologist with the specific purpose of finding out how to make life as difficult as possible for his wife.

The psychologist listened to Joe's story and then gave this advice, "Well, Joe, I think I've got the perfect solution for you. Starting tonight when you get home, I want you to start treating your wife as if she were a goddess. That's right, a goddess. I want you to change your attitude toward her 180 degrees. Start doing everything in your power to please her. Listen intently to her when she talks about her problems, help around the house, take her out to dinner on weekends. I want you to literally pretend that she's a goddess. Then, after two months of this wonderful behavior, just pack your bags and leave her. That should get to her!"

Joe thought it was a tremendous idea. That night he started treating his wife as if she were a goddess. He couldn't wait to do things for her. He brought her breakfast in bed and had flowers delivered to her for no apparent reason. Within three weeks the two of them had gone on two romantic weekend vacations. They read books to each other at night, and Joe listened to her as never before. It was incredible what Joe was doing for his wife. He kept it up for the full two months. After the allotted time, the psychologist gave Joe a call at work.

"Joe," he asked, "how's it going? Did you file for divorce? Are you a happy bachelor once again?"

"Divorce?" asked Joe in dismay. "Are you kidding? I'm married to a goddess. I've never been happier in my life. I'd never leave my wife in a million years. In fact, I'm discovering new, wonderful things about her every single day. Divorce? Not on your life."[15]

These ten practical and powerful principles will let you not just *feel* love, but *express* it so that others will know that you love them. But, as Erich Fromm says in *The Art of Loving*,[16] the practice of love, which he calls an art, requires discipline, concentration, patience, and it must be of supreme importance to you. Basic to this is the fact that the expression of love requires the indwelling power of the Holy Spirit.

LOVE AND THE LEADER

Love God; love yourself; love your neighbor. Jesus commanded this for all Christians. But it is particularly important for leaders. The leader, expressing genuine love, motivates his followers to move toward that which is beneficially permanent and fulfills their real needs. Only love is permanent. The last part of the greatest words ever written about love says, "And now abide faith, hope, love, these three; but the greatest of these is love" (1 Corinthians 13:13). Love is the greatest because only love is permanent. Faith ultimately will be fulfilled in heaven; hope, too, will ultimately be realized in heaven. However, love will continue throughout all eternity.

Practicing love is particularly important for a leader because leaders deal with people. Unlike the mechanic who deals primarily with things or the mathematician who deals primarily with ideas, the leader deals with people. And people need to be dealt with in love.

Practicing love is particularly important for a leader also because motivation by threat or influence is inconsistent with true leadership. That is the way of the dictator or power-holder. But love is the motivating factor most consistent with true leadership.

For a leader, practicing love is not something that he aspires to for himself only. Rather, he wants to build love into the lives of those who follow him as well. He should be a role model, showing how love works, demonstrating its development, its practice, and its benefits.

The Christlike Leader Eloquently Expresses Love

Just as the majestic tree expresses its life in fruit, the Christlike leader expresses his leadership in love. Paul the Apostle talks of the "fruit of the Spirit" in Galatians 5:22, 23, and he uses the singular. It would seem, therefore, that he is talking about one fruit. Punctuation is not inspired of God and I would therefore like to put Paul's words this way, "But the fruit of the Spirit is love: joy, peace, long-suffering, kindness, goodness, faithfulness, gentleness [humility], self-control. Against such there is no law."

The eight qualities mentioned are all expressions of love. Leadership imbued with these qualities moves those that are led toward the fulfillment of their *real* needs. And it moves them with grace.

In the rest of this chapter, we will look at the first six expressions of love. The last two—humility and self-control—will be considered in the next two chapters since they are two important principles of leadership themselves. These eight qualities will shine through the leader who is practicing love. Here is what his followers will see.

JOY

Joy is love's music. Only love can keep one cheerful in all circumstances. Jesus told His disciples, "These things I have spoken to you, that My joy may remain in you, and that your joy may be full" (John 15:11). But it is not a superficial giddiness that is meant here.

Our self-centered nature and society have led us to believe that happiness and joy come when we get what we want and our "needs" and "wants" are filled. We are told that joy is a new car, a bigger house, healthy children, and a bit of fame. But these things will never bring joy because we will always want more. Joy comes not from getting, but from giving. My friend Peter Gillquist expressed it this way, "Every time we have the chance in *any* way to flesh out the love of God to others, our joy cycle gets fulfilled all over again."[17]

St. Francis of Assisi expressed the Christian's way to joy through love in his famous prayer:

"Lord, make me an instrument of Thy peace.
Where there is hatred let me sow love;
Where there is injury, pardon;
Where there is doubt, faith;
Where there is despair, hope;
Where there is darkness, light;
Where there is sadness, joy.
Oh Divine Master, grant that I may not so much seek
To be consoled as to console;
To be understood as to understand;
To be loved as to love;

For it is in giving that we receive;
It is in pardoning that we are pardoned;
It is in dying that we are born to eternal life."

PEACE

Peace is love's agreement. The Bible speaks of two kinds of peace that come to a person as the result of a loving relationship with God. There is "peace *with* God" and the "peace *of* God." The first refers to the making of a peace treaty after a war is over. "Friendship with the world is enmity with God. Whoever therefore wants to be a friend of the world makes himself an enemy of God" (James 4:4). But when you become a child of God through Jesus Christ, no longer are you at war with God—no longer are you His enemy—but you are at peace with Him.

The second phrase—the "peace of God"—refers to the inner tranquillity you can have in the midst of a confusing and falling-apart world because you know that God is in charge. The fruit of the Spirit, which is love, produces peace.

There is a third aspect of peace in the life of the leader. He is to bring peace to others in this world of turmoil, for he has been given a "ministry of reconciliation."

It is often the ploy of the loveless, self-centered power-holder to create factions, skillfully foment ceaseless conflict, unrelentingly keep the parties off balance so he can control the group. This callous *modus operandi* fails in the end. The loving leader, the one who works for harmony, may lose some votes, but ultimately win the decision—for everybody's benefit. He's willing to be vulnerable. He knows that unless he's vulnerable, his leadership will never be viable. He doesn't waste adrenaline on paranoid efforts to exterminate criticism.

In 1970, I spent three weeks with one of the influential leaders of the world's largest Presbyterian church, the Young Nak Church in Seoul, Korea. I asked many questions about its celebrated senior minister, Dr. Han Kyung Chik.

"Does he ever encounter opposition in session meetings?" I asked.

"Many times."

"How does he respond?"

"Usually he'll say, 'You are good and godly men. I know you desire the will of God. Perhaps I was premature in bringing this matter up. Or, maybe it's an error to consider it. Let's pray some more about it."

"And how does Dr. Han respond to unjust criticism?"

"I remember one time when a session member made what to me was a savage attack on Dr. Han's judgment. Dr. Han wept. He said, 'Apparently I did not pray sufficiently before taking this course of action. Forgive me. I shall pray more earnestly about this.' Within a year, the entire session saw the wisdom of Dr. Han's proposal and adopted it, although he never again brought it up."

What makes this so powerful a lesson to me is that Dr. Han spends hours every day in prayer. For more than half a century he's been at prayer no later than 5 o'clock every morning. Neither I nor any of the critics are worthy to tie his shoes! His great and surpassing and sustained leadership finds its roots in love—and peace, love's agreement.

LONG-SUFFERING

Long-suffering is love's endurance. The meaning of the New Testament word for long-suffering is "to endure with unruffled temper." The long-suffering person is long-tempered. This person incarnates the words of the apostle Paul in 1 Corinthians 13, "love suffers *long* and is kind."

Dr. Han says, "When you lose your temper, you lose everything." How true that is. I recommend that every leader read, reread, and memorize Rudyard Kipling's poem "If." It begins, "If you can keep your head when all around you are losing theirs and blaming it on you. . . ."

Any leader worth "his salt" possesses a temper. The effective leader, in reliance upon God, controls his temper. The effective leader will not stoop to respond, no matter what the provocation, with smug complaisance, worldly courtesy, patronizing contempt, or a brutal vindictiveness. Rather, he responds with love's endurance—long-temperedness.

KINDNESS

Kindness is love's service. The original word for kindness in the New Testament does not refer to sentiment but to service, to helpfulness in small things—doing the little things that help, reinforce, and support. Kindness is love's service.

When I was a teenager, I listened to the spellbinding Dr. Walter A. Maier on the Lutheran Hour's "Bringing Christ to the Nations" broadcast. Sunday after Sunday I sat before the radio transfixed by the greatest radio preacher on earth. I scraped up two dollars and mailed it to him with a letter. I apologized for such a small offering but told him it was all I had. I assured him of my faithful "attendance" to his broadcast and of my fervent prayers for him and his ministry.

I was astonished a few days later when I received from him a two-page typewritten letter. It was no "canned" letter. He had typed it himself. No secretary could have been that bad! He answered my letter in detail. He told me how important my gift was. He encouraged me with the fact that "every dollar reaches 1,500 people with the gospel through our program, so your gift will reach 3,000 people!" He shared some personal insights and anecdotes. In my ecstasy, I said to myself, "When I get older, if anyone writes me, I shall be as kind to them as Dr. Maier has been to me."

Maier's response demonstrated kindness, love's service. No wonder his leadership influenced millions with dimensions of beneficial permanence.

GOODNESS

Goodness is love's deportment. Goodness is the manifestation of Godlike virtues in a person. Goodness is Joseph's fleeing from Potiphar's wife when she tried to seduce him. Goodness is Jesus' showing compassion to the woman caught in adultery without condoning her sin. Goodness is George Washington praying on his knees in the snow at Valley Forge and Abraham Lincoln on his knees in the White House—each asking God for guidance and strength to do the right. Goodness is one of Egypt's great Christian leaders living modestly on an income that does not even make provision for a car, giving himself totally because he loves the Egyptian people, even though he could enjoy a prestigious position with a good income and impressive perks.

God Himself is referred to as abounding in goodness. And goodness marks the strong leader. It reveals the strength which opposes everything evil and immoral. It drives the Christlike leader to dependence on God. This leader asks God for:

- a disposition to hate what is evil,
- a compulsion to follow after that which is good,
- wisdom to judge rightly in all things,
- increased thoughtfulness and sensitivity in dealing with all people.

The Greek word that is translated *goodness* in the New Testament never appears in secular Greek writings. Neither the Greeks nor the Romans grasped the meaning of *agape* love, nor of its offspring, goodness. They saw love and goodness as qualities to be avoided. Instead, the Greeks worshiped the intellect and the Romans worshiped power.

Love is the father of goodness. Therefore, it functions only in the area of beneficence and help. Goodness finds its anchor in love, not in legalism, nor in lackeyism. Neither the legalist nor the lackey provide beneficence or help.

The legalist forces his so-called "goodness" on others. The martinet, always poised to jump with criticism on every person who deviates from his chart of "proper" behavior, preempts leadership.

The lackey forfeits leadership not only by obsequiously agreeing with those he perceives to hold power and favor, but by shamelessly adopting their "goodness" code in an attempt to acquire their power and curry their favor. Both the legalist and the lackey violate love and, therefore, leadership.

Goodness in leadership produces a deportment that is kind but just, tender but tough, fair but firm.

FAITHFULNESS

Faithfulness is love's measure. Faithfulness has to do with a leader's staying true to his trust, to his commitment to others, to himself, and, above all, to God. It's a characteristic of the reliable leader. Faithfulness is Noah's building an ark in spite of the jeers and criticisms of others. He and his family were saved in the flood because of that ark. Faithfulness is Abraham's willingness to sacrifice his only son Isaac because he believed God would deliver him. And He did—by providing the substitute of a ram.

Faithfulness is Savonarola's defiance of the vested interests of Florence, Italy, in his proclamation of the Truth. He was hanged and his body burned, but his leadership continued hundreds of years after his death. That's the power of faithfulness in life and leadership.

Do you keep your promises? Do you pay your bills? Do you honor your appointments? Do you stay on course with your commitments? Is your word your bond? Do you go the second mile?

Motel magnate Cecil B. Day opposed everything false. He refused to alter verbal agreements at the closing of real estate transactions, even when the alterations were legally permissible and when they would profit him.

Faithfulness is love's measure. People will not willingly follow an unreliable leader. They want one who is trustworthy.

The attitude of *agape* love gives vitality and credibility to the leader's influence. Love in the leader produces in the group a desire to follow him. Love accomplishes what neither fame nor force, muscle nor manipulation can attain.

When the late Dr. E. Stanley Jones preached on love in India, a church leader complained that though he had saturated his leadership with love, one of the laymen was making a lot of trouble and threatening to split the church. The frustrated clergyman asked Dr. Jones what to do since love hadn't worked. "Increase the dosage," retorted Jones.

Leadership by love works! In business and politics, in the professions and education, the church, and the home—in every area of life, the leadership of love is the outgoing of the leader to others in beneficence and help. Leadership based upon this foundation cannot fail.

Jesus, the only *perfect* leader, set the example and promises the strength to follow it.

And that's the leadership our changing world cries for. It's the *only* leadership that holds out any hope. There is no limit on the number of such leaders needed. You have a wide open opportunity to help set the course of this changing world in the right direction. And your resource is the ultimate Super Power—LOVE!

SUMMARY

Just as vision sets a leader apart from a manager, love sets a true leader apart from a power-holder. There cannot be true leadership without love. True love is not merely a sentimental emotion, but it is an act of the will in which the Christlike leader works toward the highest good of others.

Scripture says that you are to love God exclusively "with all your heart, with all your soul, with all your strength, and with all your mind." You are to love yourself with a self-confidence that issues from the domination of the Holy Spirit in your life. And you are to love your neighbor, giving yourself freely to others in beneficence and help.

The Christlike leader expresses love because love infuses his leadership with a beneficial permanence that draws others to him. The expression of love is found in Galatians 5:22–23. The qualities listed there will be present in the life of the Christlike leader who shows love.

- *Joy* is love's music.
- *Peace* is love's agreement.
- *Long-suffering* is love's endurance.
- *Kindness* is love's service.
- *Goodness* is love's deportment.
- *Faithfulness* is love's measure.

Leadership by love works! It is the outgoing of the leader to others in beneficence and help. Leadership based upon this foundation cannot fail.

5

The Principle of

HUMILITY

Contrary to what many think, humility gives tensile strength to leadership.

To please a certain official, Abraham Lincoln once signed an order transferring certain regiments. Secretary of War Stanton, convinced that the President had made a serious blunder, refused to execute the order. "Lincoln's a fool!" he roared.

When Lincoln heard what Stanton had said, he replied, "If Stanton said I am a fool, then I must be, for he is nearly always right. I'll step over and see for myself."

Lincoln did just that. When Stanton convinced him the order was in error, Lincoln quietly withdrew it.

Part of Lincoln's greatness lay in his rising above sensitivity to the opinions of others concerning himself. One could not offend him easily. In his humility, he welcomed criticism. And he demonstrated a strength that few leaders ever match.

If you hope to rise to your potential as a leader, you'll do well to learn to meet criticism with tranquillity and pleasantness. This approach strengthens your spirit, gives added thrust to your work, and, above all, honors God.

To paraphrase the words of the late A. W. Tozer in his book *The Pursuit of God,* [18] the humble man is not a human mouse, suffering a sense of his own inferiority. In his moral life, he may be as bold as a lion and as strong as Samson, but he doesn't fool himself about himself. He has accepted God's estimate with regard to his own life. He knows he is as weak and as helpless as God has declared him to be. Paradoxically, he relies on the confidence that in the sight of God, he is more important than the angels. In himself, he is nothing; in God, he is everything. That's his motivating motto. He is not overly concerned that the world will never see him as God sees him. He is perfectly content to allow God to determine His own values. The humble man patiently waits for the day when everything will get its own price tag, and real worth will come into its own. In the meantime, he will lead for the benefit of mankind and for the glory of God, happily willing to wait for the day of final evaluation.

Humility—or meekness—is love's mood. It is love's prevailing attitude, spirit, and disposition. The humble person is free from pride or arrogance. He submits himself to others and is helpful and courteous. The humble person does not consider himself to be self-sufficient. And yet he recognizes his own gifts, resources, and achievement. He knows that he has been the object of undeserved, redeeming love. Therefore he cannot build up himself for he knows it is "all of grace." But being humble does not exclude confidence, for we are told in Scripture to "cast not away your confidence" (Hebrews 10:35).

The humble person does not take offense or fight back. He turns the other cheek to the one who hits him. And yet humility is not cowardice, for humility requires high courage. Humility makes you willing to take a lower place than you deserve, to keep quiet about your merits, to bear slights, insults, and false accusations for the sake of a higher purpose. Jesus displayed humility for "when he was reviled, [He] did not revile in return; when He suffered, He did not threaten."

Christ gave life, vitality, and glory to the word *humility*. We learn of humility through His teaching, His example, His character. He did not come in the pomp of arrogance or of pride, although He could have done so. He did not ask Herod for the key to the city. Nor did He have His associates engineer a testimonial dinner in His honor. He came in lowliness of mind, according to the prophecy in Psalm 22 and Isaiah 53.

Humility is the lowliness that pervades the leader's consciousness when he contemplates God's holy majesty and superabundant love in contrast to his own unworthiness, guilt, and total helplessness apart from divine grace. This is the kind of humility Christ welcomes. This humility makes religion neither stiff nor heavy nor pompous, but simple, relaxed, joyful, honoring to God, and helpful to people.

While it is difficult for most people to display humility, it is particularly difficult for a leader because his experiences discourage humility.

Most leaders have a ceremonial role to fill. It is the leader who must meet and entertain visiting dignitaries. It is the leader who represents his followers at official events. It is through honor given to a leader that the group also receives honor. When Prime Minister Rajiv Gandhi is treated elegantly, with honor and respect, at an official state visit in another country, all of India is being treated elegantly with honor and respect. Because of this, it is not easy for a leader to demonstrate humility. And yet humility is an extremely important principle of leadership.

One recoils at the task of writing on humility when he recognizes that even the discussion of humility can induce pride. It can be said that just as the honest person does not discuss honesty nor the pure person discuss purity, so the humble person does not discuss humility for the simple reason that humility possesses no self-consciousness. Humility is the "eye which sees everything except itself," according to Ritschl.

Someone asked Dwight L. Moody, "Are you saying that the humble person doesn't think much of himself?" Moody retorted, "No. He doesn't think of himself at all." Humility is unconscious of itself. The man who is humble doesn't know he is humble.

False Humility

Even worse than a lack of humility in a person's life is a false humility in which a person is very proud about acting in a humble way. The English author and poet Samuel Taylor Coleridge correctly said that the devil's "favorite sin is pride that apes humility."

And yet the person with false humility is fooling only himself, for people see through the pompous, self-adulatory, and arrogant person who feigns humility. The truly humble person will avoid contrived posturing. He will not play games like those who are always willing to sit at the foot of the banquet table, provided they come late enough for everyone to see them do it.

After a soloist has thrilled an audience with a glorious rendition marked by beauty, skill, and impact, it would be false humility to deny such surpassing ability in response to the comment, "That was a beautiful solo." It would be hypocrisy. The musician, recognizing that the voice, the health required to practice long hours, and the tutelage all were gifts from God, accepts the comment with grace and gratitude.

In the first century, there were some teachers at Colossae called Gnostics. They said one could obtain perfection beyond the capabilities of ordinary Christians through special knowledge ("gnosis") and through observing Jewish circumcision, feast days, new moons, and sabbaths. To these Jewish observations, the Gnostics added their own precepts and rituals. They taught that the observance of these rituals led to a special communion with angels. The rationale was that since angels are above this world, the ascetic, by divorcing himself from the things of this world, draws near to the angels and is therefore qualified to associate with them. The apostle Paul branded this as a false humility that detracts from the true worship that is due to Christ alone: "Let no one defraud you of your reward, taking delight in false humility and worship of angels, intruding into those things which he has not seen, vainly puffed up by his fleshly mind. . . . These things indeed have an appearance of wisdom in self-imposed religion, false humility, and neglect of the body, but are of no value against the indulgence of the flesh" (Colossians 2:18, 23).

Paul accused these Gnostic teachers of wanting to appear humble while they were actually laying claim to superior insights into divine truth and superior piety in their own lives. They claimed they were doing more than God required.

Unfortunately a similar false humility is all too common today. Some people imply they have a direct line to God, a line not available to other Christians. Four such people in a church business meeting, all having opposing views, create chaos. They each insist, "God told me we should follow my suggestions." Each claims to have the mind of Christ. Obviously, it takes God-honoring humility to come to a position of agreement.

The man or woman of true humility *never* criticizes an alleged lack of humility in another. Judgmentalism is foreign to true humility. But it is extremely difficult for the leader to see judgmentalism in himself. Sometimes it surfaces in the advice he gives. The leader is not omniscient, and humility will protect him from indiscriminate counsel.

Whether it be dress or speech or behavior, anything that draws attention to itself and away from Christ is displeasing to God and violates humility. It promotes pretentiousness and projects vanity.

In every age, true humility has been a rare quality. Even Christ's disciples in the first century did not always exhibit humility. Listen to them when they were interrupted by the woman of Canaan seeking healing for her daughter: "Send her away, for she cries out after us" (Matthew 15:23). Or listen again as they argue about who would be greatest in the kingdom of heaven. They did not exhibit any outgoing of beneficence and help to others.

WHY IS HUMILITY IMPORTANT?

The psalmist ascribes humility to God Himself:

> Who is like the Lord our God,
> Who dwells on high,
> Who humbles Himself to behold
> The things that are in the heavens
> and in the earth?
> —Psalm 113:5–6

God, "the High and Lofty One . . . whose name is Holy" (Isaiah 57:15) dwells in the humble heart.

There can be no real love without humility. Paul told the Corinthians that love does not parade itself and is not puffed up. Augustine said that in importance, humility is first, second, and third.

The spirit of humility frees the leader to concentrate on the real needs of others. He doesn't dissipate his energies wondering what kind of impression he is making. Refusing to "think of himself more highly than he ought to think," he does not feel insulted no matter what is said. Nor does he languish under the fear of being treated in a disrespectful manner.

> "Great peace have those who love Your law,
> And nothing causes them to stumble" (Psalm 119:165).

Humility is important for a leader because people follow more enthusiastically the leader whose motives they consider to be non-self-serving. All other things being equal, the humble leader comes closer to achieving his objectives. Why? Because his objective is the highest good of the group, not his own self-aggrandizement. The humble leader's joy comes from seeing the group move toward the fulfillment of its real needs. Leadership lacking this quality, this expression of love, inevitably loses credibility.

THE RESULTS OF HUMILITY

The Christlike leader will pray for and strive after humility because he knows it is a characteristic Christ Himself demonstrated and one He expects of His followers. But there are also a number of results that come to the one who demonstrates humility that should make it a characteristic that anyone would seek after.

Serenity

Humility fosters serenity. Activity to the point of frantic confusion, uncertainty, worry, and fear are all too common today. People feel as if they need to depend on themselves, but self-sufficiency does not give them calmness and strength. What a contrast is the leader who exhibits serenity, tranquillity, and poise because of his humility. He is not self-conscious, and he is not offended by what people may say that is not complimentary. He is too busy serving with all humility to give thought to offenses real or imagined.

The late Corrie ten Boom dubbed herself "Tramp for the Lord." Unlike the tramp who does nobody any good, Corrie moved across the world serving others with gladness of heart and with deep serenity in the midst of threatening problems.

I know two ladies who demonstrate this contrast. One is a medical doctor who, although she comes from great wealth and could live a life of ease and affluence, has chosen to bury herself in service to thousands who are hurting and diseased half a world away from her home. She lives amidst constant danger. But the serenity in her heart reveals itself in her face and deportment. She endures slights and savagery, derogation, and danger. But she continues without self-pity. She actually revels in her opportunities to serve. Five minutes in her presence reveals to the most casual observer both her humility and the resulting quiet serenity.

In contrast to this young doctor is another woman I know who focuses all attention on herself and her family. She serves nobody. Though she is a highly trained academic, her energies and training are dissipated in a passion for self-protection. Her face is a maze of misery and a mask of distress. She has retreated into a bottle of alcohol. She forms a striking contrast to the serenity the doctor exhibits because of her humility.

Enlargement of Life

Too often humility is associated with lethargy, apathy, indecision, and inactivity. Nothing could be farther from the truth. Instead of limiting the leader, humility will enlarge his life. It will lead to learning, faith, and service.

Because the humble leader will not act as if he is self-sufficient and will not have to pretend he knows all the answers, humility puts the leader in a position to draw insights from others. The person who lacks humility and pretends to be self-sufficient, however, won't accept any ideas; he restricts himself to his own little world. Instead of leading to the shriveling neglect of personhood, humility opens the door to the expansion of personality and individuality.

Humility results in an enlargement of life because the humble person is faithful and content where he is and so God can give him more.

Banishment of Fear

Humility tends to banish fear because humility is love's mood, and "perfect love casts out fear" (1 John 4:18). The humble leader knows that God is in control of the world and all that is in it. His confidence is not in himself but in God, and if God is in charge, he has nothing to fear.

Humility calls the leader to courage in adhering to truth and righteousness, no matter how pervasive the evil or how unrelenting the resistance to the truth. Because God is in charge, the leader can stand up without fear. Christ's unflinching exposure of the Scribes and Pharisees in Matthew 23 is a challenge to the humble leader, for he recognizes that assertion has a legitimate place when it comes to the defense of truth and righteousness. Humility that arises from a dependence on God and a confidence in the faithfulness of God banishes fear.

Success

Humility leads to success. Sometimes we may shy away from success (perhaps in false humility!), but it is a legitimate goal. God told Joshua to meditate on the Word of God "day and night, that you may observe to do according to all that is written in it. For then you will make your way prosperous, and then you will have good success" (Joshua 1:8).

Assuming that you know about something when, in fact, you know nothing is a dangerous cover for ignorance and confusion. Those who think themselves to be "wise and prudent" (see Matthew 11:25) are impervious to new light. Pride and prejudice prohibit spiritual enlightenment and intellectual advance. The true scholar and the legitimate leader react like Newton, the man who discovered gravity, who said, "The great ocean of truth lay all undiscovered before me." Like scholarship, leadership requires docility, not dogmatism. The man who knows everything, learns nothing, and so it is a humble attitude that sets the stage for the knowledge and know-how that lead to success.

Availability of Unlimited Resources

It is a divine principle that strength is made perfect in weakness. God's resources are available to the humble leader who is willing to recognize his weakness. The person who fails to understand this principle weakens himself and dishonors the Lord.

The apostle Paul said, "I can do all things through Christ who strengthens me" (Philippians 4:13). Another translation, which I find exciting, is "I am almighty in the One who continually keeps pouring His power in me." When Paul says, "I can do all things" or "I am almighty," it would be the raving of an egomaniac were it not moderated by what comes after: "in the One who continually keeps pouring His power in me."

The one who comes humbly to God—who comes as a little child—finds God's strength, wisdom, resources, and discernment available to him without limit.

Serenity, enlargement of life, banishment of fear, success, and availability of unlimited resources all come about through humility. There are also many other results of humility. The point is, however, that humility does not lead to a suppression of your personality and an abandonment of achievement goals. Nor does it stifle leadership. Rather, humility is the way to enlarge your personality, to achieve, in His strength, the goals God has given you, and to enhance your leadership.

HOW IS HUMILITY NURTURED?

If you wanted to lose five kilograms, you would go on a diet. If you wanted to be closer to the Lord, you would spend more time in prayer and study of His Word. If you wanted to become more knowledgeable about the history of Egypt, you would study books and listen to lectures. But how do you become more humble? Talking about humility seems to make us less humble—not more humble—because humility possesses no self-consciousness.

It is possible to develop humility, but you must do it indirectly. You must recognize those paths that lead to humility and then concentrate on those paths, not on humility itself. Humility will come. But to concentrate on humility will make achieving it impossible.

How is humility nurtured? Here are five paths to humility:

By Enthroning Christ in Your Heart

If Christ lives in your heart, humility will shine through to the degree that you yield yourself to Christ. You will want to glorify Christ, not yourself. Humility is the expression of love, which is the fruit of the Holy Spirit. Love germinates and develops as a result of the Spirit's life-giving power.

The first path to humility, therefore, is making Christ the Lord of your life. Although you are born again only once, you must constantly renew your commitment to yield yourself to the lordship of Christ because self-will is constantly trying to dethrone Christ and rule your life.

By Obeying Christ

The person who enthrones Christ in his heart will want to obey Him, for Christ said, "If you love Me, keep My commandments" (John 14:15). In obedience to Christ some very practical steps are taken toward humility.

For instance, in 2 Timothy 2:24–25, Paul says, "And a servant of the Lord must not quarrel but be gentle to all, able to teach, patient, in humility correcting those who are in opposition. . . ."

The true leader must not quarrel. He must be gentle to all, not just to those who are polite to him. He must be patient. He must lovingly share the truth. The Holy Spirit produces humility through such a commitment to obedience. There is no place for a pompous, self-promoting arrogance in the Christlike leader. At one time Paul was proud, but having been brought low at the feet of his Lord and Master, he was able to exhort others. "If it is possible, as much as depends on you, live peaceably with all men" (Romans 12:18).

Christ said many things for our instruction and guidance; we cannot review them all. But they are summed up in His words to His disciples: "If you keep My commandments, you will abide in My love, just as I have kept My Father's commandments and abide in His love. These things I have spoken to you, that My joy may remain in you, and that your joy may be full. This is My commandment, that you love one another as I have loved you" (John 15:10–12).

By Assuming the Attitude and Behavior of a Little Child

To the Greek philosophers, the ideal man was a magnificent physical figure. He was one who excelled in both sports and the intellect. Christ, however, said that the ideal disciple was as a little child. A child is trusting and innocent, not arrogant. A child knows others are more important than he is, but he also has an unshattered belief in his own ability to do things. A child is obedient.

The Christian who wants to become more humble must assume the attitude and behavior of a little child.

By Following Christ's Example in Prayer

Christ taught His disciples the simplicity and humility of prayer. And what He taught them, He also practiced. He frequently retired into remote privacy to pray, submitting Himself, the Son, to God the Father. Over and over again the Gospels tell us of Christ's prayer life.

One evening at sundown, people brought the diseased to Jesus to be healed. All the town was there, and they must have stayed a great while. And yet "in the morning, having risen a long while before daylight, He went out and departed to a solitary place; and there He prayed" (Mark 1:35).

At another time, having fed 5,000, Jesus told His disciples to get into a boat and go to the other side of the Sea of Galilee while He sent the people away. "And when He had sent them away, He departed to the mountain to pray" (Mark 6:46).

Before choosing the twelve apostles, Jesus "went out to the mountain to pray, and continued all night in prayer to God" (Luke 6:12).

Christ bathed His ministry in prayer. He prayed to God because He needed fellowship with God. He included praise and adoration of the Father in His prayers. He prayed for the needs of Himself and others. In the prayer He taught His disciples, He also showed us that we should ask for forgiveness and confess our sins in prayer. Humility comes by following Christ's prayer example.

By Following Christ's Example in Personal Relationships

Consciously, in the strength of Christ, avoid elitism, intolerance, class distinction, and self-promotion. Here again, we profit from observing the little child who is not impressed with a person's bank balance, social position, or educational attainments.

A friend of mine, an outstanding Christian leader, exploded with rage because his office had sent only a junior staff member to meet him at the airport. Later he reflected and repented. I applaud the humility his contrition showed. He's a leader!

Christ demonstrated His humility in the choice of His followers and friends. He didn't go to the "Who's Who" of Palestine to select the people whom He would choose as disciples. In fact, in 2 Corinthians 1:26 and 27, Paul says, "Not many wise according to the flesh, not many mighty, not many noble, are called. But God has chosen the foolish things of the world to put to shame the wise, and God has chosen the weak things of the world to put to shame the things which are mighty."

Christ showed His humility by His sympathy with little children and those of modest circumstances who begged Him for help. He demonstrated appreciation for the smallest offering and the simplest service (see Matthew 10:42).

In 1969, a businessman who had climbed to a top executive position with an international oil company came to the first Haggai Institute session. When he arrived at the airport, the late Dr. Ernest Watson, then dean of the Haggai Institute, met him and went with him to the baggage claim area. The oil company executive turned to Dr. Watson and said, "Where is the servant to carry my bag?" Without any reply, Dr. Watson, a man then 66 years old and a recognized world leader, smiled and picked up the bag, carrying it to the car.

On arrival at the room, the gentleman complained, "There is only one glass in my room, and I need two." Patiently and without any rebuttal, Dr. Watson secured a second glass for him. During the sessions, God did a work of grace in that executive's heart, and his spirit seemed significantly tempered by the work of the Holy Spirit who used Dr. Watson as an example.

By Serving Others

The twelve apostles came together at the Last Supper. Ordinarily a servant or a slave would have been present to wash the feet of the guests, but apparently there was not one on this occasion. Peter did not offer to do it, nor did John, nor Thomas—nobody offered to wash the other's feet. Everybody's business was nobody's business, and so nobody offered to wash anybody's feet. They had taken their positions, reclining around the table. Our Lord then rose, laid aside His outer garments, took a towel, and girded Himself with it. He then poured water into a basin and went from one disciple to another washing their feet. After He had done that and was again reclining with them, He told them He was among them as a slave, a domestic who does the most menial work. They had seen this demonstrated for themselves (see Luke 22:27).

Jesus Christ, the ultimate example of leadership, lived a life of humility. The Lord of earth and heaven dressed in the garb of a rustic! He who poured out all the waters of the earth—the Amazon, the Euphrates, the Nile, the Mississippi—bent over a well to ask a Samaritan woman for a drink. He who spread the canopy of the heavens and set the earth for a footstool, spent the night with Simon a tanner. He whose chariots are the clouds, walked with sore feet. Look at Him hushing the tempest on Galilee and wiping off the spray of the storm, sitting down beside His disciples as though He had done no more than wipe the sweat from His brow in His father's carpenter shop.

He took the foot of death off the heart of Lazarus and broke the chain of the grave against the marble of the tomb, after which He walked out with Mary and Martha without any more pretension than a plain citizen going into the suburbs to spend the evening. Look at Him jostled as though He were a nobody, pursued as though He were an outlaw, nicknamed—sitting with crooks and sinners. He was the King of heaven and earth, with His robes trailing in the dust!

The leader will always endeavor to do good to others. The leader need not go to the ends of the earth to start serving—he can start in his own house. The leader, from morning to night, should be moving people toward goals that fulfill their real needs. It should be his constant ambition to imitate our Lord Jesus Christ by being willing to bear other's burdens. Is this difficult? Absolutely. But serving others is an essential path to follow on the road to humility.

The Christlike leader will follow these five paths to nurture humility in himself in all areas of his life:

In the social area of life, he will "in honor give preference to one another" (Romans 12:10).

In the intellectual area of life, he will subordinate his intellect to the mind of Christ that it might be maximized in serving others.

In the financial area of life, he will understand the true meaning of Wesley's heart when he said, "Earn all you can and save all you can to give all you can for as long as you can." The effective leader will invest his money, counting on God to multiply it, even as the Lord multiplied the fishes and loaves so that He could feed the multitude.

In the physical area of life, he will, in humility, observe the laws of health in order that he may more effectively serve those for whom God has made him responsible. He will recognize the importance of consistent exercise that strengthens the heart and lungs and maintains the best possible circulation. He knows the body is the temple of the Holy Spirit.

In the area of family life, he will demonstrate humility in his relationship with his spouse and conduct himself so as not to provoke his "children to wrath" (Ephesians 6:4).

Love and its mood—humility—are essential principles of Christlike leadership. They are not often found among so-called leaders who are not Christlike. That is why their cultivation is so essential. These principles set the Christlike leader apart from other leaders. Only that person who subjugates himself to the place of a servant and lets Christ continually pour His power into him is equipped to deliberately exert that special influence within a group to move it toward goals of beneficial permanence that fulfill the group's real needs.

Professor Dr. Eliseo Pajaro of Manila, Philippines, who died 6 October 1984, was one such person. From boyhood, Pajaro shone as a musical talent of exceptional promise. He developed into a man of charm, achievement, and spiritual depth. He earned his Ph.D. at the Eastman School of Music in Rochester, N.Y., and not long afterward attained full professorship at the University of the Philippines.

In 1959, Pajaro became the first Filipino to receive a grant from the Guggenheim Foundation for a year's study in the United States. During that time, he composed an opera which won the Filipino Presidential Medal of Merit. Twice he received the Republic Cultural Heritage Award. His entire adult life was punctuated with honors.

Dr. Pajaro was a professor, a composer, a conductor, a performer, but above all, a leader whose thumbprint shall remain indelible and intelligible on the pages of Filipino history, culture, music, and spirituality.

When Pajaro retired in 1980, he gave his energies to composing Christian cantatas. He completed four. Just prior to his death, he told me he planned next to write a cantata for Haggai Institute.

A year before his death, I attended a Haggai Institute (Philippines) dinner meeting which included some of the elite of the Philippines: representatives of government, academia, the judiciary, the church, medicine, the media, and multinational businesspeople. I was struck by the unobtrusive way Dr. Pajaro took a chair in the back row. People rushed to sit by him. His face, a marvelously open countenance, revealed his wholehearted response to every speaker. His wife, also a retired professor, and an H.I. alumna, had a major part on the program. He beamed. Afterward, he was crowded by many of these celebrated leaders. They all wanted a word with him.

It would never have crossed Dr. Pajaro's mind to tell people he was humble. A humble man does not concentrate on his humility. When I congratulated him on his achievements, he thanked me; he didn't deny them, but he made it clear that God had so blessed him he must honor God with his talent. To use his gift for the glory of God was his quiet passion.

Eliseo Pajaro embodied the principle of humility. His influence continues after his death, independent of any public relations program or publicity scheme. He demonstrated a humility that gave his leadership a continuing beneficial influence so that "he being dead, yet speaks."

SUMMARY

Humility is love's mood. It is the lowliness that pervades the leader's consciousness when he contemplates God's holy majesty and superabundant love in contrast to his own unworthiness, guilt, and total helplessness apart from divine grace. The humble person is free from pride or arrogance. He puts himself in submission to others and is helpful and courteous. The humble person does not consider himself to be self-sufficient and yet he recognizes his own gifts, resources, and achievements. Both love and humility are characteristic of true leaders.

Even worse than a lack of humility in a person's life is a false humility in which a person is proud about acting in a humble way. The person with false humility is fooling only himself, for people see through the pompous, self-adulatory, and arrogant person who feigns humility. In every age, true humility has been rare. Even Christ's disciples did not always exhibit humility.

Serenity, enlargement of life, banishment of fear, success, and availability of unlimited resources all come about through humility. Contrary to what is usually thought, humility does not suppress one's personality nor stifle leadership. Rather, it is the way to enlarge one's personality and to achieve—in God's strength—the goals He has given.

Talking about humility seems to make us less humble—not more—because humility possesses no self-consciousness. Therefore, to develop humility, you must concentrate on other paths that lead to humility. Enthrone Christ in your heart. Live in obedience to God and His Word. Assume the attitude and behavior of a little child. Follow Christ's example in prayer. Follow Christ's example in personal relationships by avoiding elitism, intolerance, class distinction, and self-promotion. Serve others.

The cultivation of love and its mood—humility—is essential for the Christlike leader because they are characteristics not often found among so-called leaders who are not Christlike. Only that person who subjugates himself to the place of a servant and lets Christ continually pour His power into him is equipped to deliberately exert that special influence within a group to move it toward goals of beneficial permanence that fulfill the group's real needs.

6

The Principle of

SELF-CONTROL

Religious leaders, some of the world's leading intellectuals, and hundreds of others stood ten and twelve deep trying to get into a packed Miami, Florida, auditorium in 1945 to hear a young evangelist, Bron Clifford. Dr. M. E. Dodd, minister of the prestigious First Baptist Church of Shreveport, Louisiana, introduced Clifford as "the greatest preacher since the apostle Paul." Clifford held the audience spellbound. That was normal. That same year he kept Baylor University students on the edge of their seats for two hours and fifteen minutes with his address, "Christ and the Philosopher's Stone." President Pat Neff, himself an outstanding orator, had ordered the bells switched off so the evangelist would not feel time-bound.

At the age of twenty-five young Clifford touched more lives, influenced more leaders, and set more attendance records than any clergyman his age in American history. National leaders vied for his attention. He was tall, handsome, intelligent, and eloquent. Hollywood invited him to audition for the part of Marcellus in *The Robe*. It seemed as if he had everything.

Less than ten years after the Miami meeting, Clifford had lost his leadership—and his life. Drinking and fiscal shabbiness did him in. His story is one of the saddest I know.

Before Clifford died, Dr. Carl E. Bates, a Christian leader, visited him and tried to help him. Dr. Ernestine Smith, a surgeon in Bates' church, had done exploratory surgery on Clifford and knew he was near death. She had asked her pastor to visit him.

Clifford was alone, with nobody to look after him. He had left his wife with their two Down's syndrome children. Bates was appalled to find Clifford occupying a grubby room in a third-rate motel on the western edge of Amarillo, Texas. Dying of cirrhosis of the liver, he was too sick to continue his last job, selling trucks for Plains Chevrolet in Amarillo.

Bron Clifford died unwept, unhonored, and unsung. The ministers of Amarillo took up an offering among themselves to buy an inexpensive casket and ship his body back east where it was buried in a potter's field.

Clifford lacked one essential quality necessary for sustained leadership: self-control. And it is lack of self-control that brings most of the griefs in other leaders' lives, too.

WHAT IS SELF-CONTROL?

Self-control is love's mastery. It is a way of life in which, by the power of the Holy Spirit, the Christian is able to be temperate in all things because he does not let his desires master his life. The concept of self-control does not just mean that the Christian abstains from certain habits such as contentiousness, quarreling, or drunkenness. It means that all aspects of his life are brought under the mastery of the Holy Spirit. It means his life is characterized by discipline.

The Greek word for self-control comes from a root word meaning "to grip," or "to take hold of." It describes the strength of the person who takes hold of himself, who stays in full control of himself. Paul talks about athletes being "temperate in all things" when they are in training. Eating, sleeping, and exercise are all carefully regulated when one is preparing for a race or a game.

Aristotle used this same word to describe the "ability to restrain desire by reason . . . to be resolute and ever in readiness to endure natural want and pain." He further explained that the man who is self-controlled has strong desires which try to seduce him from the way of reason, but he keeps them under control.

When I was a boy, my father told me the story of Esther in the Old Testament. I never tired of it. In that story, Haman, who was made head officer of the Persian empire under Xerxes, expected everyone to bow before him and pay homage to him. When Mordecai, Esther's uncle, did not bow or pay homage, Haman "was filled with indignation." He was furious. He could have arrested Mordecai on the spot. "Nevertheless Haman restrained himself"—he exerted self-control—so that he could plan an elaborate plot to have Mordecai hanged. Haman's plot backfired, but I have always been fascinated by the way in which Haman restrained his natural desire for the moment. That was self-control.

SELF-CONTROL AND THE LEADER

Self-control is an essential attitude and characteristic for a leader. Without it, the leader diminishes his effectiveness, and he will lose the respect of his followers. With it, people view him as one who has the determination and strength to be in charge.

In spite of its importance, self-control is an attitude that is difficult for a leader to develop, as it is for those who are not leaders. For instance, the effective leader has a vivid and clear vision of what his group will be like in three or five years. The leader lives in the future. With his top assistants, he actively plans goal programs that will accomplish his vision. But self-control requires that expenditures and attitudes be geared to today's reality so that he doesn't get into trouble by spending money before he has it. The effective leader will have many people looking to him for wisdom and insight, but self-control insists that he not think more highly of himself than he ought to think. The successful leader always runs the risk of believing his own press releases—of thinking he can do no wrong. But self-control should result in an attitude of humility and caution. Successful leadership requires self-control, and yet successful leadership makes it difficult to practice self-control.

It is this tension that makes understanding self-control so important for the Christlike leader. No leader can influence others if he doesn't control himself. When Paul listed the qualifications of bishops in Timothy 3, most of them related to the bishop's control of himself or of his family:

A bishop then must be blameless, the husband of one wife, temperate, sober-minded, of good behavior, hospitable, able to teach; not given to wine, not violent, not greedy for money, but gentle, not quarrelsome, not covetous; one who rules his own house well, having his children in submission with all reverence (for if a man does not know how to rule his own house, how will he take care of the church of God?); not a novice, lest being puffed up with pride he fall into the same condemnation as the devil. Moreover he must have a good testimony among those who are outside, lest he fall into reproach and the snare of the devil (1 Timothy 3:2–7).

Lack of Self-Control Destroys Leadership

Time and time again otherwise competent leaders have been destroyed because of a lack of self-control. Bron Clifford was one such tragic example. For some, their greed and extravagance have caused them to embezzle money or cheat their organization. Others have been lured by sexual temptations that have destroyed the leader himself, his family, and his leadership ability. Talking too much and too indiscreetly has cost other leaders the respect of their followers and the loss of confidential information. Gluttony or alcohol abuse has cost others their leadership positions because of the destruction of their physical bodies. Pride and self-indulgence have cost many their leadership position because their judgment became corrupted.

No one is immune to temptations caused by lack of self-control. But leaders are particularly susceptible. What one needs to be aware of is that such loss of self-control is most likely to happen in those areas where one is the strongest, has the most confidence, feels most secure. That's exactly where trouble strikes. The apostle Peter was known for his boldness and self-confidence. He vehemently proclaimed that he would defend Jesus Christ against all opposition. It was Peter who took a sword and cut off the high priest's servant's ear when the soldiers came to arrest Christ. And yet it was Peter who denied Christ three times that same night. Too much confidence in your strong points can sabotage your self-control in the very areas of your strength.

When the leader has no control over his own spirit, the smallest consequences annoy him. The shabbiest allurements draw him into the side alleys of leadership-destroying trivia. The smallest provocation angers him. Victimized by his own undisciplined passions and losing self-control habitually, the leader loses the confidence of the group. He sinks into complete uselessness. The self-indulgent person makes himself the slave to the self-controlled person.

Self-Control Gives Courage to Stand Alone

The first step toward effective leadership is a vision—a clear picture of what the leader sees the group being or doing. The leader may listen to others, but God gives the vision to him alone. He must not be diverted from his vision by the opinion and subtle pressures of the crowd. Self-control gives the leader the courage to stand alone.

John Templeton, Wall Street's most successful financier in the field of mutual funds, spends comparatively little time in New York City. He lives on the Bahama Islands. One of the reasons he gives for distancing himself is so that he might do his own thinking without being swayed, however imperceptibly, by prevailing Wall Street wisdom. I believe that this consistent self-control is one reason Templeton has created so many ideas that have brought immeasurable help to people around the world.

Self-control gives the leader courage to stand alone when others are questioning his vision. The habit of self-control will teach a leader the importance of relying on his own evaluation and understanding of situations rather than relying on popular opinion. Most shiver at the thought of individual responsibility or liability. They don't determine their stand until they first test the direction of the wind, consult a popular poll, or detect a consensus.

Strong character is an individual thing, requiring individual nurture. An attitude of self-control develops strong character and strong character can be defined as the power to stand alone. Holiness never counts its companions; it never intimates that its validity is in proportion to the number of its admirers.

The leader realizes the importance of standing alone because continual contact with his followers weakens him. He will sink to their level. He will accommodate to their habits and fancies. Instead, he should limit the spiritual development of his character to being on God's plane. Being part of the group is far easier and more comfortable than rising above the group, but that would fail to meet the group's highest needs by giving it a vision that will result in change of beneficial permanence.

In solitude, where you recognize your need of God, you become strong. But solitude demands self-control. Alone in a desert with God, John the Baptist viewed things that matter most—and viewed them in true perspective. He never became drugged on his own fame. He knew his mission. He knew his relationship with the coming Messiah: "He must increase, but I must decrease." He paid the price in love's mastery, self-control, to exert the special influence that motivated great crowds to fulfill their real needs.

The real test of a leader's courage and ability to stand alone comes in times of crisis. Crises remove all subterfuge, double-talk, and posturing. It is in times of crisis that the leader's self-control is so important because lack of control will only aggravate most such situations.

Self-Control Draws Followers to the Leader

People want a leader whom they can trust. The effective implementation of any of the principles of leadership—vision, goalsetting, love, humility, self-control, communication, investment, opportunity, energy, staying power, authority, and awareness—will draw people to the leader. They want a worthy example to follow and these principles accomplish that. They want to have confidence in the strength of their leader, and the attitude of self-control especially will convey the leader's strength. They want to believe that the change the leader will bring about really will be ones of beneficial permanence. Living these principles communicates that.

Probably no foreigner exerted greater leadership over the people of Shaohsing, China, in the early twentieth century than Dr. Claude H. Barlow. This self-effacing medical missionary was the personification of self-control.

A strange disease for which he knew no remedy was killing the people. There was no laboratory available for research. Dr. Barlow filled his notebook with observations of the peculiarities of the disease in hundreds of cases. Then, armed with a small vial of the disease germs, he sailed for the United States. Just before he arrived, he took the germs into his own body and then hurried to the Johns Hopkins University Hospital, where he had studied.

Claude Barlow was now a very sick man. He turned himself over to his former professors as a human guinea pig for their study and experimentation. A cure was found, and the young doctor recovered. He sailed back to China with scientific treatment for the scourge and saved a multitude of lives.

When he was asked about his experience, Dr. Barlow simply replied, "Anyone would have done the same thing. I happened to be in the position of vantage and had the chance to offer my body." What humility! What self-control! What love!

No wonder multitudes followed Claude Barlow's leadership when he returned. He demonstrated love's mastery. He risked his life, to say nothing of his reputation and future ministry, by attempting the impossible. He motivated the people by his own love, the outgoing of his total being to them in beneficence and help. And the capstone quality of this love was its mastery, self-control.

It is this kind of leadership that will draw the followers to the leader.

How to Develop and Exercise Self-Control

Like all of the principles of leadership, self-control must be carefully developed and nurtured. It doesn't just happen. And there will never be a time in this life when the leader can say he has arrived and does not need to continue nurturing his love, his ability to communicate, or his self-control.

Through Dependence on God

The exercise of self-control must be done in dependence upon God. "Will-power has no defense against the careless word, the unguarded moment. The will has the same deficiency as the law—it can deal only with externals. It is not sufficient to bring about the necessary transformation of the inner spirit."[19]

The ultimate resource derives from the transformation of the inner spirit. I'm referring to the resource available to the Christlike leader who has been changed into a new creation by Jesus Christ. Belonging to Him, you can look to Him for guidance and depend on Him for help. You can develop and exercise self-control through dependence on God.

Through a Life of Discipline

A life characterized by self-control begins with an attitude of discipline. This discipline is not just in one or two areas of life, but all areas. Those who are disciplined in small things tend to be disciplined in large things as well, whereas those who are undisciplined will be that way in many areas of their lives. Regular exercise takes discipline. Maintaining an organized study takes discipline. Getting out of bed on time takes discipline. Discipline is necessary to have a daily devotional time. You may think the small areas are unimportant, but a lack of discipline in little things will affect your ability to maintain discipline in large things.

The word *discipline* for the Christian also has a specialized meaning in the sense of the classical disciplines of the spiritual life. In our age of self-gratification, these disciplines have for the most part been abandoned. They are viewed as too rigorous, too other-worldly, too time-consuming. These disciplines include meditation, prayer, study, solitude, service, confession, and worship.

What better way for a Christian leader to begin a life of self-control than with the cultivation of these disciplines of the spiritual life!

Through Making Decisions Ahead of Time

When Daniel, Shadrach, Meshach, and Abed-Nego were chosen for special training in Babylon, they purposed in their hearts that they would not defile themselves "with the portion of the king's delicacies, nor with the wine which he drank." Thus when they were actually faced with the opportunity to eat the king's food and drink the king's drink, they didn't have to make a decision under pressure. They had already made up their minds. They knew they wouldn't do it.

Self-control is made easier when you purpose in your heart how you will act in certain situations. For instance, I have decided that I will be honest if a clerk gives me too much change for a purchase. If I buy something for $3.00 and give the clerk a $5 bill, I don't have to think twice about returning the extra money if I receive $7.00 in change. It's automatic. I don't give myself the opportunity to rationalize that the store charges too much for its goods and so the error simply evens things out. Too often, if we are faced with a decision under pressure, it gives us a chance to question whether we should do what we know is right or not and we will find an excuse to do what we know to be wrong.

Self-control works best when you make your decisions ahead of time and live according to those decisions.

Through Gratitude for Adversity

It fascinates me that of all the New Testament writers, only Paul used the word *adversity*. Adversity was his constant Spirit-administered discipline. He could have become bitter about his adversities, but he rejoiced in them because he knew they were given for his benefit. He could finally say, "I take pleasure in infirmities, in reproaches, in needs, in persecutions, in distresses" (2 Corinthians 12:10).

At the peak of his career, God sent Paul a "thorn in the flesh" to buffet him lest he be "exalted above measure." What a blessing! God had equipped Paul with gifts of character, energy, and power. He possessed the capacity to command, to lead, to organize. His was a great mind which could articulate the truths of God so as to be understood by both the literati and the illiterate. However, had it not been for the presence of his infirmity, he may never have achieved for God such splendid work. He may have surrendered to self-centered confidence rather than developing self-control. He may have relied upon his extraordinary endowments instead of casting himself completely on the power of God.

Scripture assures us that suffering produces joy and "the testing of your faith produces patience." Adversity is God's refining fire. In the crucible of suffering you have the greatest opportunity to develop and exercise self-control. During Job's suffering, his wife urged him to "curse God and die." Job responded, "Though He slay me, yet will I trust Him." That kind of self-control comes as the result of adversity. You should show gratitude for those experiences God gives you that will build self-control. He gives you those experiences because He loves you and wants to see you develop love so demonstrated through self-control.

Through Ruling Your Spirit

A friend told me that he could not possibly control his temper. He attributed his ungovernable explosions of anger to his parents and grandparents. He said there were some people, like himself, who could not be expected to rule their own spirits. I asked him if he were in a heated argument with his wife and the doorbell rang, would he continue shouting. He saw my point that he really could control his temper when he wanted to. You can rule your spirit, and ruling your spirit is essential to developing self-control.

In exercising self-control, you must learn to take all sorts of punishment and abuse without retaliating in kind. This is the price you pay for leadership. When an angry person starts to vilify and abuse you—justly or unjustly—just remember that if you retaliate in a like manner, you are being drawn down to that person's level; you are allowing that person to dominate you! And in so doing, you are forfeiting your leadership, for you have allowed that person to control your emotions rather than controlling them yourself.

The Christlike leader rules his spirit. "He who is slow to anger is better than the mighty, and he who rules his spirit than he who takes a city" (Proverbs 16:32).

You will find support in developing and exercising self-control by reflecting on God's work in your own life. The mercy Paul received from God, for instance, motivated him to exercise self-control. How could Paul ever despair of others when he himself had found such mercy? How could he abandon his course when the same grace by which he was saved was given to him so abundantly to guide him and sustain him? How could he become impatient with others when he reflected upon God's long-suffering which had hovered over him and had overcome his rebellion? God's goodness provides a powerful incentive to self-control.

From the beginning to the end of his career, Paul was constrained by the one overriding thought that he had been redeemed to serve—to help meet the *real* needs of others.

Through Controlling Your Thoughts

The effective leader realizes that self-control is really a matter of thought-control, and he insists on doing his own thinking. Thinking about your vision, your mission, your goals, and the needs of your group several times daily—especially upon awaking and before retiring—will go a long way toward guaranteeing your exercise of self-control.

Picture the way you will act as a leader characterized by self-control. How will you react to people in various situations? How will self-control contribute to your goals and mission? Picture your group as you see it one year and three years from now. Putting these images clearly in your thoughts will help you act them out in reality. In addition to picturing yourself in situations as you would like them to be, replay in detail situations where you have already demonstrated self-control.

Athletes are trained in this way. They are told to relax and visualize their best performance—how they felt, what they heard, odors they noticed, the taste of the water or dirt or air, what they saw. They are told to input all of these sensory-rich impressions into their brain so that in their next contest they can reproduce and even improve their performance. Big league salesmen and notable orators have been doing this for years.

Develop your self-control by taking time each day, preferably just after your prayers and before retiring at night, to replay victories of self-control when the normal response would have been anger, fear, or intimidation.

You have the potential ability to make your thoughts do your bidding. Two impulses set your brain in motion: self-suggestion and outside suggestion. It is humiliating to realize that you are influenced by the outside suggestions of others whom you permit to place thoughts, without your examination or question, in your consciousness. You have it in your power to determine the material you will think about. Act on this ability. It will develop your self-control.

Deliberately choose the thoughts which you want to dominate your mind. Decisively deny admittance to all outside suggestions that don't square with your values and commitments. Paul commanded us to do this when he said to think on "whatever things are true, whatever things are noble, whatever things are just, whatever things are pure, whatever things are lovely, whatever things are of good report" (Philippians 4:8).

You are the product of your thoughts. You must exercise self-control if you are to influence others with your suggestions instead of yourself being influenced by random suggestions from outside. You learn to swim by swimming. You learn to exercise self-control by exercising self-control. And the key is through controlling your thoughts.

Optimum Self-Control Is Spirit-Control

Domination by the Holy Spirit makes possible the self-control that God and good leadership require. Spirit domination and lack of self-control are mutually exclusive. One cannot exist with the other. The

Holy Spirit produces in the submissive heart a disposition, a strength, a mind-set that makes an otherwise unreachable self-control possible.

WHAT SELF-CONTROL ACCOMPLISHES

You can't permanently defeat the leader who exercises self-control. Obstacles ultimately seem to melt away in the presence of such a leader. In short, love conquers, and self-control is love's mastery.

Self-control is usually seen as a restriction, a discipline that produces a harsh, joyless existence. In reality, however, just the opposite is true. Self-control produces in any person results that will make him a candidate for leadership.

Freedom

Self-control produces a wonderful freedom that comes from bringing self-centeredness and fear into subjection. Self-control cuts down on nagging decisions about whether you should do the things you know you should avoid and whether you would skip the things you know you should do. You have already made up your mind. You don't have to decide. Self-control is God's practical way of giving us freedom from the domination of sin and sinful thoughts. The freedom produced by self-control comes from knowing you have mastered your habits instead of letting them master you.

You need to experience this freedom to appreciate it because you are told every day by the world that freedom comes not from self-control but from self-indulgence. In reality, self-indulgence leads to slavery, whereas self-control leads to freedom.

Confidence

Self-control produces a confidence and assurance that you are capable of leadership.

When I met His Excellency Rajiv Gandhi a year before he became India's prime minister, I was impressed. When I returned home, I was asked if I thought he would succeed his mother, Madam Indira Gandhi.

"I think so."

"Can he fill the role?"

"I'm convinced he has the intelligence, the savvy, the charm, but I'm not sure he has enough 'fire in his belly.' He's a brilliant and gentle man, the kind you'd like as a friend, but I'm not sure he has the stomach for the rough and tumble of politics."

How wrong I was! Through the exercise of self-control, Rajiv

Gandhi has consolidated power and achieved a support base unequaled by any Indian prime minister before him, including his illustrious mother and scholarly grandfather. Self-control created in him the confidence to lead.

Joy

Joy comes from knowing you are being obedient to the will of God. Consistent, constant obedience takes self-control. That is why self-control can produce a deep, lasting joy. Richard Foster says, "Joy is the keynote of all the disciplines. . . . When one's inner spirit is set free from all that holds it down, that can hardly be described as dull drudgery. Singing, dancing, even shouting characterize the disciplines of the spiritual life."

Stability

Few people like change. We want things to stay the way they are. People look to leaders who will provide them with stability. A disciplined life does not mean there will be no change for you and your followers, but it does mean that the change will be purposeful and controlled. It does mean that there will be stability.

Leadership

Self-control produces freedom, confidence, joy, and stability. Those qualities will catapult a person to a place of leadership. Self-control also insures the flowering of every other quality of love: joy, peace, longsuffering, gentleness, goodness, faithfulness, and meekness. Through self-control, all aspects of the Christlike leader's life are brought under the mastery of the Holy Spirit.

One of the most important principles of effective leadership is certainly that of self-control. Begin today to develop it in your life.

A twenty-seven-year-old man, Dawson Trotman, with only one year of Bible school and one year of seminary, organized the Navigators, an evangelistic organization that majored on conversion and spiritual growth through complete commitment to Christ, the Bible, and others.

Daws Trotman embodied self-control in his prayer life, in his Bible study, and in putting others first to a degree I have rarely witnessed. After extended time with God, he was driven to take the promises of God seriously and to act on them. He was a constant challenge to me, and he was a leader whose leadership still exerts special influence around the world.

Trotman was bright, artistic, and highly articulate, but he emphasized the importance of complete commitment to the Lord Jesus Christ and to the Bible. He was an exhorter. No exhorter of significance is ever responded to with neutrality. People either love him or hate him. Trotman suffered some vicious attacks over the course of his life and ministry. But he continued on, fully believing the promise, "Great peace have those who love Your law, And nothing causes them to stumble."

In 1956, Daws was at Schroon Lake, New York. A girl was drowning. He dived into the water, saved the girl, but it cost him his life. He drowned as a young man. He left an organization that now ministers powerfully in more than 50 countries with a staff numbering more than 2,500.

Bron Clifford is a vapor long since dissipated. Dawson Trotman is a power continuing to influence the world. The difference in the two men is one of self-control.

SUMMARY

Self-control is a way of life in which, by the power of the Holy Spirit, the Christian is able to be temperate in all things because he does not let his desires master his life. Self-control is usually seen as a restriction. And yet it is impossible to permanently defeat the leader who exercises self-control. Self-control is love's mastery.

The Christlike leader knows that self-control is important because lack of self-control destroys leadership. The leader needs to be particularly careful that loss of self-control does not come in those areas where he is the strongest, has the most confidence, feels the most secure. That is exactly where trouble strikes. Self-control gives courage to stand alone. It allows the leader to be not diverted from his vision by the opinion and subtle pressures of the crowd. Self-control draws followers to the leader. People want to follow those who demonstrate self-control.

Like all the principles of leadership, self-control must be carefully developed and nurtured. This is done through dependence on God, a life of discipline, making decisions ahead of time, gratitude for adversity, ruling one's spirit, controlling one's thoughts, and by letting the Holy Spirit live in the leader.

Self-control is usually seen as a restriction, a discipline that produces a harsh, joyless existence. In reality, however, just the opposite is true. Self-control produces in any person results that will make him a candidate for leadership. Self-control produces freedom, confidence, joy, and stability. Those qualities will catapult a person to a place of leadership.

7

The Principle of

COMMUNICATION

Leadership begins with a vision. The commitment to that vision is a mission, which is then fulfilled by setting and accomplishing certain goals. But the leader does not do this in isolation. The leader's task is to communicate the vision, the mission, and the goals to his followers in love and humility.

The leader must be a communicator. He may have other skills because of the field in which he works, but he is to be first and foremost a communicator. Good musicianship, for instance, is a requisite for a good choir director, but many great musicians have failed as choir directors because they could not communicate effectively to the members of the choir.

The ability to effectively communicate, through speech and writing, is possibly the leader's most valuable asset. There are seven rules of effective communication which, if mastered, will help leaders maximize their effectiveness.

RULE ONE: RECOGNIZE THE IMPORTANCE OF EFFECTIVE COMMUNICATION

"What could be easier than communicating?" you might ask. "I do it every day." But communication is not as simple as it appears, and you may be only repeating words when you think you are communicating. And yet communication is the way the leader unifies and directs the group.

85

In simplest terms, communication takes place when a message has been transmitted from one person to another with both people understanding the message in approximately the same way. But there are an incredible number of barriers to effective communication. Suppose Mr. X wants to tell Mr. Y something. The figure[20] below represents Mr. X's communication to Mr. Y.

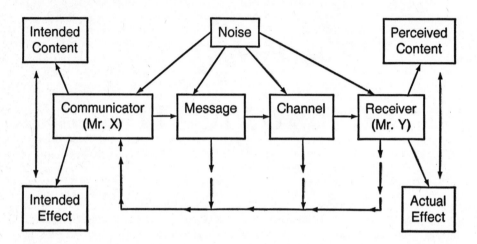

Mr. X wants his message to have a certain effect on Mr. Y. Perhaps he is compiling a mailing list and mixes up some of the addresses. Mr. X wants Mr. Y to correct the mistake. He chooses certain words to tell Mr. Y that the list is incorrect and what he should do to make it right. The technical word for this is "encoding." The encoded message has both an intended content (the list is wrong) and an intended effect (Mr. Y fixes it). Next, Mr. X transmits the message to Mr. Y through a channel. Perhaps he speaks to Mr. Y or perhaps he writes him a memo. Mr. Y then decodes the message so that he will perceive the content Mr. X is trying to communicate. The effectiveness of the communication depends on how similar the perceived content is to the intended content and the actual effect is to the intended effect.

It is important for the leader to recognize that the effectiveness of the communication depends on the *perceived* content and *actual* effect—not on his intended content, no matter how eloquently given, nor on the intended effect, no matter how pure and noble his intentions. It is the communicator's task to *make sure* the perceived content and actual effect are right, not just assume the content is understood and the effect is carried out.

Mr. Y's perception of the content and the actual effect of the message depends on many things other than the words. If Mr. X speaks Swahili and Mr. Y understands only Japanese, obviously the message will not be communicated. If the room is so noisy that he can't understand what Mr. X says, Mr. Y may smile politely and do nothing. The intended effect is not achieved. If Mr. Y has just heard that his father died and has had several other things go wrong that day, he may get angry with Mr. X. Again, the intended effect is not achieved. In addition to his words, Mr. X can communicate a great deal by his nonverbal behavior—how he stands, his facial expression, where he places his hands.

Effective communication is both an art and a science. It's an art that requires the same earnest attention, persistent practice, and careful technique as the mastery of painting, sculpture, or music. It's a science based on the tenets of psychology.

Learning to communicate effectively is important to you as a leader because you will never reach your leadership potential without it. I am convinced that only bad attitudes account for more failures of leadership than faulty communication.

Effective Communication Overcomes Isolation

Members of a group can be isolated from each other by geography, language differences, or attitudes such as class distinction, religious sectarianism, racial segregation, nationalism, or political partisanship. Isolation destroys the group and group achievement, and so the leader is compelled to overcome the isolation of members of the group. Through effective communication, the leader must encourage the kind of understanding, tolerance, and sympathy that will bring those in isolation into unity with the rest of the group.

Effective Communication Is a Factor in Reproduction

Communication is the means by which the leader reproduces leadership principles in others. He wants others in the group to catch the vision and work toward the goals that will fulfill the mission. "He who does the work is not so profitably employed as he who multiplies the doers," a man named Morley said in the early part of the last century.

"No man ever began a movement which was destined to stand the test of time but that he placed great stress on the task of teaching those who followed after him," said Dr. Herschel H. Hobbs. "Thoughts are things, beliefs are biotic, and ideas are imperishable. Leaders may come and go, personalities may live and die, but mental and spiritual concepts are immortal. These are the dynamics for changing the course of history and the lives of men and women."[21]

It is the reproduction of great thoughts, beliefs, and ideas in others through effective communication that sets a leader apart.

Effective Communication Tends to Safeguard Freedom of Speech

Those of us who live where there is freedom of speech may not fully appreciate it, but such freedom is a treasure to be guarded and defended. And yet when speech becomes insipid and banal, all the legislative enactments in the capitals of the world will not make it effective. A person in a leadership position who violates the rules of effective communication tragically imposes a greater limitation on freedom of speech than any external restriction that tyrants can impose. Free speech cannot long endure without effective speech. The leader should therefore make the development of communication effectiveness his lifelong passion and discipline.

Effective Communication Presents Worthy Thoughts Worthily

A popular assumption is that you need only "to have something to say" in order to communicate. What a dreadful fallacy! Unless that "something to say" is communicated effectively, it might as well be scattered to the wind. Having a concern only with what is being said is focusing attention on the *intended* content and *intended* effect of the communication. They are important, but the effective communicator focuses instead on the *perceived* content and *actual* effect.

How often speech fails to attain its purpose! The professor seeks to impart his important knowledge, and he finds the students confused. The lawyer pleads earnestly before the jury to accept his valid facts, but he loses the case. The salesman extols his superb products, but he makes no sales. The father wisely counsels his son, but the son shows no change in attitude or action. The political leader presents his just policies to the crowds, but he loses the election. And the preacher declares the eternal truth of the Word of the Lord, and the congregation falls asleep! In each instance, potential leadership was desecrated because effective communication was violated. Worthy thoughts were not given a chance because they were not presented worthily. The perceived content did not match the intended content, and the actual effect was not the same as the intended effect.

The effective leader leaves nothing to chance. Although he will certainly be open to the enlightenment and leading of the Holy Spirit, he prepares his verbal communication as thoroughly as the concert master prepares his musical communication. It is not enough to have worthy thoughts. Those thoughts must be communicated worthily.

Progress would be tragically stopped if all communication were prohibited. The wheels of industry would screech to a halt. Schools would shut down. Governments would collapse. Families would disintegrate. Alliances would crumble. Famine would decimate humankind across the globe. How sorely would evangelization of the world suffer if all communication were prohibited!

Communication is the means by which we transfer truth. Communication can move and mold men, individually and collectively. Communication lays the very foundation for spiritual decisions. It relates intimately to a person's relationship with God. If effective communication is so important, does it not follow that leaders, redeemed and called of God, ought to give sober attention to the most effective way of utilizing this powerful tool? The leader cannot ignore the rules of effective communication.

RULE TWO: ASSESS YOUR AUDIENCE

The leader's task as an effective communicator is (1) to make the perceived content of the message in the mind of the receiver as similar as possible to the intended content of the message that is in his own mind and (2) to make the actual effect of the message on the receiver be as close as possible to the intended effect. To do this, the leader must know the receiver—his audience.

Several years ago, I received a phone call from a young man named Jackson. He asked me for some counsel. I identified him as a young man in his mid-thirties, living in Texas, the son of a close friend whom I had known for twenty years. We set the date to meet. To my astonishment, it was someone other than the person I expected. The man who met me was also in his thirties. He also lived in Texas. His father had also been a close friend of mine for more than twenty years. However, because I had misassessed my audience, my preparation was substantially different for the young man I thought was coming than it would have been for the young man who actually came. I had failed to assess my audience.

You must know your audience thoroughly if you are going to communicate effectively and lead the people in it.

First and most basic, you must identify the audience makeup. Learn such demographic facts as gender, age, ethnic background, education, vocation, lifestyle, religious affiliation and degree of commitment to it, hobbies, and anything else that would be particularly relevant to what you want to communicate.

Second, assess your audience's attitude toward its environment and important issues. Are they happy with the social, political, cultural, and educational conditions where they live? Do the working conditions and family conditions of the area meet with their approval?

I painfully recall a dinner I had with several business leaders in a Third World nation. Their head of state had just delivered a major address. Although I disagreed with some of what he said, I told the businessmen that I was enthralled by his oratorical style. They looked at me in stony silence with eyes that seemed to say, "We didn't know you were so stupid!" They felt so strong an antipathy for the man that nothing I could say would have been construed as positive.

Third, assess your audience's attitude toward each other. Are they comfortable with each other, jealous of each other, suspicious of each other, supportive of each other? Are they homogeneous or heterogeneous?

Fourth, assess their attitude toward the subject you are dealing with. Are they familiar with your subject? Are they agreeable to what you will say? A subject such as "How to Kill Rats" might rivet the attention of farmers, but bore college students to death.

If your audience is totally unversed in your subject, you'll probably begin with the known and progress to the unknown. If your audience is not interested in the subject, you will have to show how the discussion is going to affect them and fulfill their real needs.

Finally, assess your audience's attitude toward you, the leader. Communication is a two-way street. You should tailor your communication by the feedback you get to what you say.

When I was conducting large crusades, it was standard operating procedure to send my associates ahead to learn as much as possible about the audience. Even then, on occasions we slipped up. In 1974, I made an impassioned plea in Australia for each person to vote during an upcoming election. In America, people are not compelled to vote. It is strictly voluntary. I was trying to impress my audience with the importance of every citizen taking advantage of this precious privilege of a free society. After the meeting I was told that voting was compulsory in Australia! In fact, people are fined if they do not vote. I had wasted twelve minutes of each person's time simply because I had not properly assessed the audience. Multiply twelve minutes by 2,000 people, and the 400 hours wasted still embarrasses me.

My definition of leadership presupposes a thorough assessment of the audience. How can a leader move the group toward goals of beneficial permanence that meet its real needs if he does not know who the group really is, where the members of the group really are in terms of self-image and living philosophy, and what they really want to accomplish?

RULE THREE: SELECT THE RIGHT COMMUNICATION GOAL

The first requisite to effective communication is a clear understanding of the goal of the communication. No one builds a building without asking what the function will be, and no one takes a journey without knowing where he is going. If the leader fails to target a precise goal when he communicates, the followers will respond with indifference.

Once a stranger in America stopped a man on the road and asked him, "Where does this road lead to?" The man answered, "Where do you want to go?"

Again the stranger persisted, "Where does this road lead to?"

"My friend," replied the other, "this road leads to any place in the United States."

It is the same with communication. The leader must know his destination if he wishes to arrive there. He must have a goal when he starts out. His goal may be to inform, to impress, to convince, to entertain, or to actuate. The leader usually will have the goal of actuating, but he will try to actuate the group by informing, impressing, convincing, or entertaining.

When the leader is explaining the impact of a newly enacted law on the group's activities, his goal is to inform. When he is handing out awards to the high achievers and reciting some of the historic "highs" of their achievements, his goal is to impress. When he lectures on the superiority of computerization, his goal is to convince. When he makes an after-dinner speech, his goal may be to entertain. And when he is speaking to the members of the board about the importance of spending $100,000 to purchase computers and another $100,000 a year to recruit computer technocrats, his communication goal is to actuate.

Whether you're writing a memo, composing a magazine article, preparing a sermon, presenting a radio talk, or motivating students or employees, knowing the proper communication goal will conserve time, accomplish the task more effectively and thus strengthen your leadership.

To Inform

If your goal is to inform, it means you will create understanding. This is the goal of all who seek to convey information purely as information. In this instance, the duty of the communicator is discharged when he presents the ideas so that the audience can understand them clearly. This is the goal of the witness in court. This is the great function of a dictionary. When "to inform" is your goal, you state the ideas and stop there. You state no bias, no slant.

To Impress

Impressiveness connotes vividness. The message to be conveyed is not simply to be understood, but to be *felt*. The lecturer on literature desires that in the presentation, the genius of Kahlil Gibran will not only be understood, but that it shall arouse pleasurable emotion. The evangelist, in preaching on the love of God, is concerned not only that it be comprehended, but that it will stir the soul. This is the goal of speakers at school graduations, funerals, festivals, anniversaries.

When the specific purpose is to arouse in the listener emotional association, the goal is to impress.

To Convince

When the leader has the goal of convincing, it means that he is not content for his group only to understand or feel, but he wants each person to accept the subject matter as truth. Each one must say, in effect, "That is so"; "You are right"; "I believe." This goal, however, doesn't require action. It simply relates to matters of opinion, such as which of two political philosophies exercises the greater influence or which is the better policy for world evangelization.

In every case where the dominant motive of the communicator is to secure acceptance of his idea, the goal is to convince.

To Entertain

Entertainment as a goal is concerned with amusement. This is the leader's goal when he wants to arouse pleasant feelings, interest, mild delights, or even hearty laughter.

In 1971, Hockaday, an elite girl's school in Dallas, Texas, asked me to speak. The officials warned me that the last several speakers were interrupted by the girls; they would hum on one note, causing a distraction that made the public address impossible. I told them I thought we would get along just fine.

Within fifteen seconds, through the use of humor, I had captured their attention. Twenty-seven minutes later, they gave me a standing ovation. I was actually able to say everything that was on my heart. It was the entertainment factor that neutralized the girls' antagonism. To this day, some, now mothers and career women, write to tell me what a turning point that session was to their lives.

To Actuate

When the leader has a goal of actuating the group, it means that he wants his hearers to *do* something. He wants them to take action. His dominant purpose is to move the group to act: to be, to go, to give, to bring, to join, to do.

To actuate is surely the main concern of the evangelist, the trial lawyer, the political speaker, the merchant, and the salesman—and the leader. To actuate may demand, as preliminary steps, the goals of informing, impressing, convincing, or even entertaining. But it is more than all of these. The goal of actuating seeks to make the hearer not only see, feel, and believe, but to make him validate his understanding, his feeling, his belief by his works.

The Epistle of James underlines this communication goal: "But be doers of the Word, and not hearers only, deceiving yourselves" (James 1:22).

Differences in Goals

The distinction between the various goals becomes unmistakable when we consider them in relation to a particular topic.

If my subject is Samson and I explain his conquests and his final defeat but ultimate victory without any effort to secure approval or disapproval, then the goal is *to inform.*

If I wish to arouse the emotions by showing how Samson backslid, how he was double-crossed by those whom he trusted, and how in his closing hours he honored God, then my goal is *to impress.*

If my purpose is to make the listener or reader believe that victories are possible in the strength of God and use Samson as an illustration, then my goal is *to convince.*

If I am using some of Samson's exploits such as sending the foxes through the Philistines' corn as an illustration of humor in the Bible and my dominant motive is to create pleasure, then my goal is *to entertain.*

If I am addressing a group of young people urging them to make a complete surrender of their lives to God, and use Samson as an illustration of the importance of putting God first, then my goal is *to actuate.*

Be clear, precise, and focused if you want people to follow you. This will come by having a clear communication goal. Selecting the right communication goal liberates the leader from the awful pit of indefiniteness.

Rule Four: Break the Preoccupation Barrier

Before you can communicate effectively, you must capture your audience's attention. But everyone is preoccupied. You will rarely find anyone who wants to know what you think. Moreover, everyone is bombarded with thousands of messages a day, each clamoring for their attention: "Buy Shell gasoline"; "Here's the latest in the Mideast crisis"; "You need to take a vacation in Australia"; "The price of gold went up today." Your first move, then, if you want to communicate, is to master the skill of breaking the preoccupation barrier. The key is in assessing your audience.

In 1975, I had a special speech to give. For days I thought and prayed for a way to break the preoccupation barrier. The major perceived problem troubling the largest number of people at that time was the financial crisis caused by the skyrocketing oil prices.

I began the address with these words: "I'm going to give you ten commandments for surviving the financial crisis." In seconds, you could hear an onionskin drop on the carpet, so quiet was the audience of 2,500 persons. When it was announced that the message would be available on cassette or in printed form, the telephone operators were kept busy for the next twelve hours trying to handle all the requests.

The title and cover of a book are given the task of capturing attention. Of all the books I've written, one has outsold all others combined. It has been in print for more than twenty-five years and has been translated into eighteen languages. The title is *How to Win Over Worry.* Apparently the title breaks the preoccupation barrier.

It is possible to get people's attention by forcing them to listen, but that insures neither a faithful following nor an effort on the part of the listener to decode the message. Forced attention violates the very foundation of leadership. But attention captured by self-interest lasts. This is a principle ineffective leaders ignore and good leaders grasp. A leader can force some followers to listen, but effective leadership occurs only when the leader breaks the preoccupation barrier and earns the right to be heard.

To break the preoccupation barrier, the leader must ask himself, "What are the disturbing problems the people are facing?" He then identifies the problem in a way that the listeners or readers will recognize. Next he promises a solution and fulfills the promise.

Writers of magazine articles need to quickly break the preoccupation barrier. One writer who did this effectively had the following first sentence: "You who are reading this article may die before you finish it."

It was an article on heart disease, and the writer knew what would get people's attention. The sentence is personal. It sets up a potential problem that the reader will want to know about. It is universal. If the first sentence had been, "Heart disease strikes most often at men and women around forty," the writer would have lost a large audience. Only people around forty would be tempted to read it. Or if the first sentence had been "Heart disease causes more deaths than any other ailment," the writer would have captured very few people because the sentence would be too general. Instead, the writer's sentence was striking and it was personal.

Russell Conwell built one of America's largest churches, established one of the world's leading universities, and founded Temple University Hospital. How did he raise the funds? He delivered his classic address, "Acres of Diamonds," more than 6,000 times. What made him so powerful a communicator? For one thing, he knew how to break the preoccupation barrier of his hearers.

> Friends, this lecture ("Acres of Diamonds") has been delivered under these circumstances: I visit a town or city, and try to arrive there early enough to see the postmaster, the barber, the keeper of the hotel, the principal of the schools, and the ministers of some of the churches, and then go into some of the factories and stores and talk with the people, and get in sympathy with the local conditions of that town or city and see what has been their history, what opportunities they had and what they failed to do—and every town fails to do something—and then go to the lecture and talk to those people about the subjects which applied to their locality.[22]

Conwell broke their preoccupation barrier in the first seconds of his lecture because he knew their problems and he had the solution. He could do this because he took the right steps to assess his audience.

RULE FIVE: REFER TO THE KNOWN, THE AUDIENCE'S EXPERIENCE

Jesus had many important teachings, some of which were abstract and a bit difficult to understand. Therefore, Jesus told parables, stories that referred to situations that were in His audience's experience. For instance, to those who were familiar with farming, He told the parable of the sower and the parable of the wheat and the tares.

Communication is not "unloading" on your audience. Communication carries with it the idea of involvement with others, and the leader is involved with people. The word *communication* has its root in the Latin word *communis,* which means "common." To be an effective communicator, you must impose on yourself the discipline of seeing things from the viewpoint of your people. This may be the most important lesson in communication.

The leader refers to what his listener knows—that which the listener has seen, heard, read, felt, believed, or done and which still exists in his consciousness, his inventory of knowledge. The known includes all those thoughts, feelings, and events which to him are real. It includes direct experiences—those he has experienced with his own senses—as well as indirect experiences which, while not felt and seen directly, are nonetheless accepted as second-hand knowledge. We have never seen Julius Caesar, but we accept as reality the statement that he lived and did certain things.

Only by referring to the experience of your audience will you develop credibility. You judge the truth or error of a statement by the criterion of your own experience, and what's true of you is true of others. Reference to experience is the way you make the unknown known.

You must habitually ask yourself, "How would I feel about this if I were in the audience? Would I understand this point with the background they have? Would this sound reasonable if I had been through their experiences? Would it be interesting to me if I were they?"

There are several factors to consider about people's experiences. First, we tend to remember those impressions that were initially intense. In 1975, in Tehran, I was doubled over by the pain of a kidney stone. Using that experience won't relate to most people since most have never had a kidney stone attack. But most people have had a toothache. I can use the experience of a toothache to communicate the idea of pain much more powerfully than that of a finger scratch because a toothache is far more intense.

Second, an experience will be vivid in proportion to the number of times it's repeated. Those coming from the northern hemisphere have a deep conviction that mid-year is warmer than winter. It is vivid not so much because of the original experience but because of the frequency of the experience. They have experienced summer every year of their lives. Those living south of the equator have the opposite experience; mid-year is the colder season.

Third, an experience will be vivid in proportion to the number of times it's recalled. A war veteran may have served in only one campaign, but the battles and the sieges all have their original intensity if he has frequently recollected them and retold them, keeping the mental pictures fresh. One of the great justifications for giving Christian people an opportunity to testify frequently is that it focuses their attention on the great things God has done for them. Recalling God's blessings strengthens their commitment by making those blessings more vivid.

Fourth, other things being equal, an experience is vivid according to its nearness in time. Do you remember what you had for breakfast this morning? Of course. Do you remember what you had for breakfast ten years ago? Probably not. You can remember the raging headache you had yesterday with much deeper feeling than you can the pain you had four months ago.

Just as a singer has a repertoire of songs, you must acquire a repertoire of vivid general experiences common to the average person you lead if you are to communicate with influence. These experiences must have the characteristics of intensity, recency, and frequency in recurrence and recall. Impress on your own mind those experiences. Develop the habit of seeing with the eyes of those with whom you communicate and hearing with their ears.

People today refuse to be commanded, threatened, or maneuvered into an opinion. They say, "Only through my knowledge, only through my life, shall you secure my approval. I am a person. Bring your thought in line with my mind frame, and I may join with you."

You must always ask yourself, "What references to the listeners' experience will bring my idea, with the necessary vividness, most quickly in line with the listeners' knowledge? What will cause them to say, 'I see,' 'I feel,' 'You are right,' 'I will do it,' 'I am pleased'?" Then you will know what arguments come closest to the lives of your listeners, what appeals come nearest to their hearts. Knowing this, you are able to distinguish that which appeals to all from that which appeals to a few, and in great moments you can touch the universal chord.

Rule Six: Support Your Assertions

Abstract ideas tend to chloroform people's attention. Or worse, people frequently resist abstract ideas altogether. Usually people don't believe a statement unless there is proof. And they don't act on a suggestion unless it's given logical and emotional support.

A salesman may tell me I need a computer/word processor in my study at home. I disagree. "The cost is prohibitive. I don't have the space. And I have not been trained in how to use one," I say.

He doesn't let the matter drop. He explains that his company will give me full instructions. He shows me how little space the equipment requires. He convinces me that I'm losing money by my archaic method of dictating, reviewing, and editing. He leads me to persuade myself that failure to secure the equipment is throwing money in the trash. Today, I'm writing this book on a computer/word processor because a salesman supported his assertion, "You need a personal computer/word processor."

Most of a leader's communication centers on assertions. Without supporting them, he appears to be didactic, pontifical, even dictatorial. "Support" refers to any and all material used to clarify, amplify, verify, or in any way make the assertion illuminating and valid. The assertion is the skeleton; the support gives flesh and blood—life.

You may use several forms of support. Sometimes you'll use one form; other times you'll use two or more in combination:

1. Cumulation
2. Restatement
3. Exposition
4. Comparison
5. General illustration
6. Specific instance
7. Testimony

Cumulation

You will not likely change a person's mind, inspire his devotion toward a new concept, or make him contribute to a worthy cause with an isolated statement. You need to employ a succession of statements bearing on the same point. Cumulation means "a heaping up." It's a progression of thought. It adds to the information given, offering additional proof.

If I say, "Many over sixty have done great accomplishments," my audience may question the assertion. But I may win their agreement if I use cumulation by telling of Benjamin Franklin, who was ambassador to France when more than eighty; Gladstone, who was prime minister of England at eighty-three; Chiang Kai-shek, who governed the Republic of China when he was more than eighty; and Verdi, who wrote operas when he was eighty.

Cumulation uses a succession of details, instances, and illustrations to direct the followers' attention repeatedly to the original statement until the required goal has been attained.

Normally you cannot accomplish your purpose with a single statement. You cannot make the doctrine of the Trinity clear with one sentence. You cannot stir deep feeling by simply saying, "Milton was great." If you insist that apartheid in South Africa is wrong and say nothing more, you'll not convince anyone of the validity of your opinion. An isolated declaration will not usually affect your followers.

Using cumulation, however, gives your followers the necessary time and logical and emotional support to convince them of what you are saying. Each detail, each fact, each illustration "heaps up" support to accomplish your purpose.

Restatement

Restatement offers no additional proof, puts forth no reasons, and gives no details. Restatement tends to force the listener or the reader to concentrate on the original assertion as an entity. It subtly says, "Focus your attention on this; grasp it fully." You should use restatement when you believe greater concentration on the assertion itself is required.

When the leader's goal is to inform, restatement may be necessary to break through this obscurity that results from unfamiliarity with the meaning of the words or the complexity of structure.

The statement "He (Voltaire) had exercised a function and fulfilled a mission" is obscure; it does not communicate the precise meaning of "fulfilled a mission." Therefore Victor Hugo restated it: "He had evidently been chosen for the work which he had done by the Supreme Will which manifests itself in the laws of destiny as in the laws of nature." [23]

Often restatement can be valuable as a conclusion. If the argument has been lengthy, the leader can rapidly review his several ideas and drive them home as a whole.

However, let me warn you not to use restatement indiscriminately. Nothing annoys a person more than a writer or speaker who restates an idea that is already clear and vivid.

Exposition

Exposition sets forth in simple and concise terms the meaning of an assertion.

The late Justice Louis D. Brandeis, for instance, explained the meaning of the word *profession:* "The peculiar character of a profession as distinguished from other occupations, I take to be these: First, a profession is an occupation for which the necessary preliminary training is intellectual in character, involving knowledge and, to some extent, learning, as distinguished from merely skill. Second, it is an occupation in which the amount of financial return is not the accepted measure of success." This is exposition.

Comparison

You may support your assertion by pointing out similarities between that which your audience already knows and that which it does not know. You connect the known with the unknown.

Here's how Thomas Edison explained electricity and the long-distance telephone: "It's like a dachshund (this is a dog with short legs but a disproportionately long body) long enough to reach from Edinburg to London; when you pull his tail in Edinburg, he barks in London."

You greatly increase your credibility and authority when you use comparison that refers to the experience of your audience.

General Illustration

General illustration gives details about the idea expressed in the original assertion. It amplifies, although it does not individualize.

You might say, "My alma mater is a good school. Today it's turning out some of the nation's best leaders in the fields of robotics, genetic engineering, aerospace, and computer science." The assertion about the quality of the school is clarified by the general illustration that follows. You mention robotics, for instance, but you do not name any particular leader in that field.

Specific Instance

Specific instance concerns itself with specifics—dates, times, places, names, incidents. It differs from general illustration in that it is individual, absolute, and precise.

You might make the assertion, "Greece had great men." You could clarify and support the assertion with the general illustration, "It had authors, philosophers, poets, experts in medicine." Specific instance supports the same assertion by saying, "It had Demosthenes, Aeschylus, Plato, Aristotle, Sophocles, Homer, and Hippocrates."

Testimony

Testimony is the form of support in which an authority figure verifies what you are saying. It gives you the added credibility of the person whom your audience accepts as an authority. Testimony is used widely in advertising as, for instance, when an athlete says he eats a particular brand of breakfast cereal.

Testimony corroborates the leader's assertion in the mind of the follower. Testimony will be stronger than your own assertion when your audience looks on the person or work quoted as more authoritative than you. Interestingly enough, it is not necessary for the person to be authoritative on the matter at hand—although he should be. The athlete, for instance, may not know anything about breakfast cereal but still be able to sell it effectively.

If you want to use testimony effectively, you should know your audience, have a familiar knowledge of recognized authorities and authoritative works, and constantly be alert to and gather testimony that can be used.

Let me give one caution: it is possible to use quotations and testimonies so frequently you destroy your audience's confidence in your own credibility and authority. My former professor, Dr. P. B. Fitzwater, said, "People don't come to hear through your lips what somebody else said. They come to hear what you say!"

Yet there are the occasions when testimony is essential and powerful. Added to the other forms of support, testimony can be clear and compelling.

RULE SEVEN: MOTIVATE ACTION BY THE APPEAL TO DESIRE

Most of the time the leader's communication goal will be to actuate, even though he may use one of the other goals to achieve that end. The leader should stimulate action by appealing to desire, by understanding and using the motivation that people already have.

People don't want facts for facts' sake. You can give your son a pile of facts about health, and he will be indifferent. Then one day he comes home from school all fired up to compete in a 1500-kilometer race. He goes into training and avidly studies all the facts about health he can get. What made the difference? Desire. Perhaps his coach said he had to do it or he would fail. Perhaps he wants to impress a certain young lady. But there is in him a desire to compete.

To most effectively motivate people to action—to move them toward goals of beneficial permanence that meet their real needs—you need to understand people's desires and how to fulfill them.

You do not buy a life insurance policy because the Department of Vital Statistics predicts that one out of every four people now alive will be dead in ten years. Rather, you buy the insurance because you don't want your wife to be destitute, your children deprived of an education, the estate you have built up decimated, and your reputation (after death) to be one of irresponsibility. Life insurance salesmen know that and have learned the most effective ways to appeal to these desires.

Many thinkers have tried to analyze our desires. Fifty years ago, Professor A. E. Phillips classified all desires under seven headings: self-preservation, property, power, reputation, affection, sentiment, and taste.[24] In his book *The Magic Power of Emotional Appeal,* Roy Garn refers to four basic desires: self-preservation, money, romance, and recognition.[25] The late Alan H. Monroe of Purdue University listed eighteen major desires.[26]

In one of the most significant studies of desires, Abraham Maslow suggested that there is a hierarchy of needs. The basic needs, he said, are physiological and security needs—food, clothing, shelter, security. Next, says Maslow, are social needs—needs to belong. The highest level of needs are self-actualization needs. These include the need for ego fulfillment. Maslow suggested that once a lower-level need is satisfied, a person can attend to the next higher level of need but that you can't preach an ideology to a person with an empty stomach.[27]

In this book, I will look at needs from the standpoint of self-preservation, property, power, reputation, and affection.

Self-preservation

Self-preservation is the desire for long life and health and all that makes living more pleasant and fulfilling. It includes the desire for freedom from sorrow, pain, and death. It includes the desire for heaven as opposed to hell.

Self-preservation is the primary desire that induces the majority of actions. It determines that we eat and drink. It recruits armies and organizes police forces. It demands emission controls on automobiles and environmental protection concerns on the part of industry.

Property

Property refers to the desire for wealth, goods, lands, and money. It is not just the desire for survival, but the desire to have things— whether we "need" them or not.

This desire is prevalent from the cradle to the grave. The baby cries for the toy. The worker wants an increase in salary. The capitalist wants a greater return on his investment. The child wants a bicycle.

Power

Power refers to the desire to possess skill, force, and energy. It refers to the desire for ability to be and to do. It includes the desire for strength (moral and physical), authority, and influence. Under this category come nearly all ambitions.

Reputation

Reputation refers to the desire for the good opinion of others. It is rooted in self-respect and pride. All normal people seek the favor of others. They find pleasure in being known as upright, honest, kind, generous, and scholarly.

This is a powerful desire. Some men would rather risk their life than lose a good reputation. It is this desire that makes the lazy industrious, the stingy generous, and the deceptive honest.

Affection

Affection refers to the desire for the welfare of others—a loving concern for the needs of loved ones, a town, or a nation.

No one is a leader who cannot induce others to act, and no one can induce others to act if he ignores the employment of appeal to basic desires. When Jesus said, "Give and it shall be given unto you," He appealed to the desire of property. When the apostle Paul said, "Knowing, therefore, the terror of the Lord, we persuade men," he appealed to the desire of self-preservation. When Solomon said, "Train up a child in the way he should go, And when he is old he will not depart from it," he appealed to the desire for affection.

This appeal to desire can be manipulative. However, in moving your group toward goals of beneficial permanence to meet their real needs, you must make clear that the action you're suggesting will, in fact, contribute to fulfilling their *real* needs.

Since the leader transfers his thoughts to his group through communication, it follows that only effective communication can make clear to the group their real needs and move them toward the appropriate goals to fulfill those needs. Effective communication, through speech and writing, is possibly the leader's most valuable asset. You can and must acquire it.

Make communication an ongoing study, your life-long passion and discipline. Practice, practice, practice! Study human reactions. Know what your followers are thinking. Think of ways to refer to their experience in the achievement of your objectives. Through effective communication, you will out-achieve others who may be more intelligent or more personable, but who have not developed their communication abilities.

SUMMARY

The leader must be a communicator. The ability to communicate effectively through speech and writing is possibly the leader's most valuable asset. Seven rules of effective communication will help the leader develop that asset.

1. *Recognize the importance of effective communication.* The leader is not just concerned with the words he says, but with the content his listeners perceive and the effect the content actually has as a result of his communication. The leader's task is to create understanding. Effective

communication overcomes isolation, is a factor in reproduction, tends to safeguard freedom of speech, and presents worthy thoughts worthily.

2. *Assess your audience.* The foundation for carrying out all the other rules of effective communication is to assess your audience. Learn its demographic characteristics. Assess its attitude toward its environment and important issues, assess the audience's attitude toward each other. Assess its attitude toward your subject. Assess your audience's attitude toward you.

3. *Select the right communication goal.* Having a goal clearly in mind will conserve time, accomplish the task more effectively, and thus strengthen your leadership. The leader will almost always have the goal of actuating—motivating the group to take action. But he will try to actuate the group by one of the other goals: informing, impressing, convincing, or entertaining.

4. *Break the preoccupation barrier.* Capture the audience's attention. Earn the right to be heard. To break the preoccupation barrier, identify the leading problems the people in the audience are facing, promise a solution to those problems, and then fulfill that promise.

5. *Refer to the known, the audience's experience.* Only by referring to the experiences of your audience will you develop credibility. To do this, you must acquire a repertoire of vivid general experiences common to the average person you lead. A number of factors make these experiences more memorable: intensity, how often the experiences are repeated, how often they are recalled, and recency.

6. *Support your assertions.* Abstract ideas in themselves do not capture people's attention. Abstract assertions should therefore be supported and brought to life through cumulation, restatement, exposition, comparison, general illustration, specific instance, and testimony.

7. *Motivate action by the appeal to desire.* The leader wants action. He wants to effect change. The most effective way to do that is by an appeal to the dominant desire of the particular audience. The leader should appeal to his audience's healthy self-interest, which can be expressed in needs of self-preservation, property, power, reputation, and affection. No one is a leader who cannot induce others to act, and no one can induce others to act if he does not employ an appeal to basic desires.

Make communication an ongoing study, your life-long passion and discipline. Through effective communication, you will out-achieve others who may be more intelligent or more personable, but who have not developed their communication abilities.

8

The Principle of

INVESTMENT

The small Zambian Baptist Church was poor. The members loved their pastor, Rev. Godfrey Mulando, but they were unable to pay his salary. This love was mutual, and the pastor had dedicated himself to lead his people into a close daily walk with God. However, he had been warned not to preach about money or he would frighten the people away.

When Mulando went to Singapore for leadership training in the "how" of evangelism, he was so struck by what he heard of God's commands and promises on the subject of money and possessions, he was convicted that his people should also know this truth.

When he returned to Zambia, he began to teach his people: "Stewardship is part of the gospel. A person cannot fully know God unless he knows the concept of stewardship and practices it. Worship is not complete unless you give something. When the wise men came to worship the baby Jesus, for example, they brought precious gifts."

The members of the congregation were dedicated people and they were not frightened away by God's commands to give. Rather, they were thrilled at what they heard and also ashamed of their own disobedience. They asked their pastor why he had not taught these things before. He was forced to admit that he himself had not known them.

For the first time, the people of Masala Baptist Church in Ndola, Zambia, began to tithe and give joyously of themselves and their money. In addition to meeting church expenses, they accepted responsibility for their pastor's salary and house rent. They bought the pastor a motorcycle to facilitate his visitation and evangelistic work. They also wrote to the missionary society and said, "No more money, just send your prayers and your love."

They discovered they could not outgive God, and not only were their personal lives blessed, but God also blessed the church. It grew. As the members saw God honoring His promises, they began to share their joy, themselves, and Christ with friends, neighbors, and relatives. They began bringing people to the church. It grew to such an extent the walls had to be knocked down and the building extended. A daughter church was founded in an area lacking in gospel witness. Then another, and another—until there were five churches where there had been only one struggling church.

"When my people started giving, they saw that they had a big role to play in the whole realm of evangelism. Prior to that they were just spectators in the church. When they began to tithe and give to God's work, they began to see their responsibility to witness, to bring in the people, to teach and help them, and they were so excited," said Pastor Mulando.

"Before I went to Singapore in 1974, we were 134 members; and [within only five years] I saw the church grow to 300 members (not counting the daughter congregations and 200 adherents not yet members)."

Pastor Godfrey Mulando and his people had experienced the truth of an important principle of leadership: "Give, and it will be given to you: good measure, pressed down, shaken together, and running over will be put into your bosom. For with the same measure that you use, it will be measured back to you" (Luke 6:38). This is the principle of investment.

MASTER THE MEANING OF INVESTMENT

The principle of investment says that if you invest or give something, you will receive it back many times over. The Scriptures express this principle again and again.

"Whatever a man sows, that he will also reap" (Galatians 6:7). What do you want? Sow it. Invest it. Do you want friends? Invest friendship. Do you want love? Invest love. Do you want respect? Invest by respecting others. The political dictator and corporate autocrat stumble because they invest fear and, therefore, reap fear. Their followers may fawn, but at the opportune time, they will revolt.

"Just as you want men to do to you, you do to them likewise" (Luke 6:31). This is what some have called "The Golden Rule." But as much as people give lip service to it, few seem to try to live by it.

"But this I say: He who sows sparingly will also reap sparingly, and he who sows bountifully will also reap bountifully" (2 Corinthians 9:6). It's not just a matter of receiving back *what* you invest, but also a matter of receiving it back according to *how much* you invest. If you invest little, you will receive a little in return, but if you invest a lot, you will "reap bountifully."

I use the terms *investment* and *giving* interchangeably. To many people, *giving* means a reduction in the giver's net worth. Such people have a scarcity mentality. That is not a proper understanding of giving because giving is an investment. The term *investment* carries the idea of increasing the investor's net worth. Those who understand this have an abundance mentality. They realize that the more they give away in time, money, or encouragement, the more they will receive back of time, money, or encouragement.

The motivation for giving (or investing), therefore, is self-interest, a motive not only commended by Jesus, but the only motive He ever used in the Scriptures.

Too often giving which is seen as reducing the giver's net worth is motivated by charity, sentiment, peer pressure, recognition, and even guilt. Such motivation *never* sustains meaningful philanthropy.

Robert W. Woodruff died at the age of 95 while I was writing this book. He not only built Coca-Cola® into an international giant, but he also influenced education, the arts, politics, social service, and Christian outreach. Among other gifts, he gave the largest single gift ever made to a university: $105 million to Emory University in Atlanta, Georgia.

Atlanta is the only American city with a population of more than one million that racially integrated its schools with no incidents whatever. A lot of credit goes to William B. Hartsfield, who was mayor at the time. However, he was able to put teeth in his program because of the moral and financial backing of Woodruff. Woodruff was self-giving.

As a leader, you are to understand and practice the principle of investment. If your leadership is motivated by love, humility, and self-discipline, you will reap love, loyalty, and devotion from the people you lead. If they recognize that you're investing your very life for their good, they'll be more inclined to follow your leadership. But if the group perceives you to be self-aggrandizing, you'll lose the influence you now have to move those in the group toward goals of beneficial permanence that meet their real needs. They will question the validity of the goals you state because they will question your motives.

The elders of Dr. Han's church in Korea told me that he received his pay on Fridays and often, before he had arrived home, he had given it all away. Finally, they started giving the money to Mrs. Han so she could pay the bills and buy the groceries! Dr. Han's practice of giving accords his leadership the credibility and permanence that leaders who are self-aggrandizing never attain.

But more than understanding investment and practicing it yourself, you are to instill it in the people in your group. As the result of example, of teaching, and of the vicarious experience of seeing reaping according to what you have sown, the people in your group should come to the point where they are living by the principle of investment too.

In their tremendously popular book, *In Search of Excellence,* Thomas J. Peters and Robert H. Waterman, Jr., study what it is that makes an excellent company. Among the eight factors is one that illustrates the principle of investment: "Excellent companies are close to the customer." Such companies have an obsession with quality, reliability, or service. They are committed to making the customer important, giving him the best value for his money, and being ready to serve him in any way he needs. And these excellent companies reap what they sow by gaining customer loyalty and long-term sales and profit growth. Peters and Waterman tell the story of Frito-Lay, a potato chip and pretzel company, to illustrate the point:

> What is striking about Frito is not its brand-management system, which is solid, nor its advertising program, which is well done. What is striking is Frito's nearly 10,000-person sales force and its "99.5 percent service level." In practical terms, what does this mean? It means that Frito will do some things that in the short run clearly are uneconomic. It will spend several hundred dollars sending a truck to restock a store with a couple of $30 cartons of potato chips. You don't make money that way, it would seem. But the institution is filled with tales of salesmen braving extraordinary weather to deliver a box of potato chips or to help a store clean up after a hurricane or an accident. Letters about such acts pour into the Dallas headquarters. There are magic and symbolism about the service call that cannot be quantified. As we said earlier, it is a cost analyst's dream target. You can always make a case for saving money by cutting back a percentage point or two. But Frito management, looking at market shares and margins, won't tamper with the zeal of the sales force.[28]

The result of this sowing of service is that Frito-Lay reaps more than $2 billion of potato chip and pretzel sales per year, it owns market shares of 60 percent and 70 percent in most of America (which is astoundingly high for such an undifferentiated product), and it has profit margins that are the envy of the food industry.

In mastering the meaning of investment, realize that it is important to have a spirit of giving—of wanting to help others. This makes practicing the principle of investment a natural habit. But there are two kinds of people who make up the world: the investors and the takers. By their nature the investors practice the principle of investment; the takers are the ones who do not see giving as an investment and so try to hoard whatever they have. Ultimately, the investors win and the takers lose.

Jesus was the perfect man, the only perfect man who ever lived. Unqualified and generous giving marked every moment of His life here on earth. And those who are effective leaders reflect this passion to give rather than to take.

One of my heroes is John R. Mott, who was born in 1865 and died in 1955 at the age of 90. Mott made the YMCA a significant worldwide organization. He founded the International Missionary Council. He headed up a fund-raising drive for the United War Work Council that raised more than $188 million in less than a year. He recruited more than 240,000 men and women for leadership positions on all six continents during the course of his unequaled career. He was decorated by eighteen nations. He won the Nobel Peace Prize in 1946. You cannot worship at any church of any denomination on any continent that he did not influence.

The key to John Mott's leadership was that he was an investor. He had a commitment to the principle of investment. John Mott represents the highest type of leadership. No personality cult arose around his name. Mott was generous with his concepts, his time, his energy, and his money.

I believe the secret to Mott's self-giving spirit can be found in the intimate relationship he sustained with the Lord. He began each day with an unhurried quiet time of Bible study, prayer, and meditation.

Years ago, I heard the pastor of one of America's largest churches say, "After a long study of history and a lifetime of observation, I have concluded that without exception the men whom God has used most remarkably over the years are those who are generous."

At the risk of being misunderstood, let me say that I believe the reason America is in a position of world leadership is because of its generosity. America has given more money, goods, and services to other nations than all the nations of the world in all the history of the world combined. I believe America's leadership in the world has occurred largely as a result of its investment of concern and resources in the nations of the world.

While investors win, takers lose. In the 1970s, an Indian pastor was invited to attend a meeting in Europe. He said he couldn't afford it. The people holding the meeting offered to underwrite 75 percent of his expenses. He still refused to attend. When the Indian pastor was killed a few weeks later in an automobile accident, it was discovered he had hoarded $160,000. During the course of his ministry he had complained about poverty and had taken advantage of his poor parishioners who, out of love, had sacrificially given extra money to him. He had sown deceit and distrust. And the legacy of his life is one of dishonesty and greed. He did more to harm the Christian witness in his town than all the atheists in India combined.

For nearly forty years, I have watched men and women in leadership slots. The takers ultimately lose. They lose disposition, friends, health, and respect. The investors win. As a leader you need to master the meaning of investment and study how to make giving a habit for both you and those whom you lead.

PERCEIVE THE RIGHT MOTIVE FOR INVESTMENT

If the leader wants to create joy for people in his group, he can accomplish this by motivating them to make the principle of investment the law of their life. But to do this, he has to understand the right motive for investment. The leader knows that his group will act when they have a reason. To motivate people to enjoy the enlargement of life that comes from investment, he must put forth a powerful motive.

Charity, sentiment, peer pressure, recognition, and guilt are not adequate motives for giving. They will work at times, but they are not self-motivating. Duty is a legitimate motive, but it usually fails because most people lack the character to respond. No greater motive can be put forth than the motive of love. Nevertheless, the wise leader knows that while he himself must lead from the motive of love, for many in the group, love is fluctuating and tends to rise and fall with spasms of altruism. Were we already in heaven, doubtlessly love would be the best motive to put forth. But we are still sinful.

The one and only motive that Jesus ever used is the motive of self-interest. Investment is the ultimate path to permanent gain. Every command and promise that Jesus made was based on the assumption of self-interest—that obeying the command would benefit the individual. For example, Jesus said, "Judge not, that you be not judged." He also said, "Do not lay up for yourselves treasures on earth, where moth and rust destroy and where thieves break in and steal; but lay up for yourselves treasures in heaven. . . ."

The principle of investment is so powerful because it has built into it the motivation of legitimate self-interest of the individual. "Give and it will be given to you." Everyone wins.

The farmer gains by giving. He invests his labor and seed and irrigation into the soil. He normally gets back in proportion to what he puts in. The businessman gains by widening the market. He invests money for advertising and entertainment and public relations and necessary travel and labor. He gets his money back multiplied. The athlete invests effort and gains strength and achievement in proportion to the effort invested. The effective leader will appeal to the powerful desire of self-interest to actuate his people to invest.

Some may protest that it's not right to give in order to get. I usually tell such people to argue with Jesus, not with me, for it was Jesus who said, "Give and it will be given to you." If you are a believer, why did you give your life to Christ? Most people will answer that they wanted forgiveness, salvation, and peace. Self-interest is a legitimate motive, one to which Jesus Himself appealed.

You may say you cannot please God with the wrong spirit. That is true, but the effectiveness of the principle of investment does not depend on one's spirit in the matter. If an atheist plants a thousand acres of corn, and a Christian plants one acre of corn, who is going to get the most corn? The "right spirit" has nothing to do with the harvest. The principle of investment is as inexorable a law as the law of gravitation. If I jump off the top of the Empire State Building and an agnostic jumps at the same time, I'm not going to be in any better shape than he is when we hit the ground!

You can identify a person's IQ—investment quotient—by noticing if he continues to invest under all circumstances. For instance, does the board member give as generously when he has been rotated off the board as when he was on the board? Does the church officer maintain the same level of giving when out of office as in office?

The effective leader devotes his life to bringing his group into the joy of giving. He leads by his own example. His life demonstrates to his group the validity of self-interest as the motive to which Christ appealed. The leader will bring honor to God, benefit to the world, blessing to his people, and enrichment to his own life to the degree that he is successful in moving his people to the habit of perennial investment through the motive of self-interest.

WARNINGS ABOUT CARE AND COVETOUSNESS

The principle of investment is like all of God's gifts. The gift is good. But if the principle of investment is used to get more of something that has become a god or something that is evil, we are misusing the benefits of the principle. We are to use the principle of investment to acquire money, but it is necessary to mention Jesus' warnings here against care and covetousness.

Most people hold one of two erroneous ideas concerning money. Some feel that money is inherently evil and only things of the spirit are good. This is the position that was held by many Greek philosophers and Christian monastics. However, money and matter are neither good nor evil. It is how we use material things that determines the goodness or the evilness involved. Those who believe money is inherently evil tend to be overcome with cares and concerns about material things.

The other erroneous idea is the attitude of materialism which makes matter the very center of life. Unhappily, this view has even infiltrated areas of church life. This position leads to idolatry of things, and it is against this attitude that the Bible sounds some of its sharpest warnings: "You shall not steal. . . . You shall not covet your neighbor's house; you shall not covet your neighbor's wife, nor his manservant, nor his maidservant, nor his ox, nor his donkey, nor anything that is your neighbor's" (Exodus 20:15, 17). "For the love of money is the root of all kinds of evil" (1 Timothy 6:10). "Do not lay up for yourselves treasures on earth" (Matthew 6:19). "Man shall not live by bread alone" (Matthew 4:4). Those who have made matter the very center of their lives tend to be ruled by covetousness.

Jesus warned against the perils that arise from these two ideas of material things, money, and the principle of investment. He warned against care and covetousness—the worry that one might not possess enough to meet the bare necessities of life and the desire to possess more and more. These two perils will undermine the discipline needed to employ the principle of investment.

Jesus said, "You cannot serve God and mammon" (Matthew 6:24). The word *mammon* represents wealth and material possessions, not necessarily in particular quantity, but the fact of their existence. According to Jesus, mammon is something about which people should never be anxious, over which they should never worry, something with which they should not be obsessed. Instead, the Christian is to "seek first the kingdom of God and His righteousness, and all these things shall be added unto you" (Matthew 6:33). The covetous leader and the worrying leader ultimately self-destruct.

When Jesus says we cannot serve both God and mammon, He is not saying that mammon is inherently evil. Mammon—material things—can be the vehicle to achieve the highest ends and the most God-honoring objectives. Or you can put mammon to such base uses that it will bring mischief and hurt.

E. Stanley Jones correctly said, "You can serve God with mammon, but you cannot serve God and mammon." [29] When you serve God, you are the bondslave of God, yielding to His absolute supremacy so that everything is regulated according to the divine will. Material things are not abandoned, but are brought into His service. But to serve mammon, to be the bondslave of material possessions (and poor people can be a bondslave of material possessions as well as rich people), is to bring about spiritual impoverishment and, in many cases, even financial disadvantage. When you live to serve mammon, either through worrying about what you shall eat and drink and how you shall be clothed or through covetousness, you dethrone God. And your leadership loses credibility.

Religious leaders often emphasize the need for more prayer if God is to send worldwide revival. But until these same leaders get honest with God on the money question, prayer will continue to be an exercise in hypocrisy and futility. A spirit of care or covetousness mocks prayer. Living according to the principle of investment is the attitude God wants us to have toward material goods. So, too, those who profess a concern for the salvation of the world's needy millions and pray for their salvation while withholding from God the money to give people the Good News are uttering hollow words.

Jesus warns against care, against worry. It is very easy to become concerned because in ourselves we do not know the future. Living by the principle of investment demands vulnerability. When the farmer puts the seed into the ground, he becomes a bit vulnerable. He will not see the seed again for a period of time, during which he will cultivate, water, and employ all of the agricultural techniques he knows to insure an abundant harvest. When one invests his love in another, he becomes vulnerable. When a businessman invests in a piece of property, he becomes vulnerable. Without vulnerability, there is no viability. Without risk, there is no forward movement.

But this is no excuse for care and worry. When one invests in God's work, he is given promises by God that protect the investor. Why it is that otherwise competent leaders fail to see and act upon the investment principle mystifies me. Their failure here robs them personally and their people of advantages otherwise unattainable.

Jesus also warns against covetousness, the desire to possess. The covetous sometimes camouflage their stinginess with such expressions as "prudence," or "good business," or "sound planning." God calls it covetousness—an insatiable desire for worldly gain, an obsession to get more, a preoccupation with having what is not yours.

Covetousness is David, with all his wives and concubines, wanting Bathsheba, the only wife of Uriah. That jeopardized David's leadership.

Covetousness is Saul keeping for himself, in defiance of God's ban, the finest cattle and the blue-ribbon sheep of the Amalekites. Covetousness ultimately destroyed Saul's leadership.

Covetousness is Judas, selling Jesus for thirty pieces of silver. Covetousness destroyed Judas' leadership for he had been the treasurer, a respected position.

Each suffered severe punishment. God has not moderated His view of covetousness. It is still sin. And those trapped by this sin still suffer.

Covetousness can cost you ulcers, friendships, inordinate pressure, family relationships. The costs in litigations, medical care, and forced vacations can offset the short-term gain of covetous maneuvers.

One of the major reasons for covetousness is insecurity. The insecure person, the person who is afraid, is doing his best to protect himself from feared calamity. No matter how much bravado is projected, basically the stingy person, the one who lives only for himself, is terribly frightened. And, of course, a temperament of insecurity and fear does not make for great leadership.

Since God has promised a special blessing to those who honor Him with their material possessions, then the leader sins against his followers by withholding this good news of the joy and enrichment of giving. You can't expect blessings from God if, through greed and covetousness, you block the pathway down which God sends the blessings. In short, covetousness not only betrays love, but it also blasts self-interest. It destroys leadership.

THE TEN COMMANDMENTS OF INVESTMENT

One out of every six verses in the Gospels has to do with the right and wrong use of material possessions. Sixteen of Jesus' thirty-eight parables have to do with the right and wrong use of material possessions.

Money is the most powerful tangible expression of our life. One of the great things about the famed evangelist Dwight L. Moody was his understanding of the place of money in the kingdom of God. He wasn't timid about expressing it. Time after time, he had solicited money from James Farwell. On one occasion, after Moody had asked Farwell for $10,000, Farwell complained, "Mr. Moody, must you always be coming to me for money? You have so many other wealthy friends. I've already given you $85,000 for your work."

Moody replied, "Mr. Farwell, you grew up on a farm just as I did. Did you ever take a pail to a dry cow?"

Moody's leadership developed Farwell, but Moody's influence with Farwell would have died had Farwell not known that Moody was a self-giving person who practiced what he preached. Largely through Moody's influence, Farwell became an outstanding nineteenth-century philanthropist.

The principle of investment deals with one of the most sensitive but important issues in the Christian church. The leader's attitude toward money and material possessions will affect in part the effectiveness of his leadership. Therefore, let me list ten commandments for investment. They will help you understand and master this important principle.

COMMANDMENT ONE: *Recognize That God Is the Provider*

In Genesis 22, Abraham speaks of God as *Jehovah-jireh,* which means "the Lord will provide." God had told Abraham to offer his only son Isaac as a burnt offering on a mountain in the land of Moriah. Evidently Abraham did not tell Isaac what God had said to him, for when they arrived at the mountain, Isaac said, "Look, the fire and the wood, but where is the lamb for a burnt offering?"

You can imagine the emotional turmoil Abraham was going through. He was determined to obey God no matter what the cost. He even went so far as to tie Isaac on the altar and "took the knife to slay his son." But at the same time, Abraham had tremendous faith in God, for when he and Isaac left the servant at the foot of the mountain, Abraham had told the servant they would both "come back to you." It was in the middle of this experience and in answer to Isaac's question that Abraham said, "My son, God will provide for Himself the lamb for a burnt offering." *Jehovah-jireh.*

God provides all the resources necessary to accomplish His will. We can be confident of that. For those who have the gift of generosity, those resources can be an abundance of this world's goods.

It is tragic that over the years we have equated sanctification and poverty. It is true that we are supposed to be willing to be abased. And it is very possible that God may have purposes for us that do not include driving luxury cars or living in elegant homes. But whether we are poor or rich, whatever we have comes from our Provider, God. And, we have the joyful obligation to honor Him and enrich ourselves by acting on the principle of investment.

COMMANDMENT TWO: *Keep Your Mind on the Things You Want and Off the Things You Don't Want As Long As These Are Compatible with the Will of God.*

After telling of his misery and misfortune, Job said,

> For the thing I greatly feared
> has come upon me,
> And what I dreaded
> has happened to me (Job 3:25).

Job feared the worst and he got it.

Our negative thoughts and fears become self-fulfilling prophecies. If you don't believe you will make your sales goal, you probably won't. If you are a pastor and you are afraid your new congregation won't accept you, they probably won't. If you tell a child that he will fail and never amount to any good, you'll probably be right. So many dear people see the glass half empty instead of half full. They don't comprehend that "God has not given us a spirit of fear, but of power and of love and of a sound mind" (2 Timothy 1:7).

You'll ruin your leadership potential by concentrating on the things you don't want. And, such negative attention violates the principle of investment.

But if you keep your mind on the things you want, you'll probably succeed. Keeping your mind on winning the race is the first step to making it a reality. Believing a friend can accomplish a difficult task and telling him he can do it can help to make it possible.

The leader who acts on the principle of investment tends to be positive and optimistic. This gives him personal power and influence.

COMMANDMENT THREE: *Invest What You Want*

This seems like an obvious statement. If you plant cotton, what do you get? Cotton. If you plant wheat, what do you get? Wheat. If you plant corn, what do you get? Corn. If you plant love, what do you get? Love, of course. If you plant friendship, what do you get? Friends.

Most people will agree that the statements in the previous paragraph are true. The awkward part comes when it is asked, "If you invest money, what do you get?" People usually freeze up on this point. Some say, "When Jesus says, 'Give and it shall be given unto you,' it means you give money to God, and He'll give you back peace and joy . . . spiritual blessings. He doesn't mean He'll give you monetary returns." That interpretation is fatuous spiritualizing. Why is money different from cotton or friendship?

Jesus promises that when you give money, you'll get back more money than you gave. When the leader communicates by precept and practice the principle of investment in all areas of life, he strengthens the motivation for the followers to move toward goals of beneficial permanence that meet their real needs.

COMMANDMENT FOUR: *Invest on the Front End*

Suppose a farmer were to say, "If I have a good harvest, I'll then plant the seed." Or suppose a businessman were to say, "When I receive 100 percent of the lease payments for a ten-year period, I'll build the apartment building." You would agree that that is ridiculous!

No, you invest first—on the front end.

Remember the story of the widow of Zarephath? She said that she had just enough oil and meal to make some food for her son and herself. They were going to eat and then die. Elijah said, "Do not fear; go and do as you have said, but make me a small cake from it first" (1 Kings 17:13). Be it said to her eternal credit, she violated worldly wisdom and what would seem to be sound thinking, and she made God's prophet the cake first. "And she and he and her household ate for many days. The bin of flour was not used up, nor did the jar of oil run dry, according to the word of the Lord which He spoke by Elijah" (1 Kings 17:15–16). The widow invested on the front end.

Don't delude yourself by saying, "When my ship comes in I shall give a lot of money to the work of God to help people in need." Start where you are with what you have.

COMMANDMENT FIVE: *Be Patient*

When the farmer plants, he doesn't expect a crop the next day. It takes months. You should be patient. It may be a while. You may have lots of problems before the harvest.

Can you imagine a farmer planting one day and digging down into the ground the next day to see how the seed is germinating? Relax. Keep cool. Exercise faith. Believe God. It's an attitude of patience that oftentimes distinguishes the leader.

COMMANDMENT SIX: *Do Not Be Deterred by an Occasional Crop Failure*

Just because a frost wrecks the peach crop in Georgia, does the peach farmer quit growing peaches? No, he knows that he will prosper as he obeys the laws of peach growing.

Just because a friend betrays you, does that mean you'll never trust anyone else? I hope not. You may say, "I invested love, and I was betrayed. I invested friendship, and I was insulted. I invested money, and I suffered financial disaster." Yes, you may get an occasional crop failure. But the law of planting and harvesting is as unchangeable as the truth of God. If you observe this over the long term, inevitably you will be the one who prospers.

COMMANDMENT SEVEN: *Put Your Money Where You Want Your Heart to Be*

I hear people say, "If people just get right with God, they'll give. So therefore, just build them up in the faith." But the best way to begin to build someone up in the faith is through the motivation of self-interest. And if a person invests money in a particular work, he will become involved in it through self-interest.

Charles W. Shepard, a cotton broker from Gadsden, Alabama, became interested in the work of the Haggai Institute. He gave to it and inspired others to do the same. In one year, he raised more than $30,000. He said to his friends, "Let's help John Haggai. He's strengthening the moral base of America."

In 1968 he and his beautiful wife, Kathleen, accompanied me on a major evangelistic mission in Indonesia. He enthusiastically passed out tracts and was instrumental in winning people of all ages to faith in Christ.

Two years later he was dying of cancer. My father and I visited him in the hospital and I asked Mr. Shepard when it was that he received Christ as his Savior. He said, "I don't know exactly when I became a Christian. But do you remember the first big money I put into the Haggai Institute? Well, I followed that money to see where it was going, and I ran right into Jesus Christ. I don't know exactly the day, but I know He is my Savior, and I'm trusting Him."

Put your money where you want your heart to be.

COMMANDMENT EIGHT: *Rejoice*

Even when things are not going right, rejoice. You can't think clearly when you're frowning and fretting. Don't fret because of evildoers or because of evil conditions.

You may not feel like rejoicing if you have just lost some money in a sour investment or the stock market has just gone from 1,300 to 900. While you can't control your feelings directly, you can control them indirectly by controlling your actions and sometimes by controlling your thoughts. If you don't feel the way you ought to feel, think and act the way you ought to feel, and soon you'll feel the way you are thinking and acting.

Nobody follows a griper. A griper, a complainer, is never dynamic. There are two types of people: thermometers and thermostats. The thermometer person, who registers the temperature of his environment, is up and down like a yo-yo. He reacts according to whatever happens to him. On the other hand, the thermostat person regulates the temperature of his environment. When this radiant personality, manifesting the strength of God, comes in the room, it's like turning on hundreds of lights. Yes, rejoice. Rejoice in your face. Let others, by looking at your face, know of the joy you say is in your heart.

COMMANDMENT NINE: *Expect Results*

The farmer expects results. He may not see any evidence of it for several weeks, but he expects results. The Christlike leader, living by the principle of investment, should expect results too. He should expect that when he invests encouragement in a person, he will see better performance. He should expect that when he goes out of his way to be friendly to people, he will acquire many friends. And he should expect that when he invests money in God's work, God will repay him.

The Bible says, "Abraham believed God." Every Christian believes *in God,* but it seems very few *believe God.* I am calling upon you to believe God in the financial area of your life. Believe God and expect results.

This habit will add an impressive dimension to your leadership. You'll always seem in command—focused, energized, in control of yourself. That inspires confidence and loyalty.

COMMANDMENT TEN: *Give God the Glory*

It is so easy when your investment pays off to think that you were special. You may have worked hard; you may have planned well; you may have sacrificed. But it is God who provided your reward. When discussing divisions in the church, Paul gave the credit for the successes the church had experienced, not to one faction or the other, but to God: "So then neither he who plants is anything nor he who waters, but God gave the increase" (1 Corinthians 3:7). Paul also said, "He who glories, let him glory in the Lord" (2 Corinthians 10:17).

Rejoice in God's provision and cash in on His promises. Take advantage of the principle of investment, but make sure God gets the glory since He is the Provider.

Millions upon millions of dollars haven't been tapped. Tapping them for the glory of God and the benefit of mankind would enrich not only those who would receive the money, but also the people who now have that money in their custody. As a leader, you are to teach the principle of investment by precept and example. To be an effective leader, you must be a person of faith.

When you live to impress people with your importance, to use leadership as a means primarily to gain wealth, honor, power, or pleasure, you'll wind up as did Caesar, Charlemagne, and Napoleon. But when your life and leadership incarnate the principle of investment, you'll leave a mark of beneficial permanence. "But seek first the kingdom of God and His righteousness, and all these things shall be added to you."

In 1978, I had the honor of meeting Archbishop Perreria of Bombay, India. This great Roman Catholic leader impressed me with his humanity and his spirituality. After he heard my lecture on investment, he said, "Dr. Haggai, what you say is splendid, but I cannot preach this to my people. They are so poor they cannot possibly tithe."

"Your grace," I said, "you say they have nothing. Is not the tithe of nothing also nothing? The point is, if they have a desire to honor God with their financial substance, if they have a tithing heart, I am convinced it will not be long until they will have money with which to tithe."

Two years later, the archbishop told me, "I started emphasizing what the Bible says about tithing. The people of my parish responded with gladness and today they are prospering as never in their lives or in the history of this diocese. And the church income is greatly enlarged."

I challenge you, if you have not acted on the law of investment previously, to begin today. Add a new and an exciting dimension to your life—and to your leadership.

SUMMARY

The principle of investment says that if you invest or give something, you will receive it back many times again. You will receive it back based on *what* you invested (e.g., if you invest friendship, you will have many friends) as well as on *how much* you invest ("He who sows sparingly will also reap sparingly").

The motivation for investment—or giving—is self-interest. The investor invests because it will benefit him. This is the only motive Jesus ever used in Scripture.

As a leader, you are to understand and practice the principle of investment. In addition, you are to instill the habit of giving into the people in your group.

There are two kinds of people in the world: investors and takers. The investors (or givers) by their nature practice the principle of investment; the takers are the ones who do not see giving as an investment and so they try to hoard whatever they have. Ultimately, the investors win because they receive back many times what they invested. The takers ultimately lose because they lose disposition, friends, health, and respect.

Like all of God's gifts, the principle of investment is good, but it can be used for good or evil ends. Jesus, therefore, warned against two extremes in our attitudes toward money. He warned against feeling that money is inherently evil and therefore being overly concerned about material things and worrying about them. He also warned against the extreme of making material things the center of one's life and being covetous or having the desire to possess for the sake of possessing. The Christian cannot serve both God and Mammon, but he is to learn how to serve God with Mammon.

Since God has promised a special blessing to those who honor Him with their material possessions, then the leader sins against his followers if he withholds this good news of the joy and enrichment of giving. The leader therefore will master the meaning of investment, perceive the right motive of investment, grasp the importance of investment, and follow the ten commandments for investment:

(1) Recognize that God is the provider.

(2) Keep your mind on the things you want and off the things you don't want as long as these are compatible with the will of God.

(3) Invest what you want.

(4) Invest on the front end.

(5) Be patient.

(6) Do not be deterred by an occasional crop failure.

(7) Put your money where you want your heart to be.

(8) Rejoice.

(9) Expect results.

(10) Give God the glory.

The principle of investment is summarized in the words of Christ: "Give, and it will be given to you: good measure, pressed down, shaken together, and running over will be put into your bosom. For with the same measure that you use, it will be measured back to you" (Luke 6:38).

9

The Principle of

OPPORTUNITY

Your greatest opportunities are cleverly disguised as insurmountable problems.

In the 1970s, Lee Iaccocca was the aggressive, successful president of the Ford Motor Company. He had created the Mustang, a car that sold more units its first year than any other automobile in history. He had led Ford to a $1.8 billion profit for two years in a row. He received an income of $970,000 a year and was treated royally. But he lived in the shadow of Henry Ford II, a man Iaccocca describes as capricious and spiteful. On 13 July 1978 Henry Ford fired Lee Iaccocca.

Less than four months later Iaccocca became president of Chrysler, an automobile company that had just announced a third-quarter loss of $160 million, the worst deficit it had ever had. Iaccocca found that Chrysler was not managed well—each of the thirty-one vice presidents was working by himself rather than working with each other. The oil shortage of 1979 compounded Chrysler's problems as the price of gasoline almost doubled and sales of large cars plummeted. In 1980, Chrysler lost $1.7 billion, the largest operating loss in United States corporate history.

But Iaccocca was turning his obstacles into opportunities. He had been fired. He had become president of a company most people felt would go bankrupt. But without these obstacles, Lee Iaccocca would never have had a chance to prove himself. He was determined not to quit. Union concessions, streamlining Chrysler's operations, development of new products all contributed to Chrysler's recovery.

In 1982, Chrysler made a modest profit. In 1983, it made the best profit in its history. And in July of that year, Chrysler paid off its controversial government-guaranteed loan—seven years before it was due. Chrysler introduced new cars that excited the American public: the economical K-car, convertibles, and the mini-van. Chrysler stock soared from two dollars to thirty-six dollars a share. Its investors made money and gained renewed confidence in the company. Its challenging slogan became known nationwide: "If you can find a better built car, buy it!" Lee Iaccocca became one of the most respected corporate leaders in America, and when his autobiography was published in 1984, it broke publishing sales records.

These opportunities would not have come to Lee Iaccocca if he had not had the obstacles of being fired from Ford and a near-bankruptcy situation at Chrysler. He found in these obstacles his greatest opportunities.

Every setback has within it the seed of an equivalent advance. You only have to look for it.

Joseph was the favorite son of his father Jacob. Joseph was a dreamer, but his dreams angered his eleven brothers who envied, criticized, and mistreated him. They captured him and sold him to some Midianite traders. The Midianites took him to Egypt where he became a slave of Potiphar, a court officer. The brothers, meanwhile, dipped Joseph's tunic in blood and led Jacob to believe Joseph had been killed by wild animals.

In Egypt, Joseph was thrown into jail. He had fled from Potiphar's wife when she made sexual advances toward him. Angered at his refusal to sin with her, she accused him of mocking and attacking her. Joseph was in prison as a slave in a foreign country. The obstacles he faced seemed insurmountable. But God turned them into his greatest opportunity.

Joseph was brought before Pharaoh and he interpreted Pharaoh's dreams. As a result of Joseph's faithfulness and discernment, Pharaoh made him his second in command in Egypt. Joseph was an influential leader with great power.

The significance of Joseph's opportunity was shown when his brothers came to him years later to buy grain because there was a famine in their land. They did not know who he was, and he tested them for awhile before revealing his identity to them. With love and forgiveness he said, "Do not therefore be grieved nor angry with yourselves because you sold me here; for God sent me before you to preserve . . . a posterity for you in the earth and to save your lives by a great deliverance" (Genesis 45:5, 7).

The principle of opportunity says that life is a series of obstacles, and these obstacles hold the key to your greatest opportunities if you only discipline yourself to see opportunities everywhere.

You are not perfect! Nor am I. Nor is anyone. Since you are bound to make blunders—a mistake made through stupidity, ignorance, or carelessness—you must know how to turn blunders into benefits. Anyone can make a mistake. That takes no genius. But it does take outstanding character to refrain from throwing up your hands in despondency. Learn from your blunders. Convert them to unexpected benefits!

Dealing with blunders productively contributes to outstanding leadership because it removes the paralyzing fear of making mistakes. The leader knows he will make mistakes, but he knows he can turn those mistakes to his benefit—and the benefit of the group. The more you succeed in turning blunders into benefits, the greater will become your self-confidence. When that takes place, you will lose the timidity that paralyzes the decision-making process. You will be willing to make decisions and act on the decisions even when risk is involved.

To put the principle of opportunity into practice, you need to learn how to handle mistakes, how to cope with errors, and how to profit from blunders.

First, admit the blunder the moment you know about it. You can never correct a situation if you don't admit that it exists. Moreover, mistakes multiply and get worse if they are uncorrected. Several years ago, a newscast reported that should NASA's Venus probe veer one degree off course, it would miss its target by approximately two hundred thousand miles. The NASA scientists had to carefully and constantly monitor the Venus probe so they could identify any deviation the moment it occurred.

Late in 1969, I learned that our accountant had forgotten my instructions to pay an airline bill of nearly $50,000 for bringing the participants and faculty to the first session of the Haggai Institute. While there were other bills due, they were not so pressing, and so I had made arrangements for them to be handled later. But the accountant had paid the other bills, leaving no money available for the airline.

Like the proverbial ostrich, I stuck my head in the sand, hoping the problem would go away. I didn't want to admit the blunder had been made. As a result, we lost our international airline credit cards. Repeatedly, the airline threatened us with lawsuits. It wasn't until I admitted the blunder, talked to the creditors, and transparently told them what we could do and what we could not do that the fears began to subside, the doubt melted, and the limitations seemed to disappear.

Second, assume accountability for the blunder. I am appalled at how few people want to assume accountability for anything that is not a success. Over the next two weeks, watch for it. You will find that when a stupid mistake or an honest error is mentioned—even if there is no implication that the person responsible needs to be determined—most people's initial reaction is to say in some way, "I didn't do it."

This reaction started in the Garden of Eden. When God caught up with Adam and Eve after they had eaten the fruit of the tree of the knowledge of good and evil, He asked Adam if he had eaten it. Adam's response was exactly like that people give today. He said that it was not his fault: "The woman whom You gave to be with me, she gave me of the tree, and I ate." Eve also responded that it was not her fault: "The serpent deceived me, and I ate."

Blunders are not the end of the world. No one escapes them. In fact, the people with the greatest number of achievements have frequently also scored the largest number of blunders. For years, Babe Ruth held the record for the most home runs hit in a single season of baseball. But he also held the record for the greatest number of failures through strikeouts.

To correct and profit from your blunders, you must assume accountability for them. As a leader, you must also assume accountability for the blunders of the people in your group just as you receive the credit and respect for the group's successes. A good leader does not say, "Sam did that and so it's not my problem" if Sam is a member of his group.

When I was a student pastor, my father visited my church one Sunday morning. I was ready to resign the pastorate and quit the ministry. Dad saw how disconsolate I was. He told me to assume accountability for my blunders. He said, "If you have done poorly in presenting your message, analyze why it was. If the reason lies in your failure to give sufficient preparation or to undergird it with sufficient prayer, or through any other personal faults, confess it, claim God's forgiveness, and go forward ready to honor the Lord on your next opportunity.

"If, on the other hand, the problem is outside yourself, commit that also to the Lord. If anything can be done about it, do it. If it cannot, relax and rejoice that He is more interested in His work than you are."

The world's great and not-so-great all make blunders. A blunder is not the end, but the beginning, if you assume accountability for it. So, what do you do next?

Third, evaluate the damage. Will the damage resulting from this blunder be minimal or major? Think it through carefully. Care must be taken neither to underestimate nor overestimate it. Sometimes we can get upset about a blunder that will make us embarrassed but cause little actual damage. On the other hand, when we cannot escape accountability for a blunder, our second line of defense is sometimes to minimize its importance, whereas we ought to be taking quick and drastic measures to eliminate further damage.

When God directed us to launch the Haggai Institute for Advanced Leadership Training, we took great care to determine the most propitious place to conduct the training. It should be in a neutral nation. If the training were done in the United States, the leaders, on return to some of the countries, would be eyed as Uncle Toms or as mouthpieces for America's CIA. A host of leaders from Asia, Africa, South America, and Australia affirmed Switzerland as the ideal nation.

The offer of some property in Switzerland, at an extraordinarily low price, fell through; but it helped direct our thinking to that country. Finally we found a property on a lake in the German-speaking section.

Conducting the initial seminars of the Haggai Institute in Switzerland turned out to be one of the biggest blunders we have ever made. Switzerland was not the right place. I had no choice but to admit the blunder. I then had to assume accountability for it. I called a major donor who had borrowed $100,000 to get the program started to make an appointment to see him. I would rather have taken a flogging, but I knew I had to do it.

"Why can't you tell me by phone what's on your mind?" he asked. I said, "Regarding this matter I must sit in front of you and look into your eyes." When I arrived at his home and told him the story, this dear man who could have made life miserable for me, broke out in a big grin and said, "John, you learned a great lesson by a much cheaper blunder than I did. We have just lost two million dollars on a bad overseas venture in our business!" What grace!

Our evaluation of the damage of this blunder included a loss of $55,000 in cash because the owner of the original property went back on his word. There had been signed agreements and we were advised to take him to court, but the board decided not to pursue that course of action.

It became clear that I had been influenced to move to Switzerland by superficial observations and the offer of property in a beautiful area at a low price. In other words, I had fallen prey to the trap of taking what is handy rather than securing what is really needed.

Often a church will hire an unemployed woman in the congregation because she's handy and because it can get her at half the price it would normally pay for a secretary. In many cases, the reason she's unemployed is because of her mediocre ability. To my thinking, this is a wicked mishandling of the Lord's money. However, I had fallen into the same trap of taking what is handy rather than securing what is really needed.

In addition to the cash loss, our damage included a loss of some of the momentum of the Institute and the expensive costs involved in finding a new location in another part of the world.

When evaluating the damage done by a blunder, ask yourself such questions as: What effects will it have by upsetting deadlines? How will this blunder interfere with the work of others? Will it adversely affect the "big picture"? How will it affect the testimony I have?

Fourth, do an in-depth study of the possible causes of the blunder. Blunders are the result of (1) an error in judgment, (2) poor planning, (3) insufficient information, or (4) defective follow-up. Examine all these areas in depth. To fail to study the causes of your blunder will only guarantee a repetition of the mistake.

Cross-examine yourself. To put the blame on others is leadership suicide. Identify the problem and isolate it.

Ask if the planning was defective. You may have planned most of the project, but if you overlooked any component, it can set back the entire project.

Ask yourself if you allowed enough time. Or did you select the best time to do it? I once met a godly American who had taken thirty people to an Asian country for an evangelistic thrust. He had not taken into account that it was during the monsoon season and so hundreds of thousands of dollars were wasted simply because of poor timing.

Ask yourself if the project was sufficiently funded. Did you allow for inflation? Did you identify the sources of the funds? A warning that needs to be given here is that if people of the so-called poorer areas of the world are to develop the kind of self-respect that honors God, they must stop wasting their energies writing people in other parts of the world for financial handouts. I have never seen a strong church maintained by foreign monies. Some of the largest church memberships in the world are situated in Korea. Most came out of dreadful poverty. Their strength today can be explained, in part, by their emphasis on the importance of self-support.

Ask yourself if you had adequate personnel. Did you have the various jobs slotted, and did you know exactly the person or persons required to fill each slot? Did you have a sufficient number of people both in the skilled and the nonskilled areas?

Ask yourself if you had the right kind of equipment. For example, if large mailings had to be sent out, did you have the means by which to process them? Or did the lack of equipment or persons mean that the mailing was stretched over such a long period of time as to neutralize the impact?

Ask yourself if you anticipated and made contingency plans for possible obstructions. For instance, in certain countries one must make provision for strikes. Did you allow for sickness or legitimate absenteeism? Did you make plans for securing any necessary government clearances or permissions?

Ask yourself if your information was accurate. Veteran missionary Roy Robertson made a statement to a group of leaders in Indonesia in 1968 that has stuck in my mind: "A genius with inadequate information is at a great disadvantage to a man of mediocre mentality but with superior information." He was so right!

Ask yourself if the blunder was due to a lazy worker who failed to carry out directions on time or whose violent temper caused discord among those who work with you or who did not thoroughly understand what he was supposed to do. In asking this question, however, be careful not to look for scapegoats. That is both unproductive and un-Christian. And it will demoralize an entire staff.

Do an in-depth study of the possible causes of the blunder. If the mistake was important to you and your group, you may have others help you find the answers, but ask the questions and make the evaluation yourself.

Fifth, immediately eliminate the causes for the blunder. Your evaluation in step four revealed the causes of the blunder. Now take action. Write down your plan. Work this into your goals program.

Conducting the Haggai Institute seminars in Switzerland was a big blunder for several reasons. First, the late sixties was a time of hijacking sprees. Third World leaders from the Orient and the subcontinent did not like the prospect of refueling in Mideastern capitals plagued by terrorists. Second, the climate and cuisine of Switzerland was incompatible with most Third World experiences. I have often seen people, well fed with three wholesome, nutritious meals, who feel as if they had not been fed if they did not have rice during the day.

Third, although the leaders coming for the international training all spoke English, few of them spoke German. If any difficulties with airline connections arose, it would not be easy for the leaders to contact us. Most didn't even know enough German to ask for an English-speaking telephone operator. Fourth, the facility we were using was two-and-a-half hours from the nearest airport, Zurich. Picking people up and returning them became a logistical nightmare. Fifth, when most people think of Switzerland, they think of numbered bank accounts, expensive ski holidays, and high-priced vacations. They don't think of human suffering and need. That made fund raising for a ministry based in Switzerland difficult.

Out of this blunder came a painful conclusion and a complicated transition: a move to Singapore. But in doing that we eliminated the causes for the blunder.

Singapore is just as neutral as Switzerland. It is situated in the heart of the Third World. The climate and cuisine of Singapore relates more compatibly to the lifestyles of the majority of the people in our seminars and Singapore has a good racial mix. Eighty-five percent of the people in Singapore speak English. The entire Republic of Singapore covers only 230 square miles, and so it would be difficult for a person to get lost and not be found.

Singapore is without question the cleanest major city in the world, and its very cleanliness, orderliness, predictability, and noncorrupt, highly sophisticated government are all models for observation by leaders coming from other nations.

Sixth, salvage what you can. Years ago, a company overproduced hundreds of thousands of fly swatters. It could not handle the expensive inventory and storage requirements, and so it engaged one of the world's leading persuaders, Elmer Wheeler. He looked at the fly swatters, noticed that they were square, and suggested the sales line, "These fly swatters are square so you can kill flies in the corners." In a matter of a few weeks all the fly swatters were sold. This company used good judgment. To secure the services of Elmer Wheeler cost it a fortune, but it was a wise expenditure, based on a calculated risk. The problem was salvaged.

Seventh, revise your modus operandi *so that the blunder won't be repeated.* You should be constantly evaluating what you do to see if it can be improved—not just in relation to this one blunder, but in relation to all your activities. This requires constant questioning and study.

Perennial learning insures productive leading. Learn from others. Devour biographies. Read journals relating to your particular field. No matter who you are or where you live, you can probably find in books and periodicals stories of prominent people who serve God in the area of your endeavor. These writings will review their failures and their achievements. My heart becomes heavy when I talk to aspiring Christian leaders who have not learned any Scripture in years, who have not read an average of five books a year for ten years, and who have done nothing to enlarge their knowledge or sharpen their skills.

Continually learn from the experience of others so that you won't reinvent the wheel. In your reading of biographies and in your association with other leaders, write out the application of what you learn to your everyday demands.

My own knowledge of leadership and other subjects has come from many sources. Among many others, I am indebted to John Sung of China and James Chalmers of Scotland; to Han Kyung Chik of Korea and Joseph Parker of London; to Benjamin Moraes of Brazil and John Calvin of Geneva; to Chandu Ray of Pakistan and Roland Payne of Liberia; to John Wesley of England and to Sam Arai of Japan; to John Gladstone of Canada and to Baki Sadaka of Egypt; to Martin Luther of Germany and to Neson Cornelius of India; to Saint Francis Xavier of Spain and France and to Reginald Klimionok of Australia; and to such publications as *Korean Review, Asia Week, Board Room Report, Success,* and *Fortune.* You will notice that my list covers every continent and spans hundreds of years.

Your learning has to be followed by action. Put your revision into practice. In the Haggai Institute program we used to make the error of scheduling sessions too close to the Chinese New Year. This caused great problems in logistics, image, and faculty availability. We admitted the blunder, assumed accountability, evaluated the damage, studied the cause, salvaged the situation, and revised the calendar. Today no scheduling is done near the Chinese New Year.

Eighth, begin to execute the new program immediately. If the blunder is causing your program difficulty, procrastination will only make the situation worse. Begin your correction right away.

As you embark on the new course, maintain a detailed chart of progress so that you will know exactly where you are at every stage of the program. One reason Japan has done so well in productivity allegedly derives from its having consulted a statistical physicist, Dr. Demming, who suggested that managers know by the day and even by the hour where they stand in their productivity compared with previous performances and current goals.

Ninth, use blunders as road signs. Blunders can serve as road signs that mark both where you have been in the past, as well as where you should go in the future. What you learn from the mistakes you make and the obstacles you encounter and overcome will help you to be a better leader in the future.

Charles Haddon Spurgeon of London said that when a leader commits a David-type wickedness which is made public, he should not resume active ministry until his confession and repentance are as notorious as his sin! You must openly acknowledge such blunders in order to learn from them. When you truly repent, God promises to restore the ruins.

The prophet Hosea talked about the healing of backslidings. He said that when the backslider returns to the Lord, God will heal the backsliding and "his beauty shall be like an olive tree." He promised that the restored backslider "shall grow like the lily." When the backslider has truly repented, he may grow in grace with great rapidity, whereas while living in sin he had not grown at all. The beauty of the lily is in its delicate texture and coloring. A touch or blot will mar it, and once marred, it can never be restored. The backslider need not expect to recover the virgin beauty of the lily which he had before sin blurred and bruised him. The scars of sin will remain even after the wound has been healed.

The olive tree, on the other hand, may not be in itself beautiful. It is often gnarled and crooked. Its beauty is chiefly in its fruitfulness. When the tree is full of olives, you forget the unsightliness of its trunk and branches while you gaze at the beauty of its fruit. So the restored backslider, while he mourns the loss of lily beauty, may rejoice in the beauty of olive fruitfulness.

Tenth, remember that obstacles enhance leadership. In overcoming obstacles, you improve your leadership capability by (1) the credibility you develop with others who realize you have experienced what they are experiencing, (2) the conditioning of your own spirit for service, and (3) the opportunity to demonstrate love, humility, and self-control.

The Reverend S. Arnold Mendis, an Anglican priest, returned to Sri Lanka from attending a Haggai Institute seminar and began a series of large meetings in a northern city. Some Buddhist monks openly opposed the preaching. Mendis, realizing that confrontation would neither honor God nor forward His work, stopped preaching and began cultivating the friendship of these monks. He talked with them in love. He did not seek government action to protect his rights as one with a minority status. He employed the weapons of his warfare: love and prayer. Within months he was invited by these same monks to conduct Christian services in the Buddhist temple! Today, several of those monks are committed to the person of Jesus Christ, and a few are studying for the ministry. Under God, Mendis creatively turned what could have been a severe problem into a glorious opportunity.

In 1935, my preacher father was a leader at a boys' camp in Michigan. It was in the middle of the Great Depression, and Dad had to watch every penny. One day he filled the car with gasoline to go to a city fifteen miles away. But before he got there, the car stalled; it was out of gas. A spike had punctured the gas tank. It did not take long to identify the culprit—a ten-year-old boy in the camp. I disliked this rich, spoiled, arrogant boy. I wanted my father to see that the "spoiled brat" was severely disciplined. Instead, I was appalled (and angered) to see Dad sitting on the edge of the dock with his arm around the boy, discussing calmly what had happened. He demonstrated love and compassion, and I have reason to believe the future course of that boy's life was altered for good because my father, under God, creatively turned a serious and expensive problem into an opportunity for witness.

An H.I. alumnus from a Mideast nation (who must remain anonymous) returned from the training in Singapore to be thrown immediately into prison without any charge. When released six months later, he inquired what the charge was. The officials informed him that since he had left an affluent medical practice to become an evangelist, they concluded he must hate Muslims. He smiled and said, "No, it is precisely because I love Muslims that I am spending my time telling them about Jesus Christ, the One of whom the Koran speaks so often and so glowingly. And I want to thank you for throwing me into prison because it gave me the opportunity to tell some criminals about Jesus Christ just before their execution. Had I not been in prison, I would have had no way of talking to them about Jesus."

In 1950, God blessed my wife and me with a son who was brutalized at the point of delivery by a world-famous but intoxicated doctor. Our son, Johnny, lived as an invalid for more than twenty-four years.

I never cease to be amazed by the demonstrable change in attitude and expression of those who find out that I was the father of a son with cerebral palsy. Suddenly, those who felt that I didn't know what problems were, that I lived in a fine house, drove a fine car, saw people at their best, jetted around the world, met with leaders, and wrote books, decided that just maybe I did understand their problems. Those who had considered my messages to be theoretical, although rooted in Scripture, realized that my wife and I understood suffering. Johnny was such a blessing to me personally. What could have been an overwhelming obstacle became a minister of mercy to my own life and ministry.

The leader, under God, will develop the habit of creatively converting obstacles into opportunities. This habit will enhance his leadership by inspiring those who follow him.

I need to give two words of caution. First, a leader neither attempts to shine or whine. When confronting difficulties, he must not complain that he is sacrificing. He is to be characterized by rejoicing rather than railing. Some, however, seem to label any unavoidable difficulty which they must endure as "sacrifice."

A mother can't avoid the care of a sick child. Let her not delude herself that such care is sacrifice. A father can't evade his role as breadwinner just because he'd rather be playing golf. Let him not complain, "How I sacrifice for my family!" That is an outrage! A pastor may not be provided a study by the church. Let him not call "sacrifice" his surrender to the inescapable situation. A young lady may fail to charm the wealthy young bachelor and instead marry a lowly, ill-paid day laborer. It's almost sacrilege for her to refer to her life as a "sacrifice."

Those who demonstrate a true sacrificial spirit *never* complain of sacrifice. Those who bemoan their alleged sacrifices think too much about themselves. They have not grown up.

Second, it's unrealistic and dishonoring to God to treat obstacles as though they don't exist. Nor must we fall into that heretical trap set by well-meaning but ill-advised Christians who say, "If you have enough faith, the obstacles will disappear." Hebrews 11 is the classic chapter on faith in the Bible. Verses 32 through the first part of 35 show the victories of faith, the great deliverances. However, from the last part of verse 35 through verse 40, we read of those who suffered, who experienced no physical deliverance but still had spiritual victory. They were just as much loved by God as those who were delivered physically.

Obstacles *do* exist and God does not promise that He will always deliver us from them. However, He will always help us to turn our blunders into blessing. In His strength, every obstacle can be an opportunity!

SUMMARY

Your greatest opportunities are cleverly disguised as insurmountable problems. The principle of opportunity says that life is a series of obstacles and that these obstacles hold the key to your greatest opportunities if you only discipline yourself to see opportunities everywhere.

Anyone can make a mistake. That takes no genius. You should learn from your blunders. Convert them to unexpected benefits. To put the principle of opportunity into practice, you need to learn how to handle mistakes and how to profit from blunders.

First, admit the blunder the moment you know about it. You can never correct a situation if you don't admit that it exists. And if mistakes are uncorrected, they multiply and grow worse.

Second, assume accountability for the blunder. Unless you assume accountability both for your own mistakes and those of the people in your group, you cannot correct them and profit from them.

Third, evaluate the damage. Ask yourself such questions as: What effects will the blunder have by upsetting deadlines? How will this blunder interfere with the work of others? Will it adversely affect the "big picture"? How will it affect the testimony I have?

Fourth, do an in-depth study of the possible causes of the blunder. Blunders are the result of (1) an error in judgment, (2) poor planning, (3) insufficient information, or (4) defective follow-up. Examine all these areas in depth.

Fifth, immediately eliminate the causes for the blunder. Take action. Write down your plan. Work this into your goals program.

Sixth, salvage what you can. Make the most of the assets you have.

Seventh, revise your modus operandi so that the blunder won't be repeated. Constantly evaluate what you do to see if it can be improved, not just in relation to this one blunder, but in relation to all your activities. This requires constant questioning and study.

Eighth, begin to execute the new program immediately. Procrastination will only make the situation worse. Begin your correction right away.

Ninth, use blunders as road signs that mark both where you have been in the past, as well as where you should go in the future. Learn from your mistakes.

Tenth, remember that obstacles enhance leadership by (1) the credibility you develop with others who realize you have experienced what they are experiencing, (2) the conditioning of your own spirit for service, and (3) the opportunity to demonstrate love, humility, and self-control.

There need to be two words of warning: first, a leader neither attempts to shine or whine. He must not complain that he is sacrificing. Second, it's unrealistic and dishonoring to God to treat obstacles as though they don't exist. They do.

The leader, under God, will develop the habit of creatively converting obstacles into opportunities. This habit will enhance one's leadership by inspiring those who follow him.

10

The Principle of

ENERGY

A leader without energy is like a pianist without hands or a runner without feet or an orator without a voice. The very tool needed to accomplish the purpose is missing. People follow an enthusiastic leader, and it is energy that produces enthusiasm. Some psychologists believe that the only common denominator of all leaders is energy. Not tact, not humor, not organizational ability, not vision, but energy.

Napoleon said that he owed his success to youth, health, and the ability to stand physical strain without limit. He had the "power to sleep at any moment" and a stomach which could "digest anything."

Florence Nightingale, according to her biographer Edward T. Cook, "stood twenty hours at a stretch, apportioning quarters, distributing stores, directing work, or assisting in operations."

John Wesley traveled on horseback the equivalent of ten times around the world's equator. He preached as often as fifteen times a week for fifty years. He authored more publications than any writer in the English language until the contemporary science fiction writer Isaac Asimov. He read books while making his horseback journeys. When he was past eighty, he complained that he could not read and work more than fifteen hours a day!

You can't explain the leadership of Napoleon, Florence Nightingale, or John Wesley if you ignore their tireless energy. The same is true of the late Sir Bruce Small, former chairman of the Haggai Institute (Australia) board of directors. Sir Bruce served simultaneously as a member

136

of Parliament and as the mayor of the Gold Coast in Queensland, while also heading up the largest property development company in Queensland. He is in *The Guinness Book of World Records* as the oldest man ever to run for an elective office and win. He was seventy-six at the time.

Sir Bruce insisted on having his phone number listed. He told me his constituents had a right to get to him when they needed him. His wife, Lady Lillian, told me he hardly ever slept through a night without several emergency telephone calls. His internationally heralded leadership got its thrust from a seemingly limitless energy supply.

A person may be in a position of leadership because of popularity, because of connections with the right people, because of intellectual ability, or just because he was available. But a real leader must exude energy. He must first capture the attention of those he leads. Attention requires movement. Movement demands energy. The effective leader works longer hours, reads more voluminously, wastes less time, and generally lives life optimally. He glows with energy. Energy enables the effective leader to make more contacts, write more letters, travel more miles, study more concentratedly, train more people, and make more phone calls than others. Study any area of human endeavor, and you will find a correlation between the level of energy and the effectiveness of leadership.

Energy is the "vigorous exertion of power" and "the capacity of acting or being active."[30] A leader's energy is communicated to his followers through his physical vitality, his mental alertness, his hard work, his commitment and persistence, and his attention to details. After examining how the principle of energy is demonstrated in leaders, we will also look at how to develop and nurture your own energy level. While it is true that some people seem naturally to possess greater energy than others, it is possible to increase and develop your energy level.

How Energy is Demonstrated

A leader's energy is demonstrated through physical vitality. We are all attracted to those people who have physical vitality—those who radiate good health and purposeful activity. Young people, especially, are drawn to those who are characterized by energy demonstrated through physical vitality. We can lament the way they are drawn to rock concerts and music videos while forsaking the church, but until the church starts demonstrating the same physical vitality and energy that the world's music performers do, it will be a natural reaction for young people to be attracted to them.

At the age of sixty-six, Dr. Ernest H. Watson assumed the deanship of Haggai Institute, a herculean responsibility. No one, including myself, has matched the hours he invested in the training sessions. For five weeks, he sat through every single period. In addition to that, he was available for counsel. Immediately after his quiet time in the morning, he would plunge into the Olympic-size swimming pool for fifty laps before men half his age were out of bed. Between seminar sessions, he would be writing, screening applicants, preaching, traveling, and writing extensive reports to the donors who made the program possible.

I remember a man from India coming to me and complaining that the regimen at the Haggai Institute was too demanding. He said, "It's inhuman to expect anyone to start the day at seven in the morning and continue until nine at night for five solid weeks."

I asked his age.

"Thirty-six."

"This year Dr. Watson is twice your age. Have you noticed that he has been at the morning devotions every day, at each meal every day, at each lecture period, at each tea break? He works past eleven at night and then is often awakened by one of the participants who is sick."

After this young man returned to an effective indigenous leadership role, he confessed that it was Dr. Watson's energy that made as great an impact on him as the subject matter itself.

Demonstrating energy through physical vitality lets others know you are in control. It gives your followers a feeling of confidence and well-being. Other people find it attractive because physical vitality is a desirable trait, and people follow those who have characteristics they want to imitate.

When the celebrated clergyman Dr. J. C. Massee was in his nineties, he told me, "John, you can have greater insights at my age than you did when you were thirty. You can have a greater understanding of the really important priorities. You can empathize with people much better than in your younger years. But when you lose your physical vitality, something happens. You lose your leadership power because people will not follow a man whom they perceive to be feeble."

Then he made a strange comment. "I have never seen a man without robust energy who could give an effective public invitation for people to accept Christ. I am not saying that spiritual power is dependent on human energy. But there is some kind of relationship between energy and the ability to give an invitation that God owns and honors."

It is important to emphasize that a leader does not have to have perfect health to draw others to himself by energy demonstrated through physical vitality. Franklin Delano Roosevelt, for instance, was unable to walk because of having polio, but he had boundless energy and physical vitality and is the only person in history to have served more than two terms as president of the United States.

A leader's energy is demonstrated through mental alertness. Claude Brown owns a thriving trucking business in Atlanta, Georgia. He makes decisions faster than anyone I have ever known. One day I asked him about it. He said, "Well, John, the Lord has given me an adequate mind, and I figure if I am right fifty-one percent of the time, the sheer speed with which I make decisions will put me ahead of the competition."

At sixty-seven, Claude Brown exudes more energy than many much younger people. Such mental alertness has made him successful. He's a leader. He has energy, and it is demonstrated through mental alertness.

All leaders are not intellectual giants any more than all leaders are ideal examples of physical health and strength. But all leaders do have a mental alertness as well as a physical vitality. Moreover, intelligence supported by a high energy level and governed by good character guarantees exceptional leadership. The leader who has intelligence will use it for observation, foresight, reflection, and reasoning.

The leader with intelligence will observe trends. He will see big issues and essential details. Observation lays the groundwork for wise action. The best observation constantly questions the meanings, the motives, and the relationships behind the obvious.

When World War II ended, Dr. Han Kyung Chik was teaching school in North Korea. He observed the large number of children orphaned by the war; he recognized the critical need for educational facilities. He grasped the areas of social service required to meet the needs of the people brutalized by war. Out of his keen observation came the leadership philosophy that has governed his work for more than forty years: evangelism, education, social service.

The leader with intelligence will have foresight, which implies preparedness. Foresight makes provision for every possible emergency. When Roald Amundsen made the trip that resulted in the discovery of the South Pole, he took along 97 selected dogs from Alaska. As he proceeded southward over ice barriers, he established supply stations. He marked them so well by signs and flags that when he returned he found them, even though they were hidden in dense fogs or covered by fresh snow. He thoroughly prepared for the expedition and made the 350 miles across an ice-covered plateau 11,000 feet high without difficulty.

Reflection and reasoning reveal intelligence at its highest level. It is through reflection and reasoning that the leader penetrates the heart of the profoundest problem. Reflection and reasoning pierce shams, uncover hidden secrets, command respect. They create leaders by their incisive drive. They climb to the summit of understanding and open the gate to personal achievement.

I have been blessed by the friendship of two men who, on hearing a plan, can lay bare the weakness of it with explosive speed. If you do not have this ability yourself, strengthen your leadership by making yourself vulnerable to the criticism of colleagues whose ability to reason and reflect will spare you some errors costly in time and money.

A leader's energy is demonstrated through hard work. Work is the most common expression of human energy. No sluggard ever excelled as a leader. When John Wanamaker was postmaster general of the United States, he stunned Washington society by going to work at 7:30 every morning, two and half hours earlier than official Washington. In 1920, when he was eighty-two years old, Wanamaker was at his office in Philadelphia from eight in the morning until six in the evening.

Since 1941, I have made it a point to interview men and women whom I consider outstanding leaders. Without exception, when I ask the secret of their success, they include somewhere in their response the words *energy* or *work.*

Horace Mann was a remarkable person. Until he was fifteen he never attended school more than ten weeks in a year. But when he was twenty he prepared himself so that in six months he was admitted to the sophomore class at Brown University where he graduated with highest honors three years later.

Mann practiced law, returned to the University to teach Latin and Greek and serve as librarian, and then took an interest in public affairs. After serving in the Massachusetts legislature, he became secretary of the board of education. His educational program in Massachusetts made that state's system the prototype for the rest of the United States. At fifty-two, Mann became a U.S. Congressman and then became president of Antioch College in Ohio.

His last words to students, delivered in a baccalaureate address just a few weeks before his death, were, "Be ashamed to die until you have won some victory for humanity." Often people asked how he had succeeded in this project or that. His consistent reply was, "In almost every case, it has required constant, hard, conscientious work. I consider there is no permanent success possible without hard and severe work, coupled with the highest and most praiseworthy aims."

I often chuckle at union leaders who put in a sixty and seventy and even eighty-hour week trying to get a thirty-two-hour week for the union members! Could that be why a union leader is a leader and the members are not?

A leader's energy is demonstrated through commitment and persistence. It was Thomas Edison who said that genius is one percent inspiration and ninety-nine percent perspiration. In 1878, Edison predicted that he would be able to light homes and offices with electricity. "When it is known how I have accomplished my object, everyone will wonder why they have never thought of it," he said.[31] The amazing thing about that statement is that Edison had not yet invented the electric light bulb. He had many obstacles to overcome before he accomplished his goal, but he believed he could do it. He had commitment and persistence. It took thousands of experiments, for instance, to find the right material for the filament of the electric light bulb. Platinum, beard-hair, lamp black, and every other substance Edison could think of were tried until he found success with carbonized cotton thread. Edison's commitment and incredible persistence gave the world the electric light bulb which, at the time of its invention, was considered to be the eighth wonder of the world.

Commitment and persistence require a tremendous amount of physical, intellectual, and emotional energy because it means believing in and working toward your goal against all odds. It means doing the tasks no one else will do.

Shortly before his death, Bob Pierce told me, "I honestly believe that God intended another man to do what I finally did." He mentioned the other man's name. "But," he said, "he wouldn't make the kind of total commitment necessary to achieve it. He was too lazy to lead. And so God took me, despite my lesser gifts, education, and personal charm, and used me. I was willing to commit everything to the accomplishment of that goal."

You cannot do much travel in Asia without noticing the large footsteps of this man. To describe Pierce's leadership without mention of energy is impossible. He made his last missionary journey around the world as an advanced cancer victim. He was confined to a wheelchair. To the end, Bob maintained his original commitment to help those in need and do it as a witness for Christ's love and salvation.

It takes energy demonstrated through commitment and persistence for a mother and father to maintain a proper discipline in the home, resist peer pressure in determining their child's activities, and to rear their children "in the nurture and admonition of the Lord." To stand by your convictions when those closest to you—even your own family members—strenuously object takes energy.

Henrik Ibsen said, "The greatest of men is he who most stands alone." And Henry Ford disclosed a similar spirit when he said, "I refuse to recognize any impossibilities."

American President Woodrow Wilson said to his opponents, "You can turn aside from the measure if you like; you can decline to follow me; you can deprive me of office and turn away from me, but you cannot deprive me from power as long as I steadfastly stand for what I believe to be the interests and the legitimate demands of the people themselves." That's leadership. That requires strong character, commitment, and persistence. And that demands energy.

Commitment and persistence will let you overcome opposition and persecution. The apostle Paul tells of the opposition he received:

> . . . In labors more abundant, in stripes above measure, in prisons more frequently, in deaths often. From the Jews five times I received forty stripes minus one. Three times I was beaten with rods; once I was stoned; three times I was shipwrecked; a night and a day I have been in the deep; in journeys often, in perils of waters, in perils of robbers, in perils of my own countrymen, in perils of the Gentiles, in perils in the city, in perils in the wilderness, in perils in the sea, in perils among false brethren; in weariness and toil, in sleeplessness often, in hunger and thirst, in fastings often, in cold and nakedness—besides the other things, what comes upon me daily: my deep concern for all the churches (2 Corinthians 11:23–28).

And yet in spite of the opposition and persecution he received, Paul was able to say, "I have fought the good fight, I have finished the race, I have kept the faith" (2 Timothy 4:7). Endurance impregnated his leadership with vitality. That took energy.

A leader's energy is demonstrated through attention to details. A careless attitude regarding a small matter can be dangerous. One of America's most prominent religious leaders went to Rio de Janeiro for a large evangelistic crusade. The Brazilians, with their usual charm and fiesta attitude, met the evangelist and his wife at the airport and presented his wife with a gorgeous bouquet of flowers.

She thought the flowers were beautiful, but on the way from the airport to the hotel, she found it awkward to handle them along with her carry-on luggage. At the first sight of a trash bin, she had the driver pull over and dropped the flowers into the bin. She did not know that several carloads of the greeters were following and saw her discard the flowers. Understandably, she created hostile feelings among the group without knowing it and without meaning to. A word, a look, an accent may affect the destiny of not only one person but of an entire nation. The little things make or break you. Trifles are important in determining the effectiveness of your leadership. A leader with energy takes the effort to pay attention to details.

HOW TO RAISE YOUR ENERGY LEVEL

Francis Xavier left wealth and position and set out across the world with the message of redemption through Christ Jesus. It took energy for him to labor twenty-one hours out of twenty-four, to learn to preach in twenty different languages in ten short years, to beg passage on a troop ship and later sail with pirates as he tumbled about the oceans in unsafe vessels. It took energy for him to sleep in tents with the Bedouins, cross the burning deserts and the snowy ranges of Asia. It took energy for Xavier to dare death in every form, shake hands with every ailment and disease, endure the pangs of hunger and the horrors of thirst after a decimating shipwreck and bitter persecution. But no Christian in the history of Japan has made such an impact as Francis Xavier.

We are challenged by the energy demonstrated by Francis Xavier's leadership—or by the energy of Napoleon, Florence Nightingale, John Wesley, or Ernest Watson. Leadership requires a physical vitality, a mental alertness, hard work, commitment, persistence, and an attention to details.

It is true that some people naturally possess greater energy than others. Nevertheless, it is possible to increase your energy level. The leader will want to raise his energy level to the fullest extent he can. You don't have to feel sluggish. You can be more energetic than you are now.

There are many factors that can sap your strength and deplete your energy. Being overweight, lack of exercise, poor sleeping habits, depression, stress, and tension can all make you less effective by reducing the energy you have available for leadership. You can maximize your energy level by eating right, exercising regularly, maintaining a proper mental attitude, eliminating negative emotions, and by walking in fellowship with God.

Eat Right

Your energy level is affected by what you eat. A friend of mine returned from a three-week vacation with her family during which she had eaten mostly in fast food restaurants. She felt sluggish, her joints ached, and she couldn't sleep. Her energy level was very low. By changing her diet, she was able to restore her energy level, feel younger, sleep better, and get rid of her aches.

How do you eat right for maximum energy? I do not pretend to be a nutritionist, and I know there are a number of good diets that I could recommend. Let me mention the diet given in *The Aerobic Program for Total Well Being,* by Dr. Kenneth H. Cooper,[32] the world's leading authority on total wellness. Cooper says that no matter who you are, you can be an energetic person if you will pay attention to your body and its need for right food and good exercise. The secret, says Cooper, is balance—balance in terms of *when* you eat and balance in terms of *what* you eat. In many parts of the world, people eat too much at the last meal of the day. The proper balance is to have 25 percent of one's calorie intake in the morning, 50 percent at noon, and 25 percent in the evening.

In addition, a person should have balance among the three major food types: 50 percent of what one eats should be complex carbohydrates, 20 percent should be protein, and 30 percent should be fats. Complex carbohydrates include fresh fruits, fruit juices, fresh vegetables, pasta, bread made from whole grain flour, cereals, brown rice, and bran. Complex carbohydrates are beneficial because they are high in water content and fiber, and yet their calories are low. Protein-rich foods include fish, poultry, meats (eat only lean cuts), cheese, milk, yogurt, eggs, peanut butter, and dried peas and beans. It is easy to let fats comprise more than 30 percent of one's diet. The best way to keep fat consumption down to the recommended level is to avoid fried foods, sauces, gravies, rich desserts, cold cuts, hot dogs, and excessively large meat portions. Also, limit the quantities of margarine, mayonnaise, and salad dressings. Fats from vegetable sources are much better for you than animal fats.

A similar program of eating is recommended by Nathan Pritikin. He says that eating this way "will enhance the acuity of all your senses, give you boundless new energy, take away that tired feeling, and may even reduce your daily sleep requirement. Some symptoms of aging even disappear."[33]

The Pritikin Program also recommends restricting salt and eliminating alcohol, caffeine beverages such as coffee and tea, and smoking. Salt contributes to hypertension. Alcohol is bad for the liver and for the effective functioning of the brain. It makes arthritis worse, and causes a host of other problems. Caffeine is a drug that increases the rate of heartbeat and contributes to high blood pressure. The danger of cancer from smoking is well known, but smoking also increases the risk of heart disease, stroke, and emphysema.

Eating right is not a matter of going on a diet for a week or two. It is a matter of changing the way one thinks about food—especially if processed foods are available. You have to become constantly aware of what is good for you and what is not because you may eat items that are not good for you without knowing you are doing it. For instance, sugar in one form or another is added to most processed foods and to fast foods as well. So is salt. Caffeine is found not only in coffee and tea, but in many cola drinks (which is why noncaffeinated cola drinks are now available) and also in chocolate.

I am aware that what Kenneth Cooper and Nathan Pritikin suggest is a way of eating that is more like the eating habits of the Third World than that of Western countries such as America. It is a terrible irony that our "advanced" countries have developed foods that are bad for us. But if you develop an eating habit such as I have described, you will not only live longer, be more healthy, and look better, you will feel better and have more energy.

Exercise

A regular program of exercise is essential not only for increased energy, but for a healthy body and a long life. Marie Beynon Rae in her book, *How Never to Be Tired,* says the answer to fatigue is not rest, but work.[34] She insists that boredom produces fatigue and work produces energy. I have found that during those times when my work load has caused me to go without some sleep, I have more energy, not by trying to catch an extra half hour sleep, but by spending that time in exercising.

The best kind of exercise is that which increases your heartbeat and sustains it for at least thirty minutes a day. Walking, running, and swimming are three excellent means of exercise. Isometric exercise—such as weight lifting—may serve a useful purpose in building up muscle tissue, but it does not help your heart and should not be viewed as a substitute for walking, running, or swimming.

The important thing about exercise is to do it regularly. Schedule it into your day. Make it a priority. Your increased health, feeling of well-being, and added energy will make it worthwhile.

Maintain a Proper Mental Attitude

Increased energy comes not just from conditioning your body through proper eating, exercise, and plenty of sleep, but also from conditioning your mind through developing positive attitudes and eliminating negative emotions. Your body provides you with your storehouse of energy. How much is in the storehouse depends on your physical care and development. But it is your attitude that decides how much of that energy should be released.

Do you know people who have a hard time getting up in the morning? Are any of them zealous fishermen? On a work day they would have a hard time getting out of bed by six o'clock or seven o'clock. But if they are going fishing, they know that they are to meet their friends at four-thirty and so they set the alarm for four. A few minutes before four they are wide awake! They hook up the trailer, they pull the boat to the fishing place, they slide down muddy river banks, and they get wet. They exert more energy over the next fifteen hours than during the preceding three weeks in their vocation. If they are successful in catching a lot of fish, they come back feeling better than they have felt in weeks. They seem to be aglow with energy. What makes the difference? Attitude!

If you want to be energetic, act energetic. Energy will come if you are as interested in the people you are leading—and the beneficial changes that will come to them because of your leadership—as you are in your hobbies.

Eliminate Negative Emotions

Nothing will divert your energy from constructive leadership faster than negative emotions. They will direct your energy into nonproductive channels. There are many negative emotions and effective leaders learn how to deal with them in constructive ways so they will not turn their attention from the job of leadership.

Anger is a common emotion often repressed or denied. In itself, anger is not wrong, but unless it is recognized and dealt with, it can become a matter of constant concern. Tensions, ulcers, and high blood pressure may result. Much energy can be spent needlessly by either repressing or nurturing anger. The correct approach to anger is to recognize it, analyze why you are angry, make changes where possible to relieve your anger, and accept the situation if changes cannot be made.

Hatred and bitterness are negative emotions that are wrong. They are mental and physical poison that will destroy you if you let them. Hatred and bitterness can seem to generate a lot of energy. But it is a diversion of energy from constructive to destructive purposes. Usually the harm and destruction do not happen to the person or thing hated, but to the person doing the hating. The only way to overcome hatred and bitterness is with love. Christ said, "You have heard that it was said, 'You shall love your neighbor and hate your enemy.' But I say to you, love your enemies, bless those who curse you, do good to those who hate you, and pray for those who spitefully use you and persecute you" (Matthew 5:43–44). With Christ's help, you can overcome hatred and bitterness.

Anxiety is a general sense of uneasiness or discomfort. It differs from fear in that there is no specific object or situation which is feared. This vagueness makes anxiety difficult to deal with. Focusing one's attention on anxieties leaves little energy for constructive accomplishments—precisely the thing that would help relieve anxiety. Christ warned against anxiety when He said, "Therefore I say to you, do not worry about your life, what you will eat or what you will drink; nor about your body, what you will put on. Is not life more than food and the body more than clothing?" (Matthew 6:25).

Fear can be good or bad, and like all emotions, fear produces energy. If someone approaches you with a stick to kill you, you will experience fear. That fear will give you the energy to turn and run faster than you ever thought possible. Fears that are phobias—exaggerated and irrational fears—also generate energy, but they turn energy away from constructive purposes to destructive ones. The fear of the dark, of heights, of closed places, of speaking before a crowd inhibit your development as a leader. The first step to overcoming your fears is to identify them and study them. Begin slowly to face your fears in the strength of Jesus Christ.

Guilt is a legitimate feeling because we have "all sinned and fall short of the glory of God" (Romans 3:23). But if we are not freed from guilt, it can become a demoralizing emotion, and we will look for reasons to condemn ourselves for things about which we should not feel guilty. Jesus Christ offers the only freedom from guilt. Through His salvation the guilt for our sins is removed and remembered no more. God has forgotten our sins, and we should too.

Worry, doubt, loneliness, jealousy, and depression are some of the other negative emotions that can divert our energy. Eliminating these negative emotions increases our energy available for leadership.

Walk in Fellowship with God

All things being equal, your energy level will be in proportion to the intimacy of your walk with God. When you are in fellowship with God, you walk with God, study the Word of God, spend time in prayer to God, tell other people about God, and relate all your concerns and activities and feelings to the will of God. This eliminates the energy-destroying frustrations, fears, and guilt that come from ignoring Him and walking in your own inadequate strength.

The apostle Paul said, "Be fervent in spirit, serving the Lord." That will produce energy the world cannot give and the world cannot take away, energy that gives the leader a magnetic influence.

The apostle Paul and his companion Silas, languishing in a Philippian jail, prayed and sang hymns of praise to God at midnight. Were they fatigued? Bored? Did they have the blahs? Not those two! They pulsated with the energy that vitalizes true leadership. God was their energy source.

SUMMARY

Energy attracts attention. Energy attracts followers. The leader who demonstrates enthusiasm and energy will gain the acceptance and confidence of others. Energy conveys the ideas of authority, of excitement, of success, and of purposeful activity. The principle of energy says that a real leader must exude energy, "the vigorous exertion of power" and "the capacity of acting or being active."

The leader's energy is demonstrated through physical vitality. Even though he may be older or have a physical handicap, the leader radiates good health and purposeful activity. The leader's energy is demonstrated through mental alertness. He is not necessarily an intellectual giant, but he will use his mind to its fullest for observation, foresight, and reflection and reasoning. The leader's energy is demonstrated through hard work. Work is the most common expression of human energy and the leader will enjoy it and pursue it. The leader's physical, intellectual, and emotional energy is demonstrated through commitment and perseverance as he believes in and works toward his goal against all odds. A leader's energy is demonstrated through attention to details because the little things will make or break you.

It is true that some people naturally possess more energy than others. Nevertheless, it is possible to increase your energy level. You can maximize your energy level by eating right, exercising regularly, maintaining a proper mental attitude, eliminating negative emotions, and by walking in fellowship with God.

11

The Principle of

STAYING POWER

In the late 1960s, I was asked to conduct an evangelistic crusade in Lisbon, Portugal. It was an exciting opportunity because it was the first time in the history of Portugal, which is 99 percent Catholic, that a Protestant minister had been invited to conduct meetings in public buildings.

I was an itinerant evangelist, having been a pastor for several years before that. As a pastor, I had not wanted to travel. Our only child had been victimized by cerebral palsy from birth, and in the pastorate I had repeatedly declined trips that had been offered to me. I didn't feel right being away unless it was absolutely necessary. Johnny needed me; so did my wife, Christine. Only the bedrock conviction that God was pushing me to become an itinerant evangelist led me to take that step. The conviction came when I received 420 unsolicited invitations to conduct meetings—evangelistic crusades, preaching missions, evangelistic Bible teaching seminars—during the last 18 months of my pastorate.

No sooner had the planning for the Lisbon evangelistic crusade begun than a prominent American parachurch organization (which I will call "Gospel Enterprise") sent two executives to meet with our Portuguese committee chairman. They damned our ministry with faint praise. Then the main spokesman of the two said, "I don't think Haggai will make much of a difference. But surely he can't hurt anything. We'll plan to come at a later date for a history-making evangelistic effort. You may just want to wait for us." The Lisbon leadership declined their recommendation.

Next, one of Gospel Enterprise's friends, a missionary to Portugal and a good man, used his influence to stonewall our crusade, even though he had cooperated with us enthusiastically two years earlier. It was tempting to give in to discouragement, but the Lord wanted us to persevere, and so He gave us staying power. The crusade proceeded on schedule. Toward the end, after thousands had made decisions for Christ, the missionary said he wasn't going to resist the obvious work of God any longer. He candidly told us he had been instructed by Gospel Enterprise not to cooperate, but to wait until it came with its programs to Portugal.

The late Bob Pierce flew from Dacca, Bangladesh, specifically to warn me that "Gospel Enterprise is out to stop you." He advised me to be on guard; he didn't want to see the ministry hurt.

This opposition did not surprise me, for just prior to the Portugal crusade, a family friend of one of my associates said he had sat in on an annual board meeting of Gospel Enterprise and had heard one of its executives comment that "Haggai is the only one we haven't been able to sweep under our umbrella." I had known for a number of years that Gospel Enterprise opposed our ministry.

As a pastor, I hadn't wanted to be away from home. And yet I knew God wanted me to be an evangelist. Giving up would have been easy in the face of the opposition from Gospel Enterprise—opposition I didn't understand then and I don't understand now. The opposition in Portugal wasn't an isolated incidence. I had encountered opposition earlier. No sooner had I begun my evangelistic ministry than the leadership of Gospel Enterprise attempted to end it by getting my engagements cancelled. Sometimes they used a direct approach as when they torpedoed a city-wide crusade in Honolulu that the clergy had asked me to consider.

The opposition to my ministry came from the top. Some European friends showed me a letter belittling our ministry which the head of Gospel Enterprise had written to one of the continent's highly placed Christian laymen. The favorite instruction of the head of Gospel Enterprise to his associates, when he faced a sticky situation, was known to be, "Do this. Get it done. Don't tell me how you do it; just do it." And they did it!

The active opposition continued for many years. Gospel Enterprise seemed determined to destroy our ministry. I asked God for the grace to stay true to Him and to the vision He had given me. For 15 years I tried every way possible to get an appointment with the head of Gospel Enterprise. He refused to meet with me. I had supported the organization from my college days. It was in my daily prayers. My son, Johnny, prayed with special fervency for the head of Gospel Enterprise. I never told Johnny the facts because I didn't want him to lose confidence in the people involved. I still pray for this man and the organization.

One night in Florida, a man connected with Gospel Enterprise phoned me. Since I did not know him too well, I was surprised at how determined he was to meet with me. "Fine," I said, "come over to our hotel and have dinner with us at 7 o'clock tonight."

"Oh no, this meeting must be kept in confidence. Let's meet at 11 o'clock tonight. We must not meet at a public place like your hotel or even my home." He then mentioned a remote spot where a street, deserted that time of night, dead ends into the ocean. "Let's meet there."

We met. With tears in his eyes, he said, "If you tell what I'm about to say and name me as the source, it could cost me my position with the organization. I've wrestled over whether to meet with you, but I don't want to see God's work hampered. So I determined to warn you of a vigorous attempt to eliminate your ministry." He then told Christine and me details of the efforts undertaken by Gospel Enterprise to terminate my ministry.

With a puzzled look, he said, "You don't seem surprised."

"No," I said, "I could tell you a few things. For instance, Gospel Enterprise's strategic planner, after volunteering on Wednesday to encourage the Indonesians to cooperate in a Total Evangelism—Plus project we had coming up, flew to Jakarta on Friday where he subtly denigrated the project before the chairmen of the various committees we had set up. They couldn't believe their ears. Later they played a recording of what he had said to my associate, who then went to great lengths to suggest that Gospel Enterprise was a great organization and maybe there was an innocent misunderstanding.

"Two of Gospel Enterprise's top executives went to unimaginable lengths to try to persuade the man who became Haggai Institute's executive vice president and director of worldwide operations not to join us. I could keep you here the rest of the night with documented story after documented story. I think I know every ploy, ruse, innuendo, and tactic they have used."

"And you're not upset?"

"I'm grieved, but not upset," I said. I appreciated the man's efforts to warn me of Gospel Enterprise's intentions. In the early years, I could not bring myself to believe Gospel Enterprise was deliberately obstructing my ministry and working to end it. I was the last to see it. My wife saw it. Members of my family and my friends saw it. Dr. Ernest H.

Watson, our dean, grieved over it. A multinational tycoon friend of mine, who also knew the principals of Gospel Enterprise, was so infuriated by the situation when he learned about it, he said, "I will put up $50,000 to arrange an international press conference in London. We'll blow the whistle on these folks."

"No," I said, "we cannot permit the ministry to be blamed."

"But this is dishonest. It's unjust. It's defamation by innuendo."

"Yes, but I believe they must have reasons they feel valid, although you and I cannot understand them. The Lord will take care of it all."

If we had followed a course of documented exposure and retaliation, we would have created havoc among Christians and great mischief among skeptical unbelievers who are looking for something like this to justify their rebellion against God. They fail to realize that the power of the gospel is verified by the fact that it survives such human frailties.

Gospel Enterprise's unrelenting opposition worked unspeakable hardship on us. In the early days, I went through all my savings, sold my car, and borrowed money to keep the ministry afloat. This was necessary because each time Gospel Enterprise got our meetings cancelled, we would lose all the money we had put into the preparation for the meetings—money that would normally be reimbursed by the crusade finance committee. On four different occasions we were faced with bankruptcy and closure. It could very well be that the leadership of Gospel Enterprise honestly believed we were not qualified to work in the field of evangelism. Yet for more than a decade they plagiarized our materials (one magazine article was almost word for word), and, of course, plagiarism is the most sincere form of flattery.

I rejoice in the great good Gospel Enterprise does. I know it is committed to reaching people for Christ. The fact that it has opposed our ministry can't negate that. Even though it caused us no end of grief and difficulty, God has used Gospel Enterprise to touch thousands of lives. Today, many individuals in Gospel Enterprise not only commend the work of the Haggai Institute, but several support it with their money as well as their prayers.

Whatever the motives of the leaders of Gospel Enterprise, their opposition made me and those who worked with me stronger. We had to have staying power to survive their attacks. And the exercise of staying power produces stronger staying power. God saw us through.

Cecil Day had only one wall picture in his original office. It showed a cat with eyes bulging and front paws desperately grasping a chinning bar. The cat was high above the ground and didn't want to fall. The eyes were just above the bar. The words below read, "Hang in there,

Baby." Cecil Day had staying power. That's why he appreciated the picture.

Difficulties do exist. Let's not kid ourselves into thinking they don't. Every leader has pressures and problems that can make him want to give up. The opposition I received from Gospel Enterprise made me question God's direction and my strength to fulfill the vision He had given me.

Charles Swindoll, senior pastor of the First Evangelical Free Church in Fullerton, California, decided to keep a record of the difficulties he faced in one 36-hour period:

• A mother and dad committed their teenager to a local psychiatric ward.

• A relative of a girl in our church took her own life.

• A fifteen-year marriage went up in smoke as the wife walked out. She is now living with another man.

• A young couple had their first child. It is mongoloid.

• A woman in her twenties is plagued with guilt and confusion because of an incestuous relationship with her father years ago.

• A young woman on a nearby Christian campus was raped and stabbed.

• A former minister is disillusioned. He has left the faith.

• A middle-aged husband and wife cannot communicate without screaming. Separation seems inevitable.

• An employer is embittered because his Christian employee cannot be trusted.

• A missionary wife who has returned to the States has suffered an emotional breakdown.

• Christian parents just discovered their son is a practicing homosexual.[35]

Swindoll then comments, "And then I got in my car after a late meeting last night—and it wouldn't start!"

The leader is guaranteed he will face problems, difficulties, discouragement, opposition, persecution, and betrayal. God has given you a vision, and you have established a goals program to accomplish your mission. At times it will seem as if it is impossible. Something will happen that can make you want to give up. Don't be surprised if this happens. I had to realize that I was doing the work God had given me to do as an evangelist, and the opposition I was facing did not mean I should quit. It only meant I had to exercise staying power. Moreover, God sends us opportunities to exercise staying power so that we will be strengthened to overcome greater problems and difficulties later.

Charles Swindoll lists what he calls "four spiritual flaws" about Christian maturity that show the need for staying power in the Christian's life:[36]

"Flaw 1: *Because you are a Christian, all your problems are solved.*" When I began an evangelistic ministry—one that complemented the work of Gospel Enterprise—I expected that we would work together to spread the gospel of Jesus Christ. But just because I was a Christian doing God's work did not mean all my problems were solved. Let's not promise the unbeliever that becoming a Christian will solve all his problems either.

"Flaw 2: *All the problems you will ever have are addressed in the Bible.*" The fact of the matter is, they are not. God tells us many things in the Bible, but He also requires us to walk by faith, receiving our guidance from the Scriptures, the Holy Spirit, and from the counsel of godly believers.

"Flaw 3: *If you are having problems, you are unspiritual.*" For some reason this is one of the most tenacious lies I know. It won't go away even though it isn't true. In fact, it's probably true that if you *are* spiritual and *are* doing the will of God, you *will* have problems. Job wrestled with this when his friends accused him of suffering because he was unspiritual. Swindoll says, "Some of the most spiritual men and women I have ever known have wrestled with some of the deepest problems life offers." When you have made your peace with God, you've declared open and unrelenting warfare with the devil. You *will* have problems.

"Flaw 4: *Being exposed to sound Bible teaching.automatically solves problems.*" Instruction in the Word of God will help you solve your problems, but it won't solve them for you. If you have stolen some money, the Bible will tell you that you should confess your sin to God and to the person from whom you stole and repay it. But that doesn't solve the problem. You need to be a "doer" of the word and not just a "hearer."

The apostle Paul said, "We are hard pressed on every side, yet not crushed; we are perplexed, but not in despair; persecuted, but not forsaken; struck down, but not destroyed" (2 Corinthians 4:8–9). That's staying power.

The leader will have problems and discouragements, but God wants him to persevere in following his vision. The principle of staying power says that these problems and difficulties can be overcome, but the leader has to hang in there. He has to have staying power.

Mastering other principles of leadership can take study and practice. But you can master this principle of staying power as fast as you can read these words. You don't need education, or charm, or well-connected family ties, or influential friends, or staff, or equipment, or materials, or prestige, or even profound biblical understanding. All you need is will. You don't have to wait until tomorrow; you can begin employing this principle right now. You have no excuse not to. If God wants you to be a leader, He wants you to have staying power. The question is, do you have the determination?

Staying Power Overcomes Illness

A serious and persistent illness can be one of the most discouraging obstacles to face in carrying out your goals program. Sickness will sap your physical and mental strength. And yet staying power can overcome illness.

Charles Haddon Spurgeon of London continued steadfastly with his multifaceted ministry when he was so sick he had to spend most of his time resting in southern France. His wife, who became an invalid after the birth of their twin sons, transcended her physical limitations by staying power. Though paralyzed, she directed from her bed an unprecedented book distribution effort. It is because of her staying power that Spurgeon's books are on the shelves of more people around the world than the books of any other minister.

Dr. John Sung, even when cancer was ravaging his body, continued to preach three times a day for periods of two hours and more. He did this in tropical heat, when there was no air conditioning and not even an oscillating fan. He did it thirty days consecutively and for eleven months out of every year. He did it until he died at the age of forty-four. Because of his staying power, God was able to use him to change the complexion of China and Southeast Asia.

Will Houghton, pastor in Atlanta, Georgia, and later president of Moody Bible Institute, suffered mental torture created by headaches that were so severe they could have made death a welcome relief. And yet most of us who knew Dr. Houghton had no idea of his illness. He did not speak of his great problem. His humor could put at ease all the students who would tense up in his commanding presence. This man, who demonstrated a unique leadership from the time of his spiritual conversion in the early part of the century until his death in 1946, pursued his work with a staying power that continues to challenge me personally.

Staying Power Overcomes Personal Desires

Thirty years ago I read a line that moved me and has stuck with me. "Efficiency is the willingness to sacrifice personal desires to the will to win." In every leader's experience, there are times when it would be easier to abandon a project, give in to the detractors, or take the easy road. A leader will also frequently be faced with the opportunity to satisfy a personal desire that may not be bad in itself but would interfere with the accomplishment of his goals. But efficiency is the willingness to sacrifice personal desire to the will to win. That takes staying power.

William Borden of the famous Borden family in America graduated from Yale University in 1909. While he was a student, cars were just beginning to come on the streets. One day he was looking out the window and admired a car. His roommate said, "Bill, why don't you buy one? You have the money." But Borden had different priorities. He had committed his life and his money to missions. Before he died at the age of twenty-nine, his leadership had made its impact on both sides of the Atlantic. The secret to Borden was total commitment to Christ and a leadership rooted in staying power—staying power that sacrificed personal desires to the will to win.

Staying Power Overcomes Financial Limitations

Many have demonstrated outstanding leadership by practicing staying power in the face of financial limitations. George Muller, who founded homes for orphans in Bristol, England, is a well-known example. He changed the lives of thousands of children and made a positive impact on England by his compassionate care. He did it by faith. Many times he did not have money for the food required for the next meal. He never complained. He never whimpered. He never threatened to discontinue his ministry to the orphans. Instead, he prayed. In answer to his faith, thousands of pounds came in to support the work from all over the world, much of it from people of whom he had never heard. What set George Muller apart was not his prayer life, for thousands of people around the world are faithful in fervent prayer. What made Muller unique was his staying power. His staying power gave validity to the faith undergirding his prayers.

Staying power is built on a deep commitment to the leader's vision. A weakness of many who occupy positions of leadership today but lack the qualities of a true leader is a "bail-out" mentality. When you talk with them intimately, you find out they are already making plans in case they fail. I have even heard clergy say, "If things get rough in the church, I'll move into the field of insurance. I can certainly maintain myself there." Their failure has been programmed and its arrival assured because the so-called leader lacks staying power.

Staying Power Overcomes the Peril of Prosperity

Almost nobody fears prosperity. We fear dishonesty, impurity, gluttony, jealousy, and the various sins of the flesh. But not prosperity. And yet prosperity and easy living constitute the biggest challenge staying power has. Prosperity can be a bigger danger than other difficulties.

Prosperity is also a threat to a close walk with God. The Bible never says that wealth itself is wrong (although it does say in 1 Timothy 6:10 that "the *love* of money is a root of all kinds of evil"). But wealth is the one thing that Christ said would make spirituality difficult. "Assuredly, I say to you that it is hard for a rich man to enter the kingdom of heaven. And again I say to you, it is easier for a camel to go through the eye of a needle, than for a rich man to enter the kingdom of God" (Matthew 19:23–24). And yet most Christians I know are actively pursuing wealth.

If our primary goal in life were a close walk with God, it seems clear that we would stop the pursuit of riches for the sake of amassing wealth because wealth makes such closeness more difficult. Usually, however, we rationalize our pursuit of riches by saying we need to provide financial security for our family. Or we say we want more money so that we can give more to the Lord's work. (Thank God some do give generously to God's work when they become wealthy.) Or we say that others may not be able to handle riches, but we can.

A powerful orator and a good friend of mine said several years ago, "Russia will never bury America. No matter what Khrushchev said, it just isn't so. America will bury America unless America breaks the stranglehold of self-indulgence, wanton waste, and narcissism." That could be said of many countries, not only in the West but even in the East, where preoccupation with things and self-indulgence are robbing the people of character and values of permanence.

Staying Power Overcomes Family Opposition

Fortunate is the person whose family supports the responsibilities of his leadership role. Unfortunately, it is not always so. A leader has a 24-hour, 7-day-a-week job. It requires doing unpleasant tasks as well as enjoyable ones. It is easy for members of a leader's family to feel they are getting second place.

David Livingstone, who opened much of Africa for exploration and missionary work, was not only a missionary himself, but a writer, a cartographer, and an anthropologist. He was a man of many and varied skills and achievements. Livingstone's wife, Mary, gave him such trouble, always complaining and criticizing, that it made Livingstone's work almost impossible.

Let it be said that the demands on Livingstone were great. In that day there were no jet airplanes making it possible for him to visit a city a thousand miles away and be back home the same day. However, as General Dwight D. Eisenhower said in 1945, "There are no victories at bargain prices."

The tension became so great that Livingstone sent his wife home to England for a period of more than twelve years while he suffered and bled and ultimately died in Africa for the Africans.

Staying power overcomes the obstacle of family opposition. The leader fixes his eyes on his mission and does not let opposition even from his own family move him from the path of accomplishing that mission. This is what Jesus meant when He said, "If anyone comes to Me and does not hate his father and mother, wife and children, brothers and sisters, yes and his own life also, he cannot be My disciple" (Luke 14:26). The leader's staying power must overcome family opposition.

Staying Power Overcomes Betrayal and Persecution

Polycarp, the Bishop of Smyrna, exercised enormous leadership. While he was in his eighties, for instance, he undertook a journey to Rome where many were converted to Christ. Shortly after his return home, persecution broke out in Asia. For sport, the Romans abducted eleven Christians, mostly from Philadelphia, and martyred them at a great festival in Smyrna.

The appetite of the mob was inflamed by the spectacle of the martyrdom. A cry was raised, "Let a search be made for Polycarp." Polycarp took refuge at a country farm, but his whereabouts were betrayed. He was arrested and brought back to the city where the proconsul urged him to "revile Christ," promising that if he would deny his faith, he could be set free. To this demand, Polycarp made his memorable answer, "Eighty and six years have I served Him, and He has done me no wrong. How then can I speak evil of my King who saved me?" These words only intensified the fury of the mob, which clamored for a lion to be let loose on him. The request was denied and instead timber and kindling were hastily collected, and Polycarp was placed on a pyre. With calm dignity and unflinching courage, he was martyred by being burned alive.

It wasn't Polycarp's death that accounts for his position of prominence; it was his leadership. And his leadership was characterized by an unswerving staying power. Right up to the time the flames licked his body and he breathed his last, he remained faithful to his calling and to his Lord.

One nation I have frequently visited has laws that require the death penalty for anyone who evangelizes or "converts someone to Christianity." In that country, a government informant went to a secret meeting of believers in 1982 under the guise of interest in Scripture and a desire to accept Jesus Christ as his Savior. Since the informant was to be away from his family for a few weeks and since hospitality is an important part of that culture, he was invited to live at the home of the host of the meeting. While the host, his wife, and family were out, the informant had television cameras hidden in the ceiling. The next worship service was photographed, with a clear shot of each person in attendance. As a result, each of the adult men was thrown in prison.

I have two friends in that country who have the staying power to overcome the obstacles of betrayal and persecution. They walk and work in peril of their lives. Every phone call is bugged. Every letter is censored. Every step they take is hounded. Both of these men have been offered positions of prestige which carry large incomes outside that country. But they have declined. They are leaders in their own country. Staying power keeps them there, even though both of them have been roughed up physically on occasion. Both have suffered government-sanctioned pressure, including the vandalism of their buildings. Staying power keeps them on course.

Betrayal and persecution can take many forms and come from many sources, but the leader with staying power does not deviate from his vision and goals. I mentioned the opposition I experienced from "Gospel Enterprise." Such opposition is most heartbreaking because it comes from those who are fellow believers. It is then that the leader needs staying power the most.

Staying Power Overcomes Misinterpretation of Events

The leader has a clear view of his vision and attempts to communicate it to others. But when others don't understand the vision with the same clarity as the leader, it is possible that the leader's actions will be misinterpreted. Or it is possible that some will not see how the pieces fit together. Or some may want to give in to discouragement.

The leader with staying power properly interprets the events, explains the situation to the people, and despite continued opposition, proceeds in love to insure the success of the enterprise.

When Spurgeon was hardly in his twenties, such large crowds came to the church services he held that the building could not accommodate them. He met with thirty of his leaders and suggested they build an auditorium that would seat more than 5,500 people. Allegedly, he told them that if any of them doubted the possibility of accomplishing this, they should leave. Twenty-three left! A leader without staying power would have had all kinds of doubts, but Spurgeon had the vision. The goals were clearly defined. He had the staying power to see it through. For more than thirty years, crowds packed out the Metropolitan Tabernacle morning and night, and it became the most influential Baptist church in history.

Staying Power Overcomes Impossibilities

What problem are you facing? I have mentioned the problems that can be caused by illness, personal desires, financial limitations, prosperity, family opposition, betrayal and persecution, and misinterpretation of events. But just because I haven't talked about the problem you're facing doesn't mean it can't be overcome. Every problem has its own solution, and although the solutions are different, staying power is the key to each one. If you give up, you have already failed. But if you have staying power, you will find a solution with God's help. Staying power insures success when every circumstance seems to insure failure.

When the Young Nak Church was established in 1946 with twenty-seven North Korean refugees, it met on a mountain in Seoul. All they had was a threadbare tent. One Sunday the weight of the melting snow caused the tent to collapse. All the members of the church were destitute. Not one of them had money. And yet the young pastor, Dr. Han, suggested they needed a church building. That seemed like an impossibility.

But leaders of faith don't confuse problem solving with decision making. They don't counsel their fears. They don't insist that every possible obstacle be overcome before they engage in an enterprise. They determine what needs to be done, they make the decision, and then they seek solutions to the problems. Leaders of faith know that staying power will overcome impossibilities.

One lady in the congregation said she had no money but she would give her wedding ring. Another lady said that other than the clothes she was wearing, her only possession was a quilt which she would give to the church fund. She would sleep when another woman with whom she lived was awake and use her quilt.

A third woman said that all she had was a spoon and a rice bowl. She gave that. She could borrow her friend's spoon and rice bowl.

The money began to come in.

Construction began on a magnificent church edifice. Then in 1950 the Communists came down from the north and pushed the South Koreans nearly into the sea. It was almost four years before the members of Dr. Han's church could get back to Seoul to worship in that building and during the Korean War, the Communists converted the church into an ammunition depot.

Just as the United Nations' forces were pushing the Communists back, an elder of the Young Nak Church went to the building to examine its condition. Communists were hiding in it and said they were going to kill him. Before shooting him, they granted his request for a moment to pray. If you visit the Young Nak Presbyterian Church in Seoul today, you will notice a tombstone just to the right of the front door. It is the burial place of Young Nak's first martyr.

Setbacks, discouragements, martyrdom, oppositions—all sorts of impossibilities—have been faced by the members of the Young Nak Church. And yet their staying power, which comes from their faith in God, kept them going. Today the church is the largest Presbyterian church in the world.

> "Got any rivers you think are uncrossable;
> Got any mountains you can't tunnel through?
> God specializes in things tho't impossible;
> He does the things others cannot do."[37]

Whatever impossibility you are facing, have faith in God, and He will give you the staying power to see it through. We are all faced with a series of great opportunities brilliantly disguised as impossible situations. Staying power lets you see the great opportunity in your own impossible situation.

How to Maintain Your Staying Power

You need staying power to maintain your staying power. Every leader gets discouraged. Most leaders at some time question whether they ought to quit. When those moments hit you, you can renew your staying power. But don't wait for discouragement to come. Begin now to practice strengthening your staying power—

By Remembering Your Vision

Your leadership began with a vision. You had a clear picture of what your group could be or do. You saw how you could move the group toward goals of beneficial permanence that would fulfill the group's real needs. The vision you had was valid when you started and the need was real. The goals were worthy ones. You can maintain your staying power by remembering your vision and renewing your commitment to it. Doing that will put your problems in perspective.

By Focusing on Your Goals

Remembering your vision will give you the motivation to maintain your staying power. You will renew your commitment to the calling God has given you. Yet individual problems are overcome by focusing on your goals. If I were to think only of my personal vision of world evangelization, I would be overwhelmed. There are too many people in the world. There is too much that needs to be done. Where should I start? But focusing on one or two goals is manageable.

Goals are the specific, measurable steps designed to achieve the mission that arises from the vision. Focus on your goals and tackle them one by one. The progress you see in accomplishing them will strengthen your staying power.

By Visualizing Your Goals As Accomplished

I have noticed that leaders frequently talk as if what they want to see accomplished has already been done. A president of a company may tell you of his large chain of retail stores, how much business they do, and where they are located when, in fact, the first store has not yet opened. The president is not lying to you. If he is an effective leader, he has visualized his goals as being accomplished so often that to him his stores *are* a reality. And he is setting new goals as if the stores were fully operational.

The late Max Stoffel of Liechtenstein, whose Stoffel linens are known around the world, practiced visualizing his goals as accomplished. He told me that every morning he would get a cup of coffee, return to bed, prop himself up on some pillows, sip his coffee, and in a state of complete relaxation, he would mentally rehearse his plans for the day. If he had some appointments, he would mentally rehearse the opening words, what the tone of the conversation would be, the expression on the faces. He said, "I attribute my success as much to this as any other one discipline. Actually, when I left my house to go to the office, I was simply replaying the role I had already experienced. It relieved a lot of pressure and dissipated a lot of stress."

By Relaxation

Tension is the enemy of staying power. Most outstanding leaders know how to relax. They understand and practice the habit of solitude. In addition to a quiet time with God, they spend time with their own thoughts, planning, thinking, dreaming.

Interestingly, it is possible to be alone in a crowd. One of my associates used to spend two hours a day commuting by bus to work in New York City and back. Moving to another part of the country reduced his commuting time to less than half an hour by car, but he said he missed the bus ride because it was a time when he could relax, be alone, commune with God, and review his vision and goals.

By Reading Biographies

Biographies of great people will strengthen staying power because they let you see how God worked in the lives of others. Thousands have been inspired by the story of Dwight L. Moody's response to the challenge that "the world has yet to see what God can do with one man totally committed to Him and who doesn't care who gets the credit." Moody said, "By God's grace, I will be that man." His commitment changed thousands of lives through his preaching and through the establishment of Moody Bible Institute and its many ministries. But his commitment has also changed many lives because of the example it has set for those who have read Moody's biography.

By Living in Communion with God

Living in communion with God enhances the leader's staying power by helping the leader to focus his thoughts not on himself but on God, His majesty, His power, His goodness, His mercy, His love. Focusing on God tends to put the leader's own problems and obstacles in an eternal perspective, making them seem smaller and less overwhelming and making the vision God has given the leader more important.

Dr. Han Kyung Chik can be found in church at daybreak, spending time in prayer every morning of the year. During the day, whenever he begins a new task or a new meeting, he quietly bows his head in prayer without obtrusiveness, without awkwardness, without rudeness. If he goes to visit a person, for instance, he will take a moment, just after shaking hands, to silently commit the interview to the Lord. It does not matter if the person is a preacher of the gospel or a head of state. Dr. Han lives in communion with God. And God has given him staying power.

Staying Power Insures Success

Problems and discouragements will face the leader, but he can overcome them with staying power. It seems as if many of the world's famous leaders faced some of the greatest difficulties and discouragements in carrying out their visions.

Christopher Columbus, for instance, concluded from information he acquired from his travels and from studying charts and maps, that the earth was round and that he could reach Asia by sailing west. But he needed a patron to finance such an expedition. He first tried John II, King of Portugal, without success, and then the Count of Medina Celi in Spain. The Count encouraged Columbus for two years, but never actually provided him with the money and supplies he needed. Ferdinand and Isabella, king and queen of Castile in Spain, were then contacted. A review of Columbus' plans by a committee appointed by the queen resulted in the conclusion that his ideas were vain and impractical. But they kept talking.

After the better part of a decade of trying to find a patron, Columbus was in despair, but he didn't stop. He had staying power. He believed in his mission, but he held out for high terms from Ferdinand and Isabella. He asked that the rank of admiral be bestowed on him right away and that he be made viceroy of all that he should discover. In addition, he would receive one-tenth of all the precious metals discovered within his admiralty. His conditions were rejected and negotiations were again interrupted. Columbus left for France. However, the queen had a change of mind and sent for him. In April, 1492, Ferdinand and Isabella agreed to subsidize the expedition on Columbus' terms.

It seemed almost impossible to get crews together even in spite of the indemnity offered to criminals and "broken men" who would serve on the expedition. But Columbus demonstrated once again his staying power and finally three ships, the *Niña,* the *Pinta,* and the *Santa Maria,* set sail 3 August 1492. Three days later, the *Pinta* lost its rudder. They had to quickly and secretly repair the boat because three Portuguese ships were trying to intercept Columbus. The voyage was punctuated with experiences that unsettled the crews and put them on the threshold of mutiny more than once. It wasn't until 12 October 1492 that they landed on North America.

Columbus did not visit the Grand Khan of Cathay as he had hoped. But he did discover two new continents. He was successful because he had staying power.

SUMMARY

Difficulties exist. Every leader has pressures and problems that can make him want to give up. But if God has given you a vision and you have established a goals program to accomplish your mission, you need staying power to overcome these difficulties. The principle of staying power says that problems and difficulties can be overcome, but it takes staying power. The leader has to hang in there. Moreover, God sends us opportunities to exercise staying power so that we will be strengthened to overcome greater problems and difficulties later.

Charles Swindoll warns against the "four spiritual flaws" that show the need for staying power in the Christian's life: (1) "Because you are a Christian, all your problems are solved"; (2) "All the problems you will ever have are addressed in the Bible"; (3) "If you are having problems, you are unspiritual"; (4) "Being exposed to sound Bible teaching automatically solves problems."

The leader does not need education, charm, well-connected family ties, or influential friends, staff, equipment, materials, prestige, or even profound biblical understanding to master the principle of staying power. All you need is determination. You can do it today.

Staying power is essential to overcoming problems. Staying power can overcome illness, personal desires, financial limitations, the perils of prosperity, family opposition, betrayal and persecution, misinterpretation of events, and a host of other impossibilities.

Many leaders at some time question whether or not they ought to quit. When those moments hit, they can strengthen their staying power by remembering their vision, by focusing on their goals, by visualizing their goals as being already accomplished, by relaxation, by reading biographies, and by living in communion with God.

Staying power assures success. Problems and discouragements will face the leader, but he can overcome them with staying power.

12

The Principle of

AUTHORITY

For years I have admired an insurance salesman named Ben Feldman. He has broken every sales record in insurance history, and yet he lives in a small city in Ohio, not in a metropolitan center. He sells more insurance than 70 percent of the insurance companies in the United States.

When I arrived home from the office one evening, my wife, knowing of my fascination with Feldman, said, "Ben Feldman was just on television."

"What does he look like?" I asked, thinking he would have an impressive physique, a compelling voice, and good looks.

"Like a kind, short, somewhat overweight Jewish man. He is not what you would call handsome. He is certainly not imposing. Nor is his speech impressive."

"Then I wonder what the secret of his success is."

"The camera went on his eyes," she said. "When you saw his eyes you could understand his success. There was an authority that is hard to describe. It was indefinable, but it was there."

I have since met Ben Feldman on two occasions. He is gracious and respectful. Although not physically impressive, he has an authority about him that nearly knocks you over. It's not that he has an aggressive personality. He is quiet, subdued, and speaks softly. I believe Ben Feldman could be put down in any place in the world, totally unknown, and would shortly rise to the top. He has that kind of authority. He is a natural leader.

William Golding's novel, *Lord of the Flies,* tells the story of a group of school boys who are stranded on an island after a plane crash. No grown-ups survived—only the children. The boys all meet on a beach, get to know each other, and wonder what they will do and how they will be rescued. One of the first things is to "vote for a chief." A boy named Ralph is elected, although, says Golding, "The most obvious leader was Jack. But there was a stillness about Ralph as he sat there that marked him out."[38] Besides, he had the conch shell, which became the symbol of the leadership of the group. The story of the book centers on the struggle between Ralph and Jack for leadership. Both of them have an air of authority about them to which the other boys respond. Both of them are natural leaders.

Charles G. Finney, a lawyer of great intellect and scholarship, became an evangelist after his conversion and made a greater impact on America than anyone else of his time. He had no entourage, no press corps, no public relations advance team, no public address system. Yet under his preaching, 30,000 people professed faith in Christ each week during one six-week period.

His most vigorous detractors begrudgingly admitted he had an air of authority about him that commanded attention and respect. They told of one time when he walked into a textile mill in New York State. Before he was introduced, before he had said a word, all eyes turned toward him. And even more remarkably, many asked how to get right with God. Nearly the entire work force repented of their sins and professed faith in Christ. He had an authority that captured their attention. He was a natural leader.

It is true that the twelve principles of leadership found in this book will help you understand and practice effective leadership. They are all important. But a natural leader will be a leader without studying any of them. A person with a charisma, an air of authority, a strong force by which he exerts influence over those with whom he comes into contact, will become a leader and will "naturally" practice many of these principles. We say that such a person is a "natural leader." He has internal authority. Ben Feldman has it. The fictional Ralph and Jack had it. Charles Finney had it. Haile Selassie, Achmed Sukarno, Winston Churchill, and Jan Christian Smuts all had it.

"It" is an internal authority that causes a person to command the respect of others and by which the person can exert a powerful influence over others by virtue of his own charisma and personality. It is visible in a person. It's not dependent on his club membership, his social position, his race, or his intellectual ability. This internal authority sets the possessor apart from other people. Internal authority is different from external authority.

External authority causes a person to exert an influence over others by virtue of symbols or position. The conch shell Ralph held gave him external authority. External authority depends on entourage, automobiles, membership in particular clubs, and many other status privileges. External authority can be taken away from a person; internal authority cannot. External authority can impress people, but it will not cause a person to command the respect of others and exert special influence to move a group toward goals of beneficial permanence that fulfill the group's real needs. That comes only from internal authority.

The principle of authority recognizes the distinction between internal and external authority and says that the leader should develop and enhance his internal authority. I am firmly convinced that every person of normal mind, spirit, and body possesses the seeds of internal authority, some in greater measure than others. I am also convinced that it can be developed to the benefit of the people led and, above all, to the glory of God.

INTERNAL AUTHORITY

Internal authority is difficult to define. In this respect it's like life itself, which seems to defy precise scientific and legal definition. But nonetheless, internal authority is the quality that makes a person a leader. Let us examine what internal authority is not, give some examples of it, and identify some characteristics of internal authority.

Internal authority has nothing to do with physical properties or actions. The person with internal authority may be short or tall; he may be fat or thin; he may be handsome or ugly; he may be eloquent or halting in his speech.

Internal authority has little to do with wealth, social position, or status. The person with internal authority may be rich or poor, famous or unknown, socially prominent or an ordinary person. Internal authority may be used to bring riches, fame, and social prominence to a person if those are his goals in life, and I would guess that a higher percentage of rich, famous, and socially prominent people exhibit internal authority than those who are not. But it is important to realize that these things are one *result* of internal authority—not the cause of it.

Internal authority has little to do with success. Like riches, fame, and social prominence, success can be a result of internal authority, and the person with strong internal authority will have a better chance of success than the person without it. But internal authority does not guarantee success.

Internal authority does not mean that you feel you are better than others. Rather, it is a conviction that you can move the people in your group toward goals of beneficial permanence. It is not pride, but it is a belief that your vision, your ideas, and your leadership will benefit your group. At some point, every leader realizes that he is actually able to make a difference. People will act and be different because of what he says and does. That's the realization of internal authority.

Apparently the apostle Paul had this internal authority. Paul was plain looking, without an impressive physique, and not eloquent. But he must have had an internal authority to capture the attention of the world's leaders, as well as people on the extreme opposite sides of the social and economic spectrum.

Of course, Jesus was the ultimate example of a person with internal authority. We are not told that He had a commanding physical presence. He did not have wealth, social prominence, or status. He was not a success by the world's standards. And yet He commanded the respect of others and exerted a powerful influence over others by virtue of His authority. After recording the "Sermon on the Mount," Matthew says that Jesus "taught them as one having authority, and not as the scribes" (Matthew 7:29).

Nicodemus was one of the seventy most important Jewish people in Judea. As a member of the Sanhedrin, he helped rule the nation. Religiously, he was without peer. He knew 400 ceremonial laws by heart. He fasted two days a week and prayed four times a day. In contrast, Jesus had no position, no status. Undoubtedly, Nicodemus was older than Jesus. And yet when the two met, Jesus was the undisputed leader. Nicodemus opened their meeting by addressing Jesus as "Rabbi," meaning "Teacher." Jesus possessed an internal authority that no one, not even His detractors, denied.

When Jesus drove the money-changers out of the Temple, He was confronted by the chief priests and elders precisely on the point of authority. They asked, "By what authority are You doing these things? And who gave You this authority?" (Matthew 21:23). Jesus did not answer their question although His authority came from God. He also had authority over unclean spirits (Mark 1:27) and could convey to His disciples the power over demons and to cure diseases (Luke 9:1).

One ingredient of internal authority is individuality. Internal authority sets the possessor apart from other people. As a result, others regard the possessor as unique, not as one of any group or class or crowd. Others want to be in that person's presence because of the person himself. His individuality is apparent. It is *always* in existence. It is not something he can turn on when people see him.

Another ingredient is a realistic assessment of the leader's own authority and a sense of humility. The person with internal authority is not flattered by people, nor does he feel the need for flattering others unnecessarily. He neither looks up to any person, nor down on any person. While he is receptive and gracious, he is not a flatterer, and he never condescends. The Christlike leader who possesses this internal authority simply lays every compliment, as a tribute, at the feet of Jesus Christ Whom he serves.

The person with internal authority is never a weak, flabby, or jellyfish type. He may be physically aging and weak, but he exudes an impression of strength.

Most important, the person with internal authority has self-confidence and a strong sense of self-esteem. His awareness of his own personal dignity is wholesome. He is not dependent on outside support to determine who he is, how much he has achieved, or what people think of him. He monitors himself in the most objective terms. He does not need anyone to give him the key to the city to verify his importance. It would never dawn on him to manipulate a testimonial dinner in his honor. He has a sincere belief in himself that is developed through understanding, forgiving, and accepting himself. It is this self-esteem that gives the natural leader his internal authority.

EXTERNAL AUTHORITY

External authority, on the other hand, derives its influence not from personal strength and ability, as internal authority does, but from external signs, symbols, and manipulations. It is an authority that can be taken away from a person, which indicates that the person never really possessed it in the first place. It is an authority immediately recognizable to those who know how to read the signs.

In the army, everyone's relative authority is clearly marked on his sleeve or chest for all to see. The general is more important and can exert more influence over more people than the sergeant, who is more important and can exert more influence over more people than the private. The authority each has comes from his position, which is reflected in his uniform. The general can do certain things because he is the general with external authority, not because he has the ability, strength of character, or intelligence—the internal authority—to do them, although it is hoped that he will.

There are many groups in which one's position of external authority is indicated by clothing. Policemen indicate authority by uniforms. Certain American Indian tribes indicated it by the kind and number of feathers in the warriors' headdress. Medieval knights indicated authority by gold spurs. In theory, signs of external authority are to be given only to those with a strong internal authority. However, it is no secret that people quickly realized that by acquiring the sign or symbol, they could bypass the discipline of developing real authority—the internal authority.

In his book, *Power: How to Get It, How to Use It,* Michael Korda describes the symbols that constitute external authority in the American business world.[39] A limousine is one such symbol. "Rented limousines are less prestigious than ones that are owned, a Rolls Royce carries more prestige than Cadillacs, and nothing equals a Mercedes 600 with the chrome painted black and the rear windows tinted to make the occupant invisible." A telephone in the limousine is a standard symbol of authority, and you can even buy a dummy telephone aerial so that others will think you have a phone in your car, even though it isn't connected to anything.

Telephones themselves are not just a means of communication, but another element of external authority. One telephone may be adequate, but two, three (or more!) phones in a person's office indicates more authority or power. Korda tells of executives who insist on having a telephone brought to their table at a restaurant to indicate how important they are. But for all the phones he may have, a person who is intent on developing external authority should never place a call himself. He has someone else do it for him. "With rare exceptions, power people do not dial telephones, use Xerox machines, add up figures themselves, type, or sharpen pencils. The first sign of a rise to power is often creeping helplessness."

Even shoes can be part of what gives a person external authority. "Powerful people generally wear simple shoes," says Korda. "—Peal & Co., Ltd. five-eyelet shoes from Brooks Brothers for example, and always put the laces in straight, not crisscrossed, and use round, waxed shoelaces. Shoes that have square toes, or high heels, or large brass buckles, or stitching in odd places, or are cut like jodhpur boots, are all definitely not power symbols, and to be avoided."[40]

A key to the executive washroom, a parking place with one's name on it, a certain kind of briefcase, a second secretary, a large salary, and many other symbols are the signs which constitute external authority.

External authority is also developed by manipulating situations and people. Korda says, for instance, that receiving telephone calls does not develop external authority, but placing them does. Therefore, one should do whatever is necessary not to actually take phone calls, but to get phone messages and return calls to people. If you spend enough time making calls, you probably won't be able to receive many anyway.

Upstaging others is another manipulation tactic that I personally find wearisome. No matter what you may say and no matter how innocently, there are some people who will upstage you. If you mention you have been to London, they have been with the queen. If you have visited Houston, they have just declined an invitation to be the first person in their professional group to fly on the next Challenger shuttle. If the waiter is a foreign student, studying at the local university, they must immediately tell you, with every conceivable embellishment, how their children have established new academic records and I.Q. levels.

Acquiring symbols of authority and learning how to manipulate people and situations are the means of developing external authority, an authority that is contrived and artificial. The Christlike leader seeks to develop his internal authority, an authority that is powerful and permanent. But there is a relationship between the two kinds of authority. For instance, the person who exhibits internal authority and as a result becomes head of a division of a company will get a larger office, his own secretary, and other symbols that give him external authority. To the extent that the person with internal authority seeks after and uses the symbols and manipulations of external authority, he denigrates his internal authority. But he should be aware of the symbols and manipulations, although he does not pursue them as an end in themselves.

A friend of mine who was a department head of a large publishing company was made vice president and given the external authority symbols that went with his new position: invitations to high-level meetings, a company car, a new parking place, a new title. He found that those symbols did not just give him greater status, but they were important for everyone who worked for him as well. They were interpreted to mean that the whole department was more important.

The Christlike leader seeks to develop his internal authority and not rely on external authority. However, if he is aware of his leadership (see chapter 13) and develops it by developing his internal authority, he will also be aware of what are considered the symbols and manipulations of external authority in his situation. Although he will subordinate it to his internal authority, he will nevertheless make external authority work for him.

DEVELOPING YOUR INTERNAL AUTHORITY

You have within yourself an internal authority. If through failure to exercise it or through lack of self-esteem you do not exhibit that internal authority, you must take steps to develop it if you are going to be a leader.

First, though, let me mention this: I do not believe that anyone should exercise authority over others until he has first learned to accept authority over himself. Moreover, even when a person is in a position of authority, he must be accountable to others. Perhaps the person in authority is accountable to an individual—as in a company or in churches with an episcopal form of government. Perhaps the person in authority is accountable to a board of directors or to stockholders. In some situations, Christian leaders are becoming part of an accountability group in which the members of the group make themselves accountable to one another and seek spiritual direction from each other. Lack of accountability leaves even the best-intentioned person open to the misuse of his authority. God wants each of His servants to be accountable not only to Him, but to Christian brethren of spiritual maturity as well.

Discover Yourself

Developing your internal authority begins by discovering yourself. You must know who you are, and you must be happy with what you know. Though you are a Christian and realize that you are a sinner who has been saved by grace, you also realize that having been saved, you are superior to the angels.

Do you know yourself? Too often we try to keep our real selves secret even from ourselves. To most people, the possibility of discovering themselves is frightening. They hide behind images they create of themselves or behind a fear of rejection or a fear of failure. Don't try to be somebody else. Your internal authority is yours alone and reflects your personality. To use it effectively, you must first discover yourself.

The only way to discover yourself is to walk closely with God. Commune with Him. Immerse yourself in His Word, the Bible, enough so that you begin to see things as God sees them. Then, regularly spend some time each day reflecting on the things you did and the things you learned during the day. View them not from the standpoint of your own selfish interests, but see them from God's viewpoint. Gradually a pattern will emerge letting you discover yourself.

Develop Self-Confidence

Self-confidence or self-esteem is one of the most important factors contributing to internal authority. Therefore, the development of self-confidence is essential, and one begins developing self-confidence by eliminating the fear of failure. Fear of failure is not usually a fear of the failure itself, but a fear that if one fails, his friends will forsake him, he will be humiliated and ashamed, and he will lose his self-esteem. Fear of failure can be overcome if you realize that the results of failure are not loss of friends and/or humiliation. Your friends will not condemn you for missing the mark, but they will criticize you if you never even try. Good people never abandon the courageous, honest, enterprising loser. They will admire your effort at trying. They will abandon you only when your fear of failure has caused you to abandon yourself. It is far better to attempt to do something great and fail than attempt to do nothing and succeed. In fact, as I have often said, you should attempt something so great for God, it's doomed to failure unless God be in it. The first step to self-confidence is eliminating the fear of failure.

Guilt also stifles self-confidence. Perhaps you have been programmed to feel guilty for having special gifts or power or skills. Those are gifts from God, and you should not feel guilty about them. Perhaps you feel guilty because of your sins and mistakes. If you are a Christian, God has forgiven you. "As far as the east is from the west, so far has He removed our transgressions from us" (Psalm 103:12). God has forgiven and forgotten your sins. Now you need to forgive and forget them too. You must reject guilt caused by sins that God has already forgiven. Affirm His forgiveness. Say it aloud!

God has not only forgiven you, He has accepted you as you are. Have you accepted yourself? Perhaps you are not happy with a habit you have. Perhaps your personal appearance or a physical handicap bother you. If you cannot change these things, accept them. Accept yourself just as you are.

Next, compliment yourself. Thank God for your pluses. If you really accept yourself just as you are, you will find certain things about you that are worthy of gratitude. Each of us has negative things about us, but we all have positive things as well. Recognize those things out loud. Say, "By God's grace I am a generous person" or "God has given me an exceptional mind" or whatever those things are of which you are most proud.

Only after accepting yourself and complimenting yourself for your existing good points should you try to improve yourself. The Christian is first accepted by God just as he is, and *then* God begins a work of sanctification in his life, making the Christian more like Jesus Christ. So, too, you should accept yourself as you are, and *then* begin to improve yourself. Perhaps you should begin a program of vocabulary building or a diet to lose weight or a careful plan of increasing your wealth. Whatever it is, your improvement will mean change for the better. And positive change means hope. Having a vision for a change, planning the change, and seeing the change occur will develop your self-confidence which will strengthen your internal authority.

Believe in the Importance of Your Mission

It has been my observation that people who are completely immersed in the importance of their life work, who with singleness of mind pursue their mission, tend to reveal a greater internal authority than others. The difference is that the person who is totally immersed in his mission knows where he is going. The others, while generalizing what they want to accomplish, seem to be ceaselessly looking for some new fad, some new activity that will get the attention of the public. Moreover, the person who is immersed in his mission has committed himself to people, projects, and causes and has had an opportunity to assume responsibilities. Those responsibilities create self-confidence, for responsibility fulfills the need to be needed.

Remember Your Relationship with Others

In developing internal authority, the leader must be careful in his relationships with others and the impression he leaves.

Don't reveal fatigue. If you are committed to a goal and you are enjoying working toward that goal, you can sometimes overlook your fatigue warnings. Others will notice it, and it tends to dilute your internal authority. When you are tired, get out of the public view. Get your rest. Let people see you only when you are vigorous. You may be the boss, the page-one celebrity, the lauded athlete, but the moment others see you fatigued, they instinctively jump to the conclusion of considering you to be equal with everyone else.

Keep your own counsel. Sharing your joys and woes, your achievements and setbacks, and finding a sympathetic ear all give comfort, but except in rare instances—as between a husband and a wife, or between a person and his mentor—it dilutes internal authority. Benjamin Franklin said, "Let no man know thee thoroughly; men freely ford that see the shallows." This does not mean that you are to be furtive or devious; it simply means that you are your own person. Let your counsel be shared with God, of course, but with few others.

Respect the rights and emotions of others. There are hundreds of guidelines that could be given, but I'll list only a few. Let people know you are aware of them. Be sensitive to their individuality, their achievements, their position. Give "honor to whom honor is due," but don't do it obsequiously. Show regard for the concepts, the intelligence, the abilities of others. You don't tell the carpenter how to do his work, nor the doctor how to diagnose your physical condition. Use good manners, be courteous. Practice the Pauline dictum, "In honor preferring one another." Show as much respect for the person who answers the telephone in an office as you would for the president of the company. Show knowledge of and concern for the culture of another person. When you are in Rome, do as the Romans do, unless doing so would violate your own value system.

Respect the personhood of others, and in so doing, you will be demonstrating the principle of love, for love delivers you from rudeness or criticism or inconsiderateness. And showing love is one of the best ways to develop your internal authority.

Strive for Excellence

In all you do, do the best you can. Excellence brings its own satisfaction, and doing your best will reinforce your internal authority in the eyes of your followers.

Everyone can excel in some area. Look at those areas of strengths you found when you discovered yourself. Those are the areas you should concentrate on in your striving for excellence because those are the places where you can most naturally achieve excellence and where you will enjoy doing so the most.

Believe in Your Own Success

Having committed yourself to the principles set forth in this book, visualize yourself as the exponent and practitioner of them. This develops your internal authority. Visualize yourself as already in possession of the qualities that enhance leadership and honor God. See yourself under His leadership, demonstrating the fruit of the Spirit in every facet of your life.

It is vital that you develop a strong belief in your ability to succeed.

And if you practice the twelve principles of leadership, you will succeed and your internal authority will blossom.

A PORTRAIT OF AUTHORITY

She systematically shuns all symbols of external authority. She owns only two changes of clothing. When she was given a white Lincoln Continental convertible with red leather seats, she auctioned it off to benefit the poor. Her office contains only a single telephone line, and for a while she was not sure whether even that was necessary. She travels in the third class compartments of trains. Her organization has no public relations officials and keeps a low profile.

Without any of the symbols of external authority that most people think are so necessary, Mother Teresa has founded an order of dedicated nuns and brothers who now work on five continents. She has become an international symbol of goodness and is honored by kings, popes, journalists, and the rich and powerful of this world. In 1979, she received the Nobel Prize for Peace because "the loneliest, the most wretched, and the dying . . . have at her hands received compassion without condescension." The $192,000 she received went to build a leprosarium in India.

Born in Skopje, Yugoslavia, in 1910, the daughter of an Albanian grocer, Agnes Conxha Bojaxhiu (the name given to Mother Teresa at birth) was called to be a nun at the age of twelve. She became one of the Sisters of Loreto and a missionary in eastern India. In 1946, she received a second call, this time to leave the convent and help the poor while living among them.

This tiny lady founded the Missionaries of Charity. One of her first projects was a home for dying destitutes in Calcutta. Here the homeless and forsaken could die in peace, experiencing at the end of their lives love and tenderness. One project led to others: an orphanage for abandoned children, a colony for lepers, a home for the elderly and bewildered, a workshop for the unemployed, and a free lunch program. Today, the Missionaries of Charity minister to the sick, dying, and destitute in thirty-one countries.

Mother Teresa exhibits internal authority that affects people around the world. She is quoted and respected. Malcolm Muggeridge, the British journalist, called his book about her *Something Beautiful for God* and describes her as a person "through whom the light of God shines." That is the key to her internal authority. She radiates the love of Jesus Christ, and when she holds a child, washes a putrefied wound, or feeds a dying mother, she does it as if she were doing it for Christ Himself. Mother Teresa is a person who demonstrates internal authority. She is a leader. And the source of her internal authority is the love of God.

SUMMARY

Internal authority is the charisma, the self-esteem, the personality that causes a person to command the respect of others. It is the element that characterizes all "natural leaders." External authority, on the other hand, is derived from the symbols and manipulations attached to a person's position. The principle of authority recognizes the distinction between internal and external authority and says that the leader should develop and enhance his internal authority.

Internal authority has nothing to do with a person's physical characteristics or actions, with his wealth, social position, or status. Nor is it derived from success. Rather, internal authority is a conviction that you can move the people in your group toward goals of beneficial permanence. The person with internal authority is an individualist with a strong sense of self-esteem.

External authority derives its influence not from personal strength and ability, as internal authority does, but from external signs, symbols, and manipulations. It is an authority that can be taken away from a person. It is an authority that is immediately recognizable to those who know how to read the signs.

You have within yourself an internal authority. If you are going to be a leader, you must take steps to develop this authority. First, though, it must be said that no one should exercise authority over others until he has first learned to accept authority over himself. Internal authority is developed by discovering yourself so that you know who you are and so that you are happy with what you know. It is developed by acquiring self-confidence. It is developed by believing in the importance of your mission. It is developed by not revealing fatigue, by keeping your own counsel, and by respecting the rights and emotions of others. It is developed by striving for excellence. Internal authority is developed by believing in your own success.

All of the principles of leadership are important, but not all are absolutely essential. Cultivating the principle of authority is. It is essential that a leader have and demonstrate to others internal authority and use to his benefit the symbols of external authority that go with his position.

13

The Principle of

AWARENESS

Awareness undergirds excellence. This is true not only of leaders, but of athletes, musicians, orators, businessmen, dancers, and writers— it is true in every area of life. To excel, a person must be aware of the elements that contribute to excellent performance and constantly measure his own performance against the standard of excellence he has set for himself. There are some people who are "natural" leaders or "natural" athletes or "natural" orators. They can do well following their natural talent and instinct. They can heighten their skill through training. But whether they train or not, it is essential that they be aware of their skills.

A musician should make his performance appear effortless so his presence does not interfere with the audience's enjoyment of the music. But although it may seem as if the music is just happening, the musician must constantly be aware of tempo, dynamics, chord progressions, and expression, as well as what the other musicians with whom he is playing are doing.

A writer's goal is to communicate effectively without calling attention to the writing itself. To do that, he must constantly be aware of many elements of writing, such as grammar. Do the verbs and nouns match? Are adjectives and adverbs used correctly? Do pronouns have identifiable antecedents? The excellent writer has made such things second nature to himself. He is constantly aware of them.

A boxer gets into the ring only when his awareness is heightened and prepared. He must be aware of his footwork, his hands, his pacing, his breathing—and that of his opponent. To let down his awareness for only a few seconds can mean the end of the match.

Could a teacher be effective while unaware of teaching principles? Or a physician while unaware of the principles of healing? Or a jurist while unaware of the principles of jurisprudence? Or a mother while unaware of the principles of child care? Of course not. Neither can anyone attain the level of effective leadership who fails to be constantly aware of leadership principles.

The principle of awareness says the leader will be aware of his own leadership, constantly monitoring his performance of the leadership principles against a standard he has set for himself so that he can achieve excellence. Awareness is the keystone in the arch of leadership. Knock out the keystone, and the arch, which consists of leadership principles, comes crashing down.

Awareness of how to be a leader requires sensitivity and exacting self-discipline over a period of time. One isolated experience of a group following a person's suggestions does not mean he is a leader. For example, suppose a fire rages through a building. A young man clearly and commandingly gives directions for those trapped inside. He tells some to go out one door, others out another, and still others down an outside staircase. His lightning-quick response to the crisis and his brilliant command of the situation make it possible for everyone to get to safety.

The young man would seem to have an aptitude for leadership. Nevertheless, that one instance does not assure solid and continuing leadership effectiveness. If he is to be an effective leader, he must be aware of his leadership and, by discipline, develop the principles of leadership.

The importance of awareness lies in the fact that it is the basis of the self-image the leader must have if he is to be effective. The leader cannot mistake weakness for humility, reluctance for waiting on the Lord, willfulness for individuality, excessive socializing with effective sociality. Awareness of his leadership role, of what leadership is, and of how to exercise it will sustain the discipline the leader needs for effectiveness. At times, a leader will experience loneliness that cries out for companionship, weariness that cries out for understanding, and risk-taking responsibilities that sound the sirens of fear. But an awareness of his leadership role will reinforce the leader's commitment. That commitment is essential to sustain the exacting discipline required for effective leadership. His leadership will collapse without both awareness and commitment.

THE LEADER IS AWARE OF HIS OWN LEADERSHIP ROLE

Leaders are aware of their own leadership role. They know they are in charge. They enjoy the privileges and bear the responsibilities that go with giving direction to the group's future. On the one hand, the effective leader will have many people look to him with admiration and loyalty, which puts him in an influential position. He knows that if he suggests to his followers something needs to be done, he can expect it will be done. He knows he will have a significant effect in people's lives for he has a vision, and by exerting special influence he will move the group toward goals of beneficial permanence. He is aware of the impact and influence he has on other people's lives.

On the other hand, leadership brings with it an awesome responsibility, and the leader is constantly aware of this. Ultimately, the leader is responsible for the well-being of the group. If there is a serious threat to the group's welfare, it is the leader who must find a solution. Others can comment, criticize, or have the luxury of merely talking about the problem. But the leader must find a solution. The people in the group expect him to do it.

The leader is part of the group, but he is also set apart; to some extent, he must distance himself from the other members of the group. This contributes to making the leader aware of his leadership role.

The early church leaders held a council in Jerusalem to discuss the divisive issue of whether Gentiles needed to be circumcised before they became Christians. There was much debate. After an appropriate time of interaction, James, the leader of the church, declared, "Therefore, I judge. . . ." He was keenly aware of his leadership role, which allowed him to listen to certain controversial issues, consider God's leading in the matter, and make the decision for the group.

THE LEADER IS AWARE OF THE MEANING OF LEADERSHIP

Leadership is the discipline of deliberately exerting special influence within a group to move it toward goals of beneficial permanence that fulfill the group's real needs.

Reread this definition of leadership. Think about it. Memorize it. Analyze it. Begin by centering your awareness on each of the components. Then think about that component's interaction with every other component. It will take time and effort, but the leadership our changing world demands deserves your best attention.

Leadership is a discipline. It is hard work. It takes effort and concentration. It takes staying power.

Leadership is deliberate. The leader leaves nothing to chance. Daily he's fine-tuning his leadership skills. Having carefully thought out his plan of action, the leader deliberately exerts special influence. His vision is deliberate (even when he receives a divine call, he deliberately responds). His choice of the group is deliberate. His selection of goals is deliberate. His assessment of the real needs of the group is deliberate. The orientation of his leadership to beneficial permanence is deliberate.

Leadership exerts special influence geared to change. When people want an improved lifestyle, they look to a leader for direction. The leader can change the course of history for God and for good. When the infant mortality rate is shockingly high, people look to a leader for an improved change. When thugs terrorize the public so that people are afraid to leave their homes at night, they look to a leader who will give direction.

John Sung, the Chinese scholar-preacher-leader, visited Indonesia for a few months in 1938. He organized five thousand evangelistic teams, each team composed of three young men. So great was his leadership that long after he had left Indonesia, the teams continued their work. Many observers have concluded that the influence and impact of these 15,000 young men, middle-aged by 1965, contributed toward the abortion of the Communist-attempted coup. Change calls for leadership and the leader exerts special influence geared to change.

Leadership sets goals of beneficial permanence. The leader takes his role seriously and sets goals that are continuing, enduring, and lasting, and in harmony with God's will for the group.

Leadership focuses on fulfilling real needs. This means that the leader understands his people well enough to distinguish between what they say they want and what they really need. The leader maintains a sensitivity to and a keen awareness of the people for whom God has given him responsibility.

THE LEADER IS AWARE OF THE PRINCIPLES OF LEADERSHIP

It will be good for us to review what we have discussed as the principles of leadership because leaders are aware not only of their own leadership roles and the meaning of leadership, but they are aware of the principles of leadership. These principles are the essential elements of effective leadership. Just as the writer is constantly aware of rules of good grammar while he is writing, the leader is constantly aware of the guidelines to effective goalsetting or the necessity of exhibiting energy while he is leading.

The Principle of Vision

Leadership begins with a vision. A vision is a clear picture of what the leader sees his group being or doing. A vision could be of health where there is sickness, of knowledge where there is ignorance, of freedom where there is oppression, or of love where there is hatred. The leader is wholeheartedly committed to his vision, which involves beneficial change for the group. The leader is aware of the importance of his vision and makes it the driving force behind his leadership.

The leader also seeks to communicate his vision to his followers. He captures their attention with his optimistic intuition of possible solutions to their needs. He influences them by the dynamism of his faith. He demonstrates confidence that the challenge can be met, the need resolved, the crisis overcome. If his followers grasp the vision, the group will become more cohesive and be able to work together toward a common goal. The significance of a person's leadership depends on the "bigness" of his vision; the effectiveness of a person's leadership depends on how well he moves the group toward the fulfillment of that vision and their needs.

Since the leader's vision is the basis of his leadership and since he is to be wholeheartedly and enthusiastically committed to the vision—that commitment is called the mission—the leader must be constantly aware of his vision. It must be before him always so that he will not grow weary in working toward the vision's fulfillment, nor will he be sidetracked into doing things that do not contribute to the fulfillment of the vision.

A God-given vision is an awesome responsibility. Fulfillment can lead you to heights of tremendous service to God and your fellow humans. Or failure to follow the vision will deprive others of the leadership they need. The leader must constantly be aware of his vision, be aware of whether he is effectively communicating it to the people in his group, and be aware of whether the group is moving toward fulfilling the vision.

The Principle of Goalsetting

Having a vision is not enough. There must be a commitment to act on the vision. That is called a mission. There must also be a set of specific, measurable steps designed to achieve the mission. Those steps are called goals. Goals design the program for achieving the mission and thus fulfilling the vision.

Goals must be S-M-A-R-T: specific, measurable, attainable, realistic, and tangible. The leader must also predicate his goals on his own behavior rather than on hoped-for behavior of others. He should let his mind soar and not limit God when he sets his goals. The leader should write out his goals in detail. He should also state his goals positively, and he should make his goals personal ones.

Because goals need constant review, the leader must constantly be aware of the goalsetting process. Goalsetting is not a one-time exercise. Rather, it is an ongoing discipline. As soon as one goal is accomplished, another goal—which also contributes to fulfilling the vision—takes its place.

Effective goalsetting demands a constant awareness of the leader's goals: goals that have just been accomplished, goals on which the group is now working, and goals that are about to be adopted. An awareness of the goals that have just been accomplished will be a great encouragement to both the leader and the group as they consider other goals.

The Principle of Love

There cannot be leadership without love. *Love* as used here refers to a mindset, an act of the will. It includes unconquerable consideration, charitableness, benevolence. It means no matter what people do by way of humiliation, abuse, or injury, the Christlike leader works toward their highest good. Without this kind of love, leadership fails the ultimate test—permanence.

The exercise of the principle of love demands awareness. Love relates to the real needs of people and the leader must, therefore, know what those real needs are. He must be aware by constantly searching them out because the needs change. What the needs were last month is different from what they are today. Also, the leader cannot show love only when he wants to or when he has the time. The essence of showing love is that it must be done when the other person needs it or wants it. It takes awareness and perceptiveness to determine when those times are.

In chapter 4, ten principles were given of how to express love to our neighbor. Each one demands a high degree of awareness to make it work. For instance, consider, "It takes a conscious effort to nurture an authentic interest in others"; "It will always take time—often a long time—to understand one another"; "Simply be there to care, whether you know exactly what to do or not"; "Emphasize the strengths and virtues of others, not their sins and weaknesses." All these principles demand awareness.

Love sets a true leader apart from a power-holder. If one is a power-holder, he does not have to be aware of his followers if his position is defended securely. But if one leads by love, a high degree of awareness is essential. The goal of a leader, however, is not just to practice love himself, but also to build love into the lives of those who follow him. He should be a role model, showing how love works, demonstrating its development, its practice, and its benefit.

The Principle of Humility

Humility is the lowliness that pervades the leader's consciousness when he contemplates God's holy majesty and superabundant love in contrast to his own unworthiness, guilt, and total helplessness apart from divine grace. The humble person is free from pride or arrogance. He is willing to submit himself to others and is helpful and courteous. The humble person does not consider himself to be self-sufficient, and yet he recognizes his own gifts, resources, and achievements. Both love and humility are characteristic of true leaders.

It is not accurate to say that the leader is aware of any aspect of his humility, for humility has no self-consciousness. There is a sense in which the humble person is *not* aware. He is not aware of wrongs done to him; he is not aware of presumptuous attitudes of others; he is not aware of his own humility. However, the spirit of humility frees the leader to concentrate on the real needs of others. He doesn't dissipate his energies wondering what kind of impression he is making. While the leader is not aware of his own humility, he is watchful of those things in himself that would violate humility.

The Principle of Self-Control

Self-control is a way of life in which, by the power of the Holy Spirit, the Christian is able to be temperate in all things because he does not let his desires master his life. Self-control is usually seen as a restriction. And yet it is impossible to permanently defeat the leader who exercises self-control, for self-control brings freedom, confidence, joy, stability, and a stronger sense of leadership.

Self-control is an essential attitude and characteristic for a leader. Without it, the leader diminishes his effectiveness and will lose the respect of his followers. With it, people will view him as one who has the determination and strength to be in charge.

Awareness is an essential ingredient in the development of self-control. This is because successful leadership requires self-control and yet successful leadership makes it difficult to practice self-control. Therefore, it is only by being constantly aware of the need to practice the steps to self-control that it will happen. Our natural tendency is to revert to a state of a lack of discipline and control. Self-control is developed through dependence on God, through a life of discipline, through making decisions ahead of time, through gratitude for adversity, through ruling your spirit, through controlling your thoughts, and through control by the Holy Spirit.

Self-control is love's mastery. It is something most people rebel at or avoid. But strength and power in leadership come from developing self-control. Awareness can produce self-control, but self-control will also produce in you a greater awareness of yourself and others.

The Principle of Communication

The ability to communicate through speech and writing is possibly the leader's most valuable asset. To develop this ability takes careful attention to the seven rules of communication. To use this ability on a day-to-day basis takes an awareness that makes these rules second nature.

The leader needs to be aware of the importance of effective communication. Each time he speaks or writes, he must be aware of the need to create understanding, not just to repeat words.

The leader must be in the habit of assessing his audience. He must determine its characteristics and attitudes before he starts to speak or write. He must be aware.

The leader must select the right communication goal. The goal is determined by his assessment of the audience and the purpose of his communication. An awareness of the goal will permeate everything he does while he speaks or writes.

The leader must break the preoccupation barrier. He must be aware of the concerns and desires of his audience and what will attract the audience's attention. While he is speaking, the leader should be aware of the audience's reaction so that he can tailor what he says and how he says it to the particular audience.

The leader must refer to the audience's experience. Again, the leader must know his audience. However, his assessment is not static, and he must be aware of changes in the audience. He must be sensitive to the audience becoming hostile, tired, enthusiastic, or agreeable. Awareness is the key.

The leader must use cumulation, restatement, exposition, comparison, general illustration, specific instance, or testimony to support his assertions. The leader must be aware of what will work best in his particular situation.

The leader must motivate action by an appeal to desire. He wants action. He wants to effect change. The most effective way to do that is by an appeal to the dominant desire of the particular audience.

Awareness is the key to effective communication. The leader must be aware of his audience, aware of the communication principles he is using, and aware of the effect they are having on his audience. Communication is a process; it is not static. The leader should constantly evaluate his communication, based on the feedback he receives from his audience, to see if it needs to be changed. That takes constant awareness.

The Principle of Investment

Wise investment demands awareness. A profitable investment is possible without awareness, but it would be the result of happenstance, not planning. The wise investor does not depend on happenstance, but instead he studies industry trends, market conditions, government regulations, and other factors that may have an impact on his investment in order to be in control. He is aware.

The principle of investment for leaders says that if you invest or give something, you will receive it back many times over. If you invest friendship, you will have friends. If you invest love, you will be loved. If you respect others, you will be respected. And if you invest money, you will receive it back many times over. It is possible to benefit from the principle of investment without being aware, but that is the result of haphazard action. The effective leader will want to plan his use of the principle of investment to maximize its benefit to his group.

The effective leader will be aware of and practice the ten commandments for investment:

(1) Recognize that God is the provider.
(2) Keep your mind on the things you want and off the things you don't want as long as these are compatible with the will of God.
(3) Invest what you want.
(4) Invest on the front end.
(5) Be patient.
(6) Do not be deterred by an occasional crop failure.
(7) Put your money where you want your heart to be.
(8) Rejoice.
(9) Expect results.
(10) Give God the glory.

There are two kinds of people in the world: the investors and the takers. The investors, by their nature, practice the principle of investment; the takers try to hoard whatever they have or spend it on themselves. Ultimately the takers lose. They lose disposition, friends, health, and respect. The investors win.

The leader is aware of the principle of investment and the ten commandments for investment. He seeks to master them and to make giving a habit both for himself and for those whom he leads.

The Principle of Opportunity

Your greatest opportunities are cleverly disguised as insurmountable problems. The principle of opportunity says that life is a series of obstacles and these obstacles hold the key to your greatest opportunities if you only discipline yourself to see opportunities everywhere.

Exercising the principle of opportunity, therefore, takes awareness. The effective leader looks for opportunities. Exercising this principle also demands an attitude that knows how to handle mistakes and turn blunders into benefits. Cultivating this attitude will heighten your awareness of opportunities.

In 1970, James Howard was the 42-year-old head of the sixth largest public-relations agency in America. But he felt "out of control." He was unhappy with the way he saw some of his clients doing business and he had a nervous breakdown. He sold the agency, moved to the quiet of Vermont, and began to put himself and his career back together.

It would seem as if James Howard had failed. But out of the obstacle of his nervous breakdown came Howard's greatest opportunity. He took the time to discover himself. He wrote out his vision and mission and a new set of goals. He analyzed four sample brokerage businesses he might want to pursue: farm and timber, solar homes, real estate, and small businesses. From this emerged Country Business Services, America's most successful small-business brokerage firm. James Howard carefully and systematically turned his obstacle into an opportunity.

These are the ten steps to successfully dealing with blunders so that the greatest awareness of available opportunities can emerge:

First, admit the blunder the moment you know about it.

Second, assume accountability for the blunder.

Third, evaluate the damage.

Fourth, do an in-depth study of the possible causes of the blunder.

Fifth, immediately eliminate the causes of the blunder.

Sixth, salvage what you can.

Seventh, revise your *modus operandi* so that the blunder won't be repeated.

Eighth, begin to execute your new program immediately.

Ninth, use blunders as road signs.

Tenth, remember that obstacles enhance leadership.

The Principle of Energy

Energy attracts attention. Energy attracts followers. The leader who demonstrates enthusiasm and energy will gain the acceptance and confidence of others. Most people are drawn to the person with energy because energy conveys the ideas of authority, of excitement, of success, of purposeful activity, and people want to be identified with those things.

The leader's energy is demonstrated through physical vitality. Even though he may be older or have a physical handicap, he radiates good health and purposeful activity. The leader's energy is demonstrated through mental alertness. He is not necessarily an intellectual giant, but he will use his mind to its fullest for observation, foresight and reflection, and reasoning. The leader's energy is demonstrated through hard work. Work is the most common expression of human energy, and the leader will enjoy it and pursue it. The leader's physical, intellectual, and emotional energy is demonstrated through commitment and perseverance as he believes in and works toward his goal against all odds. A leader's energy is demonstrated through attention to details because he knows the little things will make him or break him.

The effective leader is aware of the importance of energy to a person in a position of leadership and consciously tries to build up his own energy level. He does this through eating right, exercising, maintaining a proper attitude, eliminating negative emotions, and walking in fellowship with God.

The leader who understands the principle of energy is aware of the importance of demonstrating energy before his followers. They will not be more enthusiastic or more energetic than the leader himself is. He knows that the organization will not rise above the level he exhibits. He therefore carefully cultivates the principle of energy in himself.

The Principle of Staying Power

Difficulties do exist. The leader will have problems and discouragements. But God wants him to persevere in following the vision He has given. The principle of staying power says that these problems and difficulties can be overcome, but the leader has to hang in there. He has to have staying power.

Every problem has its own solution, and although the solutions are different, staying power is the key to each one. Sometimes God's answer to a problem is that He will not remove the problem from us, as was Job's experience. In those instances, staying power is especially needed. Staying power can overcome illness, personal desires, financial limitations, the perils of prosperity, family opposition, betrayal and persecution, misinterpretation of events, and a host of other impossibilities.

Many leaders at some time question whether they ought to quit. When those moments hit, they can strengthen their staying power by remembering their vision, by focusing on their goals, by visualizing their goals as being already accomplished, by relaxation, by reading biographies, and by living in communion with God. Staying power insures success because it indicates a strong awareness to a commitment.

I believe it was Ho Chi Minh who explained why the North Vietnamese would eventually win the war in Viet Nam. He said that he could lose ten soldiers to every American soldier killed because eventually the Americans would get tired and leave as the French had done. Ho Chi Minh's comment showed a terrible disregard for human life, but he was in part correct. Historians will long discuss the actual factors contributing to the American withdrawal from Viet Nam, but certainly the staying power of the North Vietnamese was one of them.

It seems as if many of the world's greatest leaders found some of the greatest difficulties and discouragements in carrying out their visions. But what made them great was their success that came because of staying power.

The Principle of Authority

Authority demands awareness. A leader cannot exercise the principle of authority without being aware of what he is doing and why.

Consider the biblical story of Joseph. Alert to the prospect of God's prophesied famine, Joseph, during the preceding seven years of prosperity, ordered all the inhabitants of Egypt to surrender their surplus grain. He would save it until the famine, during which time he would ration it. Surely Joseph's order angered many of the Egyptians. But his superior leadership, marked with authority, served the real needs of the people and sustained them throughout the famine. Joseph was aware of the use he was making of his authority and probably used not only his internal authority, but his external authority as well.

Internal authority is that which causes a leader to command the respect of others and by which the leader can exert a powerful influence over others by virtue of his own charisma and personality. Internal authority has nothing to do with a person's physical characteristics or actions, with his wealth, social position, or status. Nor is it derived from success. Rather, internal authority is a conviction that you can move the people in your group toward goals of beneficial permanence.

The person with internal authority is an individualist with a strong sense of self-esteem.

External authority, on the other hand, causes a person to exert an influence over others by virtue of symbols or position. External authority is developed by manipulating situations and people. External authority can be taken away from a person; internal authority cannot.

The principle of authority recognizes the distinction between internal and external authority and says that the leader should develop and enhance his internal authority. Internal authority is developed by discovering yourself so that you know who you are and so that you are happy with what you know. It is developed by acquiring self-confidence. It is developed by believing in the importance of your mission. It is developed by not revealing fatigue, by keeping your own counsel, and by respecting the rights and emotions of others. It is developed by striving for excellence. Internal authority is developed by believing in your own success.

Every normal person possesses the seeds of internal authority, some in greater measure than others. Those seeds can be developed through cultivating awareness of authority to the benefit of the people led and, above all, to the glory of God.

THE LEADER IS AWARE THAT GOD IS HIS RESOURCE

The leader is aware of his own leadership role, he is aware of the meaning of leadership, and he is aware of the principles of leadership. As he lives in the awareness that he is a leader, he may react, "But I feel so unworthy." Of course he feels that way. Any rational, spiritually sensitive person feels unworthy to the task of Christlike leadership.

Paul the apostle said that he was "the least of the apostles." He admitted freely that he was not perfect, but he learned that God's grace was sufficient and that God's strength was made perfect in weakness.

Jeremiah said, "Behold, I cannot speak, for I am a youth." But God told Jeremiah to stop complaining. He said, "For I am with you to deliver you. . . . Behold I have put My words in your mouth. See, I have this day set you over the nations and over the kingdoms to root out and to pull down. To destroy and to throw down. To build and to plant" (Jeremiah 1:8–10).

When nineteen-year-old Charles Haddon Spurgeon was invited to become pastor of the new Park Street Church in London, he honestly believed that there had been a mistake and the invitation was meant for another man by the same name! But Spurgeon became the most influential Baptist pastor in history. He understood that his strength came from the Lord.

A few weeks before writing this, I was in Japan, the guest of a close friend and director of Haggai Institute. Unashamedly, this multinational businessman, who uses his vocation as a conduit for Christlike leadership, said, "Without Christ, I could do nothing."

You must rely on supernatural resources. This presupposes that you live in the awareness of God's presence and power. While you may feel unworthy, you must not despair. Your resources are in God, but you must exercise the faith and discipline to appropriate them.

God is calling leaders. Not power-holders. Not Madison Avenue hype artists. Not mutual congratulation experts. Not influence peddlers. Not crowd-manipulating, exhibitionistic demagogues. God is calling leaders!

Will you respond to this call in dependence on God Himself for your strength?

SUMMARY

Awareness undergirds excellence. This is true in all areas of endeavor. The principle of awareness calls for the leader to be aware of the elements that contribute to excellent performance and constantly measure his own performance against the standards of excellence he has set for himself. Awareness is the keystone in the arch of leadership. Knock out the keystone, and the arch, which consists of leadership principles, comes crashing down.

The leader is aware of his own leadership role. He knows he is in charge. He is aware of the impact and influence he has on other people's lives. He enjoys the privileges and bears the awesome responsibilities that go with giving direction to a group's future.

The leader is aware of the meaning of leadership. Leadership is the discipline of deliberately exerting special influence within a group to move it toward goals of beneficial permanence that fulfill the group's real needs. The leader knows each component of that meaning and how the components interact with each other.

The leader is aware of the principles of leadership:

(1) The principle of vision. Since the leader's vision is the basis of his leadership, he must be constantly aware of his vision, of whether he is effectively communicating it to those in the group, and of whether the group is moving toward fulfilling the vision.

(2) The principle of goalsetting. Because goals need constant review, the leader must constantly be aware of the goalsetting process. Goalsetting is an ongoing discipline.

(3) The principle of love. Love relates to the real needs of people and the leader must, therefore, be aware of what those real needs are.

(4) The principle of humility. The leader is not aware of his own humility, for humility has no self-consciousness. But the leader is watchful of those things in himself that would violate humility.

(5) The principle of self-control. Awareness is an essential ingredient in the development of self-control because successful leadership requires self-control and yet successful leadership makes it difficult to practice self-control.

(6) The principle of communication. Communication is a process that is always occurring. The leader needs to communicate effectively by being constantly aware of the seven rules of communication and making them second nature to himself. Awareness is the key to effective communication.

(7) The principle of investment. It is possible to benefit from the principle of investment without being aware, but that would be the result of haphazard action. The effective leader will want to plan his use of the principle of investment to maximize its benefit to his group.

(8) The principle of opportunity. A person's greatest opportunities are cleverly disguised as insurmountable problems. Through awareness, the leader must discipline himself to see opportunities everywhere.

(9) The principle of energy. The effective leader is aware of the importance of energy to a person in a position of leadership and consciously tries to build up his own energy level.

(10) The principle of staying power. Difficulties do exist. There will be problems. But these difficulties and problems can be overcome (not necessarily eliminated) by staying power.

(11) The principle of authority. A leader cannot exercise the principle of authority without being aware of what he is doing and why. He is aware of both his internal authority as well as his external authority.

(12) The principle of awareness says the leader will be aware of his own leadership, constantly monitoring his performance so that he can achieve excellence.

The leader is also aware that God is his resource. He understands that his strength comes from the Lord.

Recommended Reading List

Adler, Mortimer J. *How to Speak, How to Listen.* New York: Macmillan Publishing Company, Inc., 1983.

Augustine, Saint. *Saint Augustine's Confessions.* New York: Penguin Books, 1961. Published every year or two since 1961.

Bennis, Warren, and Burt Nanus. *Leaders: The Strategies for Taking Charge.* New York: Harper and Row, 1985.

Blamires, Harry. *The Christian Mind: How Should a Christian Think.* Ann Arbor: Servant Books, 1963.

Bogardus, Henry S. *Leaders and Leadership.* New York: Appleton-Century-Crofts, Inc., 1934*.

Bounds, E. M. *Power through Prayer.* Louisville: Pentecostal Publishing Company.

Bready, J. Wesley. *Faith and Freedom.* New York: American Tract Society, 1946.

———. *Freedom Whence.* Winona Lake: Light and Life Press, 1956.

Brion, Marcel. *Attila, Scourge of God.* Translated by Harold Ward. London: Cassell and Company, Ltd., 1929.

Brown, Barbara B. *New Mind, New Body.* New York: Bantam Books, 1974.

Burr, Agnes Rush. *Russell H. Conwell and His Work.* Philadelphia: John C. Winston Company, 1926*.

Butterfield, Fox. *China, Alive in the Bitter Sea.* New York: Bantam Books, 1982.

Chambers, Oswald. *My Utmost for His Highest.* New York: Dodd, Mead & Company, 1935.

Colson, Charles W. *Born Again.* Old Tappan, New Jersey: Chosen Books, distributed by Fleming H. Revell Company, 1976.

———. *Life Sentence.* Lincoln, Virginia: Chosen Books distributed by Word Books, 1979.

———. *Loving God.* Grand Rapids: Zondervan Publishing Company, 1983.

Connelly, Thomas L. *The Marble Man: Robert E. Lee and His Image in American Society.* New York: Alfred Knopf, 1977.

---

* Although these books are out of print, I feel you would find it worthwhile to find copies and read them.

Cooper, Kenneth H. *The Aerobics Program for Total Well Being.* New York: M. Evans and Company, 1982.

Curtis, Richard Kenneth. *They Called Him Mr. Moody.* Garden City, New York: Doubleday and Company, Inc., 1962.

Daniels, Peter J. *How to be Happy Though Rich.* Unley Park, South Australia: The House of Taylor, 1984.

Dasgupta, A. *Some Management Skills.* Delhi: Department of Business Management and Industrial Administration, University of Delhi, 1968.

Dobbins, Gaines S. *Learning to Lead.* Nashville: Broadman Press, 1968.

Drakeford, John W. *Psychology in Search of a Soul.* Nashville: Broadman Press, 1964.

Drucker, Peter F. *The Effective Executive.* New York: Harper Colophon, 1985; New York: Harper Row Publishers, 1966.

Edersheim, Alfred. *The Life and Times of Jesus the Messiah.* Grand Rapids: William B. Eerdmans Publishing Company, 1947.

Egri, Lajos. *The Art of Dramatic Writing: Its Basis in the Creative Interpretation of Human Motives.* New York: Simon and Schuster; A Touchtone Book, 1960.

Eims, Leroy. *Be the Leader You Are Meant to Be.* Wheaton: Victor Books, 1975.

Engel, Peter H. *The Overachievers.* New York: Dial Press, 1976.

Engstrom, Ted W. *The Making of a Christian Leader.* Grand Rapids: Zondervan Publishing Company, 1976.

Erwin, Gayle D. *The Jesus Style.* Palm Springs, California: Ronald N. Haynes Publishers, Inc., 1983. Assigned to Word Books, Publishers, 1985.

Eubank and Auer. *Discussion and Debate.* New York: F. S. Crofts and Company, 1946.

Fitzwater, P. B. *Christian Theology.* Grand Rapids: William B. Eerdmans, 1948*.

Flesch, Rudolf. *How to Write, Speak, and Think More Effectively.* New York: The New American Library of World Literature, Inc., Signet Books, 1960.

Forbes, B. *America's Twelve Master Salesmen.* New York: Forbes and Sons Publishing Company, Inc., 1952.

Forbes, Rosalind. *Corporate Stress.* Garden City, New York: Doubleday and Company, Inc., 1979.

_____. *Life Stress.* Garden City, New York: Doubleday and Company, Inc. 1979.

Garfield, Charles A. *Peak Performance.* Boston: Houghton Mifflin Company, 1984.

Garn, Roy. *The Magic Power of Emotional Appeal.* Englewood Cliffs, New Jersey: Prentice Hall, 1960.

Geneen, Harold. *Managing.* Garden City, New York: Doubleday and Company, 1984.

Gillies, John. *Memoirs of Reverend George Whitfield.* Hartford: Edwin Hunt, 1845*.

Greenleaf, Robert K. *Servant Leadership.* New York: Paulist Press, 1977.

Griffin, Emory A. *The Mind Changers, The Art of Christian Persuasion.* Wheaton, Illinois: Tyndale House Publishers; Eastbourne, England: Coverdale House Publishers, Ltd., 1976.

Haggai, John. *How to Win Over Worry.* Grand Rapids: Zondervan Publishing House, 1959.

_____. *New Hope for Planet Earth.* Nashville: Thomas Nelson Publishers, 1974.

_____. *My Son Johnny.* Wheaton, Illinois: Tyndale House Publishers, Inc., 1978.

_____. *How to Win Over Loneliness.* Nashville: Thomas Nelson Publishers, 1979.

_____. *The Steward.* Atlanta, Georgia: Haggai Institute, 1983.

Harvey, Paul. *The Rest of the Story. . . .* Compiled by Lynne Harvey. Chicago: Paulynne, Inc., 1969.

Hayes, James L. *Memos for Management: Leadership.* New York: AMACOM, 1983.

Hiebert, Paul G. *Cultural Anthropology.* Grand Rapids: Baker Book House, 1976.

Hopkins, C. Howard. *John R. Mott, 1865-1955, A Biography.* Grand Rapids: William B. Eerdmans Publishing Company, 1979.

Hughes, John. *Indonesian Upheaval.* New York: David McKay Company, Inc., 1967.

Iaccocca, Lee. *Iaccocca, An Autobiography.* New York: Bantam Books, 1984.

Jones, E. Stanley. *A Song of Ascents: A Spiritual Autobiography.* Nashville: Abingdon Press, 1979.

Josey, Alex. *Lee Kuan Yew: The Struggle for Singapore.* London: Angus and Robertson Publishers, 1976.

Kiev, Ari. *A Strategy for Daily Living.* New York: Free Press, a division of Macmillan Publishing Company, Inc., 1973.

Knight, James Allen. *For the Love of Money.* Philadelphia: Lippincott, 1968.

Kriegel, Robert, and Kriegel, Marilyn Harris. *The C Zone, Peak Performance Under Pressure.* Garden City, New York: Anchor Press/Doubleday and Company, 1984.

Laszlo, Ervin, et al. *Goals for Mankind.* New York: E. P. Dutton, 1977.

Lee, Josh. *Public Speaking.* Oklahoma City: Harlow Publishing Corporation, 1936*.

Levinson, Harry. *Executive.* Cambridge: Harvard University Press, 1981.

Liechtenberger, Henri. *The Third Reich,* Translated and edited by Koppel S. Pinson. Freeport, New York: Books for Library Press, 1969.

Lyall, Leslie. *Flame for God: John Soong and Revival in the Far East.* London: Overseas Missionary Fellowship, 1976.

Mackay, John A. *Christian Reality and Appearance.* Richmond: John Knox Press, 1969.

Macmillan, D. *The Life of George Matheson.* London: Hodder and Stoughton, 1908. The story of this blind Scot inspires me as do few biographies.

Marshall, Catherine. *A Man Called Peter, The Story of Peter Marshall.* New York: McGraw Hill Book Company, Inc., 1951.

Marts, Arnaud C. *The Generosity of Americans: Its Source, Its Achievements.* Englewood Cliffs, New Jersey: Prentice Hall, Inc., 1966.

Matthews, Basil. *John R. Mott, World Citizen.* New York: Harper and Brothers, 1934.

McCartney, Clarence E. *The Making of a Minister, Autobiography of Clarence E. McCartney.* Great Neck, New York: Channel Press, Inc., 1961.

McCormack, Mark H. *What They Don't Teach You at Harvard Business School.* New York: Bantam Books, 1984.

McLoughlin, William G., Jr. *Billy Sunday Was His Real Name.* Chicago: University of Chicago Press, 1955*.

Meyer, Paul J. *Dynamics of Goal Setting.* Waco, Texas: Success Motivation Institute, 1977. Lesson manual, cassette tapes and plan of action. I highly recommend all materials produced by Success Motivation Institute, Post Office Box 7614, Waco, Texas 76714–8018.

————. *Dynamics of Personal Motivation.* Third Edition. Waco, Texas: Success Motivation Institute, 1983. A kit consisting of: "Lesson Manual," "Cassette Tapes," and "A Plan of Action"—covering 16 lessons.

Montgomery, Field-Marshal. *Path to Leadership.* New York: G. T. Putnam and Sons, 1961.

Morgan, G. Campbell. *The Crises of the Christ.* Old Tappan, New Jersey: Fleming H. Revell Company, 1903.

Muir, Sir William. *The Life of Mohammed.* Edinburgh: John Grant, 1923.

Mulando, Godfrey. *How Much Shall I Give?* Ndola, Zambia: Copperbelt Christian Publications, 1977.

Naisbitt, John. *Megatrends, Ten New Directions Transforming Our Lives.* New York: Warner Books, 1982.

Nehru, Jawaharlal. *The Discovery of India.* New York: John Day Publishers, 1946.

Nixon, Richard. *Leaders.* New York: Warner Books, Inc., 1982.

Nizer, Louis. *Thinking on Your Feet.* New York: Norton Company (Liveright Publishing Company), 1963.

_____. *The Jury Returns.* Garden City, New York: Doubleday and Company, 1966.
Ogilvy, David. *Confessions of an Advertising man.* New York: Dell Publishing Company, 1963.
_____. *On Advertising.* New York: Vintage Books (A Division of Random House), 1985.
Ostrander, Sheila; and Schroeder, Lynn; with Ostrander, Nancy. *Super-Learning.* New York: Dell Publishing Company, Inc., 1979.
Otto, Herbert A. *Guide to Developing Your Potential.* New York: Charles Scribners Sons, 1957.
"Paths Toward Personal Progress: Leaders Are Made, Not Born." *Harvard Business Review* (1980).
Peters, Tom, and Austin, Nancy. *A Passion for Excellence.* New York: Random House, 1985.
Phillips, Arthur Edward. *Effective Speaking.* Chicago: The Newton Company, 1922*.
Pierce, Earl V. *The Supreme Beatitude.* Old Tappan, New Jersey: Fleming H. Revell, 1947.
Pollock, John. *The Man Who Shook the World.* Wheaton: Victor Books, 1972.
Reischauer, Edwin O. *The Japanese.* Tokyo: Charles E. Tuttle Company, 1977.
Roeder, O. G. *The Smiling General, President Soeharto of Indonesia.* Jakarta: Gunung Agung Ltd., 1969.
Roman, Kenneth, and Raphaelson, Joel. *Writing That Works.* New York: Harper and Row, 1981.
Rusher, William A. *How to Win Arguments.* Garden City, New York: Doubleday and Company, 1981.
Rutt, Richard. *History of the Korean People.* Seoul: Taewon Publishing Company, 1972.
Ryle, J. C. *Christian Leaders of the Eighteenth Century.* Edinburgh: The Banner of Truth Trust, 1885*.
Sadat, Anwar. *Sadat, An Autobiography.* London: Fontana/Collins, 1978.
Sandburg, Carl. *Abraham Lincoln: The Prairie Years and the War Years.* New York: Harcourt Brace, 1954.
Sangster, W. E. *The Secret of a Radiant Life.* Nashville: Abingdon Press, 1957.
Sarnoff, Dorothy. *Speech Can Change Your Life.* New York: Dell Publishing Company, 1970.
_____. *Make the Most of Your Best.* New York: Doubleday, 1981.
Scammell, Michael. *Solzhenitsyn.* New York: W. W. Norton and Company, 1985; London: Hutchinson, 1984.
Schilder, K. *Christ on Trial.* Grand Rapids: William B. Eerdmans Publishing Company, 1945.
_____. *Christ In His Suffering.* Grand Rapids: William B. Eerdmans Publishing Company, 1945.
_____. *Christ Crucified.* Grand Rapids: William B. Eerdmans Publishing Company, 1945.
Seabury, David. *How to Get Things Done.* Garden City, New York: Halcyn House, 1938.
Seagrave, Sterling. *The Soong Dynasty.* New York: Harper and Row, 1985.
Sharpe, Robert F. *Before You Give Another Dime.* Nashville: Thomas Nelson Publishers, 1979.
Simonton, Carl O.; Simonton, Stephanie Matthews; and Creighton, James L. *Getting Well Again.* New York: Bantam Books, 1978.
Spurgeon, Charles Haddon. *C. H. Spurgeon's Autobiography.* 4 Vols. London: Passmore and Alabaster, 1899–1900.

Swindoll, Charles R. *Hand Me Another Brick.* Nashville: Thomas Nelson Publishers, 1978.

———. *Leadership.* Waco: Word Books, Publisher, 1985.

Taylor, Jeremy. *Taylor's Life of Christ.* London: William Pickering, 1849*.

Taylor, Robert Lewis. *Winston Churchill.* New York: Pocket Books, Inc., 1952.

Templeton, John M. *The Humble Approach: Scientists Discover God.* New York: Seabury Press, 1981.

Torrey, R. A. *The Power of Prayer and the Prayer of Power.* Grand Rapids: Zondervan Publishing House, 1924.

Townsend, Derek. *Gigsaw: the Biography of Johannes Bjelke-Petersen.* Brisbane, Queensland, Australia: Sneyd and Morley, 1983.

Tzu, Sun. *The Art of War.* Translated by Samuel B. Griffith. London: Oxford University Press, 1963.

Villari, Pasquale. *The Life and Times of Girolamo Savonarola.* Translated by Linda Villari. New York: Charles Scribner Sons, 1888*.

Vitz, Paul C. *Psychology As Religion: The Cult of Self-worship.* Grand Rapids: William B. Eerdmans Publishing Company, 1977.

Waitley, Denis. *The Winner's Edge: the Critical Attitude of Success.* New York: Times Books, 1980.

———. *Seeds of Greatness.* Old Tappan, New Jersey: Fleming H. Revell, 1983.

Wallace, Lew. *Ben Hur, A Tale of the Christ.* New York: Harper and Brothers, 1880.

Wall Street Journal Staff. *Here Comes Tomorrow: Living and Working in the Year 2000.* Princeton: Dow Jones Books, 1966.

Weber, Max. *On Charisma and Institution Building.* Chicago and London: The University of Chicago Press, 1968.

Wesley, John. *The Journal of John Wesley.* 8 Vols. London: Epworth Press, 1938.

Williamson, Porter B. *Patton's Principles.* New York: Simon and Schuster, 1979.

Wills, Garry. *Nixon Agnoistes, The Crisis of the Self-made Man.* New York: New American Library, 1971.

Wonder, Jacqueline, and Donavan, Priscilla. *Whole-brain Thinking: Working Both Sides of the Brain to Achieve Peak Job Performance.* New York: W. Morrow; Valentine Books, 1984.

Wood, A. Skevington. *The Burning Heart, John Wesley: Evangelist.* Exeter, Great Britain: Paternostra Press, Ltd., 1967.

Youssef, Michael. *Revolt Against Modernity: Muslim Zealots and the West.* Leiden: E. J. Brill, 1985.

———. *The Leadership Style of Jesus.* Wheaton: Victor Books, 1986.

Notes

[1] W. C. H. Prentice, "Understanding Leadership," *Harvard Business Review,* Number 61511, September-October, 1961, quoted in *Paths Toward Personal Progress: Leaders Are Made, Not Born* (Boston: Harvard Business Review, 1980), page 1.

[2] William Pfaff, editorial, *International Herald Tribune,* 26 June 1983.

[3] Quoted in Stephen B. Oates, *Let the Trumpet Sound: The Life of Martin Luther King, Jr.* (New York: Harper & Row, 1982), pages 260–261.

[4] Peter J. Daniels, *How to Be Happy Though Rich* (Unley Park, South Australia: The House of Taylor, 1984), pages 113–123.

[5] Wilbur M. Smith, *Will H. Houghton, A Watchman on the Wall* (Grand Rapids, Michigan: William B. Eerdmans Publishing Company, 1951), page 82.

[6] Edward J. Green, "Management Objectives" in William K. Fallon, editor, *AMA Management Handbook* (New York: AMACOM, 1983), pages 1–32.

[7] Harold Geneen, *Managing* (Garden City, N.Y.: Doubleday, 1984), reprinted in *Best of Business,* volume 6, page 6.

[8] John Naisbitt, *Megatrends* (New York: Warner Books, 1982), page 85.

[9] Ari Kiev, *A Strategy for Daily Living* (New York: Free Press, 1973), pages 2–3, 30.

[10] Carl O. Simonton, Stephanie Matthews Simonton, and James L. Creighton, *Getting Well Again* (New York: Bantam Books, 1978), pages 97, 173–184.

[11] Willam Funk and Norman Lewis, revised by Norman Lewis, *Thirty Days to a More Powerful Vocabulary* (Garden City, New York: Doubleday, 1984).

[12] Geneen, page 14.

[13] Denis Waitley, *Seeds of Greatness* (Old Tappan, N.J.: Fleming H. Revell, 1983), pages 27–28.

[14] Ted W. Engstrom with Robert C. Larson, *The Fine Art of Friendship* (Nashville: Thomas Nelson Publishers, 1985).

[15] *Ibid.,* pages 128–130.

[16] Erich Fromm, *The Art of Loving* (New York: Bantam Books, 1956), pages 90–92.

[17] Peter E. Gillquist, *Love Is Now* (revised edition) (Grand Rapids: Zondervan Publishing House, 1978), page 132.

[18] A. W. Tozer, *The Pursuit of God* (Harrisburg, Pennsylvania: Christian Publications, Inc., n.d.), page 113.

[19] Richard Foster, *Celebration of Discipline* (San Francisco: Harper & Row, 1978), page 5.

[20] James F. Engel, *Contemporary Christian Communications: Its Theory and Practice* (Nashville: Thomas Nelson Publishers, 1979), page 39.

[21] Herschel H. Hobbs, *Who Is This?* (Nashville: Broadman Press, 1952), page 53.

[22] Russell H. Conwell, *Acres of Diamonds* (New York: Harper & Brothers, Publishers, 1943), page 2.

[23] Victor Hugo's lecture on Voltaire, quoted by Arthur Edward Phillips in *Effective Speaking* (Chicago: The Newton Company, 1922), page 178.

[24] *Ibid.*, page 48.

[25] Roy Garn, *The Magic Power of Emotional Appeal* (Englewood Cliffs, N.J.: Prentice Hall, Inc., 1960), pages 20, 37ff.

[26] Alan H. Monroe, *Principles and Types of Speech* (revised edition) (New York: Scott, Foresman and Company, 1939), pages 132–145.

[27] S. Stansfeld Sargent, "Maslow, Abraham H. (1908–1970)," *International Encyclopedia of Psychiatry, Psychology, Psychoanalysis and Neurology,* 1977 ed., Vol. 7.

[28] Thomas J. Peters and Robert H. Waterman, Jr., *In Search of Excellence,* pages 164–165. Copyright © 1982 by Thomas J. Peters and Robert H. Waterman, Jr. by permission of Harper and Row Publishers, Inc.

[29] E. Stanley Jones, *The Way,* 5th edition (London: Hodder and Stoughton, 1963), page 155.

[30] *Webster's Ninth New Collegiate Dictionary* (Springfield, Mass.: Merriam-Webster, Inc., 1983), page 412.

[31] Quoted in Sterling North, *Young Thomas Edison* (Boston: Houghton Mifflin Company, 1958), page 115.

[32] Kenneth H. Cooper, *The Aerobics Program for Total Well Being* (New York: M. Evans and Company, 1982).

[33] Nathan Pritikin with Patrick M. McGrady, Jr., *The Pritikin Program for Diet and Exercise* (New York: Bantam Books, 1980), page xx.

[34] Marie Beynon Rae, *How Never to Be Tired* (New York: Bobbs-Merrill Company, 1954).

[35] Charles Swindoll, *Three Steps Forward, Two Steps Back* (Nashville: Thomas Nelson Publishers, 1980), pages 13–14.

[36] *Ibid.*, pages 18–19.

[37] "Got Any Rivers," copyright 1945. Renewal 1973 by Oscar Eliason. Assigned to Singspiration, Inc.

[38] William Golding, *Lord of the Flies* (New York: Capricorn Books, 1954, 1955), page 19.

[39] Michael Korda, *Power: How to Get It, How to Use It* (New York: Ballantine Books, 1975), page 219.

[40] *Ibid.*, pages 209–210. 209–210.

Index

Abed-Nego, 78
Abraham, 20, 56, 115
"Acres of Diamonds," 95
Action: as communication goal, 93; motivation for, 101–3, 186
Activity, purposeful, 137
Adulation, perils of, 39
Adversity, gratitude for, 79
Aerobic's Program for Total Well Being, The, 144
Affection, as basic desire, 103
Agape, 45, 55, 56
Ah Tua Teo, 21
Alertness, mental, 139–40, 189
Amin Dada, Idi, 6
Amundsen, Roald, 139
Anger, 146
Anxiety, 112, 147
Arai, Sam, 131
Aristotle, 48, 73
Artaxerxes, king of Persia, 14
Art of Loving, The, 51
Asimov, Isaac, 136
Assertions, support of, 97–98
Assessment, personal, 170
Atienza, Max, 21
Attention, capturing of, 94–95, 137
Attitude, mental, 145–46
Audience: assessment of, 89–90, 186; involvement of, in communication, 95–97

Augustine, Saint, 14, 62
Authority: and demand for awareness, 190–91; external, 168, 170–73, 190–91; internal, 167–70, 173–77, 190–91; principle of, 166–78, 190–91; summary of principle of, 178
Awareness: and meaning of leadership, 181–82; and need for energy, 189; as keystone of leadership, 180; as key to communication, 187; of demand for authority, 190–91; of God, as resource, 191–92; of leadership role, 181; of need for communication, 186–87; of need for perseverance, 189–90; of need for self-control, 185–86; of need for wise investment, 187–88; of opportunity, 188; of principle of humility, 185; of principle of love, 184–85; of principle of leadership, 182; of responsibility, 181; of vision, 183; principle of, 179–93; summary of principle of, 192–93

Balance, 144
Baptist Tabernacle (Atlanta, Ga.), 20
Barlow, Claude H., 77
Barnardo, John, 2
Bates, Carl E., 72–73
Beavan, Jerry, 21

Hartsfield, William B., 107
Hatred, 146–47
Health, 38, 137–39
Heraclitus, 7
Hinson, Bill, 15
Hitler, Adolf, 2, 5, 6
Hobbs, Hershall H., 87
Ho Chi Minh, 190
Hosea, 132
Houghton, Will H., 20, 155
Howard, James, 188
Howard, John, 2
How Never to Be Tired, 145
Hugo, Victor, 99
Humility, 48, 170; and availability of un-
    limited resources, 64–65; and ban-
    ishment of fear, 64; and enlarge-
    ment of life, 63–64; and serenity,
    63; and success, 64; as attribute
    of God, 62; as Christ-likeness, 59;
    as love's mood, 59–60; description
    of, 58–60; false, 60–61; importance
    of, 62; nuture of, 65–71; results of,
    62–65; principle of, 58–71, 185;
    summary of principle of, 71

Iaccocca, Lee, 123–24
Ibsen, Henrik, 141
"If," 54
Illness, 155
Illustration, as communication technique,
    100
Imperfection, fear of, 39
Impossibilities, 160–61
Impressiveness, as communication goal,
    92
Individuality, 170
Influence, exercise of, 182
Information, conveying of, 91
In Search of Excellence, 108
Inspirational dissatisfaction. *See* Dissatis-
    faction, inspirational
Intelligence, 139–40
Interest, on investment, 117
International Telephone and Telegraph
    Corp., 34
Investment: in material possessions, 114–
    15; meaning of, 106–10; principle
    of, 105–22, 187–88; right motives
    for, 110–11; ten commandments
    for, 114–20, 187–88; summary of
    principle of, 120–22. *See also*
    Money

Isaiah, 16, 47
Isolation, overcoming of, 87

James, Saint, 14, 181
Jealousy, 147
Jeremiah, 8, 191
Jesus, 5, 9, 44, 46, 47, 55, 66, 103, 110,
    112, 147, 158, 169; as leader, 57;
    as Lord of life, 65–66; emulation
    of, 67–68; example of, 67–68; hu-
    mility of, 59, 67–69; obedience to,
    66
Job, 79, 116, 154
John Paul II, pope, 3–4
Jones, E. Stanley, 57, 113
Joseph, 55, 124, 190
Joshua, 29–30
Joy: as expression of love, 52–53; result
    of self-control, 83
Judas, 114

Kaiser, Henry, 26
Kennedy, John F., 13
Kiev, Ari, 38
Kim, Helen, 9
Kindness, as expression of love, 54–55
King, Martin Luther, Jr., 11–12
Kipling, Rudyard, 54
Klimionok, Reginald, 131
Korda, Michael, 171–72

Leader. *See* Leadership
Leadership: and change, 6–7; and covet-
    ousness, 113–14; and family life,
    157–58; and goal setting, 183–84;
    and humility, 60, 62, 69–70, 185;
    and investment, 107, 109–10; and
    love, 51–54, 184–85; and principle
    of authority, 166–78; and principle
    of awareness, 179–93; and princi-
    ple of communication, 85–104;
    and principle of energy, 136–48;
    and principle of goal setting, 25–
    43; and principle of humility, 58–
    71; and principle of investment,
    105–22; and principle of love, 44–
    57; and principle of opportunity,
    123–35; and principle of self-con-
    trol, 72–84; and principle of stay-
    ing power, 149–65; and principle
    of vision, 11–24; and vision, 11,
    183; and need for communication,
    186–87; and need for energy, 189;

RECLAIMING PATRIOTISM

OTHER BOOKS BY AMITAI ETZIONI

Happiness Is the Wrong Metric: A Liberal Communitarian Response to Populism (2018)

The New Normal: Finding a Balance between Individual Rights and the Common Good (2015)

Privacy in a Cyber Age: Policy and Practice (2015)

Security First: For a Muscular, Moral Foreign Policy (2007)

From Empire to Community: A New Approach to International Relations (2004)

My Brother's Keeper: A Memoir and a Message (2003)

The New Golden Rule: Community and Morality in a Democratic Society (1996)

The Spirit of Community: Rights, Responsibilities, and the Communitarian Agenda (1993)

The Active Society: A Theory of Societal and Political Processes (1968)

RECLAIMING PATRIOTISM

AMITAI ETZIONI

University of Virginia Press

CHARLOTTESVILLE AND LONDON

University of Virginia Press

© 2019 by the Rector and Visitors of the University of Virginia

All rights reserved

Printed in the United States of America on acid-free paper

First published 2019

9 8 7 6 5 4 3 2 1

Library of Congress Cataloging-in-Publication Data

Names: Etzioni, Amitai, author.
Title: Reclaiming patriotism / Amitai Etzioni.
Description: Charlottesville : University of Virginia Press, 2019. | Includes
 bibliographical references and index.
Identifiers: LCCN 2019001722 (print) | LCCN 2019012876 (ebook) | ISBN 9780813943251
 (ebook) | ISBN 9780813943244 (cloth : alk. paper)
Subjects: LCSH: Patriotism.
Classification: LCC JC329 (ebook) | LCC JC329 .E77 2019 (print) | DDC 323.6/5—dc23
LC record available at https://lccn.loc.gov/2019001722

OCT 0 4 2019

For all those who have served their country honorably,
including four generations of Etzionis

Patriotism is when love of your country comes first; nationalism, when hate for people other than your own comes first.

—CHARLES DE GAULLE

CONTENTS

RECLAIMING PATRIOTISM

INTRODUCTION
"GOOD" NATIONALISM—SAVING DEMOCRACY
THROUGH NATIONAL COMMUNITY BUILDING

How to Cope with Polarization

D emocratic governments, from the US to Israel, from Hungary to Venezuela, from Turkey to Indonesia are in crisis—although some are much more challenged than others. If democracy is to be saved, more will be required than political actions such as changing the agendas of the parties (e.g., making them more "populist") or forming new parties or coalitions.[1] A major social transformation is called for—the rebuilding of the national community on which all democracies rely. This book spells out the reasons this transformation is essential and the ways it can be brought about. Polarization involves people who are divided from one another by more than whom they vote for. They also are divided by whom they socialize, talk, and work with, by whom they befriend and even marry.[2]

In the US, 77 percent of self-identified Republicans and Democrats are married to or living with someone who identifies as a member of the same political party. Fewer than 10 percent of people who identify as either a Republican or a Democrat have spouses or partners from the opposing political party.[3] Fifty-five percent of Republicans say they have just a few or no friends who are Democrats, while 65 percent of Democrats say they have just a few or no Republican friends.[4] One out of five millennials (22 percent) has broken up with someone over political differences.[5] Michael Bloomberg reports: "In 1960, only 4 to 5 percent of Democrats and Republicans said they would be upset if a member of their family married someone from the opposing party. In 2010, one in three Democrats and one in two Republicans said they would disapprove of such a marriage."[6] In other democracies polarization is also rising.[7]

Because polarization has become so widespread and encompassing,[8] it is no longer contained by a shared understanding of the common good, which could limit the paralyzing effects of social polarization on politics and provide the underpinning for shared action among opposing parties. A major social development that bedevils democracies is the loss of the commitment to the common good, a commitment that can help to balance particularistic interests, needs, and values.

I am often asked, How can one have a major effect on society, indeed on history? When I respond by suggesting that this is a rather easy question because there is only one answer, this tends to surprise people. As I see it, the one and only way to achieve truly transformative social change is to launch or join a social movement.[9]

Key examples include movements on behalf of civil rights, gender equality, economic fairness, environmental protection, national liberation, and religious freedom. These movements differ greatly from one another, especially in their values and strategies for achieving their goals. They share, however, an underlying sociological feature: they withdraw legitimacy and support from a declining regime while laying foundations for a new one. To give but one illustration: The American civil rights movement challenged the legitimacy of discriminatory laws in such basic social practices as voting, working, education, and housing. It provided for de jure and de facto voting rights, made racial discrimination illegal and uncouth, elected thousands of African American officials, and increased interracial marriages. (The percentage of African Americans married to people of other races has increased dramatically since 1980. In 1980, only 5 percent of African Americans were in interracial marriages; that figure climbed to 18 percent by 2015.)[10] To be sure, the movement has far from eliminated racism, but it did introduce major social and political changes.

Many Americans, as well as citizens of other democracies, are concerned that the guardrails of democracy—the institutions and laws on which it relies—are being weakened. To restore them requires a new social mandate. A mere change in the composition of the legislature will not suffice. One should recall that even when the Democrats controlled both houses of Congress and the presidency, from 2009 to 2011, the GOP and Red State Democrats blocked major reforms.

For the kind of sweeping changes now called for to save democratic regimes and make governments functional again, a major social movement will have to provide a mandate that will cut across party lines and force both sides to work together. This is what the environmental movement achieved when it led President Richard Nixon to form the Environmental Protection Agency and Congress to pass a whole list of environmental protection laws. This is what the civil rights movement achieved in the early 1960s. No such mandate is now available. Only a sweeping patriotic movement can bring about a wide-reaching democratic rebuilding.

The Model of Marital Conflict

To argue that democracies now need a social movement that formulates core values that a strong majority can embrace is a call not to eradicate differences and divisions but, rather, to contain them. An analogy from family life may help. Studies show that stable and happy marriages are not strangers to conflict. Couples fight, seeking changes (e.g., in the division of labor between the spouses) but also to maintain the union. There are rules for such contained conflicts, those that seek to maintain the common good, that include not demonizing the other side, validated communication, not going for the "pound of flesh," and focusing on the future rather than recriminating the past. In politics, these rules have sometimes been described as those followed by the "loyal opposition."

"Loyal opposition" refers to a minority party whose opposition to the party in power is constrained by loyalty to the fundamental interests and values governing the state[11] while continuing to offer plans and policies that claim to better serve the interests of the state and the people.[12] The US Senate used to be such a "club" but has largely lost its common ground as partisanship, reflecting swelling social divisions, carries the day. To move forward, we need new social formations—chapters of a patriotic movement yet to be fashioned—that will include people of different political persuasions, backgrounds, and parties all committed to consenting on and advancing the common good. For a more extensive discussion on the marital conflict model, please refer to chapter 2.

Incorporating the White Minority

In recent years many whites in the US have come to see themselves as a persecuted, excluded minority.[13] This sentiment has arisen in the wake of large demographic changes. Reports claim that the nation will have a majority of minorities by 2044. Increases in minority populations and a decline in the white majority in the US have driven several African American leaders, including Jesse Jackson and former New York City mayor David Dinkins, along with a few Hispanics, such as Fernando Ferrer, a candidate for the 2002 mayoral election in New York City, and some on the white left to champion a coalition of minorities to unseat the "white establishment" and become the power-holders and shapers of America's future.[14] When Jesse Jackson launched his Rainbow Coalition, I teased him a bit, pointing out that the colors of the rainbow do not include white. He shrugged his shoulders, suggesting that leaving out whites was not necessarily detrimental. Calls for minority governing coalitions that exclude white Americans—intentionally or otherwise—have resulted in many whites seeing themselves as a persecuted minority group.[15]

Arlie Russell Hochschild spent five years interviewing and living with whites in Louisiana, most of whom later voted for Trump, documenting their perception shift. She found that many of them felt abused by a world in which they see themselves as climbing a steep hill only for "others" (minorities and immigrants, most of whom are not white) to cut ahead of them in line.

Both sides are allowing one identity to trump all others rather than building on the fact that we all have multiple identities.[16] Many vote their race, and their race affects their views on most issues, overriding other identities.[17] Above all, they ignore that whatever their race, they are also Americans, or French, or Danes, and so on—in essence "they are citizens of somewhere."[18]

Minorities and whites can come together under the big tent of the patriotic movement if they come to see that they often suffer from common maladies, such as the actions of narrowly based interest groups. Thus, when banks sold millions of Americans mortgages that the banks knew people could not afford and hence were able to evict many people from their homes, both whites and black suffered, not equally, but all to great personal loss. When Americans pay many times more for medications, a major source of health expenditures, than people pay in other countries, because lobbyists got Congress to enact laws that prohibit Americans from purchasing medications overseas, the pocketbooks of people of all colors are squeezed. When millions of Americans consume vitamins that have not been tested for safety—because the industry pressured Congress to exempt vitamins from FDA regulations—people of all backgrounds are endangered. When Chlorpyrifos, a common insecticide, continues to be used in agriculture across the globe even though it has been clearly linked to defective alterations in brain structure and in the cognition of children, all kinds of children are hurt.[19]

A major example: Purdue Pharma—the company that invented the highly addictive painkiller OxyContin—claimed until 2007 that it was not addictive, although a Department of Justice report shows Purdue's awareness of significant OxyContin abuse shortly after the drug was introduced to the market in 1996 and that this information was intentionally concealed.[20] Moreover, Purdue employed an aggressive marketing campaign that paid substantial bonuses to sales representatives who worked with physicians prescribing high volumes of OxyContin, as well as a promotional campaign that included providing health-care professionals with all-expenses-paid trips to Purdue Pharma symposia at luxury resorts and widely distributing OxyContin-branded gifts.[21] The campaign led many physicians to prescribe OxyContin even when it was not needed.[22] As a result, 52,000 Americans died of opiate-related causes in 2016,[23] a number five times greater than in 1999.[24]

Narrowly based special interest groups (more about them in chapter 9) have become so powerful that they pose a great threat to people of all backgrounds. This is particularly evident when observing what happens after their wrongdoings are uncovered—in most cases, no substantial penalty or reform follows.

We learned that if one citizen forges one check, he may well end up in jail for ten years. When banks hired staff to forge signatures on thousands of mortgages, not a single banker went to jail. During the late 1990s and early 2000s, nineteen major Wall Street firms were found to have committed fifty-one cases of antifraud law violations. The SEC got them to promise not to violate the law in the future—and when they did violate it again, the SEC asked them again to behave better.[25] No wonder they were not impressed. Indeed, some violated the law time and again and again.

When *60 Minutes* reported that a hospital chain automatically orders a whole slew of tests for anybody who walks into its ER rooms, whether they need them or not, and pressures its doctors to admit at least half of these visitors to fill hospital beds, the chain suffered no pain. These and countless other examples make clear that people from all walks of life have much to gain if they join together to curb special interests.

The fact that times call for a social movement that will rebuild the common ground, the bonds that contain conflict, and the foundations on which public policies with strong majorities' support will rest is the central thesis of the book. One may well ask, But what about overcoming inequality, eliminating poverty, protecting the environment, providing affordable health care, and many other such worthy social goals?

I suggest that making major progress on any and all of these fronts presumes a strong sense of community without which it will not be possible to form the kind of strong majorities that support major reforms.

And, it is worth reiterating, there is no reason for various groups fighting for progress on any of these fronts to cease promoting their agendas—as long as they do so while supporting rather than undermining the communal bonds. Last, many books and articles have been written on how to tackle the various specific policy issues that challenge democracies. This book need not add to these volumes other than to stress that their agendas will not be advanced far unless people are willing to make sacrifices for each other and the common good, find middle ground, and yes, even compromise. To advance specific agendas, people must see each other as members of one overarching community, one with shared values and, for better or worse, a shared destiny.

No Ending of Identity Politics

When I refer to community, I am not thinking about some kind of "kumbaya," a love fest in which all differences disappear, but about the realization that we are members of one overarching community with a shared set of core values and interests and, ultimately, a shared future. For the same reason, the quest to redefine and recommit to the common good is not a quest to end identity politics; rather, it's a call to those who see one particularistic identity as defining them to make room for a more complex combination of shared and particularistic identities.[26]

This is not a case of being against individual or group rights but a recognition that rights need to be accompanied by a strong sense of social responsibility to the other, and above all to the common good. Preparing for my classes at the Harvard Business School, I read a report showing that though young Americans felt strongly about their right to be tried by a jury of their peers, they were exceedingly reluctant to serve on a jury. I argued in class and later in my book *The Spirit of Community* that it is morally obscene to take and not to give, that strong rights presumed strong responsibilities, and that if young people did not serve on juries, then there would obviously be no juries of their peers.[27] Many Americans demand more government services while raging against raising taxes, or advocate a stronger army while counseling their children against military service. In line with a popular sentiment expressed by President John F. Kennedy, the times call for asking what you are willing to do for the common good, to protect the environment, to help those unable to help themselves, to secure us from terrorist attacks.

To put it differently, all societies experience centrifugal forces that pull them apart. In many societies these have been especially strong in recent years. We cannot, and need not, eradicate these forces, though they can be mitigated. What is needed are centripetal forces to balance the centrifugal ones, that is, nation building. To use a still different metaphor, we do not need a melting pot but a mosaic, in which the pieces— though different in color and size—are held together by a framework.

The Nation Is a Community Invested in a State

The term "community" applies to many different kinds of sociological entities, including groups defining their common life around ethnicity and culture (e.g., Jewish community), sexual orientation (e.g., gay community), religion (e.g., Muslim community), vocation (e.g., scientific community), international security and cooperation (international community), among many others. This book is focused on a particular one, *a community that is invested in a state, the proper definition of a nation.* Summoning loyalties to a nation evokes intense passions. I realize when I call for renewed patriotism, when I write about commitment to the good of one's nation, about love of country, that patriotism is a highly contentious idea. Many associate it with xenophobia and jingoism.

At its core, patriotism points to passionate concern for one's fellow citizens and the community they share, a resolve to love one's nation despite its defects and to work for its flourishing. This is what I mean by "good" nationalism.[28] Several political commentators have mentioned the need to distinguish between "bad" and "good" nationalism (without going into the weeds to sort out what this entails), including Lawrence Summers, who has issued a call to "responsible nationalism,"[29] and David Brooks, who has extolled "civic nationalism."[30] These conceptions of nationalism are offered in contrast to toxic forms of ethnonationalism, blood-and-soil nationalism, or outright tribalism. Yascha Mounk is reported to have suggested that "liberals can counter Trump's 'ethnocentric' nationalism with a nationalism of their own. The trouble, as he puts it, is that American liberals are 'increasingly directed toward a radical rejection of the nation and all its trappings.'"[31] Patriots do not overlook their country's flaws and darker periods but seek to address them rather than allow them to undermine their commitment to the country's common fate, history, and future. And they do not diminish other communities, let alone seek to lord over them, but appreciate that those in those communities, too, love their country.

William Galston distinguishes between patriotism and nationalism in the following terms: "*Patriotism* denotes a special attachment to a particular political community, although not necessarily to its existing form of government. *Nationalism,* with which patriotism is often confused, stands for a very different phenomenon—the fusion, actual or aspirational, between shared ethnicity and state sovereignty." He adds, "It is perfectly possible to love one's own without becoming morally narrow, or unreasonable, let alone irrational."[32] George Orwell differentiates nationalism, as a position "inseparable from the desire for power," from patriotism, which is "devotion to a particular place and a particular way of life, which one believes to be the best in the world but has no wish to force on other people."[33]

Devotion to one's country can be fully separated from aggressive foreign policies, a mark of nationalism, and can be fully reconciled with commitment to foreign aid and humanitarian contributions and providing peace-keeping forces. No country maintains this distinction perfectly, though Canada, the Scandinavian countries, Costa Rica, and Uruguay come close. Germany and Japan paid a very heavy price before they learned the difference but showed in the decades that followed World War II that a nation can forego nationalism and still exhibit patriotism.

The Communitarian Bases of Democracy

The following discussion applies to all democracies. They all need to contend with populism, polarization, alienation, dysfunctional governments, and pernicious forms of nationalism. Democratic societies differ in the extent to which they are challenged, but not in the basic nature of these challenges. While many of the examples in the following chapters are drawn from the American experience, readers will have no trouble finding parallels in their nation, with one notable exception. The intrusion of private interest groups into the public realm is much more severe in the US than in most democracies.

Some view democracy as based on free and open elections, a political system that requires a free press, contending parties, and a civic-minded citizenship.[34] All this is true, but one should not ignore that ultimately democracy presumes a set of communal commitments. Citizens are willing to abide by decisions of the majority not merely because they believe in the legitimacy of the democratic process but also because they see others as members of the same community and hence are willing to make some sacrifices for them and for maintaining the community.

Above all, they share the values of the community that provide the normative criteria upon which elected officials need to draw if their decisions are to be accepted by the populace. Émile Durkheim pointed out that all contracts are based on precontractual commitments. Democracy is a contract that assumes communal commitments, and when those are lacking, democracy suffers. Charles Taylor observed, along the same lines: "A citizen democracy can only work if most of its members are convinced that their political society is a common venture of considerable moment, and believe it to be of vital importance that they participate in the ways they must to keep it functioning as a democracy. This means not only a commitment to the common project, but also a special sense of bonding among people working together in this project."[35] (I return to this point in chapter 7, in which I explore which values new members of a national community, immigrants, must embrace—and which they must not—and how these values may be transformed to accommodate the newcomers and other historical changes. See especially the discussion of national ethos.)

The core of shared values and bonds that nations need has been weakening in democratic societies under the impact of globalization, sluggish economic growth, polarization, concentration of power, and reaction to large-scale immigration. In some countries, such as Poland and Hungary, the response has been nationalistic rather than patriotic. In some, the polity has nearly unraveled, as in Turkey and Venezuela. One can see most clearly the results of very weak national loyalties in many nondemocratic countries, in which national bonds and shared values are even weaker, much weaker, than in democracies. The result is often civil war. Thus in Afghanistan, in which the primary loyalty is to one's tribe and not nation, the war is not so much between the government and some insurgents, as the war is often depicted, but to a considerable extent between Pashtuns and other tribes. In Iraq, it is between Shia and Sunnis, among other groups. These are countries in which the model of marriage conflict was not followed; in effect the various sides are fighting as if they are seeking divorce or to kill the other partner. Lacking patriotism, they developed instead aggressive forms of tribalism. This is what happens when national loyalties weaken beyond the level one finds in democracies, a warning to all of them.

The Outline of the Book

I turn next to outline the processes through which the members of the patriotic movement can form new shared moral understandings—the values to which they are going to dedicate themselves—by studying the ways other social movements have achieved such shared understandings. The historical examples in chapter 1 provide "how-to guidelines" for national moral dialogues of the patriotic movement.

Both libertarians and liberals—many on the right and on the left—view individuals as the key actors who shape history.[36] I cite evidence that in order to be effective actors, most individuals need to be members of communities and hence that communities play a cardinal role in shaping history. Communities, we shall see in chapter 2, provide the best antidote not just to polarization but also to the populism that appeals to people who lose their communities and to those who feel that their communities are being threatened. For reasons spelled out below, the most relevant community for the issues at hand is the nation, not local nor global ones.

I next explore topics on which moral dialogues, led by the patriotic movement, may focus. These dialogues may well reveal that there is more common ground, or at least overlapping policy consensus, than is widely believed. (Overlapping policy consensus refers to agreements among people who have profound value differences but agree on one or more policies. For instance, pro-life and pro-choice groups worked together in St. Louis for better childcare.) Topics for moral dialogues—trade, immigration, and rights—are discussed in chapter 3.

A key concept that underlies much of the following discussion is the thesis that people have moral commitments and obligations to take action not only for themselves and their loved ones but also to advance the common good, often that of their country.[37] Given that this is an often maligned concept, I try to show in chapter 4 what it entails and argue that it is well grounded. In the same vein, I point out that a good society cannot be centered only on liberty and individual rights but also must attend to the common good, expressed in terms of social responsibilities to others and to one's communities.

The tensions between individual rights and the common good, and the ways they may be worked out, are examined in two case studies. The first, in chapter 5, deals with new regulations that seek to treat personal information as private property, hence requiring an individual's consent for all usages of personal information. I show that such a conception conflicts with the common good and ask how these two may be reconciled. In chapter 6, the second case study provides a key example of where the needed balance between rights and responsibilities has not been reached and details the dire consequences for national security that follow.

Chapter 7 offers a sociological design that defines the grounds and scope for social diversity and clarifies boundaries that must be respected if the national community is to thrive. Chapter 8 examines a particular form of fighting with one hand tied behind one's back and how to advance the agenda of various groups without undermining the national community. It illustrates a way for members of communities to vie with one another.

Any narrative of our condition has to answer the question, Who are the "bad" players who undermine democracy, prevent effective governing, and stand in the way of progress? It is widely agreed that polarization has led various communities to view other communities as the enemy. Often these divisions fall along racial lines or between immigrants and old-timers. Actually, the main enemy lies elsewhere; chapter 9 identifies the greatest threat to the common good and the national community as the capture of shared assets by special interests. How to curb these interests without running afoul of the Supreme Court rulings that, in the name of protecting free speech, have allowed those with deep pockets to funnel large amounts of money to politicians is the subject of chapter 9.

For a social movement to be able to redesign society, the local communities and chapters of the movement must be combined into a community of communities, which makes for the national community. The reasons the community of local communities needs to be, for the foreseeable future, national rather than global are spelled out in chapter 10. It reveals that while nationalism is to be condemned, patriotism ought to be rehabilitated and reembraced. On the international level, we need global governance backed up by a global community, because many of our problems are global. However, the sociological conditions for extending national communities into a global one (or even regional ones) or adding a global layer on top of the national ones are not in place. Hence much trouble arises when international organizations and their champions try to advance various forms of postnational government without first forging the essential communal foundations.

The closing chapter of the book suggests that a patriotic movement will need to challenge the legitimacy of affluence and points to core values that serve best to shore up democracy and provide for human flourishing.

The ideas laid out in the following pages apply to all democracies. Granted, they are not all equally challenged. However, globalization, automation, populism, dysfunctional government, polarization, and the rising inequity of assets and power are evident in varying degrees in all of them. Although most of my examples are drawn from the American experience (and the EU), I believe readers will have no difficulty in applying the ideas to their particular society and government.

I
NATIONAL MORAL DIALOGUES

Democracies should not be led by individual charismatic leaders who capture the following of the masses and override the decisions made by deliberative bodies and courts. Instead, individual citizens need to come together and decide among each other which direction their country is to follow and what values are to be advanced.

One can readily see how dialogues can unite citizens in common purpose and goals within a small group, maybe even in groups as large as those that come together in town hall meetings.[1] However, much of public policy these days must be addressed on the national level. Pollution does not heed state lines. Immigrants flow from one community to another. Defense is a national business. To achieve genuine, lasting change, dialogues about pressing values must be national. I will show that they can be, indeed often are. Moreover, although observers often point to unresolved conflicts—say, about abortion—new shared moral understandings frequently do arise.

Members of the patriotic movement must face the fact that the values that people of many nations used to share with their compatriots have lost their legitimacy, their compelling power. True, these values—say, those that united the American people in the 1950s—included many normative positions few find compelling today. However, there is no denying that at the time they were widely endorsed, even by many of those they excluded. The fact that these values have been largely discarded is a major sign of progress. The problem is that they have not been replaced with a new set of national unifying values. Hence, the agenda of the patriotic movement is not to move back to the old, discarded values but to form new normative content for nationally shared values.

A new dialogue about core values hence is essential, in effect a prerequisite for any future effective social movement that will rebuild democracy and the national community.[2] One may well wonder how a nation could hold a moral dialogue that would help opposing groups find a common ground—without the dialogue devolving into ideological opponents screaming at each other, adhering to party lines, and re-inforcing political differences. Critics may well say that the culture wars illustrate the futility of national moral dialogues. This chapter looks at previous national dialogues to show they have led to major new shared moral understandings and unpacks which processes they employed to cultivate success. It turns out that such dialogues follow a fairly clear design, a design that the patriotic movement should employ in sorting out a new core of shared values for the nation to embrace.

Moral Dialogues Defined

Moral dialogues are social processes through which people form new shared moral understandings. These dialogues typically are passionate, disorderly, and without a clear starting point or conclusion (in contrast to elections or debates in a legislature). However, moral dialogues often do lead to profound changes in the moral positions of those who engage in them. Although moral dialogues never change the values of all involved, they often, as we shall see, change the moral positions of a sufficient number of people so that actions and policies that previously had little support (e.g., environmental protection) and actions and policies considered morally inappropriate by many (e.g., same-sex marriage) gain widespread moral approval.

Moreover, we shall see that when moral dialogues mature, the new shared moral understandings that arise have profound sociological effects well beyond changes in values, norms, and attitudes. These new or changed moral understandings lead to new laws or significant changes in law and, more importantly, to major changes in voluntary behavior. For instance, the shared understanding that we have a moral obligation to be stewards of the environment led to the founding of a new government agency (the Environmental Protection Agency); scores of new laws and regulations; construction of walkable neighborhoods and bicycle lanes; improved public transit; and considerable changes in voluntary personal behavior, including recycling, preferences for sustainable sources of energy (a factor in purchasing cars, appliances, and solar panels), donations, and voting. True, these changes were also affected by other factors, especially changes in economic incentives. However, the restructuring of these incentives reflects in part changes in a shared moral understanding. This chapter focuses on the dynamics and effects of moral dialogues that lead to significant changes in shared moral understandings (SMUs).

The analysis combines two methods. It follows historians by studying the development of various moral dialogues over time in a particular community or nation, in a given period. It follows sociologists in that it seeks to identify the recurring social factors on which moral dialogues draw to bring about new SMUs. These elements are next listed and then analyzed.

To study moral dialogues one needs to start with a *baseline,* to show where the shared moral understandings were before the moral dialogues changed them. Next the chapter examines the *sociological dialogue starters* that lead to the initiation of moral dialogues (and their differences from historical "firsts"). The next section deals with the attributes and dynamics of moral dialogues. These include a review of intensive, interlinked multiple group discussions—which we shall call *megalogues*— that are required for moral dialogues to take place on a large scale; the *distinct attributes* of moral dialogues as compared to rational deliberations and culture wars; and the crucial role of *dramatization.* The chapter then turns to show that moral dialogues that reach *closure* have significant sociological consequences. These are revealed in changes in shared values, laws, and behavior when one compares the end state to the baseline.

Following these sections, a case study illustrates the various elements in one specific historical development, the change in the SMU about same-sex marriage. The importance of moral dialogues for community building is briefly discussed. The chapter closes by pointing to a particularly challenging question: How is one to determine whether socially shared moral understandings, which basically reflect moral consensus, are indeed moral?

This chapter leaves for future discussion the study of the effects of external structural factors on moral dialogues, such as differences in political and economic power, social inequality, race, and gender. The chapter seeks to introduce moral dialogues as distinct from reasoned deliberations, expressions of emotions, and culture wars and leaves to a separate examination the important effects of structural factors on moral dialogues, a major subject all by itself.

One can readily envision moral dialogues within a family or a small community but may well wonder if a society that encompasses many millions of people can engage in a moral dialogue. We shall see below that such society-wide dialogues take place by linking millions of local conversations (between couples, in neighborhood bars, in coffeehouses, during carpooling, next to water coolers at work, and so on) into a society-wide moral give-and-take.

Moral dialogues tend to follow a set pattern. I choose my words carefully. Not all moral dialogues follow all the stages next outlined. The pattern next unveiled should hence be viewed as an ideal type.[3] It serves as an analytic matrix for the study of various specific dialogues and the comparison of one to others. In presenting the pattern (some would call it "natural history"), I draw on illustrations from the American experience, although its presence in other societies and transnational dialogues is self-evident.[4]

Baselines

To assess the effects of any given moral dialogue, one must establish what the shared moral understanding was before the dialogue took place. For instance, to assess the effects of moral dialogues on our moral obligations to "Mother Earth," about our stewardship of the environment, one must start by noting that in the 1950s, there was no shared sense of such a moral responsibility. People dumped garbage in lakes and streams, drove cars that emitted large amounts of pollutants, and used coal as a major source of energy without any concern about the environmental implications of their actions. In the same period, racial segregation was legally enforced and widely supported. Women were expected to be homemakers and submissive. Gay people were considered sinners and deviants. Smoking in public raised no moral issues. People felt obligated to do "all they could" for their loved ones until their heart and lungs stopped functioning. Researchers can readily find some academics, clergy, or visionaries who made a moral case against any one of these established mores. However, they did not start moral dialogues and did not have a significant effect on the nationwide shared moral understanding.

Sociological Dialogue Starters

Moral dialogues often start with the articulation of what might be called a "moral brief," akin to what lawyers file before they argue a case before the Supreme Court. It typically includes a criticism of the prevailing moral culture and society and a substantive statement of what a new shared moral understanding should contain. One should note in this context that some protest movements and organizations mainly provide a criticism of the prevailing order but offer little content—or only exceedingly vague content—about the core values intended to replace those of the old order. These are more disruptive than transformative. Major changes in SMUs require that briefs also include statements about the new SMU to replace the old one (a point that was not fully taken into account by several groups that brought down old regimes during the Arab Spring).

Betty Friedan provided such a brief for a moral dialogue about women's rights and status in her 1963 book *The Feminine Mystique*. Rachel Carson provided such a brief for the environmental movement in her book *Silent Spring*, published in 1962. Ralph Nader did the same for the consumer protection drive in his book *Unsafe at Any Speed*, published in 1965. Other moral dialogues were started by a declaration, for instance Martin Luther's 95 *Theses*, which prompted the Protestant Reformation. A Harvard committee provided a brief for changing the definition of death to one that occurs when there is a "brain death." Sometimes moral dialogues are triggered by an event rather than a brief, such as the Three Mile Island accident, which started a dialogue about nuclear safety. However, in all the cases examined, a brief followed.

In examining moral briefs, it is important to distinguish between *historical antecedents* and *sociological takeoff points*. When a book or trial or event leads to a new moral dialogue, historians will often point out that rather similar ones have already been published or have taken place before. For instance, before *The Feminine Mystique*, other books on the topic had been published, including *The Second Sex* by Simone de Beauvoir in 1949. However, these previous developments were only precursors as they did not mobilize major moral dialogues that could lead to new SMUs. For the purpose of studying changes in SMUs, one must focus on those briefs and events that served to initiate the kind of dialogues and societal changes next described. We are after catalysts that spurred lasting systemic change rather than those that fizzled out.

Some studies refer to the selection of dialogue starters as "agenda setting," the process through which people attribute a higher importance to some issues as compared to others. According to H. Denis Wu and Renita Coleman, "For more than thirty years, the main concept in agenda setting theory has been the transfer of issue salience, or how media emphasis of certain issues raises their importance for the public."[5] A common finding is that the media largely determines the issues on which the public focuses.

The content of the brief, how well it is argued and presented, or the nature of the starting events, is often not the most important factor determining whether it will serve merely as a historical first or will lead to a sociological takeoff. Much more important is whether or not the sociological conditions that would allow the changes to take off are in place. Thus, for instance, briefs for liberal democracy in societies of the kind the US found in Afghanistan in 2003 are unlikely to lead to a takeoff.[6] In contrast, it seems that The Feminine Mystique led to takeoff not necessarily because it was better argued or had more evidence than previous books on the same subject, but because it was published after many women had worked in factories and some had participated in the military during World War II and were thus open to suggestions that they are able and entitled to play roles other than that of homemakers.

Finally, one should note that many moral dialogues take off but then lose altitude and need to be relaunched if they are to lead to a new SMU. For instance, dialogues about inequality in the US are following this pattern. Figure 1 presents Google Trends data showing the popularity (relative to other searches of the term on Google over time) of the term "social inequality."[8] Interest in inequality is lacking a definitive spike; instead it consistently wavers.

Moreover, some moral dialogues that do take off never produce a new or changed SMU. For instance, briefs that called for the formation of a global government, in particular the 1947 Montreux Declaration by the World Federalists as part of the World Movement for World Federal Government,[9] initiated a measure of moral dialogues, but these petered out without gaining a new SMU.

Megalogues

For a starter brief or event to lead to a new SMU, it must be followed by processes that would lead a large number of people to reexamine their moral values, giving up on what they long believed was right, and accept a new set of values as morally valid.

Some advocates of moral causes believe that if the president were to make a powerful speech or conduct "fireside chats" as President Roosevelt did, this would lead to a new SMU and change the direction of the nation.

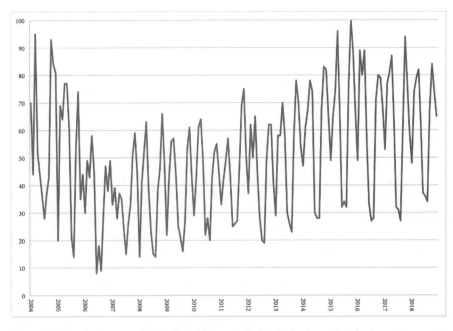

Fig. 1. Relative frequency of term "social inequality" searched on Google

President Kennedy's speech that urged Americans not to ask what their country can do for them but what they can do for their country is credited with engendering a historical change; however, although the speech is often quoted, there is precious little evidence that, by itself, it had much of an effect. President Jimmy Carter tried to make Americans treat the saving of energy as a test of their moral fortitude in his famous "malaise" speech—with mainly negative effects. President Obama spoke eloquently for many causes, especially for finding common ground, but the nation became more polarized. Such speeches can have high motives and aspirations, but as noted earlier, other sociological factors must be present for them to have the sought-after societal effects. Systemic change depends on more than speeches or verbal persuasion in general, however evocative and well-meaning they may be.

Instead, when a topic takes off, or "gets hot," it becomes the subject of extensive discussion in personal settings (over dinner, at the water cooler, in bars, firehouses) and in local meetings of voluntary associations and clubs (Rotary, PTA, places of worship). These, in turn, are amplified and linked through national organizations during their meetings (such as AIPAC, League of Women Voters, NAACP, Sierra Club,

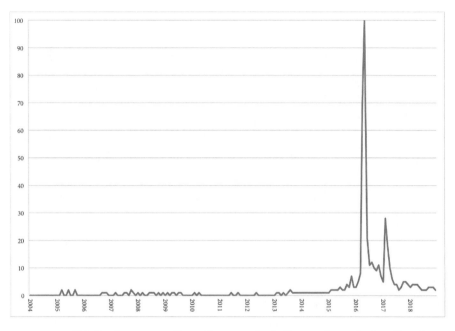

Fig. 2. Relative frequency of term "transgender bathrooms" searched on Google

Conference of Catholic Bishops, National Council of Churches, etc.) and through the media (call-in shows, commentaries and debates on TV and radio) and social media.

To illustrate, in 2016–17 a subject that was only sporadically discussed in previous years became a focus of a nationwide moral dialogue in the US, namely the rights of transgender people. Figure 2 is a Google Trends graph showing the relative popularity of the search term "transgender bathrooms" in the US from January 2004 to December 2018.[10]

Distinct Attributes

Moral dialogues differ sharply from both expressions of emotions and from rational deliberations. In effect, they constitute a hybrid that has qualities of its own, different from the composite elements. Moral statements contain emotions in contrast to sheer statements of facts or logic. At the same time, these statements contain justifications—that is, they are intellectually accountable—in contrast to emotions. When one discloses that one hates or loves or declares any other emotion, it suffices to state "because this is what I feel" (de gustibus non est disputandum).[11] In contrast, if one states that a given condition is immoral—say, not fair—one is expected to spell out the reasons and give a basis for this statement. And one may be challenged with arguments that such a statement is inconsistent with previous ones, or violates a general ethical position to which the person subscribes, or with still other arguments—and one is expected to justify one's moral judgment or modify it. This is what I mean by intellectual accountability.

Moral statements differ from rational statements that are focused on facts, as well as from logical conclusions that can be drawn from these facts. People are invested emotionally in moral statements, and hence when new facts arise or new arguments are made based on evidence, people will not change their positions readily. True, much has been written to point out that facts and values cannot be completely separated and they often bleed into each other. Still, there is a clear difference between what have been called *is* versus *ought* statements. Reasoned deliberations are about *is,* moral dialogues are about *ought.*

To illustrate, one may argue whether or not a death penalty is justified as a crime deterrent on empirical-logical, rational grounds by comparing crime rates in states that have versus those that do not have death penalties, or before and after such sentences were carried out in states that either dropped or adopted this penalty. In contrast, if one holds that it is morally wrong for the state to deliberately take a life, statistics about the effects on crime rates will matter little (or only if one can show that the result leads to a higher loss of lives).

Quite a few previous discussions of the attributes of dialogues suffer from the curse of dichotomies. The main case in point is the growing recognition that the assumption that people are rational creatures, able to collect and process the information needed to make rational choices, is a false one.[12] It is assumed ipso facto that therefore people are irrational, unable to make sensible judgments, because the analysis started from a binary position. If not A, then it must be B. Actually, as Talcott Parsons pointed out long ago, there is a whole third realm, that of the nonrational. This realm includes "otherworldly" matters that deal with questions and views about the afterlife, deities, the meaning of life, why we were born to die. And with the selection of moral values, especially when two or more of these values are in conflict.

I am not arguing that rational deliberations and moral dialogues do not affect each other. However, when one examines particular dialogues, one can, as a rule, readily determine which statements are moral versus factual, and see differences in the give-and-take between those that are evidence-centered and those focused on moral issues.

We can gain some insight into the issue from mental experiments. A father finding out that his young son has been smoking may merely yell at him, demanding that he stop (sheer emotion), or he may strongly express, in emotive terms, his concern for his son's health and also explain the risks involved to him and others around him. For the purposes of moral dialogues, it matters not in this case if the argument that the father made was merely a rationalization that followed his emotions or one he developed on the basis of information he garnered and understood. What matters is that his son is less likely to be swayed when exposed to sheer emotion as compared to emotion accompanied by reasoning. Moral dialogues draw on both emotional expressions and reason. Otherwise they are shouting matches, guilt trips, or expressions of blind love, shame, and other such emotions.

Some accord a great role to the media as a moral persuader. For instance, when it shows graphic pictures following an earthquake or typhoon, millions of donations flow to the people in the devastated area, based on the emotions the pictures evoke. However, on closer inspection, one notes that the pictures do not so much shape one's moral disposition as direct where it is applied. One can determine this by noting that large donations will come from Americans because voluntary donations are part of the American moral tradition. In some other countries, the same pictures will lead to greater demands on the government to act. And in still others, very few donations will be forthcoming. Bernard Cohen made this point well when he observed, "It [the press] may not be successful much of the time in telling people what to think, but it is stunningly successful in telling its readers what to think *about*."[13]

In further deliberating on the question at hand, one can draw on firsthand experience in moral deliberations. Thus, when we serve on a committee that considers whether or not to disclose to the public or the authorities some unethical conduct or acts that might be illegal—for example, bullying or unconfirmed reports about inappropriate sexual advances made by a coach—we note that our emotions are surely engaged but that we also take into account moral arguments.

Moral dialogues resolve differences and are thus able to lead to new SMUs in their own ways, frequently without relying on new empirical evidence. One procedure often used in moral dialogues is *to appeal to an overarching value* that the various parties to the sorting-out process share. Robert Goodin in effect is using this rule when he seeks to pave the road for a community that must sort out a course between the rights of nonsmokers and those of smokers.[14] At first, this may seem like a typical clash between two values: the rights of one group versus those of another. However, Goodin points out that *both* groups are committed to the value that one's liberty does not allow that person to violate the "space" of the other. In popular terms, my right to extend my arm stops when my fist reaches your nose. Goodin argues that this value applies because nonsmokers, in their nonsmoking, do not penetrate the smokers' space, whereas smokers do violate nonsmokers' space in public situations, thus nonsmokers' rights should take priority. Using such arguments, American communities reached the SMU that lies at the foundation of the new restrictions on smoking in numerous public spaces. (The fact that these new regulations have met very little opposition shows that they, unlike Prohibition, were based on a thoroughly shared moral understanding.)

Another procedure is *to bring a third value into play when two diverge or clash*. For instance, those who recently tried to restore the Black-Jewish coalition of the 1960s in the US argue that both groups share a commitment to liberal causes. Additionally, attempts to create an interfaith coalition pointed to the shared commitment to fight poverty, as the participants struggled to work out a joint position.[15] Groups that strongly support pro-life public policies and those that strongly support pro-choice ones agreed to work together to improve the care of children, whom both groups cherish.[16]

"Culture wars" is a term that was used originally to refer to the conflicts between social conservatives and liberals about issues such as abortion and divorce. More generally, it is used to refer to "a conflict between groups with different ideals, beliefs, [or] philosophies."[17] It implies persistent, unresolved value differences such as those between Protestants and Catholics in earlier eras, Shias and Sunnis, and secular and ultra-Orthodox Jews more recently. One may view culture wars as failed moral dialogues, in part due to higher levels of emotional involvement compared to moral dialogues. However, one should note the findings of an excellent study by the historian Stephen Prothero that shows that, over time, even these dialogues often lead to new SMUs, for instance about same-sex marriages, use of contraception, and divorce.[18] This may even be true about gun control; however, in this realm moral consensus has not yet led to significant changes in voluntary behavior, and the law moved away from the SMU.

Dramatization

So far this analysis of moral dialogues has focused on communications, on members of a community, however small or large, exchanging moral viewpoints, discussing moral issues with one another, reexamining their moral positions, and reaching (often) common ground. One should not ignore, however, that *all* such dialogues also contain acts that serve to dramatize the moral issues under discussion, such as sit-ins, demonstrations, occupying administrative buildings on campuses and at corporations, sit-downs in traffic lanes, and spilling blood on fur coats (by animal rights activists). Court cases such as the Scopes Trial, congressional hearings regarding Joseph McCarthy, and the confirmation hearing of Associate Justice Clarence Thomas also serve to dramatize the issues. If words, deliberations, and communications entail two dimensions, dramatizations are three-dimensional.

These dramatizations serve two main purposes. One is to nurture the dialogues. Following dramatizations, especially those with novel rather than merely routinized elements, one finds a spike in dialogues. For instance, the spike in dialogue cited above was associated with lawmakers in North Carolina passing a law that prevents transgender individuals from using bathrooms that correspond with their gender identity, by requiring individuals to use public bathrooms in alignment with the sex given on their birth certificate, and by the dramatic response of the US Departments of Justice and Education that threatened to deny billions in federal funds to North Carolina and any other state that followed the same course. The importance of dramatization has risen since the advent of TV. Pictures are highly evocative, whereas verbal dialogues rarely lend themselves to dramatic footage. Hence, dramatizations on TV are a particularly effective means to promote moral dialogues, to keep the issues under discussion in the public eye, and to mobilize participation.

Second, dramatizations engage people's emotions, whereas verbal give-and-take relates more to intellectual accountability elements. Dramatization thus helps ensure that people who may be swayed by an argument will also refigure their emotional commitments accordingly.

Closure

To reiterate, even when successful, the change in an SMU encompasses merely a large segment of the people who engaged in these dialogues;

there always remain some who do not change their moral position. Moreover, some moral dialogues fail, for example, between the pro-choice and pro-life groups. Many take off, slow down, and are relaunched before a significant level of SMU is reached (e.g., the dialogue on inequality). However, when these dialogues take off and mature, they change the moral positions of large segments of the populations, often creating new moral majorities.

More importantly, the great significance of SMUs is that they lead to voluntary *changes in behavior—well beyond changes in attitudes*. Thus, people who acknowledge that they have a moral obligation to the environment are much more likely than others to recycle, use recycled paper, bike and walk, buy low-emission cars that use fuel efficiently, support public policies that protect the environment, use solar panels, and so on. True, these behaviors are also affected by changes in economic incentives and legislative acts. However, for reasons next outlined, it makes a very great difference (*a*) if the changes in behavior are mainly voluntary, due to changes in what people consider the right behavior versus mainly due to economic and legal incentives, and (*b*) if the changes in incentives and laws are supported by an SMU or not.

The role of SMUs in affecting behavior rather than just attitudes is of great significance and hence deserves some elaboration. In a very extensive study of what motivates people,[19] a study whose findings were replicated and augmented many times,[20] I showed that people can be motivated to engage in pro-social behavior that they would not have engaged in otherwise, in three ways. They can be coerced; motivated by economic incentives or disincentives; or convinced of the moral rightness of changing their behavior. The study shows that people resent being coerced and will try to deviate from forced patterns of behavior whenever they believe they can get away with it. Hence compliance will be costly, unreliable, and far from satisfactory.

People who are paid to behave—read a book, come to class, work, etc.—will be less alienated than those who are coerced, but they will also seek to gain the incentives while giving in return as little as possible because in their view their preferences are not compatible with what they are paid to do.

In sharp contrast, people who find their tasks morally compelling will feel ennobled and highly motivated to complete them well, even if unsupervised. (Those in hybrid situations will act accordingly; e.g., the feelings and behaviors of physicians who are morally compelled to treat their patients while also receiving financial reward for their service will fall somewhere between those physicians driven only by economic incentives or only by moral principles.)

There are those who hold that each person is out to pursue their self-interest and, famously, that an invisible hand will ensure that as a result, the economy will thrive and all will do well. Whether this is true or not for the economy need not examined here; however, this certainly does not hold true for society. The problem of social order, as Dennis Wrong put it, is that people need to be motivated to engage in pro-social behavior.[21] However, no society can provide a sufficient number of police officers, accountants, border patrols, etc. to coerce a satisfactory level of pro-social behavior. Moreover, such enforcement is costly, as the US discovered when it incarcerated people en masse, spending more on prisons than on higher education, trying but failing to curb substance abuse. Last but not least, such enforcement faces the often-cited challenge, Who will guard the guardians? Many enforcement agents are corrupt and engage in antisocial behavior themselves: They shoot unarmed African Americans. They smuggle contraband into prisons. They harass inmates.

In contrast, to the extent that most people do at most times much of what needs to be done—go to work, take care of their family, pay taxes, avoid polluting, and so on—because they view their responsibilities as legitimate and morally compelling, compliance will be high, costs will be low, and inclination to rebel, minimal. An interesting example is tax compliance. It has been shown that if people believe that taxes are fair and legitimately used, they pay more of the taxes owed.[22]

When SMUs are formed, they enable a society to limit coercive enforcement and rely much more on self-regulation. For example, when public smoking bans were enacted, they caused little opposition and resulted in general compliance because they followed public education (especially on secondhand smoke risks) and moral dialogues.[23] On the other hand, Prohibition failed miserably because public consensus on the issue was lacking; the law was not backed up by a shared moral understanding.[24]

Although, as we have just seen, the main benefit of new SMUs (or the reworking of an old, obsolete one) is an increase in voluntary adherence to the social norms that define pro-social behavior, SMUs also lead to new *laws and regulations* or to changes in them. That is, the new SMUs tend to become legally embedded and reinforced. This is the case because (*a*) many social functions cannot rely only on moral persuasion and voluntary compliance (or economic incentives); and (*b*) even if only a relatively small number of people ignore social norms, their conduct can unravel voluntary compliance in the larger population over time because law-abiding citizens would feel like "suckers" who are taken advantage of and treated unfairly. Thus, if a growing number of people speed or park illegally with impunity, more and more will follow. Hence, mature SMUs should not only be expressed in changes in voluntary behavior but also should be embedded in laws. Thus, the rise in the SMU that we have a stewardship over the environment led to the formation of the EPA and scores of laws limiting pollution. The rise in the SMU that African Americans were treated unfairly led to Affirmative Action, the formation of the Equal Employment Opportunity Plan (EEOP), and court cases banning several forms of segregation, among other such moves.

Those who tend to favor enacting moral changes should note that in many cases *gaining a new SMU precedes the enactment of laws* that express and undergird the values agreed upon. Dialogue about women's rights advanced before Title IX became the law of the land. The same is true about gay rights before the Supreme Court ruling that made same-sex marriage legal across the country, and before legal segregation was struck down.

A Case Study: Dialogues about Same-Sex Marriages

Baseline

The moral dialogue about same-sex marriages is a subset of a much more encompassing moral dialogue on homosexuality, a dialogue not here examined. In 1970, no US state allowed same-sex marriages. Even civil unions for same-sex couples did not exist as an alternative. According to the Supreme Court, it was not even a substantial federal question (implying that same-sex marriage was not something to be considered), a statement the Court made in 1972 when refusing to hear a case on the issue. Over a decade later, in 1986, as a result of the Supreme Court's decision in *Bowers v. Hardwick,* states maintained their ability to criminalize gay sexual relations.[25] In 1996, the Defense of Marriage Act (DOMA) was passed with 79 percent approval in the House[26] and 85 percent approval in the Senate,[27] which declared that for federal purposes, marriage was between one man and one woman.[28] It was signed by President Clinton, whose statement on DOMA declared, "I have long opposed governmental recognition of same-gender marriages and this legislation is consistent with that position."[29] In terms of public opinion, a 1996 Gallup poll found that 68 percent of respondents thought same-sex marriage should not be valid.[30] Data from the Pew Research Center taken from the same year show a similar figure of 65 percent.[31]

Sociological Dialogue Starters

There were several "historical starters," such as the 1993 case in which the Hawaii Supreme Court suggested that it may be unconstitutional to reject same-sex marriage.[32] However, this prompted a backlash, and "by 2001, thirty-five states had passed laws limiting marriage to a union of one man and one woman [including Hawaii]."[33] One should not mistake this legislation as a reflection of a new SMU; rather, it was a codification of the status quo, which had previously been seen as unnecessary. Vermont's recognition of same-sex civil unions in 2000 can be viewed as a "sociological starter," though it provided an alternative to same-sex marriage rather than a redefinition of marriage.

A takeoff point was reached in 2004, when Massachusetts became the first state to legalize gay marriage.[34] As such, because of the DOMA provision denying federal benefits to same-sex couples, it put state and federal law at odds.[35] The decision in Massachusetts prompted a backlash of state constitutional amendments banning same-sex marriage.[36] California voted for Proposition 8 in 2008, which banned same-sex marriage in the state. But "advocates could show the nation that allowing gay and lesbian couples to marry had no negative consequences."[37]

Billion-Hour Buzz

The legalization of same-sex marriage by Massachusetts in 2004, with the media portraying happy gay and lesbian newlyweds, helped trigger a national debate on the subject. In 2004, 2005, and 2006, proposed amendments to the Massachusetts state constitution were discussed at what were called constitutional conventions: "Each convention generated extensive local and national media coverage, and drew large crowds of demonstrators on both sides." Ultimately no amendments were made, and same-sex marriage remained legal.[38]

During this time, marriage equality remained a salient issue across the country. In order to gauge where the public stood after the Proposition 8 vote in California, there were focus groups, roundtables, and thirty groups created a survey together.[39]

In Maine, same-sex marriage was legalized in 2008, repealed by voters in 2009, and then was supported on a ballot measure in 2012. To prepare for the 2012 referendum, a new type of canvassing was introduced, one that involved "in-depth conversations, in which the canvasser asked open-ended questions designed to invite respondents to share their experiences." More than 200,000 such conversations took place, and it is estimated that these conversations changed the stance of 12,500 Maine voters.[40] One of the televised political ads in Maine at the time closed with the statement: "This isn't about politics. It's about family and how we as people treat one another."[41]

Television played a key role in moral dialogues on marriage equality. The portrayal of gay and lesbian characters in the media has increased,[42] and there is evidence that this had an impact on public opinion: "According to a 2012 *Hollywood Reporter* poll, 27% of people who had changed their minds about gay marriage from anti- to pro- in the last decade said that they made their decision after watching gay characters on shows like *Modern Family* and *Glee*."[43]

When President Obama came out in support of same-sex marriage in 2012, it had a significant impact on the amount of conversation taking place.[44] On blogs there was more than a 60 percent increase in statements on same-sex marriage after Obama's announcement, and the percentage was even greater on Twitter: "For the week of May 7–11 [2012], Obama's comment on May 9 in favor of same-sex marriage was the No. 1 topic on blogs and the No. 3 subject on Twitter."[45] Furthermore, "there have been nine previous weeks [since 2009] when the subject [same-sex marriage] was among the most discussed on blogs or Twitter."[46]

In 2013, the Human Rights Campaign (HRC) introduced an image of a pink equal sign against a red backdrop in support of marriage equality as part of a social media campaign in connection with the Supreme Court's consideration of *Hollingsworth v. Perry* and *United States v. Windsor*, two cases that had implications for marriage equality. The logo went viral, with many people replacing their Facebook profile picture with one that included it, prompting news headlines such as "How the Red Equal Sign Took over Facebook."[47] HRC provides the following description of the phenomenon of the red logo: "The red marriage equality logo first appeared on HRC's Facebook page at 2 p.m. on March 25, 2013. Within 24 hours, HRC's Facebook post to encourage digital activists to change their social media profile pictures to a red and pink version of its ubiquitous logo received 189,177 shares, 95,725 likes, appeared over 18 million times in Newsfeeds, created upwards of 10 million impressions worldwide, and inspired countless memes. Facebook recorded a 120 percent increase in profile photo updates, and they deemed the effort the most successful campaign in their history."[48] Pew Research Center did a study of news coverage both leading up to and during the Supreme Court hearings; the study looked at five hundred stories about marriage equality during an eight-week time frame, concluding that the coverage indicated "strong momentum for same-sex marriage."[49] Although this number is by no means inclusive of every relevant news story during the selected time frame, it illustrates the extent to which marriage equality was being discussed. Pew also noted that the "Gay Voices" microsite of the *Huffington Post* "produced so much coverage that it was examined separately from the rest of the news media."[50]

Dramatization

The movement for same-sex marriage used court cases to dramatize the issues at the heart of the moral dialogue and drew on protests to engage public attention. For example, after the Proposition 8 vote, protests were widespread in California,[51] which kept the issue in the media. At the Sacramento Capitol, 2,500 protesters gathered, and other large protests occurred outside of religious institutions that had supported the measure to ban same-sex marriage.[52] Same-sex marriage was also promoted in pride parades in many cities. In 2013, DOMA was ruled unconstitutional by the Supreme Court decision in *United States v. Windsor*,[53] which furthered the momentum of the same-sex marriage movement.

Closure

In June 2015, the US Supreme Court decision in *Obergefell v. Hodges* recognized a constitutional right to same-sex marriage.[54] It applies to all fifty states, though some states still have laws banning same-sex marriage and now seek to obstruct it in other ways. A month prior to the decision, a Gallup poll showed that 60 percent of respondents thought same-sex marriage should be legal.[55] The tide had turned, and Justice Anthony Kennedy recognized that Americans had reached a new SMU. He wrote that "new insights and societal understandings can reveal unjustified inequality within our most fundamental institutions that once passed unnoticed and unchallenged."[56]

Community Building and Power Structures

When moral dialogues mature, they become a major source of community building and nurturing. Communities are not merely places where people bond and have affection for one another. They are also places where people have a shared moral culture and shared values from which specific norms are derived. However, moral cultures are continually challenged by technological, economic, and international developments, among others. To respond to these challenges, moral cultures draw on moral dialogues. The dialogues either shore up or revise the core values needed to keep various contending factions from eroding communal bonds and the core of shared values.

Social scientists and social philosophers have long worried that the social transformation accompanying the Industrial Revolution—when most people moved from the tightly knit communal life of villages into cities with "atomized" affiliations—caused the loss of essential social moorings. This thesis is often referred to as a shift from *Gemeinschaft* (community) to *Gesellschaft* (society).[57] True, we have since learned that communities can be found in industrial societies, for instance in such ethnic neighborhoods as Chinatown, Spanish Harlem, Greenwich Village, and in the gated complexes in which many millions of Americans live.[58] However, there is still considerable evidence that a large number of people lack the social bonds essential for their flourishing—hence the call for rebuilding communities in which moral dialogues play a major reconstructive role.

Major liberal scholars hold that each person should define the good and that the state should be morally neutral. Hence some have suggested that the state should stop issuing marriage licenses altogether and leave the various religions' functionaries and civic bodies to determine what marriage is. Moreover, liberals feared that even if the state remains morally neutral, as long as the society forms strong SMUs, these will be embedded in laws.[59]

In contrast, communitarians point out that social order requires a core of shared values. Some of the reasons have already been cited, such as the need for social order to rest on voluntary compliance. Further, various factions with rival interests and values need to form shared public policies as well as procedures to resolve differences so that disagreements do not spin into unresolved standoffs and violence. Developing SMUs is the process that can keep these essential core values intact or allow them to adapt rather than unravel in times of change.

I refer to a set of "core" values because the difference between core and other values is crucial for several reasons. First, much attention has been paid in recent years to the polarization of American politics, reflected in more and more people identifying themselves with either a conservative or a liberal position and fewer and fewer as somewhere in the middle—as well as a growing adamancy in the positions held by both camps. Polarization is viewed as a key reason the government is in gridlock and held in low regard by the overwhelming majority of the American people. From a communitarian viewpoint, the main question is whether the polarization concerns secondary values—and hence differences can be settled by appealing to core values—or is holistic, leading to irreconcilable differences. If the breakdown of moral consensus is holistic, moral dialogues will either fail to lead to SMUs, or they will restore the needed consensus by leading to the formation of a new core of shared values.

Relativism?

The term "moral" implies that one approves whatever is so judged. However, there is no a priori reason to hold that just because the overwhelming majority of the people of a given community come to an SMU, the content of this understanding will be in line with what a particular person will consider moral. For example, the majority of Americans used to hold that "separate but equal" was a fair SMU (reflected in the 1896 Supreme Court decision *Plessy v. Ferguson*). Another example is the Defense of Marriage Act, which held that for the purposes of federal law, marriage is between a man and a woman, as well as gave states the right to decide whether or not to recognize same-sex marriages that had taken place outside their jurisdiction. Many will not find these SMUs to be moral.

In short, moral dialogues are just that—dialogues about what the majority considers moral—not what is moral by some ethical theory or anyone's standards. One must hence keep in mind that whatever SMU a community or society or transnational body might reach—which might have all the functional merits I discussed earlier, such as making society more peaceful, functional, and effective—that SMU may nevertheless be immoral by your or my standards, or those of the Bible, Kant, Rawls, utilitarianism, Aristotelianism, or virtue ethics. Those troubled by the substance of any SMU are hence called upon to continue to reexamine it and, if found objectionable, to work to change it through moral dialogues.[60]

The Need for a New Dialogue

The reason that members of the patriotic movement now need to engage in major national dialogues on the core values that should guide the nation is that the prevailing polarization cuts much deeper than political disagreements. Many democracies have lost a shared understanding of the basic values that serve to contain conflicts and provide a foundation for forming shared directions for public policies and allocation of resources. There is no going back to the old consensus, which was biased against women and minorities. A new consensus needs to be formed from the ground up.

The patriotic movement will have to find its way through all the steps other movements did: it needs to form a brief (to which this book seeks to contribute); insert it into local dialogues and launch megalogues; find ways to dramatize its cause; and ensconce the new shared understanding yet to arise into laws and public policy.

2

COMMUNITIES ARE ESSENTIAL BUT SUSPECT BUILDING BLOCKS

The Me Needs the We to Be

The dominant ideologies in the West are individualistic. Libertarians, who have a much larger following than the number of people who vote for libertarian candidates for public office would suggest, see the world as composed of individuals acting as free, autonomous agents. As they see it, the aggregation of their votes guides the polity just as the aggregation of their purchases guides the economy. In their judgment, any intervention in their preferences is suspect and should be minimized. *Laissez-faire* conservatives hold similar viewpoints. The government that governs least governs best. Liberals are much more attuned to social factors, yet to the extent that they are preoccupied with human and individual rights, they too are individual-centered.

However, as communitarians like me have shown, individuals—at least the kind who can be reasonable and responsible citizens—are the product of communities and need communities to ensure their stability and flourishing. As I once put it, in a popular vein: The Me needs the We to Be. The patriotic movement will have to take note that the erosion of community is a major factor that drives populism, which in turn undermines both democracy and social stability. As Yoram Hazony put it, "National cohesion is the secret ingredient that allows free institutions to exist, the bedrock on which a functioning democracy is built."[1] Hence this movement will have to make shoring up communities a key element of its agenda.

The idea of community evokes various responses—including hope, a sense of connectedness, fear, and cynicism. This variety is understandable; community is a complex, variegated concept. Communities can be morally uplifting or highly troubling, because they can promote rather different values. Gangs are communities. So are the chapters of the KKK. It is best to think about communities (and the social bonds they entail) as pipelines: the stronger the bonds, the more social "business" the community can carry. However, what flows in these pipes, the content of the values the social bonds help introduce and enforce, can vary a great deal. We shall see that a new core of national values is what is now called for. We do not just need to shore up communal bonds; we need also to ensure that they support the appropriate values.

Social movements typically form new communities. There was no working class before socialism. There were workers, to be sure, but they had no sense of shared communal bonds, values, agenda, and future before Fabian socialists and Marx. There were no environmentalist communities before Rachel Carson. Now people from various social groups need to come together to form new communities, to provide the social base for the patriotic movement.

There is a widely held belief that if people of different backgrounds meet, they will listen to each other and form new bridges. (A whole school of sociology at the University of Chicago was based on this assumption.)[2] Such meetings, however, often reinforce rather than transform their participants' prejudices, including about each other. A study found that Republicans and Democrats formed even more conservative or liberal views, respectively, after being exposed to messages from elected officials, thought leaders, and think tanks from the opposing party on Twitter.[3] When people meet as partisans, framing their encounter with each other in terms of their party identifications, they tend to fit new facts into their old gestalts by interpreting the facts to suit their predispositions.[4] Hence the importance for the patriotic movement to fashion new meeting grounds that encourage people to draw on other identifications they have—we all have multiple identities—and be more inclined to form new gestalts.

For instance, if people meet at firehouses as firefighters or emergency medical services (EMS) providers rather than as Democrats or Republicans, they will tend to leave behind their political preconceptions and work together for a common cause. (Of the 1.2 million registered fire department personnel in the US, approximately 865,000 are volunteer workers, and 195,000 are classified as "mostly volunteer" workers.)[5] These meeting grounds serve as a good example of places in which one can find or develop the kind of leaders and founding members the patriotic movement needs to take off and grow.

Many veterans are similarly well suited to launch patriotic chapters because many of them are accustomed to and comfortable with speaking in terms of service to the nation. Historically, veterans groups in the US have been associated with conservative causes, and liberals often have ceded patriotism to the Right. Richard Rorty called the American Left "unpatriotic," claiming: "It refuses to rejoice in the country it inhabits. It repudiates the idea of a national identity, and the emotion of national pride."[6] However, just as liberals have learned not to cede family to the Right (but to redefine it), liberals now need to reembrace patriotism (and help ensure it does not turn into xenophobia and jingoism). Veterans should join with others to refurbish the national bonds that can contain and curtail polarization and enable the democratic polity to function again. One may view the fact that many of the most successful Democratic candidates in the 2018 election primaries were veterans as a sign that this approach has political legs.

Political Implications

To proceed, the patriotic movement needs to develop a political strategy that puts on one side the people, the public, the 99 percent; and on the other side the small elites, those with deep pockets, the special interest groups, the 1 percent. It differs from strategies that seek to build coalitions based on color or gender or age, or some combination of these, strategies that, by definition, leave out one or more major segments of the population. The patriotic movement should view all Americans as potential allies and not a priori write off anybody. This strategy does not prevent anyone from pursuing identity-specific agendas, but they should follow those through other associations. Just as the environmental movement does not deal with women's right to choose or absorb the missions of the ACLU, the patriotic movement should focus on issues directly tied to its missions and that speak potentially to most if not all members of society.

A Preliminary Platform

The patriotic movement's platform must rise from a national moral dialogue—and cannot, and should not, be forged by some public intellectual or a handful of them. I can imagine that such a platform would include the following:

The Patriotic Movement: A Platform

The Patriotic Movement is seeking to promote national unity and the common good.

As patriots, we love our country. We are not blind to its flaws but refuse to allow these to define who we are, as we dedicate ourselves to work for a "more perfect union."

We strongly favor candidates for public office who are committed to supporting the common good while they advocate for the special needs and interests of the various constituents or social groups they represent or speak for.

We are troubled by the polarization that prevents effective government. We hence strongly favor candidates for public office who do not consider working with the other party a betrayal, who do not demonize their opponents, and who compete fairly.

We strongly favor candidates who are seeking campaign finance reforms that limit the role of private money in public hands.

We are keen to protect our national sovereignty. We support multilateral and international institutions but only to the extent their policies do not harm my country's interests and do not violate its values.

(I use the phrase "strongly favor" to indicate that I realize that the extent to which a candidate is patriotic cannot be the only factor determining one's support. However, it should be a very major consideration.)

The Patriotic Movement is out to promote:

- A year of *national service* for all Americans. Initially, enrollment will be voluntary but encouraged by colleges and employers according special recognition to those who served, akin—but not equivalent—to the recognition awarded to veterans.
- *Teaching civics* in all public and private schools. These classes should be dedicated to introducing the next generation to the values we all share and the nation we cherish.
- *Welcome English.* Finding volunteers to teach new immigrants English. In the process volunteers would learn to know the immigrants personally, introduce immigrants to the values of their new homeland, and, in turn, learn about the contributions immigrants can make to the community.

- Conducting *local and national moral dialogues* on defining the common good and ways to advance it.

One may well ask, What is the position of the patriotic movement on inequality, the wars in the Middle East, and many other issues? Some of the answers can be derived from the principles already laid out; others will arise out of moral dialogues. However, one should not expect the patriotic movement to have a position on all issues. Thus one may draw on another organization if one is keen to promote animal rights or oppose gentrification and so on.

I further can imagine people creating a lapel pin composed of their nation's flag and a "P" imposed on it, an image they would carry as well on the cover of their laptops, notebooks, and T-shirts.

Patriotic Projects

Naturally, to a significant extent, the initial efforts of the patriotic movement will be focused, like other movements before it, on mobilizing support, finding members, and forming local chapters. At the same time, the movement will need to launch and nurture moral dialogues to develop its platform beyond the elementary planks outlined above that flow from the essence of the movement's nation-building purpose. The patriotic movement will be well served if it adds activities or projects for its members to engage in, above and beyond the "normal" ones of forming positions and promoting them through the political process through voting and lobbying.

One major candidate for such projects is to find volunteers to teach English to immigrant adults, many of whom experience great difficulties when they seek to find such classes. The greater the number of immigrants who learn English, and the more quickly they do so, the more they will find their way into society, and the easier it will be for current members of society to learn to know them. Moreover, the volunteers would "automatically" share American norms with their immigrant students. And the volunteers' personal relations with the immigrants would help the volunteers to see the immigrants as humans rather than viewing them in terms of the labels "foreign born" and "undocumented immigrants."

The same may be said about mentoring. Mentorship programs exist in many forms. Some of the most common include community members mentoring at-risk youth by providing educational support and life coaching, often through a structured program such as Big Brothers Big Sisters; university-level mentorship, where academic or professionals provide guidance and support for undergraduate or graduate students studying in the same field; peer-to-peer mentorships, where youth separated by only a few years cultivate a mentor-mentee relationship; sports mentorships, where an adult volunteers time and energy to coach youth and foster relationships with team members; and professional mentorships, where a mentor teaches a protégé the trade.

Studies consistently show that students in mentorship programs have fewer unexcused absences than students who are not in mentorship programs, have better attitudes toward school and education, and demonstrate a greater investment in their studies.[7] Undergraduate students receiving mentorship typically demonstrate higher educational attainment and are more likely to return to school the subsequent year.[8] Students in mentorship programs are less likely to abuse drugs and alcohol than their nonmentored peers.[9] Further, individuals who are career mentors are found to be more satisfied by their job, more committed to the organization, and have higher perceived career success than those who are not mentors.[10]

Civic Education: Essential but Woefully Inadequate

An important way to promote patriotism is to include it in the curriculum of school education on all levels, in a form of enriched, "thicker" civics education. True, civics education of any kind has never been paramount in the US. And it has been on the decline since the early 2000s, as growing pressure by parents and policy makers to teach "academics" has resulted in schools devoting more educational resources to math and sciences and cutting civics classes.[11] Currently, only nine states and the District of Columbia require a year of "government" or civics, while thirty-one require simply a half year of either.[12] Moreover, "many of the failures in civic education seem to originate from a disagreement regarding what a civics education should include."[13]

Further, many states focus on knowledge acquisition such as explaining the differences among the three branches of government, how bills become laws, and so on.[14] However, civics education typically does not teach students how to be a responsible citizen, to care about the common good, and to embrace the core values of the nation. Yascha Mounk holds that civics education should take a historical long view of both liberal democracy's successes as well as its injustices, writing, "One integral part of this education should be an account of the reasons why the principles of liberal democracy retain a special appeal."[15]

A still thicker conception is called for. Thick civic education should include the kinds of communitarian ideas that have long played a key role in the American faith, although at various periods have been neglected. E. J. Dionne Jr. sees American history as an "ongoing tension between two core values: our love of individualism and our reverence for community."[16] Dionne finds that all Americans hold these values to varying degrees and that what is now needed is a balance that accepts commitment to both individualism and community.[17] Indeed, communitarians have shown that the US tilted too far toward individualism following the Reagan era (and the Thatcher era in the UK), and hence the age requires a rededication to communal values.[18]

For all these reasons, the patriotic movement should promote the teaching of civics in all levels of school and college.

National Service: Voluntary and "Expected" for Now

Among the major efforts that can be undertaken to shore up the national community, national service is often mentioned. Its advocates hope that it will bring together people from different backgrounds and instill in them the value of service to the common good.[19] It is mandatory in some liberal democracies (such as Denmark and South Korea) and has strong supporters in countries where it is not.

Retired US Army general Stanley McChrystal supports a voluntary but socially expected "service year" where "young Americans from different income levels, races, ethnicities, political affiliations and religious beliefs could learn to work together to get things done."[20] Brookings Institution scholar Isabel V. Sawhill favors a universal national service that may not be mandatory but is socially encouraged. Sawhill says national service has strong bipartisan support: Republicans regard it as an obligation or responsibility of citizenship, and Democrats see the value in youth earning work experience.[21]

Having served myself, I have never doubted the merits of national service, both in terms of forming social bonds among people of different backgrounds and promoting patriotism. However, I was concerned about the high costs involved, and I feared that unless meaningful tasks could be found for those who serve, national service would not bring about an enhanced level of patriotism. However, Isabel Sawhill came up with an ingenious proposal, namely that those who serve be hosted in homes of people who volunteer to take care of them, the way many families do for foreign students. And having observed the Zivildienst in Germany, I have concluded that it is possible to make national service meaningful. I still hold that it would be best to start by making such service expected rather than mandatory, for instance, by asking applicants for work and candidates for public office if they had served. The patriotic movement should encourage its members—and all others—to serve and host, and treat those who served with the respect now accorded to veterans of just wars.

These are but a few examples of projects that patriotic movement members can undertake to combat growing polarization. They all create continual and meaningful relations among people from different backgrounds and engage in pro social activities.

Patriotism Meets Globalism

The patriotic movement will find itself challenged, opposed, and confronted by globalism. Given that this is a relatively new concept and often loosely defined, a few lines follow on what it entails. Globalism approaches issues from a postnational perspective, imagining or fighting for a world in which national values and bonds and hence borders matter much less than they mattered in earlier years. Indeed, some advocates of globalism call for overriding national loyalties altogether. A dictionary defines globalism as "the attitude or policy of placing the interests of the entire world above those of individual nations."[22] Greg Ip of the *Wall Street Journal* writes that globalism is a "mind-set that globalization is natural and good, that global governance should expand as national sovereignty contracts."[23]

A major globalist tenet is support of free trade policies that allow goods and services to flow across countries without regard for state borders. Another calls for open borders, allowing people to move freely from one nation to another. Still another promotes universal advancement of human rights. To the extent that human rights advocacy is not combined with a recognition of moral commitments to one's local and national community, this is an exemplary globalist position. Many public intellectuals, policy makers, and hundreds of millions of citizens subscribe to one or two of these positions but not necessarily to all of them. Globalists may be defined as those who subscribe to several of these positions.[24]

Anand Giridharadas points out that globalist ideology allowed corporations to pursue "a vision of globalization in which they owed nothing to any community." The ability to tap into global markets resulted in companies no longer acting with a sense of citizenship or loyalty to the nations in which they started. These corporations skirt the responsibility of serving the community that made them possible by moving their business across the globe to the location that allows them to maximize profits.[25] Dani Rodrik points out: "The reality is that we lack the domestic and global strategies to manage globalization's disruptions. As a result, we run the risk that the social costs will outweigh the narrow economic gains and spark an even worse globalization backlash."[26]

Globalists can draw on the works of some very highly respected and influential philosophers and public leaders. They can draw on Immanuel Kant, who hoped that eventually all states could order their polities on these principles and form a global political community. On Woodrow Wilson, who sought a world governed like a federal state.[27] And on Peter Singer, who suggests that the utilitarian maxim to seek the greatest happiness for the greatest number of people entails that we owe as much to children on the other side of the world as we owe to our own.

Globalists typically hold at least one of the following three positions: support for free trade; open or more-open borders; and recognition of universal human rights.

Free trade: Milton Friedman, a leading figure of the Chicago school of economics, exemplified globalist trade policy by asserting that "since Adam Smith there has been virtual unanimity among economists, whatever their ideological position on other issues, that international free trade is in the best interests of trading countries and of the world."[28] Think tanks such as the Adam Smith Institute in London explicitly state that they are "Globalist in outlook"[29] as they advance "free markets to create a richer, freer, happier world."[30]

Open borders: Several noted academics have proposed that state borders are inherently unjust and that people should be allowed to move more freely across them. The libertarian scholar Alex Tabarrok made a case for open borders to allow for the free movement of people on economic and moral grounds.[31] Joseph Carens has argued that borders should "generally be open" as there is a moral imperative to allow people from developing states to freely move to more developed states to gain access to a higher quality of life.[32] Jacob Hornberger writes, "Freedom entails the right to live your life any way you want, so long as your conduct is peaceful." Thus, "There is only one libertarian position on immigration, and that position is open immigration or open borders."[33]

Universal human rights: Organizations such as Human Rights Watch and Amnesty International give primacy to international human rights and humanitarian law over the laws of any particular state. Members of these organizations work to hold state officials and citizens to international law irrespective of whether a given country is a signatory to relevant human rights treaties.

Samuel Huntington coined the term "Davos Men" to describe globalist elites who "have little need for national loyalty, view national boundaries as obstacles that thankfully are vanishing, and see national governments as residues from the past whose only useful function is to facilitate the elite's global operations."[34] Jonathan Haidt proposes that the song "Imagine" by John Lennon serve as the anthem of globalists. Speaking of "Imagine," Haidt quips: "It is progressive in that it looks forward to a utopian future. It is anti-nationalist and anti-religious. It is, in essence, *anti-parochial.* Anything that divides people into separate groups or identities is bad; removing borders and divisions is good."[35] As globalist sentiments grow, "local ties weaken, parochialism becomes a dirty word, and people begin to think of their fellow human beings as fellow 'citizens of the world' (to quote candidate Barack Obama in Berlin in 2008)."[36] Theresa May may not be an outstanding prime minister, but she put it well when she stated: "Too many people in positions of power behave as though they have more in common with international elites than with the people down the road, the people they employ, the people they pass in the street. But if you believe you're a citizen of the world, you're a citizen of nowhere. You don't understand what the very word 'citizenship' means."[37]

Many who hold one or more globalist positions are willing to allow some qualifications, for instance, exempting farmers from free trade. Martha Nussbaum writes that the Stoics held that "we should give our first allegiance to no mere form of government, no temporal power, but to the moral community made up by the humanity of all human beings."[38] At the same time, she argues that while it is "permissible" to be concerned with local and national issues, being global is the best way to advance national goals. Nussbaum argues that nations should develop education systems that give special attention to the history and current affairs of their own country but teach children that—above all else— they are citizens of the world.[39]

Yuval Noah Harari thinks people are able to maintain nested loyalties, wherein loyalty to the global community does not diminish one's loyalty to the nation, community, or family.[40] As I see it, national and global commitments often come into conflict, for instance when international law and national laws point to different conclusions, and when people must choose between foreign aid and aid to the domestic poor. Harari commented: "In order to confront climate change, we need additional loyalties and commitments to a level beyond the nation. And that should not be impossible, because people can have several layers of loyalty. You can be loyal to your family and to your community and to your nation, so why can't you also be loyal to humankind as a whole? Of course, there are occasions when it becomes difficult, what to put first, but, you know, life is difficult. Handle it."[41] This flippant line ignores that there are major conflicts between the national level and the global one and that in order to combine them one needs difficult and complex deliberations on how to proceed. For instance, when national laws should take international laws into account and when to ignore or even flout them. Moreover, no one has yet found a way to develop loyalty for the global community akin to the loyalty many hundreds of millions of people feel for their nation.

Globalists tend to view nationalism as a dangerous anachronism. For instance, Jamie Mayerfeld argues that nationalism has the pernicious potential to transpose the darkest parts of human nature onto an extremely powerful entity and that those who identify with it often fail to perceive the violence they perpetrate: "Nationalism is dangerous because it encourages the unjust use of violence. The perpetrators may not see themselves as using violence unjustly. This is not a consolation, however; it is the heart of the problem. When we identify closely with the nation, we are predisposed to see it in a good light, and therefore have difficulty perceiving the injustice it commits."[42]

These globalist views fly in the face of often-cited communitarian studies that show that:

(a) Isolated individuals exhibit major psychological problems. James House, Karl Landis, and Debra Umberson, for instance, found that "more socially isolated or less socially integrated individuals are less healthy, psychologically and physically, and more likely to die."[43] John Cacioppo and Louise Hawkley demonstrated that perceived social isolation engenders a ripple of health risks, including depleted ability to cope with stressors, poor sleep, slower healing, hypertension, and so on.[44] The same researchers in a later review of the literature concluded that "loneliness is the social equivalent of physical pain, hunger, and thirst."[45] With the literature showing the serious health risks associated with social isolation, the UK has even decided to appoint a minister of loneliness.

(b) People are much more content in meaningful, lasting relationships than in isolation. A study across seventeen countries showed that married people, for example, report significantly higher levels of happiness than unmarried people.[46]

(c) People cut off from their social moorings are more likely to turn to hostile demagogues for meaning in a society that they believe has alienated them. Sociologists and critical theorists, including the proponents of "mass society theory" in the mid-twentieth century who built on earlier work by Émile Durkheim, have long held that an atomized citizenry of isolated individuals is more easily mobilized by extremist leaders.[47] Social media allows charismatic leaders to reach directly to the masses, whereas in the past such communications were largely mediated via the press and local leaders. The individual who is able to deliberate and make considered choices — the basis of both the democratic polity and free market economics — is found among people who feel emotionally secure. That is, if liberalism is to endure, people who have developed communitarian bonds are much more likely to have the temperament that demands than are those who lack such involvement. (Recall that we are dealing with a continuous variable. The reference is not to people who have versus those who do not have communitarian bonds, but to people who have more or less of such support.) In short, a liberal society assumes a communitarian foundation.

Many rest here. However, communitarian bonds provide people with much more:

(d) A core of shared values promoted by informal, noncoercive means. In other words, communities enable people to regulate each other and sort out a great deal of social business without recourse to the power of the state. Bans on smoking in select public places in recent decades, for instance, have resulted in very widespread compliance without the coercion of law enforcement.[48] The stronger the communitarian bonds, the less need for policing.[49] True, the bonds can become oppressive when they grow too strong; however, this is hardly the case in societies in which populism thrives. (Amy Gutmann has charged that communitarians want Salem but without witches, suggesting that bonds ipso facto go with oppression.[50] My answer up to a point is that firm social bonds minimize coercion, but like many other good things, they can become overpowering.)

(e) Nationalism is not dead or dying. On the contrary. Attempts to form more encompassing communities, like the European Union, are halting. For now at least, in many societies, especially in developed ones, the nation is a very powerful community, as evidenced by citizens' willingness to die to protect it. In an informal survey asking which layer of society people feel most connected to, David Brooks found only 5 percent of respondents felt most connected to humanity as a whole.[51] The French philosopher Ernest Renan elucidated the virtue of nationalism by describing the "essential conditions of being a people: having common glories in the past and a will to continue them in the present; having made great things together and wishing to make them again. One loves in proportion to the sacrifices that one has committed and the troubles that one has suffered."[52] I return below to the matter of how thick a community needs to be to counter centrifugal forces and what this entails.

(f) Globalists tend to vastly overestimate the capacity of deliberate social change. They, in effect, hold that even if it is true that people are keen to maintain their identity communities and sense of nationalism, these positions can be reformed through public policies. Hence the notion that the US could construct a liberal society in places such as Iraq and Afghanistan; promote human rights and democratic regimes in scores of other countries; and the thesis that free trade will bring with it a growing commitment to a liberal world order. The failure of these policies in the Middle East and Africa is obvious. The EU is losing support precisely because its commissioners assume that they can centralize decision-making in the EU capital and overcome national sentiments that oppose such changes. Actually the record shows that deliberate social change (i.e., social engineering) is very difficult even within one's own nation, as we see from the great difficulties of dealing with drug abuse, reducing inequality, curbing global warming, among other issues.

Far from preparing the ground for liberal regimes, attempts to over-come nationalism actually feed populism. Realistic responses to populism must accept identity communities and nations as given and seek to effect the values they embrace rather than ignore or seek to minimize these major sources of communitarian bonds.

Among the recent studies of the essential role of communitarian bonds, Amy Chua's *Political Tribes* stands out.[53] It is mostly dedicated to showing the high costs of public policies that ignore communities both overseas and within the US. Failing to understand, for instance, the tribal lines extant in Vietnam led American strategists to misjudge the contours of the conflict and to attempt to implement doomed-to-fail pro-capitalist reforms: "The group identity America offered the Vietnamese was membership in a puppet state—the ultimate affront in a country where many Vietnamese soldiers wore trinkets dedicated to the Trung sisters, symbolizing resistance to foreign invaders at all costs."[54]

More recently, Chua shows, American policy makers' poor understanding of the web of tribes in Iraqi society led to historic blunders in the region, especially following the 2003 invasion: "The Shias had a collective ax to grind, and the Sunni minority had every reason to resist and fear majority rule. Yet most of America's foreign policy makers, politicians, and thought leaders seemed to think that the Sunni-Shia divide was no big deal, repeatedly minimizing its significance."[55]

In contrast, Francis Fukuyama, in his *Identity: The Demand for Dignity and the Politics of Resentment* (2018), sees the loss of community as the source of much that ails us. People, he holds, have a profound need for recognition and respect (to which he gives a Greek name, *thymos,* defined by Fukuyama as "the seat of judgments of worth"). *Thymos* in turn is based on one's sense of identity and community. As we have lost these, we have been beset by alienation, populism, Brexit, and Trump.

Communitarian Bonds Are Primordial, but Differ Greatly in Their Normative Content

To reiterate, communitarian bonds are a force of nature; they can be re-shaped to some extent, but when they are ignored or attempts are made to eradicate them (as globalists are prone to do), such moves engender backlash, often in the form of populism.

If one grants that communities—on both the national and subnational levels—will continue to be a major source of essential communitarian bonds, it does not follow that we should ignore their illiberal tendencies. To cope with these tendencies, an essential distinction is needed. Communities have some built-in, hard-wired attributes that are widely considered negative from a normative viewpoint. The most important is that, by definition, they are exclusionary. Communities divide members from nonmembers and exclude the latter. Indeed, there is no community that opens its membership to one and all and sets no limits on its numbers. To seek elimination of communal boundaries entails elimination of communities per se. In short, borders must be tolerated.

In sharp contrast, one can seek to ensure that the bases for membership will not be discrimination against people who differ in color, religious or sexual orientation, and other such protected statuses. Communities can insist that all members' homes adhere to a given building style, respect resting periods, and thousands of other such considerations (as long as they do not serve as an indirect way to discriminate along the banned lines).

In effect, much of American national history, over the longer run, has moved in the direction of making the nation less illiberal. Thus, voting rights were first extended to non–property owners, then to women, then to African Americans, and to younger people. The civil rights movement has a long way to go to achieve its goals, but the US is less racist than it was in earlier generations.[56] In recent years, same-sex marriage was legalized. Most recently, moves have been taken to develop the rights of transgender people. The process of reform on the national level is a familiar one and needs no retelling here.[57] Making headway on liberal values does not imply that history is irreversible or without serious setbacks. One notes, first of all, though, that nations can move in the opposite direction (in contrast to Fukuyama), as we have seen in Poland, Hungary, Venezuela, and Turkey, among others.[58] And that the march of rights, combined with an expansion of free trade, automation, and immigration, can drive illiberal populism. Hence the patriotic movement needs to ensure progress in the face of continued efforts to reintroduce illiberal policies.

I turn next to ask what can be done to promote liberalism in conjunction with communitarian bonds—without engendering more populist pushback.

Liberal Bonds

More Durkheim

Before I review some suggestions for specific positions the patriotic movement may wish to consider, a general observation is called for. It concerns the relative importance of economic versus sociocultural responses to populism.[59] I write *relative* importance because clearly both responses are needed. Before the recent rising interest in populism, Benjamin M. Friedman showed that economic growth "more often than not fosters greater opportunity, tolerance of diversity, social mobility, commitment to fairness, and dedication to democracy," that is, economic factors are considered the main determining factor of social and political well-being.[60] Along similar lines, several analyses of populism are mainly economics-oriented, focusing on class rather than culture.[61] They see the fact that American workers' wages have largely stagnated since the 1970s, with the effects of the 2008 Great Recession, automation, and loss of jobs to other nations as the driving forces. Hence, their response is couched largely in terms of restoring jobs, improving wages and benefits, guaranteeing free college tuition, and so on.

This approach featured heavily during the 2016 presidential race in the rhetoric and platform of Senator Bernie Sanders, who vowed to take on a "rigged economy" and "the one percent." In his stump speech, Sanders called for increasing the minimum wage, making public colleges free of tuition, installing single-payer health care, and increasing taxes on wealthier Americans. While his campaign was themed on both "economic and social justice," the candidate notably said little about community or identity.

"In its early stages, the populist revolt appeared to be motivated by economics," commented William A. Galston. However, Galston points to larger forces at play: "This narrative was valid as far as it went. But a purely economic explanation obscures the more complex reality, which includes fears about immigration, concerns about culture, and frustration with politics itself."[62] Among those who focus on economic factors but who are fully cognizant of the importance of social and cultural factors, two works stand out. Paul Collier, in *The Future of Capitalism,* provides a valuable and imaginative attempt to bridge the economic and ethical, which leads him to the following suggestions: make corporate directors legally liable when they do not take into account the public interest in their decisions; tax people who benefit undeservedly from capitalism, such as the owners of land whose value rises for reasons that have nothing to do with their endeavors; and place a tax on every financial transaction.[63] And of special interest is Isabel Sawhill, who, in *The Forgotten Americans,* supports vocational training and adjustment assistance for workers left behind by the global economy; a broad-based tax credit to increase wages; the private sector improving its workforce training programs; and a social insurance system that supports education and family care, as well as retirement.[64]

Others note that workers who were believed to have voted for Trump because he promised to bring back the coal and steel industry stuck with him when his policies did not achieve much on these fronts. These workers felt that he represented their values in matters concerning immigration, cultural issues (e.g., transgender bathrooms), and nationalism.[65]

Poland's recent history reveals the same interplay of sociocultural anxiety and populist politics. According to Jordan Kyle and Yascha Mounk, Poles succeeded in tamping down a populist near-takeover in the early 2000s only to re-create the conditions for another rise: "For eight years, Poland went back to being relatively stable. Thanks to a highly competent government, the country barely suffered during the Great Recession. But many voters were frustrated with the prominent role that some former communists continued to play, afraid of rapid cultural change in a country long dominated by Catholicism and livid at a series of corruption scandals."[66]

In short, those who believe that populism is mainly driven by economic deprivation ought to pay more mind to the challenges to communitarian bonds and values engendered by globalism, mass immigration, and culture wars. It follows that an effective response to populism must include major communitarian elements, the kind of factors Émile Durkheim flagged, addressing social, cultural, and normative deficits rather than focusing solely on economic considerations.

Community Building Lite

There is merit in fully recognizing the value of communitarian bonds; however, this understanding alone cannot bring about the kinds of Durkheimian changes that are needed. Proclamations of national unity, often vague if well-intentioned, were President Obama's stock-in-trade. At the 2004 Democratic National Convention, then senator Obama famously declared: "There's not a liberal America and a conservative

America; there's the United States of America. There's not a black America and white America and Latino America and Asian America; there's the United States of America."[67] Such worthy sentiments need to be backed up with richer narratives and related policies in order to be effective.

Amy Chua suggests that the first step to reestablishing a unified American identity is for individuals to come to know each other personally, to engage each other, across tribal divides. To support this idea she refers to Gordon W. Allport's 1954 work *The Nature of Prejudice,* which theorized that face-to-face interactions between members of in-groups and out-groups could reduce mutual prejudice.[68] Yet a few pages later, Chua herself acknowledges that "merely putting members of different groups in the same space is not enough and indeed can aggravate political tribalism."[69] Chua is correct—prejudice is multicausal, and even Allport's contact theory proposed that a significant reduction of prejudice would occur only under conditions that were strict and hard to attain.

Furthermore, we learned that even when people of different backgrounds are placed in the same environment, they tend to interact with each other sparingly.[70] In any case, it is difficult to imagine millions of members of liberal communities going out for dinner and drinks with coal miners or steelworkers, or millions of Trump supporters "engaging" with one kind of progressive people or another. It is heartwarming when it happens; one finds instances of such dialogues, some of which even lead to increased mutual understanding and tolerance. However, they are few and far between and cannot begin to carry the burdens that must be shouldered.

Chua adds that one of the US's greatest achievements was to build a "super group" in the form of a national identity that is not mono-ethnic, resulting in a nation that has been able to accommodate and embrace a variety of ethnic communities.[71] She points out that much of super groupness is being lost, as we now face white mono-ethnic movements, egged on by leftist identity groups: "But white identity politics has also gotten a tremendous recent boost from the Left, whose relentless berating, shaming, and bullying might have done more damage than good."[72] In response, she calls for restoring the super group. "It's not enough that we view one another as fellow human beings," she writes; "we need to view one another as fellow Americans. And for that we need to collectively find a national identity capacious enough to resonate with, and hold together as one people, Americans of all sorts—old and young, immigrant and native born, urban and rural, descendants of slaves as well as descendants of slave owners."[73] She wonders if the moment is ripe for such a reconstruction of America as a super group but offers no way this might be achieved.

Democracy Per Se Is Too Thin

Mark Lilla argues that progressives should dispense with identity politics and instead secure power by appealing to a sense of citizenship. According to Lilla, today's identity politics are the product of the excessive individualism of the Reagan era (or a shift "From We to Me," to use his words).[74] And, while the civil rights movement pushed solidarity, sacrifice, and a call for Americans to live up to their founding principles— particularly, "all men are created equal"—Black Lives Matter, Lilla says, appeals to group difference, outrage, and calls for a societal indictment.[75]

Lilla holds that one ought to recognize that we have a duty to fellow citizens and that our destinies are intertwined. This recognition is particularly important as America moves toward its inevitable status as a majority-minority state. That is, "because America has become more diverse and individualistic in reality, there is greater, not less, need to cultivate political fellow feeling."[76] In other words, the more diverse we become, the more citizenship seems the sole potential source of solidarity.

The idea needs to be unpacked. Lilla stresses the importance of what he calls democratic citizenship—the notion that we are all political equals and should be treated as such—which is a sound idea. However, politics are mainly not processes through which three hundred million-plus individual choices—all equally weighted—can be harmonized to form public policies. They are, to a large extent, a give-and-take among *groups* of citizens who have different values and interests and seek common ground. Voters come, to a large extent, in packages called communities. In other words, in a pluralistic, diverse society, one cannot ignore group differences in politics—but one can ensure (*a*) that they are not radicalized to the point that parties refuse to compromise and negotiate, and (*b*) that they are contained by a core of shared values. Democratic citizenship, to the extent that it treats people as atomized individuals, is one of the forces driving populism rather than its antidote.

To his credit, however, Lilla views citizens not only as voters and the bearers of rights but also as people who have duties to serve each other and the common good. This observation suggests that we need a much more profound sense of civility than can be achieved by promoting citizen education, political awareness and participation, and mutual tolerance.[77] What is needed in addition are shared understandings of what these duties entail and what core values they draw on.

Yascha Mounk recognizes that the post–Cold War momentum toward supranational institutions and identities is failing and that renascent nationalism is rippling throughout the international system. "Institutions like the European Union," he writes, "are on the back foot."[78] According to Mounk, liberals today act futilely when they try to reject or transcend nationalism. He notes that liberals/progressives view nationalism as inherently suspect and have abdicated their role in constructing their nation's identity. Instead, he argues that liberals ought to reclaim nationalism: "To win the fight for an inclusive form of patriotism, countries will have to do much more to facilitate a real sense of community among all citizens and ease lingering fears about future migration."[79] So far, so good.

Mounk's suggestions regarding what can be done start from a similar point as those of Lilla. In fact, both thinkers point to President Obama's 2015 speech on the fiftieth anniversary of the march from Selma to Montgomery: "What greater expression of faith in the American experiment than this, what greater form of patriotism is there, than the belief that America is not yet finished, that we are strong enough to be self-critical, that each successive generation can look upon our imperfections and decide that it is in our power to remake this nation to more closely align with our highest ideals?"[80]

The question, though, is, What is going to be the normative content of the "good" nationalism (sometimes referred to as patriotism)? And how can it also speak to the communitarian needs of those now driven to populism and "bad" nationalism? In Mounk's view, one ought to make nationalism as inclusive as possible. The first step he proposes is to monitor and reduce discrimination to the fullest possible extent, especially through reforms in education. By the same token, Mounk argues that nations cannot afford exemptions on cultural grounds to practices like domestic violence and female genital mutilation. Mounk goes on to propose practical policy fixes in the areas of taxes, housing, jobs, and social security.[81] Although these all may be sound liberal ideas, they need a communitarian underpinning that these policies cannot provide.

For a Thick Patriotism

To curb populism and polarization, to enable democracy to function effectively, commitments to the overarching community—the nation—must be strong enough so that when they come into conflict with commitments to subnational communities, the national commitments will take precedence. This is in contrast to the view that these subnational communities are disappearing or can be kept out of politics, the ending of identity politics.

Much has been written about the need to ensure that nationalism will not be aggressive. More needs to be said about how to make its bonds sufficiently potent in those countries in which the national community was never strong or commitments to it have weakened unduly. I turn next to outline key elements needed for such community building:

(*a*) Communities find meaning, and public policies and regimes find legitimation, in *historical narratives*. These must, in the main, be affirmative, a source of pride, an account with which one wishes to be identified. There is no need to whitewash darker periods, but they cannot dominate the narrative. For example, one can retell the story of slavery but focus on the great sacrifices the nation made to end it rather than dwelling mainly on the shame of introducing it in the first place. One can point to the progress made since 1865 for the rights of African Americans while acknowledging that the effects of slavery still linger and need to be countered. In contrast, arguing that little progress has been made and that racism has mainly changed only its form will not do. The same holds for other darker parts of the shared history, for instance the treatment of Native Americans, Japanese Americans, or women.

(*b*) Communities do best when they have a *core of shared values, a sense of shared destiny and purpose.* While initially major segments of the American public were quite reluctant to join the fight in World War II, once the US did, many saw a compelling virtue in fighting fascism. The US saw itself as championing liberty against tyranny. After the war was won, the US prided itself in turning two enemies, Japan and Germany, into flourishing democracies and allies. The US soon embraced the virtue in fighting communism during the Cold War. And following the Cold War, it saw itself as bringing democracy to the rest of the world.[82] Since 1990, however, these narratives have lost their power. Democracy is in retreat in many countries. Russia and China are asserting themselves. Many have come to fear the challenge of terrorism. Restoring a sense of purpose is now called for. There is nothing wrong with seeking to make America great again. The question is, How does one define greatness?

(c) *An America that works for everyone.* No one public intellectual—or even a conclave—can develop a compelling new vision of America that will be both liberal and sufficiently communitarian to guide the forces that are out to arrest populism and launch a period *of reconstruction* of the institutions, norms, and bonds that populism has undermined, and in the process provide the conditions needed for restoring the guardrails of a liberal democracy. However, one can help nurture the dialogue about such a vision by sketching what its main contours might look like. Because currently, to Americans who see themselves as besieged minorities—including working-class whites—a vision of America as a *fair society,* in which nobody faces discrimination and everyone gains their due share, may have wide appeal.

It first of all entails that everyone will be treated with respect, that nobody is written off as deplorable or ignorant or "undereducated." It entails that everyone who seeks work should be able to find a job and that workers in all types of employment situations, including independent contractors and part-time employees, be provided with benefits.[83] Menial labor should be accorded the same standing as white-collar and knowledge work. (A movement in this direction is California's rebranding campaign to eliminate stigma from technical education programs and career options.)[84] Health insurance should be available to all. Expanding earned income tax credits should ensure everyone has the income needed to obtain basic creature comforts.

(d) *Shoring up a community of communities.* As far as subnational communities are concerned, there is no way to keep them out of public life, and their proper involvement is part of a legitimate democratic process. Armenian Americans can quite legitimately call on the US government to declare the Turkish massacre in Armenia to have been genocide. Irish Americans can favor independence for Northern Ireland. Jews and evangelicals can support Israel and so on. Issues arise only when these secondary loyalties conflict with the primary one, to the US as the nation. This issue was raised when Catholic candidates were running for public office and critics claimed that they would take their lead from the pope, and when leftist candidates were held to take their lead from Moscow. Some suggested that Latinos would not have to fight if the US were to engage in a war in Latin America. However, as long as those involved show that the nation will trump when their particularistic concerns come into conflict with national loyalties, ethnic identities can be part of "normal" public life.

The trouble with some of the more extreme forms of identity communities is that they see the primary loyalty to their group and not to the encompassing society—the nation. In the most extreme forms, some groups on the right, as well as Antifa, do not even support peaceful resolution of differences and legitimate use of violence against their opponents. And they view all compromises as treason. These radical forms of identity need to be curbed, but not identity politics per se.

(e) *The importance of the third sector.* For many decades, much of the public debate about policies in the US and in other Western nations has focused on the relative role of the government versus that of the private sector. In the process one often loses sight of the importance of the third sector, which includes hundreds of thousands of not-for-profit corporations, ethnic, religious, racial, and professional associations, voluntary associations, and communities. These bodies often provide the highest-ranked social, cultural, health, and elder care services. Expanding the third sector—instead of more privatization or government expansion—will make society more communitarian.

To proceed, communities should be allowed to keep the institutions around which their social life tends to center, such as a local school, public library, or post office, even if consolidating these into regional institutions is less costly. Urban design can facilitate community building by carving out public spaces in parks, promenades, and pedestrian zones, among others.

(f) *The driving force.* New visions and public policies need a social force behind them. Otherwise they are like a shiny new car without an engine. Lilla's and Mounk's books are basically aimed at the center wing of the Democratic Party. For the sake of emphasis, let me repeat that, as I see it, there is only one "driver" strong enough to carry the massive changes in culture and society and politics that are needed, the same kind of driver that led to major social changes in the past: a social movement. Major changes did not come about because one party or another formulated a new platform and lined up voters to support it. They came about as a result of social movements such as the civil rights, environmental, women's rights, and LGBT rights movements. What is needed now is a new social movement that will seek to bring about an America that works for everyone. Call it the patriot movement.

The Model of Marital Conflict

The restoration of shared bonds and core values, a major priority if not *the* priority of the patriotic movement, is the ultimate social foundation that allows democratic politics to work. This cardinal mission, to reiterate, entails neither suppressing differences in the name of gaining harmony, nor the end of identity politics. It merely requires that various politically active groups vie with each other to influence public policies and allocation of resources in line with their values and interests, and compete in ways that maintain the union and commitments to the common good.

I refer to this kind of competition as the "marital conflict model" because couples that stay together seem to not experience conflict at significantly different rates than those who break up but rather they fight in different ways. The couples that endure are those that fight with one hand tied behind their back, so to speak. The wife may want her husband to do more household chores, or a husband may want to cut back work and spend more time on his hobbies—or the other way around—but both seek to resolve such differences in ways that keep the marriage going rather than threatening it. The same must hold true for various political and social groups that vie for the power to advance their particular agendas in democratic nations.

In part, the marital conflict model is achieved by following *rules of engagement*. These involve not "demonizing" one another, attacking the issue but not the person, treating all with elementary respect, searching for a third option when two sides are dug in, and not treating compromises as betrayals or violations of principles. Nebraska senator Ben Sasse has added that addressing complex issues "require[s] vigorous debate. And we should always worry that calls for civility can be reduced to a demand to accept the status quo, which tends simply to favor those with status. But again, my point is that even as we debate these contentious issues passionately, we have to maintain the republic that allows us to do so. And so *even* on these absolutely essential issues, we must approach our opponents in these debates as people created with dignity—and we must demand that both we and they dig in as sincere, fellow countrymen rather than as enemies to be trolled."[85]

Attempts to delegitimize President Obama by claiming that he was not American-born; McConnell blocking a Senate vote on President

Obama's Supreme Court nominee Merrick Garland; John Boehner, when discussing Obama's agenda, declaring, "We're going to do everything—and I mean everything we can do—to kill it, stop it, slow it down, whatever we can"; and Democrats trying to find out what videotapes Robert Bork rented during his Supreme Court hearing to smear him are all examples of kinds of conflicts incompatible with the marital conflict model. The model assumes that people will fight fairly.

A key example of fighting unfairly is the gerrymandering of congressional districts. Both parties are guilty of the tactic. The patriotic movement should support those who call for districts to be drawn by nonpartisan commissions.

The Senate used to follow many of the elements of the marital conflict model. Norman Ornstein and Thomas E. Mann note:

> Senators were intensely loyal to the Senate as an institution; they identified first as senators rather than as partisans or through their ideology, and they were fiercely protective of their prerogatives vis-à-vis the president or the House of Representatives. The rules and procedures of the Senate were a key to its unique role as the world's greatest deliberative body; and even those who were frustrated by them and by their application, especially when an intense minority thwarted the will of the majority, were respectful of their centrality to the Senate itself.[86]

Members of each chamber crossed the aisle to find common ground on pressing issues—such as ensuring equal rights through the Civil Rights Act of 1964—to uphold the norms of their institution, placing country over party. The patriotic movement seeks to restore such a "club" not only in the Senate but in the nation.

Trust is essential. It is slowly built when different sides live up to commitments they made to each other, and it is undermined when such understandings are betrayed. Trust is like capital; one can accumulate it and be richer for it, or squander it and be left high and dry. John Gottman and Nan Silver offer insight from marital relations on how to overcome gridlock and find common ground. They advise that competing sides each create two circles, one containing their core, non-negotiable principles and the other including their positions that are more flexible. Gottman and Silver say the first circle should be small, while the second is more expansive. By clarifying core and flexible positions, the two opposing sides can conduct meaningful negotiations that provide room for compromise.[87]

To move forward, we now need, first on the local level, new social formations—chapters of a patriotic movement yet to be fashioned—that will include people of different political persuasions, backgrounds, and parties all committed to consenting and advancing the common good.[88] This position stands in sharp contrast to those who call for the formation of third parties or centrist parties. These are by definition fragments, which provide one more division when what is called for is finding a common ground. This position is also in sharp contrast to those who argue that we shall not find a common ground until either the Left ideology or that of the Right prevails and becomes the common ground. As the distinguished historian Michael Kazin put it, "Until the left or the right wins a lasting victory, America will remain a society rent in two."[89]

What is called for is society coming together under a "big tent." The term is often used to refer to making a particular political party more inclusive; I use it to refer to an even bigger tent, one that will include people from different parties and independents. As noted by President Obama after securing a second presidential term: "By itself, the recognition that we have common hopes and dreams won't end all the gridlock, resolve all our problems or substitute for the painstaking work of building consensus and making the difficult compromises needed to move this country forward. But that common bond is where we must begin."[90]

The marital model assumes that all parties seek to maintain the union. It cannot succeed if one of the parties is willing to risk a breakup, say, if he or she threatens divorce whenever the other side does not yield. In such a marriage one does best to attempt to get the uncooperative party to restore its commitment to the union, but if this fails, all bets are off. The model, however, does not call for one party to keep making concessions in a desperate attempt to keep the union going in the face of such obstruction.

What Makes a Great America?

Age-old debates about patriotism and what constitutes a good American have taken on a new significance in the Trump era. Trump's rhetoric often draws heavily on respect for the nation and its symbolic expressions, such as the flag and the national anthem. He points to athletes taking a knee while the national anthem is played as an act of disloyalty and proudly defines himself as a nationalist.

Many Democrats, especially in the left wing of the party, view the very concept of a "nationalist" as being associated with white supremacy and xenophobia. In a seminal essay in the *New York Times,* Trip Gabriel describes how the Democrats' view of patriotism is different from that of the GOP.[91] Gabriel finds that Democrats do not consider dissent as unpatriotic but, rather, as the essence of patriotism. During his Senate campaign, Beto O'Rourke declared: "I can think of nothing more American" than protesting. James Baldwin is quoted as saying, "I love America more than any other country in the world and, exactly for this reason, I insist on the right to criticize her perpetually."

The right to differ—to disagree—is indeed very American. However, when it is regarded as the essence of patriotism, one overlooks that the foremost meaning of patriotism is love of country. *There is a world of difference between showing appreciation for the nation while seeking to cure its flaws and considering the nation to be deeply flawed.* Thus, to view America as a racist society dominated by white supremacists is not to dissent but to question the very nature of the American enterprise—its basic goodness. That is quite a different perspective from the one that holds America to be a "shining city upon a hill" that has developed some serious difficulties that urgently need to be remedied.

A telling example is the attitude toward the military. To argue that the military must be subject to civilian control, that the president should not go to war (or more precisely, continue to fight) without authority from Congress, and that the military should not discriminate against people based on sexual orientation can be readily reconciled with patriotism if one acknowledges that one is proud of the millions of young men and women who are risking their lives to keep us safe. However, if one views the military with suspicion and refuses to collaborate with it and considers working on security issues as unpatriotic (as many of the employees of high-tech firms do), one crosses a line.

One can cherish the right to dissent, including the notion that burning the flag is a constitutionally protected expression of free speech. However, one must also note that if people seek to dissent while acknowledging their basic loyalty to the country, they must recognize that there are some symbols that express such loyalty and hence draw on the numerous other ways to protest rather than assaulting the already weakened expressions of national unity.

A similar distinction arises when one finds that many Democrats view pluralism and diversity as major elements of patriotism. Gabriel quotes a Democrat who gives voice to this viewpoint when she says, "I feel very patriotic that I want this country to get back to . . . a place of being who we truly are, which is a very diverse, very eclectic, beautiful mix of all kinds of people."

While it is true that the US is a nation of immigrants and that diversity makes us better in many ways, the essence of American society has always been that diversity must be contained within a framework of unity. Thus, it is fine for Americans to express special concerns for the countries from which they, or their parents, immigrated—as long as their primary loyalty is to the US. And it is fine for Americans to seek more equality for people of different ethnic and racial backgrounds, incomes, and sexual orientations, but not to deny the significant progress America has made, on all these fronts, one generation after the other.

In short, just as the GOP version of patriotism is truncated because it tends to view dissent as unpatriotic and diversity as undermining unity, the version of patriotism championed by many Democrats—especially in the left wing of the party—is flawed. It views the nation as basically defective, a nation that needs to be transformed rather than reformed. Oddly, combining the two visions may provide a sound concept of patriotism: love of country with tolerance for a critical but loyal opposition; diversity bounded by a core of shared values and a sense of community.

In Conclusion

Globalists contribute to populism when they ignore or seek to override communal bonds both on the national and subnational level. True, communities can foster values many find morally troubling. Hence these values need to be examined. Some are relatively benign and ineradicable and can be tolerated as a price one pays for securing communitarian bonds and for curbing populism—for instance, the tendency of communities to view themselves in a positive light and to view others less favorably. Other attributes—racial, gender, or religious discrimination, for example—ought to and can be curbed by public education and law enforcement.

The same holds for nationalism. The fact that many see their nation as exceptional and cast other nations in a less favorable light can be tolerated. The same is not true about aggressive policies. Ensuring that patriotism does not turn into aggressive nationalism entails more than the promotion of individual rights and democratic designs; it includes providing the communitarian underpinnings patriotism requires. These underpinnings include a shared history, a shared vision and a core of shared values, a well-developed third sector, and a community of communities. We have seen that the main engine that could drive such a movement for a good society (a liberal communitarian one)[92] is a social movement, not a political party.

3
TOPICS FOR NATIONAL DIALOGUES: TRADE, IMMIGRATION, RIGHTS

The discussion so far has focused on processes (national moral dialogues) and social formations (local and national communities, social movements) rather than on the content of the core values of a patriotic movement. This focus was called for because I hold that the new core of shared values will have to arise from intensive moral dialogues. However, one can discern a fair number of issues that are ready for a new shared understanding. Some concern areas in which there can be a policy consensus even among people and communities who subscribe to rather different values. This chapter covers three such areas: trade, immigration, and the balance between individual rights and communal obligations.

Countering Globalists

Many political commentators have characterized the 2016 US presidential election as a contest between enlightened, rational, cosmopolitan globalists and prejudiced, parochial, know-nothing nationalists. (The same perspective has been applied to Brexit.) Globalists articulate three main reasons why we ought to see nationalism as xenophobia: nationalists oppose global free trade in order to protect their own country's economy; they oppose immigration—especially immigration from cultures with different values—to safeguard their sense of national identity; and they oppose universal human rights in the name of national exceptionalism and sovereignty.

The self-congratulatory tone of many globalists is illustrated by an August 2016 *New Yorker* article by Pankaj Mishra, which appeared under the title "How Rousseau Predicted Trump." Mishra sees in Trump's America—and in Europe, India, and Russia—whole countries that "seethe with demagogic assertions of ethnic, religious, and national identity." These movements threaten "the great eighteenth-century venture of a universal civilization harmonized by rational self-interest, commerce, luxury, arts, and science." Nationalists reject the wisdom of the great thinkers of the Enlightenment, Mishra writes, and instead follow in the wake of Jean-Jacques Rousseau, whom Isaiah Berlin once called "the greatest militant lowbrow in history."[1]

During the campaign, much less attention was paid to the communitarian views that Hillary Clinton extolled in her 1996 book *It Takes a Village,* which pointed out that to raise children well (and to do well in the moral sense), all community members must bear responsibility for one another's well-being. The thesis that every citizen has not only rights but also responsibilities is a communitarian keystone. True, her vision of community is hardly one that nationalists hanker for; still, it is a good starting point for a better understanding of what globalists miss.

As I see it, the rise of right-wing populism in the US and Europe can be attributed to no small extent to the profound misunderstanding globalists have of community and communitarian values. Globalists tend to view society as composed of freestanding individuals, each of whom has his or her own individual rights and is keen to pursue his or her own self-interest. As a result, globalists assume that, given the proper information, their fellow citizens will see that their aging societies are refreshed by immigration, that free trade raises the standard of living for everyone, and that individual rights outweigh tribalism.

The trouble with this view of society is less in what it claims and more in what it leaves out: namely, that people are social creatures whose flourishing and psychological well-being depend on strong, lasting, meaningful relationships with others and on the sharing of moral and social values. These relationships and values are found in national and subnational communities (including families, which are microcommunities). By definition, communities are circumscribed rather than all-inclusive and are inevitably parochial rather than global.

If a major goal of the patriotic movement is to reduce right-wing populism, violence, prejudice, and xenophobia, then communities must be nurtured, a goal that cannot be advanced by denigrating parochialism. Rather, globalists must understand that parochialism—an attribute of all communities—can be reconfigured in terms of its content but cannot, and should not, be eliminated.

The miscomprehensions of today's globalists are reminiscent of how Enlightenment thinkers such as David Hume viewed religion, and how quite a few rationalists still do.[2] In the eighteenth century, some thinkers placed religion in the same category as witchcraft and black magic, reducing it to a set of traditional values that made people act irrationally and held back the progress of humanity. David Hume wrote in *The Natural History of Religion* in 1757 that "the primary religion of mankind arises chiefly from an anxious fear of future events; and what ideas will naturally be entertained of invisible, unknown powers, while men lie under dismal apprehensions of any kind, may easily be conceived."[3] Most of us have learned that people have a profound need to grant meaning to parts of life that science—and more broadly, reason alone—cannot address: What is the purpose of life? Why are we born to die? What is it that we owe one another? Religion provides an answer to these questions. Enlightenment thinking does not and is not about to replace religion.[4]

On the contrary, religion is thriving around the world, even in places like Russia and China. After decades of suppression by the former Soviet government, the church is resurgent in Russia. In 2014, 72 percent of Russians identified as Orthodox Christian, up from 31 percent when the Soviet Union disbanded in 1991.[5] In China, the number of Protestants alone has grown by 10 percent per year since 1979, and China may well soon have a larger Christian population than any other country in the world.[6] In Latin America and Africa, the Catholic and Anglican churches are being challenged not so much by secularism as by the rise of evangelical and Pentecostal churches.[7] Polling indicates that a majority of Muslims in many countries would like to see Islam—and, specifically, Islamic law—play a still greater role in their lives.[8] And religion continues to hold a significant place in the lives of scores of millions of Americans and Europeans.

The Communal Costs of Free Trade

Free trade, according to Robert Bartley, is a panacea. He claims that "economic interdependence will not only avoid major wars but forge a new world civilization based on political democracy and open markets, a world of political and economic freedom."[9] Prominent publications such as the *Wall Street Journal* and the *Economist* extol globalist economic principles, favoring what they deem an inevitable push to a "flat" global economy through ever-reducing barriers to trade. Public support appears to be in their favor, as a global Pew survey found 81 percent of respondents in favor of trade.[10]

When globalists champion free trade, they tend to ignore the "externalities." The fact is that many developing nations can produce cheap goods because they pay little attention to the welfare of their workers or to the environmental consequences of mass production. Trade agreements are supposed to curb these social costs and help workers in countries that pay higher wages to compete with workers in countries that do not, but such curbs have only limited effect. True, free trade lowers the costs of consumer products at Walmart and Target, but how does that help people whose jobs are outsourced? Promises to retrain them and find them other jobs—for instance, to make computer programmers out of coal miners—are often unrealistic. (Thomas L. Friedman of the *New York Times*, Robert J. Samuelson of the *Washington Post*, and writers in the *Economist* all argue that job losses are more attributable to technological developments than to free trade. But this is like saying you should not mind being kicked in the stomach because you hurt more when being hit over the head.)

Above all, globalists ignore the effects of free trade on people's essential communitarian needs. Economists often fail to understand people who are reluctant to move from, say, West Virginia to Montana when the coal industry is declining but the gas industry is growing. These globalists do not sufficiently consider that people lose their communal bonds when they make such moves. People leave behind the friends they can call on when they are sick or grieving or would like to share new joys—and the places where their elders are buried. Their children miss their friends, and everyone in the family feels ripped away from the centers of their social lives: school, church, social club, union hall, or American Legion post. And when these people finally bring their families along and form new communities, changes in free trade often force them to move again. Thus, after a boom in Montana, prices of oil and gas have fallen, and so many of the workers who moved there now need to relocate again. A reliable evaluation of the benefits of free trade should take into account the destructive effects that churning the labor force can have on communities. The patriotic movement should at least show that it feels the pain of the casualties of free trade and offer realistic means to deal with it rather than denigrate the victims of free trade and view them as redneck boors who just do not get it.

Paying mind to the social costs of increased transnational trade does not mean that nations should stop trading with one another; rather, it means that those who worried about the social effects of new trade treaties are not know-nothing, parochial nationalists but, rather, are people with valid concerns. It means that making trade deals fairer to workers in developed nations is a reasonable demand and that one has to invest much more in finding out what can be done for those who lost jobs due to trade and technology and cannot find new jobs or can find only jobs that pay poorly and provide few benefits, if any—for instance by securing a basic income or providing work in a publicly financed conservation or infrastructure corps.

The Communal Effects of Immigration

Globalists favor the free movement of people across national borders. Scholars such as Alex Tabarrok have made the economic and moral case for borders to be eradicated completely.[11] They strongly support the Schengen Agreement, which removed border controls among many members of the European Union. They cheered Angela Merkel, the German chancellor, for welcoming millions of immigrants to Germany. And they view Trump's call for building a wall on the Mexican border and restriction on immigration from Muslim countries as typical right-wing, xenophobic, reactionary policies.

In contrast, the social psychologist Jonathan Haidt views mass immigration as the trigger that set off the authoritarian impulses of many people in many nations. He concludes that it is possible to have moderate levels of immigration from "morally different ethnic groups"—so long as immigrants are capable of assimilation into the host culture—but that high levels of diverse immigration groups without adequate assimilation are likely to cause an authoritarian backlash. Haidt suggests that immigration policies ought to take into account three factors: the percentage of foreign-born residents at any given time; the degree of moral difference between the incoming group and the members of the host society; and the extent to which assimilation is being achieved by each group's children. Globalists do not approve of this approach.[12]

American patriots may well favor a path to citizenship for millions of undocumented immigrants. However, they should also pay better attention to the further acculturation of this large group than many globalists do. Adding a sizable number of people to a society, especially if many are culturally distinct from current members, is very likely to engender social tensions. The answer is not to draw up the bridges or build walls but to adopt realistic sociological strategies for absorbing immigrants into their new, host communities.

One such strategy I call "Diversity within Unity," which can help lower social tensions in countries that accept relatively large numbers of immigrants by welcoming diversity without requiring full assimilation. (This strategy is explored in chapter 8.) The US has in effect followed this policy, with surprising success, compared with the more assimilationist European nations, as well as Japan and South Korea.

Assimilation, in its strongest form, requires that immigrants abandon their distinct cultures, values, habits, and connections to their country of origin in order to integrate fully into their new country. France stands out as an archetype of this approach. In contrast, Diversity within Unity is a combination of partial assimilation and a high level of tolerance for differences. It presumes that all members of a given society will respect and adhere to certain core values and institutions that form the basic shared framework of the society (this is the *unity* component). At the same time, every group in society, including the majority, is free to maintain its distinct subculture—those policies, habits, and institutions that do not conflict with the shared core (this is the *diversity* component). Respect for the whole and respect for all are essential to this approach; when these two come into conflict, then respect for the national community (which itself may change over time) is to take precedence.

Among the core values are adherence to the law, acceptance of democratic processes to resolve differences and create public policy, and belief in civility in dealing with others. Religion, a core value for many European societies, need not be a tenet of unity. However, a measure of patriotism should be expected, especially when loyalty to the new, host nation clashes with commitments to the nation of origin. (Thus, if the US were to go to war with another country, our immigrants from that country would be required to support our effort.) Under Diversity within Unity, all immigrants are expected to learn the national language but are welcome to keep their own and speak it with their children as a secondary language. Immigrants can celebrate their own holidays (Chinese New Year, say) but are expected to participate in the national ones, such as the Fourth of July.

Nobody can decide exactly where to draw the line between the elements of unity and those of diversity, and the line shifts as historical conditions change. However, the main sociological design remains: allowing immigrants and minorities to keep intact their immediate communities— often ethnic ones—in places like Chinatown, Spanish Harlem, Little Havana, and numerous American suburbs—while maintaining their membership in the national community.

Even a global community, if one can be forged, would have to be constructed on top of local, regional, and national communities, rather than replacing them and forming a single community to encompass more than seven billion individuals, each with individual rights but with no particularistic social bonds and set of values. Thus, universalism and parochialism can be combined, but attempts to maximize either position are sure to lead to deeply troubling, socially disturbing consequences.

Reconciling Rights and Community

The greatest social and philosophical challenges for members of the patriotic movement arise from situations in which their passion for human and individual rights clashes with their understanding of communitarian values. However, there are ways to reduce the tensions between these two core elements of a good society.

Globalists hold that all human beings are created equal, that people living in Kansas City and in Kandahar are essentially the same, and that they are all entitled to the full measure of individual rights as spelled out in the UN's Universal Declaration of Human Rights. Some globalists favor using force to prevent large-scale violations of human rights, under a United Nations precept called the Responsibility to Protect, and to establish liberal democratic regimes in those nations that do not rush to the light—a strategy referred to as regime change. These globalists view local communities (in particular, gated ones) as discriminatory if not racist. And they hold that people who have a hard time accepting gay marriage and the march toward equal rights for women and minorities are longing for a Norman Rockwell vision of America that never existed or was hopelessly prejudiced.

One would do well to avoid the trap of dichotomies, of either/or, and see the merits of synthesizing universalist elements—first and foremost the respect for rights—with respect for communal bonds and a shared moral culture. This synthesis is the cornerstone of tolerant, liberal-minded communities.

One way to illustrate how such communities can be fostered is to look at the gated communities in which many millions of people live. Scorned and criticized by globalists, these places offer their members social bonding, solace, and comfort. Once again, a two-layered approach is called for: gated communities should not be allowed to discriminate, ban books, suppress speech, infringe upon the freedom of religious expression, or violate anyone's rights. However, in other matters, these communities should be welcome to form their own norms and policies, to create rules for the appearance of their communities (homes, lawns), restrict certain types of behavior in its members (e.g., loud music after midnight), and address numerous other matters, in accordance with the distinct cultures of these communities.

To illustrate: When some localities resisted allowing transgender students to use bathrooms of a gender other than the one indicated on their birth certificate, the federal government threatened to withhold billions of dollars in federal funds, putting at risk the education of hundreds of thousands of their citizens, especially poor and minority children. A less zealous approach to the rights of transgender people would have found policies that could satisfy both sides, for example, by adding gender-neutral bathrooms.

In 2015, the Supreme Court ruled that the right to marry applied to same-sex couples. A few clerks refused to issue marriage licenses to gay couples because they felt that such acts violated their faith and that God's law takes precedence over human law. In some states they were reassigned to other duties, but no gay couple was refused the license due them. Several globalists held that these clerks should be fired. Instead, globalists might have shown empathy for the strong beliefs of such people, without accepting this or any other violation of individual rights. (Much more about this topic in chapter 9.)

Communitarian sociologists have been pointing out that, for two centuries, the rise of modernity has threatened the communal bonds and shared moral cultures that are essential for a person's sense of identity, emotional stability, and moral order. Studies of the rise of Nazism show that communities serve as the best antidote to the mass appeal of demagogues. The kind of reasoned, self-governing, tolerant, civil person whom globalists favor is much less likely to be found among individuals outside the bonds of community than among people with stable social bonds, imbued with a proper moral culture. Hence, globalists have strong reasons to shore up communities.

In Conclusion

The patriotic movement must take into account that nobody can bond with seven billion people, and almost everyone feels more responsibility toward those closest to them. People have profound needs for lasting social relations and shared moral beliefs. And the patriotic movement must recognize that several globalist values can be combined with national, parochial ones. For instance, demanding that communities not violate individual rights while allowing them to foster bonds and values for their members in numerous other matters.

Local communities need to be nurtured rather than denounced, not only because they satisfy profound human needs but also because they anchor people to each other and thus help to dilute appeals to their worst instincts. Championing fair trade, fostering diversity within a framework of unity and shared values, and accepting many kinds of communities as long as they respect rights—all are positions that will help shore up the national bonds that are the foundation for stable and effective democracy, which is the agenda of the patriotic movement.

4
WHAT IS THE COMMON GOOD?

Central to my analysis is the idea that communities, local and national, serve the common good. This idea provides an important antidote to the tendencies of fragmentation, a centripetal force to limit centrifugal forces. Some critics contest the very concept of a common good. This chapter grapples with these critics.

Jeremy Bentham, for instance, characterized the concept of community as "fictitious."[1] Margaret Thatcher stated, "There is no such thing as society."[2] Proponents of such individualistic ideologies see the good as individually defined and social direction as arising out of the aggregation of individual choices and preferences.

Communitarian ideas contest individualistic ideologies and take two major forms. Some are authoritarian, as found in many East Asian countries that extol social obligations and the importance of the common good and accord much less weight to autonomy and rights. Liberal or responsive communitarianism, the other major form, holds that people face two major sources of normativity, that of the common good and that of autonomy and rights, neither of which in principle should take precedence over the other. I subscribe to the liberal communitarian viewpoint and have contributed some to its development.[3] This book draws on this social philosophy.

Some point to nations in which the common good has been allowed to dominate and trump individual rights as a reason to see it as a dangerous concept. For instance, Singapore has been characterized as an authoritarian communitarian state. The one-party government holds that individuals must make sacrifices for the betterment of the communal whole but makes short shrift of individual rights.[4] The state not only limits individual rights but also influences citizens' everyday choices. Japan also exerts strong pressure to serve the common good and fulfill social responsibilities, but this pressure is less often directed by the state and more often promoted through social processes. For instance, even an act as simple as placing your bicycle in the wrong place can result in public rebuke and a request to change your behavior.[5]

I am not denying that the concept of the common good, like most others, can be usurped and abused. However, given this risk, I see only more reason to stress that the common good can be balanced with commitments to individual rights, interests, and pursuits—rather than oppression. To call for a patriotic movement means ipso facto to call for formulating—or, more accurately, restoring while reformulating—conceptions of the common good, those of the nation.

The Common Good Defined

The common good (also referred to as the "public interest" or "public goods") is the sum of those goods that serve all members of a given community and its institutions, including goods that serve no identifiable group, as well as those that serve members of generations not yet born.

For many economists, the common good is the aggregation of individual goods.[6] It grows out of economic exchanges, and hence there is no need for the state to promote the common good.[7] The term "the common good" is contested on a number of fronts. First, there are those who argue that it does not exist at all. Ayn Rand wrote, "Since there is no such entity as 'the public,' since the public is merely a number of individuals, the idea that 'the public interest' supersedes private interests and rights, can have but one meaning: that the interests and rights of some individuals take precedence over the interests and rights of others."[8] Political scientists who adopt the assumptions of economics see little need for the concept of the public interest.[9] These political scientists hold that in a liberal democracy, competition among interest groups—which reveal and are guided by the preferences of individuals (i.e., private goods)—gives rise to a public policy that maximizes general welfare. Critics of that view argue that discrepancies in wealth, power, and social status grant various groups varying measures of leverage over the government. As a result, public policy—based on interest group politics—does not serve the common good but rather the interests of the powerful groups.[10]

In contrast, communitarians hold that the common good encompasses much more than the sum of all individual goods. Moreover, contributions to the common good often offer no immediate payout or benefit to anyone, and it is frequently difficult to foresee who will be the beneficiaries in the longer run. Members of communities invest in the common good not because their investment will necessarily benefit them but because they consider it a good in itself, for example, defending the nation or nature. Economists do recognize that there are situations in which the market fails to provide "public goods" that benefit society at large, making government promotion of these goods legitimate.[11] Such public goods include defense, basic research, and public health (e.g., fluoridation and vaccinations).[12]

A criticism of the common good from the left holds that the concept serves to conceal class differences in economic interests and political power so as to keep those who are disadvantaged from making demands on the community.[13] However, the fact that a concept is abused does not mean that it is without merit.

Finally, several academic communitarians, in particular Michael Sandel and Charles Taylor, have shown that conceptions of the common good must be formulated on the social level and that the community cannot be neutral in this matter.[14] Moreover, unless there is a social formulation of the good, there can be no normative foundation for resolving conflicts of value among individuals and groups.

To state that a given value is a common good of a given community does not mean that all the members subscribe to it, and surely not that they all live up to its dictates. It suffices that the value is recognized as a common good by large majorities and is embodied in law and in other institutions. At the same time, a value to which members merely pay lip service cannot qualify. This chapter will show that it is essential for solid analysis to consider the extent to which values are institutionalized as a continuous variable rather than as a dichotomous one. Some values are relatively highly institutionalized (e.g., marriages in the US in the 1950s). Others are largely aspirational (e.g., the belief that the US should promote democratic regimes overseas). The common good may be promoted and enforced by the state, but this is not necessarily the case. Indeed, often values are promoted by informal social controls, by peer pressures, and by communities.

Particularly important and challenging is my observation, spelled out elsewhere, that references to the common good should be read as if the emphasis is on the "common" and not on the "good." For the following discussion, the main issue is whether a value is widely shared and institutionalized—not whether a particular ethicist would judge it to be morally good. Thus, for example, a society may define the common good as giving precedence to economic development over political development—or expect that all members adhere to a particular religion. Many may not consider it a good society, but it is the "good" the given society has formulated as its common good. Shared values unify; whether the resulting union is one you and I judge morally sound is a separate consideration. As I noted above, one should not automatically assume that communities are "good"; they are needed, but one needs to pass moral judgment about the kind of values they promote. This why I am not a communitarian but a liberal communitarian.

Several scholars oppose the kind of balancing approach here followed.[15] They argue that rights are a common good, and hence the very opposition of the two goods—rights and the common good—that the balancing analysis presupposes is a false one.[16] This view is held particularly with regard to freedom of speech, taking inspiration from Justice Oliver Wendell Holmes's dissent in *Abrams v. United States* that the "ultimate good,"[17] both for the individual and society, is "better reached by free trade in ideas."[18] It is expressed in the Federal Communications Commission's opinion that "the public interest is best served by permitting free expression of views."[19] Likewise, Scott Cummings points out that many believe that "strong protection for individual rights is itself advancing the public interest."[20]

In response, one next notes that many common goods are not recognized as rights either in the US Constitution or the Universal Declaration of Human Rights.[21] There is no right to national parks, historic preservation, public health, or basic research.[22] One can of course aspire to add these rights, but until they are recognized as such, it is best not to dismiss the normative claims for these goods because they are "merely" common goods and not individual rights.

Indeed, some common goods cannot be reasonably defined as individual rights.[23] The National Archive in Washington, DC, houses the original copy of the Constitution. This preservation is a clear common good.[24] However, to argue that individual Americans have a right to have the Constitution preserved is stretching the concept of a right to the point that it becomes meaningless and has no foundation, either in American core normative concepts or in legal traditions.

National Creed vs. Constitutionalism

Some consider the core of the American faith a commitment to abide by the law, to play by the rules, to support democratic government and individual rights. This is one key interpretation of what is called constitutionalism. This concept is an essential element of the core values the patriotic moment needs to shore up, but it is also woefully inadequate. We need a much richer, "thicker" set of core values.

Various conceptions of the American Creed get closer to what is called for. William Tyler Page wrote a version of "The American's Creed" in 1917, later passed as a resolution by the US House of Representatives on April 3, 1918, that reads:

> I believe in the United States of America, as a government of the people, by the people, for the people; whose just powers are derived from the consent of the governed; a democracy in a republic; a sovereign Nation of many sovereign States; a perfect union, one and inseparable; established upon those principles of freedom, equality, justice, and humanity for which American patriots sacrificed their lives and fortunes.
>
> I therefore believe it is my duty to my country to love it, to support its Constitution, to obey its laws, to respect its flag, and to defend it against all enemies.[25]

Gunnar Myrdal provides a different version,

> where the American thinks, talks, and acts under the influence of high national and Christian precepts, and, on the other hand, the valuations on specific planes of individual and group living, where personal and local interests; economic, social, and sexual jealousies; considerations of community prestige and conformity; group prejudice against particular persons or types of people; and all sorts of miscellaneous wants, impulses, and habits dominate his outlook.[26]

This much richer, thicker concept includes the ideas encompassed by constitutionalism but adds substantial values. These are needs to be continually revisited by moral dialogues. However, whatever is agreed upon needs to be reinforced for all citizens and be introduced to new ones, whether they are youngsters entering the school system learning the ways of their country or if they are immigrants. Civics education and national service are two ways to promote these core values, part of the much more encompassing agenda of the patriotic movement.

In Conclusion

Shared recognition of a common good can hold otherwise fractious societies together. However, members of the patriotic movement should be clear that the common good does not trump individual rights but, rather, provides a balance to these rights. National moral dialogues will provide the opportunity to develop an understanding of the common good—of the responsibilities patriots should foster and the rights that must be honored.

5
RIGHTS AND RESPONSIBILITIES

Much of the current dialogue in democratic societies follows the advocacy model, which assumes that the clash of two strong one-sided views will lead to a just conclusion, reasonable judgments, and sound public policies. In contrast, the liberal communitarian approach favors the model exemplified by the *agora* in ancient Greece,[1] the *jirgas* of Afghanistan,[2] and the US Senate in earlier decades:[3] one of dialogue, in which opposing sides engage in a civil discourse, give-and-take, and commit to finding a widely acceptable course.

We all face two fully legitimate normative and legal claims—those of individual rights and those of the common good—and the fact that neither can be maximized nor can the two be fully reconciled. It follows that some balance must be worked out between the conflicting claims. The liberal communitarian model assumes from the outset that a democratic nation ought to be committed to advancing both individual rights and the common good and that neither should be assumed to a priori trump the other.[4] (Social responsibilities are the specifications of the common good. For example, a common good may be protecting the environment; recycling is a social responsibility.)

Reasonable Searches

The Fourth Amendment provides an important text for the liberal communitarian philosophy when it states, "The right of the people to be secure in their persons, houses, papers, and effects, against unreasonable searches and seizures, shall not be violated."[5] By banning only *unreasonable* searches and seizures, it recognizes that there are *reasonable* ones—those that serve the common good (or, to use a term more familiar to the legal community, the public interest).

Moreover, the Constitution provides a mechanism for determining which searches are reasonable: the courts. What the courts consider reasonable searches changes as conditions of public security and order change. For instance, after a rush of skyjacking in 1972, the courts deemed legal the newly introduced screening gates in airports where millions of travelers are searched. These gates stopped skyjacking within roughly a year. The courts, as a rule, do not use the term "common good" but refer to the "public interest." Although they have given different rationales for authoring a considerable variety of searches, many even without a warrant, they seem to be morally grounded: searches are legitimate if the gains for the public interest greatly outweigh the harms of intrusion on privacy.

A review of Supreme Court rulings shows that the Court has a broad understanding of public safety, which allows diverse intrusions into the realm of individual rights to serve this common good.[6] The most basic element of public safety is upholding law and order, and the deterrence and prevention of crime. A second element of public safety relates to preventing accidental death and injury. Thus, the Court allowed suspicionless, random drug and alcohol testing of train engineers in the wake of a series of train accidents[7] as well as random sobriety checkpoints on highways to prevent deadly car accidents resulting from drunk driving.[8] A third element of public safety is the promotion of public health.[9] Thus, the Court held that the public interest in eradicating the smallpox disease justified compulsory vaccination programs despite the resulting intrusion on privacy,[10] and held that search warrants for Occupational Safety and Health Act (OSHA) inspections do not require "probable cause in the criminal law sense."[11] In short, there are ample precedents to hold that when the common good of nations, in particular public safety and security, is concerned, individual rights can be curbed, *especially if the intrusion is small and the gain to the public interest is significant.*

Achieving a communitarian balance does not mean invariably opting for the *same* golden middle ground between rights and responsibilities. Rather, it requires consideration of how changes in historical conditions might shift the equilibrium point. The September 11, 2001, attacks against the US heightened the country's need to attend to homeland security. One can argue that the US overreacted and introduced unnecessary security measures, but one cannot deny that the event showed that some additional attention and resources had to be committed to prevent more such attacks, that is, that some correction in the balance between rights and responsibility was called for.

The patriotic movement needs, as part of developing its agenda through moral dialogues, to determine where the current balance lies between individual rights and the common good, and what corrections ought to be introduced. To illustrate the issue, first a short example follows, in which a victory of individual rights was recently declared, although actually a rebalancing occurred, namely the protection of privacy by treating information as private property. Chapter 6 provides a case study in which the common good seems to have been undermined.

Is Personal Information Akin to Private Property?

Treating personal information like private property is a popular solution to the threats to privacy in the cyber age. The essence of the idea is that if someone wants to use a piece of personal information, then they will need to get one's permission (and if one wishes, pay for this privilege). And if one disclosed personal information to another party, then that party can use it only for the purposes one agreed to and will not be allowed to share it with others without the original owner's explicit consent.

Among those who advocate this idea is Andy Kessler, a former hedge fund manager and columnist for the *Wall Street Journal*, who championed it in the article "A Better Way to Make Facebook Pay."[12] He notes that the US is a country founded on property rights. Hence "Congress can deliberate for 90 seconds and then pass the Make the Internet Great Again Act. The bill would contain five words: 'Users own their private data.'"[13] Under this solution, users' Facebook data—photos, "Likes," ads that have been clicked on, and much else—would be kept in a "virtual locker." It would be up to individual Facebook users to decide how these data may be used. And Facebook would pay the owners of the information for using it.

For homeland security and public safety the suggested approach raises major difficulties. It is widely understood that under most circumstances the government cannot legally search anyone (i.e., violate privacy) unless it has shown to a court that it has probable cause to suspect that the person is a criminal or terrorist. Much less attention is paid to the question of how the government can gain such information if it is not allowed to search before it gets a warrant. The answer lies in large part in drawing on personal information that people disclose to others, for instance when they open a bank account, purchase a house, get credit, and so on. Under the third-party doctrine, if a person discloses information to another party, then he or she no longer has a "reasonable expectation of privacy" and the government may obtain the information without a warrant. If the government must ask suspects for their consent prior to accessing these kinds of personal data, then not only is consent unlikely to be obtained, but the suspects will also be tipped off that the government is investigating them. Thus, ending the third-party doctrine would severely set back homeland protection and law enforcement.

Research would be bedeviled as well. A medical researcher tried some years back to get personal consent from several thousand people to interrogate their medical records. He found that some people could not be found, others were six feet under, and quite a few refused. He spent most of the funds set aside for his project on trying to gain consent— and ended up with a very unrepresentative sample of the population, given that the older and the less educated patients refused more often than others. One may suggest he could use the data after removing personal identifiers, a process referred to as anonymization. However, under the new doctrine, he still would need their consent for their data to be included in the study in the first place.

Finally, personal information about a given person is used at least seven hundred times a day. If each such usage would require permission from the "owner," then people would have to spend a good part of their day refusing or agreeing to share their information (as well as exploring various offers for trading privacy for coupons).

The fact that all these concerns are far from theoretical ones can be seen in a closer look at the European Union's General Data Protection Regulation (GDPR).[14] The GDPR is often hailed as an example of a sound way to protect privacy by maintaining ownership of one's personal data.[15] Indeed, the GDPR states that any secondary use of personal information released by a person or collected about him requires the explicit prior approval of the original individual "owner" of the information and that this consent cannot be delegated to an agent or machine. The details of the GDPR are complex and changing. However, it deals with all the issues I raised above by making exceptions to the ownership rule in many areas, including when the data are needed for the purposes of research, public health, or law enforcement, among others.

The GDPR makes repeated reference to Member States retaining the ability to process personal data for archiving purposes in the public interest, scientific or historical research purposes, or statistical purposes, given that Member States provide appropriate safeguards[16] and allow individuals to object to the processing of their data—unless the task is considered to be in the public interest.[17] The GDPR's parameters for processing data in the public interest (not related to national security) extend to "the field of employment law, social protection law including pensions and for health security, alert purposes, the prevention or control of communicable diseases and other serious threats to health."[18] The GDPR's parameters for scientific research are similarly expansive, as the text requests it be "interpreted in a broad manner including for example technological development and demonstration, fundamental research, applied research and privately funded research defined."[19] Finally, the GDPR makes several references to security, most notably declaring, "This Regulation does not apply to the processing of personal data by the Member States when carrying out activities in relation to the common foreign and security policy of the Union."[20] In short, the new EU data protection measures, which have been touted as a great step forward for protecting privacy, in effect are careful not to harm a variety of common goods. It is a model the patriotic movement is advised to follow in other areas in which the balance between individual rights and social responsibilities needs to be recalibrated.

In Conclusion

As the patriotic movement is developing its agenda, it needs to be leery of a tendency in liberal deliberations to focus on the question of whether or not an individual right has been violated—privacy, for instance. The implicit assumption is that any legal act or public policy that impinges on a right is on its face illegal and ought to be condemned. It should be recalled that no right is absolute and that the American Constitution, as well as the constitutions of other democracies, recognizes that in effect there are tradeoffs. Often when the violation of the right involved is minimal and the gain to the public interest (or common good) is substantial, the act or policy is considered legal by the courts. A study of privacy illustrates this point. Although at first blush it may seem that the new European General Data Protection Regulation makes privacy trump all other concerns, in effect the GDPR allows the limitation of privacy in the interest of a whole slew of common goods. It provides a model for other policy analyses the patriotic movement ought to follow.

6
PRIVACY VS. THE COMMON GOOD: A CASE STUDY

Discussions of privacy vs. the common good often take place on a very high level of generalization. Some hold that individual rights in many democracies are endangered by invasive surveillance and by authoritarian tendencies exhibited by governments that are justified by fearmongering. Others hold that we have lost much of our sense of responsibility to the other and the common good by extolling the individual.

In this chapter, I provide a case study to illustrate that finding the right balance between privacy and the common good (or more generally, between individual rights and the public interest) is often complicated by technological and economic factors that affect what otherwise may seem to be mainly moral and legal considerations. The case examines the policies concerning encryption, sometimes referred to as the Crypto Wars.

A Brief History

The Crypto Wars began in 1993 with the Clipper Chip proposal, but even then the encryption debate was not new.[1] For instance, "In January 1991, Senator Joe Biden inserted new language into the draft of an anti-terrorism bill, expressing a Sense of Congress that electronic communications service providers and equipment manufacturers *shall ensure that communications systems permit the government to obtain the plaintext contents of voice, data, and other communications when appropriately authorized by law.*"[2]

The Clipper Chip, a microchip designed for placement in a telephone, was developed to facilitate law enforcement's access to information relevant to their investigations; the chip would encrypt the conversations, but the government would hold the key, giving it the ability to intercept phone calls provided it had "lawful authorization."[3] The government was concerned with criminals using encryption to hide from law enforcement and saw the Clipper Chip as a reasonable approach that was in the general public's best interest.

According to a 1993 White House Press Release: "We need the 'Clipper Chip' and other approaches that can both provide law-abiding citizens with access to the encryption they need and prevent criminals from using it to hide their illegal activities."[4] The Clipper Chip proposal met with widespread opposition. There were security concerns about the concept of key escrow; entrusting keys to a third party was seen as a vulnerability. The idea of key escrow also sparked privacy concerns, with many people distrusting government to be in charge of encryption keys.

From a business angle, companies worried that the Clipper Chip was the first step toward banning encryption that did not include a back door.[5] Stewart Baker, chief counsel at the National Security Agency (NSA), wrote an article in *Wired* magazine in an attempt to dispel the concerns being raised about the Clipper Chip. Addressing privacy advocates, he wrote: "The key escrow proposal is not about increasing government's authority to invade the privacy of its citizens. All that key escrow does is preserve the government's current ability to conduct wiretaps under existing authorities."[6] Baker then turned to the concerns of businesspeople, taking a stern approach yet assuring them that their ability to innovate remained intact: "So where does this leave industry, especially those companies that don't like either the 1970s-vintage DES or key escrow?" he asked. "It leaves them where they ought to be— standing on their own two feet. . . . If companies want to develop and sell competing, unescrowed systems to other Americans, if they insist on hastening a brave new world of criminal immunity, they can still do so—as long as they're willing to use their own money. That's what the free market is all about."[7]

After discovering a flaw in the Clipper Chip technology, the government abandoned it and moved on to a new, yet similar proposal: that of focusing on "commercial key escrow."[8] The proposal was to be implemented by companies themselves and would apply to software as well as hardware. Unlike the Clipper Chip, the keys would be kept by government-certified private escrow agents rather than the government itself. Public fears were not alleviated. Opposition continued, including from some lawmakers.[9] In the words of Senator John Ashcroft: "We do not provide the government with phone jacks outside our homes for unlimited wiretaps. Why, then, should we grant government the Orwellian capability to listen at will and in real time to our communications across the Web?"[10] Ultimately the government abandoned its key escrow proposals, and no mandatory back doors were imposed on encryption technology.[11]

Aside from the key escrow debate, there are two other significant aspects of the Crypto Wars. First, the Communications Assistance for Law Enforcement Act (CALEA), passed in 1994, reflects compromise between government interests and privacy concerns. It contains major concessions for those favoring strong encryption. For instance, the legislative history states that "nothing in this paragraph [47 USC § 1002(b)(3)] would prohibit a carrier from deploying an encryption service for which it does not retain the ability to decrypt communications for law enforcement access."[12]

Second, there was a battle over export controls on encryption technology during the 1990s (at the time, encryption products were classified as munitions). However, by 1999, the White House announced it would remove almost all restrictions on the export of encryption products. Encryption technology was gaining a foothold in foreign markets, and continuing to impose restrictions would have hurt American businesses. This policy shift marked the end of the Crypto Wars.[13] As Andi Wilson Thompson, Danielle Kehl, and Kevin Bankston summarized, "The Crypto Wars ended with a broad policy consensus: ensuring Americans' ability to use and distribute strong encryption free of government backdoors was critical to maintaining the nation's economic security and information security, as well as maintaining Americans' constitutional rights to privacy and free speech."[14]

A second round of the encryption wars started in 2014, following the introduction of a new, much more powerful end-to-end encryption where the server cannot decrypt incoming communication; only the devices used to send and receive messages have the necessary key.[15] This enhanced security provides a very high level of privacy for ordinary citizens, criminals, and terrorists alike.

Many companies have incorporated end-to-end encryption into their products. For example, Apple uses end-to-end encryption to secure communications sent over iMessage and FaceTime.[16] The messaging app WhatsApp (which has been acquired by Facebook) also uses end-to-end encryption, and it is now an option (although not the default) on Facebook's Messenger app.[17] Google Allo is another messaging app that allows communications to be sent using end-to-end encryption, although as with Facebook, it is not the default option—users must choose to activate "incognito mode."[18]

Until the Snowden revelations, American high-tech corporations showed limited interest in developing and marketing high-power encryption software. After these revelations, many customers—especially overseas—became very concerned about their privacy. Some nations, such as Germany, India, and Brazil, considered forging their own internet networks.[19] American high-tech companies viewed these developments as highly threatening to their business.

Although Apple's iMessage service already used end-to-end encryption prior to the Snowden leaks, its security protocols were increased to allow users to erase their phone's data after a certain number of incorrect passcode attempts. WhatsApp added end-to-end encryption post-Snowden,[20] and Google announced that it would develop end-to-end encryption for Gmail.[21]

Law enforcement and government officials are concerned that securing personal information through high-end encryption and other settings that tech companies themselves cannot decrypt or override poses a security risk. (From this point on, any type of encryption or security setting that leaves devices and messages impenetrable is referred to as ultimate encryption, or UE.) Then FBI director James Comey, for example, warned that "encryption threatens to lead all of us to a very dark place" and that UE "will have very serious consequences for law enforcement and national security agencies at all levels." He added: "It's the equivalent of a closet that can't be opened. A safe that can't be cracked."[22] Former British prime minister David Cameron has asked: "Do we want to allow a means of communication between people which even in extremis, with a signed warrant from the home secretary personally, that we cannot read? . . . My answer to that question is: 'No we must not.'"[23]

FBI vs. Apple

The encryption debate exploded after the US government found a phone used by a terrorist, Syed Rizwan Farook, and could not unlock it. On December 2, 2015, Farook and his wife had killed fourteen people in a terrorist attack in San Bernardino, California. The FBI asked for Apple's help in gaining access to the contents of the phone; when Apple demurred, the FBI turned to the courts, which ordered Apple to comply with the FBI's request.[24]

An intensive public debate followed between the supporters of Apple (major parts of the media, law professors, and public intellectuals) and a smaller number of supporters of the FBI. After holding back, President Obama stated in a speech on March 11, 2016, that never allowing government access to someone's smartphone would be equivalent to "fetishizing our phones above every other value" and that it would not "strike the balance that we have lived with for 200, 300 years."[25] The FBI ultimately found a way to access the phone without Apple's help, and the case became moot, but the underlying encryption debate was not resolved.

British authorities faced a similar issue after Khalid Masood carried out a terrorist attack in London that killed five people on March 22, 2017. It is known that his phone connected to WhatsApp right before the attack, although it is unknown whether he sent or received a message. The attack has reignited the encryption debate in Britain. Home Secretary Amber Rudd stated the need "to make sure that organisations like WhatsApp . . . don't provide a secret place for terrorists to communicate with each other."[26] And acting metropolitan police chief Craig Mackey called out tech companies for acting unethically, saying, "If you're going to have ethical statements and talk about operating in an ethical way it actually has to mean something."[27]

In the wake of the Apple vs. FBI dispute, two senators tried to resolve the problems caused by UE by suggesting it be banned. Senators Richard Burr (R-NC) and Dianne Feinstein (D-CA) issued a draft bill that would require "'intelligible information or data' or the 'technical means to get it'" to be provided if required by a court order.[28] The proposal caused public outcry and opposition by tech companies. Apple hired a high-profile lobbyist for its Washington office,[29] and trade groups that represent tech companies started lobbying Congress, expressing concerns regarding privacy and the effects of weakening encryption on business.[30]

WikiLeaks has also played a role in the encryption debate. In March 2017 it released documents demonstrating some of the CIA's hacking capabilities, including its ability to hack Apple and Android devices, as well as Chrome. However, according to Apple, "the alleged iPhone vulnerability affected iPhone 3G only and was fixed in 2009 when iPhone 3GS was released," and "the alleged Mac vulnerabilities were previously fixed in all Macs launched after 2013."[31] Google's director of information security and privacy, Heather Adkins, stated that "security updates and protections in both Chrome and Android already shield users from many of these alleged vulnerabilities," adding that their "analysis is ongoing and [they] will implement any further necessary protections."[32] Google has "always made security a top priority and we continue to invest in our defenses," she added.[33] That is, these corporations argue that the arms race between the government and the privacy protectors continues and that they are winning.

Enter Massive Leaks

A new wrinkle in this continual tug of war took place when Julian Assange offered tech companies "exclusive access to the additional technical details we [WikiLeaks] have, so that fixes can be developed and pushed out so people can be secured."[34] In a move that seemed to demonstrate Apple's wariness of being seen as too friendly with Assange, the company announced that it has "not negotiated with WikiLeaks for any information."[35] Apple did, however, suggest that WikiLeaks "submit any information they wish through our normal process under our standard terms," adding, "Thus far, we have not received any information from them that isn't in the public domain."[36] Microsoft behaved similarly, stating that its "preferred method for anyone with knowledge of security issues, including the CIA or WikiLeaks, is to submit details to us at secure@microsoft.com so we can review information and take any necessary steps to protect customers."[37] Microsoft also stated that WikiLeaks did make "initial contact via secure@microsoft.com" and reported they "have followed up" and are "treating [WikiLeaks] as we would any other finder."[38]

These leaks present multiple legal issues for tech companies. Although some lawyers are convinced that the leaked documents are within the public domain due to their wide distribution, Stewart Baker, former legal counsel for the NSA, maintains that "the unauthorized release of classified documents does not mean it's unclassified."[39] Baker added, "Doing business with WikiLeaks and reviewing classified documents poses a real risk for at least their [tech companies'] government contracting arms and their cleared employees."[40] There is also a third consideration, namely the potential for being charged with negligence if tech companies' products are hacked and they had refused WikiLeaks' help.[41]

As demonstrated thus far, the issue regarding the "warrant-free zone" created by encryption is very much alive. Nobody on either side disagrees with the observation that the way this issue will be resolved will have major implications for national security (especially terrorism), public safety (especially crime), privacy, personal security (e.g., protection from identity theft), and the business interests of the corporations involved.

From a Fourth Amendment viewpoint, it seemed Apple should have complied with the court order. Furthermore, it would at first seem that the government had a particularly strong case. Unlike many other instances where government surveillance is conducted based on suspicions or circumstantial evidence, there is no doubt that the phone was used by Syed Rizwan Farook, the San Bernardino terrorist—and because he is deceased, he has very diminished privacy rights. (Moreover, the phone was owned by the San Bernardino County Public Health Department, which was happy to grant permission to search it.) In short, this case seems to be an unusually clear-cut case in which the value of security should trump the remaining privacy rights of someone who is both a known terrorist and deceased. This is, though, not the way Apple, other tech corporations, and their supporters saw it. They thought that the government was using this case to set a precedent for searching millions of other phones (more about this below). Further, they believed that even in this case there were strong legal arguments to deny the government's request.

Apple argued that weakening encryption software to allow government surveillance of phones (putting in a "back door") would not only diminish the privacy of many millions across the world but also jeopardize their security. Apple states that "at stake is the data security of hundreds of millions of law-abiding people," meaning that it sees itself as protecting not just Americans but iPhone users around the world.[42] This, Apple holds, is because other governments and criminals would come in through the same back door. That is, Apple rejects the very legal and ethical way this and other issues have been framed—as a tension between the common good and individual rights—and the ensuing question of which values should take precedence in a given conflict. Apple argues that it is out to protect *both* core values. For this reason, Apple repeatedly refers to the FBI request for Apple to develop a key able to unlock encrypted phones as "dangerous."

Tim Cook, the CEO of Apple, spells out the dangers people face if the government's demands were to be heeded and the protection Apple provides were to be weakened by introducing a back door into the software. "Bad actors" could bring down power grids, cause people dependent on medical devices to suffer a heart attack, and track the locations of peoples' children.[43] Apple's vice president of software engineering, Craig Federighi, raised similar concerns: "The threat to our personal information is just the tip of the iceberg. Your phone is more than a personal device. In today's mobile, networked world, it's part of the security perimeter that protects your family and co-workers. Our nation's vital infrastructure—such as power grids and transportation hubs—becomes more vulnerable when individual devices get hacked. Criminals and terrorists who want to infiltrate systems and disrupt sensitive networks may start their attacks through access to just one person's smartphone."[44] Supporters of Apple argue that the government should instead compel the phone owners to divulge the password. However, this is impossible to do to with terrorists who commit suicide or are shot dead. For others, the government often needs to keep them under surveillance before it tips them that they are suspects. Hence it needs access to phones, pursuant to court orders, without disclosure to the phone owners. (For the same reason, corporate arguments that customers should be alerted about government requests for their communications, i.e., lifting "gag orders," are not compatible with elementary procedures of law enforcement in all democratic nations.)

Losing Control of the Key

High-tech corporations and their supporters are concerned that if a key were created, the software would be stolen or leaked. Cook warned: "In the wrong hands, this software—which does not exist today—would have the potential to unlock any iPhone in someone's physical possession. . . . The FBI may use different words to describe this tool, but make no mistake: Building a version of iOS that bypasses security in this way would undeniably create a backdoor. And while the government may argue that its use would be limited to this case, there is no way to guarantee such control."[45] In response, I suggested on March 7, 2016, that Apple (and other high-tech corporations) leave the encryption software as it is—thus avoiding vulnerabilities or a back door—but develop a key to unlock phones, a key they would keep. Once a court orders that a given phone must be unlocked, the FBI would bring it to Apple (or Google or whatever other tech corporations were involved)—and they would unlock the phones they produced and turn over to the FBI any information that's found—but not the key. (To apply the same idea to phones still in the hands of bad actors requires considerable additional collaboration between the FBI and the tech corporations, but the same principle could be applied.)

Several artificial intelligence (AI) experts have commented on this suggestion. Many thought that although Apple has the technical capability to create a key, the real issue would be keeping it secure. Steve Bellovin from Columbia University's Department of Computer Science responded that although "a key can be readily available or it can be secure, it can't be both."[46] According to Philip Schrodt, a senior research scientist, "The problem is not the technology, it is people getting careless about how they use the technology."[47] David Bantz, chief information architect for the University of Alaska system, noted that "NYC and [the] FBI have hundreds of phones they want to unlock. That would entail a process involving many people and loading the OS on many phones. That makes it possible maybe even likely that one of those people entrusted with that power is coerced or bribed or is clumsy enough to put it in the hands of criminals."[48]

I was surprised to hear during a meeting on May 11, 2016, at the Council on Foreign Relations (a rare one, on the record) District Attorney Cyrus Vance informing the audience that until September 2014 his office was able to routinely send phones to Apple; the phones would be opened and sent back with the relevant information within a day or two.[49] The reason Apple stopped, Vance implied, was that in September 2014, it started advertising itself as the only company that sold phones whose encryption could not be broken.[50] It seems that concern over profits, a fully legitimate concern, played a key role in Apple's sudden refusal to cooperate with law enforcement and national security authorities.

In response to tech corporations' oft-repeated claim that such a key cannot be kept secure, even if it stayed on their premises under its own encryption protection, I note that Coca-Cola kept its formula secret for many decades. And that leaks about secrets from the FBI, during the previous twenty-five years, have been very rare. Further, if the key were "leaked," tech corporations would modify their encryption software by patching it up, as they often do, or developing new keys. In effect, this is what Apple sought to do when it learned that the FBI had found a way to unlock Apple's iPhone. Most importantly, I agree with Vance, who argued that one must weigh "the risk of maintaining the ability to open a phone by the company . . . versus . . . the consequence to law enforcement of not being able to access those phones."[51] The answer seems self-evident.

Rights and Responsibilities

Corporations would not exist without society granting them a special privilege, that of limited liability. Without this provision, it would be impossible for corporations to amass the large amounts of capital that modern enterprises require. It stands to reason that in exchange, society can demand that corporations pay back by absorbing some losses if, as a result, security could be much enhanced.

Moreover, communitarians have pointed out that rights presume responsibility.[52] Thus, as far as individuals are concerned, the right to be tried before a jury of one's peers means little if the peers do not see serving on the jury as their responsibility. The right to free speech will not be sustained if people do not realize that they need to accept listening to offensive speech. And the right to life will not be secured if those who seek it do not assume the responsibility to pay for national defense and public safety.

Corporations often claim that they should have the same rights as individuals. For instance, they assert that their commercials and labeling of products should not be regulated because such regulations violate their right to free speech and that they should have political free speech rights in the form of making campaign contributions. They had previously been granted due process rights and Fourth Amendment protections by the Supreme Court.[53] Society hence should expect that they also assume responsibility like individual members of the community and contribute to the common good.

In Conclusion

Whether one sides with Apple or the FBI, whether one holds that privacy concerns outweigh national security concerns or insists that ways can be found to prevent the formation of warrant-free zones, one may well agree that, as the patriotic movement develops, its general positions on the balance between privacy (and other rights) and security (and other common goods) need to address the question of where the proper balance lies within the current historical context and that these positions will need to be "translated" into specific policies. These policies, in turn, will face a large variety of technical and economic challenges, as the preceding case study illustrates. Nobody should expect that developing a new agenda for the patriotic movement is going to be an easy task.

7
DIVERSITY WITHIN UNITY

mmigration, as previously discussed, is a major force that drives populism, as scores of millions of people—especially in the EU but also
in the US—view large-scale immigration as challenging their identity,
national community, security, and jobs. In chapter 3, I suggested that
dismissing these concerns as a sheer reflection of bigotry and simply
calling for "open borders" is neither justified nor politically productive.
In the following discussion, I seek to show that the greater the capacity
of societies to acculturate new immigrants, the higher the levels of immigration they can accommodate without undue social disruption. In
the process, nations need to change what they consider their core values rather than merely expecting immigrants to buy into the prevailing
ethos. Building up the capacity of absorption should be a major element
of the agenda of the patriotic movement.

A key question arises in this context as to what level and kind of acculturation a patriotic movement should call for. I will show that major
forms of assimilation, often favored in Western states, tend to pose unnecessary burdens on acculturation processes, and I suggest a different
model, which I refer to as "Diversity within Unity." Given that this issue
is much more acute in the EU than in the US, the discussion focuses on
the EU.

Rising Alienation

Even before the recent massive immigration to Europe of people of different faiths and cultural backgrounds, many European societies and
the EU faced multiple challenges. These included very low economic
growth; high levels of unemployment; political fragmentation and polarization; increased interpersonal and intergroup violence; a rise in terrorism and right-wing parties and movements; the negative effects of
globalization (and growing disaffection with the EU). Several European
societies, most notably Germany, Sweden, Greece, and Italy, now face

the challenge of absorbing a much larger number of immigrants than at any other time in recent history. The immediate concerns—such as limiting the flow of immigration, separating asylum seekers from economic migrants, and finding housing and work for the newcomers—have already received much attention and hence are not discussed in this chapter. Rather, I focus on strategies to absorb immigrants into their new home societies and cultures. In particular, I ask whether integration requires that these immigrants embrace the prevailing national values, or do these values need to change? This question confronts all nations that face large-scale immigration, but especially those whose immigrants are from very different cultures, for instance those who arrive in a major European metropolis after having fled a war zone in Libya or Afghanistan or, say, a rural village in Senegal.

Even prior to the recent influx of migrants, many European nations had seen a significant increase in immigration. Between 2001 and 2011, the foreign-born population in England and Wales grew by 62 percent.[1] In Norway, the number of immigrants and their children nearly tripled between 1995 and 2011.[2] In Spain, the increase was more dramatic still: in 2000, the country had fewer than 1.5 million immigrants, but by 2009, the number had risen to 6.5 million, more than a 300 percent spike.[3] Even before these immigration surges, many countries had sizable minorities that were not well integrated. The result is what might be termed a normative distribution wherein European nations are struggling not only with integrating newcomers into the prevailing moral cultures but also with articulating what those moral cultures are and thus which values immigrants *ought* to embrace.

Some conceptualize nations as merely states and economies and focus on ensuring that new immigrants comply with prevailing laws and find adequate jobs. However, to reiterate, nations are communities invested in states. People are not merely citizens but also members of societies animated by a particular shared history, bonds, ideals, and hopes. To become full-fledged compatriots, immigrants need to wrestle with and embrace their new homelands' moral and social values. Otherwise, much of Europe and quite a few other nations will experience increased levels of intergroup violence and terrorism. Moreover, failure to integrate the immigrants, old and new, is *one key factor* among several others that contributes to the rise of right-wing and xenophobic reactions in the host societies, the fracturing of national unity and stability, and the undermining of the EU. This failure is a key reason that the centers of political gravity in entire nations have shifted to the right, including in Germany, Hungary, Austria, and Poland, with others likely to follow. (An Autumn 2017 Eurobarometer poll found that across all EU member states, a clear majority of respondents had a negative view of immigration from non-EU countries.)[4]

Each nation must determine the most effective ways to absorb immigrants into their societies, their communities, and above all into their moral cultures. This is a major challenge because (*a*) many of these societies are unclear about what their distinct values are; (*b*) absorbing large numbers of new immigrants may well entail recasting these values to some extent; and (*c*) large-scale absorption is always a challenging process. Unless nations do much more to integrate immigrants on a normative level, including editing their own values, many cities are likely to come to look like the suburbs of Paris. This chapter seeks to outline how the patriotic movement should contend with this challenge.

Assimilation, Unbounded Pluralism, and Diversity within Unity

The various approaches tried by different European societies and favored by the European Commission fall on various points of a continuum. At one end of this continuum is total assimilation; at the other end, unbounded pluralism. These bookends are ideal types; no society fully adheres to either, but many are fairly close to one end or the other of the continuum. Diversity within Unity (DWU) falls in the middle of this continuum.

Assimilation is a term used in different ways by different social scientists and policy makers, and it translates into different policies.[5] In its strongest form, assimilation requires that immigrants abandon all of their distinct cultures, values, habits, and connections to countries of origin in order to fully integrate into their new home.

France stands out as close to an archetype of this approach. For many years it was regarded as discriminatory—in the Republican tradition— to officially recognize French citizens' country of origin or religion.[6] France made it much easier than did other European countries for new immigrants to obtain citizenship, but it also made stricter demands of newcomers to "become French." In 2004, France passed a law banning all ostentatious religious symbols from public schools, although students are allowed to carry "discreet" religious symbols. Although concerns over the hijab were the initial impetus for the law, it does not single out any particular religion, meaning that crucifixes and yarmulkes are also forbidden in schools. The law is so far-reaching and has been interpreted so broadly that several schools have forbidden female Muslim students to wear long dresses.[7] More recently, schools in several French towns have decided to stop serving pork-free meals.

This approach is prone to failure because it requires immigrants to give up values and behaviors that are central to their identity. Such excessive homogenization undermines rather than facilitates integration, as we shall show below in some detail. Moreover, placing such severe, inflexible assimilation requirements on immigrants creates unrealistic expectations of homogeneity among the native population. The fact that there is a high level of alienation among immigrant and minority communities in France—and also among the native majority—reveals that this approach is not satisfactory.[8]

Unbounded pluralism holds that there is no need for immigrants to modify their behaviors, habits, and customs (as long as they do not violate existing laws) and that, instead, the host societies are to abandon their core of shared values, demands for loyalty, and national identity in order to accommodate various differences—above all normative ones—between the host society and various immigrant groups and minorities.

No society in Europe follows such a policy (Canada claims it does). Such an approach was advocated by the Commission on the Future of Multi-Ethnic Britain, whose widely discussed Parekh Report concluded that the United Kingdom had become a territory that English, Scottish, Welsh, West Indian, Pakistani and other groups inhabit like tribes resting next to each other. They had and needed few shared values or other commonalities; the government should avoid promoting any set notion of national identity and culture in order to avoid offending or injuring any of the various groups.[9] Along similar lines, the political scientist Jamie Mayerfeld has argued that national identity is a form of group identity that—like identities based on race, religion, and ethnicity—arouses sentiments that exaggerate feelings of injury and exerts pressure on people to undertake acts of aggression and violence.[10] In short, strong national identities are best avoided.

Although no European nation is currently following a full-blown unbounded pluralism policy, one can find it reflected in particular domains. For example, several countries have taken an approach to religious symbols that reflects unbounded multiculturalism. Sweden allows on-duty police officers to wear turbans, headscarves, or yarmulkes instead of the police hat that had previously been worn by all officers. Similarly, the UK permits police officers to wear various religious head-coverings.

Unbounded pluralism cannot be made to work as a general policy for a number of reasons. First, despite growing diversity, a strong sense of national identity is far from dead or dying in most European societies. Indeed, it seems to have been reinforced in response to the mass immigration and the weakening of the EU. Second, in those countries in which national bonds are weak, we see rising tensions and conflicts. David Goodhart notes that as societies become more diverse, there are fewer shared values and thus less solidarity or willingness to redistribute resources.[11] The institutional paralysis one witnesses in Belgium, which some have termed a failed state,[12] reflects such a division between the Flemish and Walloons—a division that is exacerbated by the absence of a sufficient normative shared core. This lack of a shared core, in turn, makes it difficult to integrate immigrants, as there is not one normative framework into which they can be integrated.

Several countries that had previously embraced multiculturalism (some forms of which are a mild form of unbounded pluralism) are retreating from this position. For example, in the 1980s, the Netherlands adopted a policy of multiculturalism that promoted respect and support for cultural diversity and allowed minorities to maintain their cultural and religious differences but paid much less attention to the unity realm. The Dutch attitude of accommodation was built upon the "pillarization" that developed in the seventeenth and eighteenth centuries that allowed various groups (originally Catholics and Protestants, and later others) to have their own semi-autonomous institutions for education and social services.[13] However, in 2004, following the murders of Pim Fortuyn and Theo van Gogh, the Dutch government officially rejected multiculturalism and "accommodation" by adopting a new strategy that requires new immigrants to "become Dutch" not only through language acquisition but also in a cultural and moral sense.[14]

There are also some indications that Germany is moving away from pluralism in the wake of an unprecedented intake of refugees and asylum seekers in 2015. In Cologne, a series of sexual assaults and harassment by gangs of men described by the authorities as having "a North African or Arabic" appearance during New Year's Eve celebrations resulted in a backlash against the German government's previous attitude.[15] Labor Minister Andrea Nahles wrote in February 2016: "If you come to us seeking protection and wanting to start a new life, you have to stick to our rules and values. If you signal that you can't integrate, your benefits will be cut."[16] Germany requires an "integration course" that consists of language and culture classes. An official German government description of the "integration course" says that attendees will discuss "important values in German society, e.g., freedom of worship, tolerance and equal rights."[17] Whether the curriculum of these classes is well formed, the teachers are properly prepared, and these classes are effective is far from clear; however, the direction in which the policy is shifting is quite evident.

A third approach is that of Diversity within Unity (DWU).[18] It presumes that all members of a given society will fully respect and adhere to select *core* values and institutions that are considered part of the basic shared framework of the society (the unity component). At the same time, every group in society is free to maintain its distinct subculture—those policies, habits, and institutions that do not conflict with the shared core (the diversity component). Respect for the whole and for all is the essence of this position, with respect for the community (which itself may be recast over time) taking precedence over diversity if and when these two come into conflict (unless the claims of community infringe on basic liberties and minority rights). No European nation fully adheres to this model; the US comes closer and has been more successful in absorbing immigrants than have many EU members.

Each of the three positions discussed here (assimilationist, unbounded pluralism, DWU) can be represented through visual metaphors. The melting pot is often used to depict society under an assimilationist model, in which all differences are melted down, resulting in a high degree of homogeneity. A salad bowl is used to represent a multicultural society in which various groups are tossed together but each maintains its original flavor and form, remaining largely unchanged by contact with other elements. DWU is akin to a mosaic that is richer for the difference in size and color of its pieces but that also has a shared frame and glue that holds the various pieces together, a frame that can be recast but not abandoned. Because I hold that DWU is the most promising approach and the one that the patriotic movement ought to champion, it is next spelled out.

Citizenship and Membership

The DWU approach is based on the observation that immigrants are not only joining a state with a particular polity, laws, and institutions but also a community with a distinctive history, values, and affiliations. States have citizens; communities have members. The requirements of citizenship are relatively limited: obey the law, pay taxes, follow public affairs, and vote. Some countries require various forms of public service of their citizens, including military service. The patriotic movement should embrace the idea that all young people provide some form of national service. Membership in a community requires learning and embracing its core values and forming bonds of affinity with other members in accordance with these values. It combines respect for individual rights with social responsibilities to the common good.

If one examines, from this viewpoint, the classes and tests required by various European societies of new immigrants, one finds that many are focused on verifying that immigrants are ready to become good citizens. Occasionally, they also include some, albeit rather limited, preparation for membership in a community. For instance, tests introduced in 2006 by the German state of Baden-Württemberg ask questions such as, "Is it right for women to obey their husbands, and for men to beat their wives when they are disobedient?" and, "If your adult daughter dressed like a German woman, would you try to prevent her from doing so?" In the German state of Hesse, the citizenship test asks, "If someone described the Holocaust as a myth or folktale, how would you respond?"[19] In the Netherlands, would-be immigrants, prior to immigration, must take a "civic integration test" that quizzes them about their command of the Dutch language, history, and culture. In addition, the Dutch pre-immigration test requires viewing a video entitled *Coming to the Netherlands* that includes images of female nudity and homosexual men kissing. In addition, imams of Dutch mosques must also attend a mandatory course on "Dutch law, including the rights of women and freedom of speech."[20] A British citizenship test introduced in 2003 seeks to tease out whether a person is ready to engage others in a proactive rather than antisocial or violent manner: "What should you do if you spill someone's pint in a pub?" The correct answer in this case is, "Offer to buy them another."[21] One can argue about whether one question or another is appropriate or well-worded. However, from a DWU perspective, which seeks to make immigrants not only citizens but also members of the national community, incorporating society's values and norms in civics education is essential and deserves more attention.

The discussion next turns to examine which required behaviors and elements belong to the unity realm—to which all members of the society are expected to adhere—and which belong to the diversity realm. To reiterate, although a realm of normative unity, of a core of shared values, must be maintained if the society is to hold together and the polity is to function, these values may be reexamined and adjusted over time. There is room for differences of opinion over which elements belong to which realm, and these distributions tend to shift over time and from one society to another. Nevertheless, to endure and flourish, nations—at any given point in time—need to clarify which behaviors must be "unified" (so to speak) and which can be left "unbound."

Shared Values—Core but Not All

The term "national ethos" refers to the values, traditions, identity, and vision of the future (or "destiny") of a given nation.[22] The DWU model holds that integration of immigrants does not require that the immigrants adopt all the elements of the national ethos but only the core values—in sharp contrast to an assimilationist approach. To proceed, nations in the process of planning for massive absorption of immigrants need to sort out which values are part of the core and which are not. This requirement is challenging for members of many European societies that have only a vague sense of what would constitute such a core.

Assimilationists avoid this issue because, as a matter of principle, they view all shared values as obligatory for immigrants' adoption. Unbounded pluralists avoid the question by assuming that immigrants need no new values. However, if one grants, even for the sake of argument, that DWU might work better, one must inevitably ask, What is the core of shared values?

Granted, many difficulties arise once one seeks to determine which values are "core" and which are not. Many of the values various European societies may regard as defining their nation are universal, for example, respect for human rights. Other values are European—for example, strong support for a social welfare state as opposed to American capitalism—but do not necessarily define what it means to be French or a Swede or an Italian. (A wit captured this dilemma by asking if warm beer and fish and chips are what makes one a Brit.) Former Norwegian prime minister Kjell Magne Bondevik stated at the 2004 Conference on European Values: "In Europe . . . to some extent we all have a spiritual and intellectual heritage from Athens—democracy, Rome—the rule of law, and Jerusalem—the Judeo-Christian values."[23] Well put, but it does not define national differences in core values.

One set of values cited by some European leaders as part of the core is a Christian heritage or worldview. Former French president Nicolas Sarkozy said: "The roots of France are essentially Christian. . . . To take away those roots means to lose meaning, to weaken the cement of national identity."[24] Former British prime minister David Cameron argued that Christianity had played an important part in shaping the country's identity, stating: "These are values we treasure. They are Christian values and they should give us the confidence to say yes, we are a Christian country and we are proud of it."[25] Public schools in many European countries in effect incorporate Christian values as part of their curriculum.

This position has to be reexamined given the need to absorb millions of Muslims. European societies have two basic choices: separate state and religion and relegate religion to the private realm of diversity or provide equal expression to several religions. For example, starting public events with a blessing from a priest, an imam, and a rabbi and perhaps a reading of a humanist text by an atheist. (While this may sound far-fetched, quite a few public events actually are implementing this policy, though atheists are typically excluded.)

There are some signs that Europe is moving in the direction of scaling back the role of Christianity in public life. Thus, Scandinavian countries that had long-standing official state churches have disestablished their national churches in recent years. Norway's parliament voted in 2012 to separate the Norwegian Church from the state but to continue to finance the church "on par with other religious and belief-based societies."[26] Similarly, Sweden disestablished its official Lutheran church in 2000, and the government now allocates money to other faiths as well, with individual taxpayers deciding what their taxes will fund.[27] These changes illustrate what I meant by saying that integrating immigrants needs in part to be achieved by changing the core values rather than those of the immigrants.

Another challenge to defining the national ethos for the patriotic movement is fear of endorsing insular nationalism that can spill over into nativism and xenophobia. In the 1990s, a group of political theorists began to argue for "liberal nationalism," which sought to preserve the sense of belonging, loyalty, and solidarity embodied in nationalism while removing chauvinist and racist elements and incorporating the personal autonomy embedded in classical liberalism.

Despite all these difficulties, one cannot disregard that each European nation has some shared values so central to communal bonds and practices that ignoring them offends or violates communal identity. One possible approach to articulating these values is for various societies to combine universal and "European" values, each in their own way. Thus, the Nordic countries may put more focus on social egalitarianism than does the United Kingdom, while the Netherlands may place more emphasis on personal liberties than does France. The UK may place less emphasis on the social welfare state than most other European societies, whereas France may stress the separation of state and church more than the rest of Europe, and so on. Further, each society has its own historical narratives, national heroes, and celebrations, which are all elements to consider in determining which particular values are to be included in the core and which are not.

In sorting out the historical values, the patriotic movement needs to take special note of the norm that accession to membership in a national community, and enjoyment of the benefits that such membership bestows, must be accompanied by an assumption of the nation's burdens. Just as one who joins a family via adoption or marriage cannot claim they are entitled to part of the new family's assets but none of its liabilities, so upon becoming a member of a new society, one cannot merely benefit from its accumulated wealth while disowning its past misdeeds and obligatory reparations. Thus, a new British citizen cannot claim to be an heir to the tradition of civil liberties passed down from the Magna Carta onward, yet disavow any implication in the legacy of British imperialism. Similarly, a new German cannot pride himself on the achievements of Kant, Goethe, and Bach—or *Dichter und Denker*—without also sharing in the national shame of the Holocaust.

The fact that the line between the unity realm, which all members of a society must enter, and the diversity realm, in which they are welcome to differ, is not always observed is illustrated by the following case in point. A website launched by the Federal Center for Health Education in Germany in 2016 seeks to provide sex education mainly to Muslim immigrants. The online guide seeks to teach them about the impropriety of groping women, respect for gay people, and manners for conversation with German women. But the guide also uses exceedingly graphic images and language to introduce immigrants to the "joy of sex," for example, by showing various sex positions and the details of oral sex.[28] Education of the latter kind seems unnecessary to impart core values, and respect for diversity in attitudes about such matters should be part of the patriotic movement platform.

Education: 80 Percent Shared

The assimilationist model assumes that immigrants and minorities will attend public schools and learn basically the same material as other members of society. An unbounded diversity model calls for setting up separate schools and allowing distinct curricula for various ethnic and religious groups from kindergarten to grade 12, such as separating Muslim or Jewish schools, and not merely as "Sunday" schools but as full-time schools.

The DWU model calls for a significant core curriculum (comprising perhaps 80 percent of the total curriculum) for all students. This core curriculum is to include the normal elements of a modern education (math, sciences, language arts, etc.) as well as classes that teach core values and prepare students for citizenship and membership in the society. For the remaining 20 percent, students would be free to choose between classes that nurture their particular religious or cultural values; for example, students might be able to take a course on the history and traditions of their (or their parents') country of origin or a theology course taught by a vetted religious leader.

Several European nations lean in this matter toward the unbounded pluralism model. For example, the British government provides financial support to a variety of religious schools; although the majority of these schools are Christian, there are also Muslim, Jewish, Sikh, and Hindu faith schools.[29] The extent to which the government requires some measure of shared core values curriculum in these faith schools varies depending on their status.[30] However, serious failings have been found at some of these schools; an official investigation determined that "seven hundred children attend schools where inspectors considered that pupils were not being adequately prepared for life in modern Britain."[31] Among the failings were students who thought that France was a part of Britain, a book in one school's library that asserted that women were less reliable witnesses than men, and older pupils who did not know the term "government" or understand the democratic process. Such findings confirm the DWU view that if students are segregated into religious schools, a strong core of shared teaching needs to be assured.

Some countries have taken actions that move diverse schools somewhat closer to the DWU model. For example, Finland's National Core Curriculum gives guidance on helping immigrant and other foreign-language students develop both cultural identities, instructing that schools should "support students' growth into active and balanced members of both the Finnish linguistic and cultural community and their own linguistic and cultural community."[32] From a DWU viewpoint, ideally all children should attend the same public schools—to ensure the element of unity and reduce tribalism as all intermingle socially—and all schools should include in their curricula classes that teach history, literature, civics and social sciences, as well as core values. If students attend private or religious-based schools, they should still be required to include these elements in their curriculum. It would also be beneficial if these students were expected to participate in some interscholastic events and activities, not just in competition against each other but also in cooperative events, for example, participating in activities such as building homes with Habitat for Humanity, to protect and restore the environment, or joint field trips to local historical sites.

At the same time, there should be room for respect for diversity. For instance, in Germany, an eleven-year-old girl requested to be exempt from coed swimming lessons at school because she did not want to swim with boys, arguing that Islam forbade her to see male classmates shirtless. A federal court ruled, however, that the girl must continue, insisting that coeducation was an important component of learning to live in a pluralistic society.[33] A DWU approach favors allowing diverse accommodations in such situations. If a significant number of students hold similar views, schools could offer gender-segregated swimming lessons. Otherwise, individual students could use the time to pursue other scholarly or extracurricular activities approved by the school. Diversity in student attire (wearing the hijab or Islamic headscarves, yarmulkes, etc.) should be accommodated, and used to teach tolerance, as long as students are able to socialize and learn together.

In Switzerland, when two Muslim students from Syria asked to be excused from shaking a female teacher's hand at the beginning and end of the school day, the local school district accommodated the students' request. The arrangement, however, became a national flashpoint. There was strong consensus that a refusal to shake the teacher's hand shows disrespect for Swiss fundamental values. Hence the canton in which the school was located overruled the decision and instituted a five-thousand-dollar fine for students who refuse to shake hands with their teachers.[34] Every act and custom can be turned into a polarizing symbol. In my judgment, this specific practice is innocuous and should serve as an occasion to promote vibrant diversity and find substitutes. Thus students may salute their teachers rather than shake their hands. Indeed, all students may be asked to change their behavior accordingly (an especially good idea in flu season).

Primary and Secondary Loyalties

Strict assimilation models hold that any vestiges of loyalty to one's country of birth are problematic and jeopardize loyalty to the host country. According to this view, loyalty is a zero-sum game. The Netherlands' policy on citizenships reflects this view, as immigrants wishing to obtain Dutch nationality through naturalization are usually required to forfeit their other nationality.[35]

DWU does not suggest, as do assimilationists, that adopting the identity of the host country implies discarding loyalty to immigrants' countries of origin. Rather, DWU suggests layered identities where various immigrants maintain subidentities (Turkish Germans, for example, or Dutch Moroccans) that are situated within an overarching shared identity. Dual citizenship is acceptable under this framework. However, when the two loyalties clash, loyalties to the new home nation must take priority in liberal democracies. Thus, refugees from conflict zones might be expected to have special concerns about the fate of people in the countries they came from, to send remittances, and to urge their adoptive country to help restore order in places such as Syria and Libya. However, if the new home nation were to send troops to fight in the old home country, immigrants must side with their new home, or they would be considered ill-integrated.

While the DWU approach demands primary loyalty to the national community from all its members, immigrants' affinity to their respective homelands need not be discouraged. In fact, such diversity can be enriching to the host society, contributing new holidays, cuisine, and other cultural attributes.

Language(s)

The assimilationist model emphasizes acquisition of the national language(s) and advocates for a ban on using other languages in official business, courts, ballots, and street signs. In the Netherlands, anyone receiving social assistance benefits must be able to communicate in Dutch; if a claimant has not attained a considerable level of language proficiency, they may have their benefit reduced and eventually discontinued.[36] In some cases, assimilationists even seek to limit second languages in the private sphere. Austria, for example, passed a bill in 2015 that requires imams to speak German.[37] Some think any use of immigrants' native languages signals a refusal to integrate. They take offense at shops that display foreign signage and street signs with "foreign" languages.

Unbounded multiculturalism opposes the recognition of any one language as official and seeks to provide a coequal status to multiple languages (sometimes a rather large number) in courts, official documents, and so on. The nearest example of this sort of linguistic pluralism is Belgium, where French, Dutch, and German are all official languages, and there are further languages and dialects that are recognized by regional authorities. As already noted, Belgium is one of the least integrated European countries, barely able to support a state.[38]

A DWU approach recognizes the considerable advantages to social cohesion of having a shared language and teaching it to all immigrants, members of minority groups, and people whose education is lagging for other reasons. However, it does not oppose the state provision of translators and translated documents for those who have not yet acquired the shared language, even if this reduces the motivation for immigrants to learn the prevailing language. Thus, Sweden guarantees *mödersmålundervisning*, or the right to receive instruction in and develop one's native language. State-funded schools offer classes in indigenous minority languages, as well as Arabic, Farsi, etc. while also teaching Swedish as a second language to students who require it. The DWU model would operate on the assumption that these measures are transitional, helping immigrants bridge the gap until they are fluent in the national language rather than facilitating the long-term conducting of official business in their native language.

The patriotic movement should mobilize members of its chapters to act as volunteers, teaching immigrants the national language or languages. In this way, not merely will acculturation be much accelerated

but also the immigrants would get to know the old-timers on a pro- .
longed personal basis (as distinct from going out to dinner together here
and there).

In Conclusion

Many nations face the challenge of integrating large numbers of immigrants, which entails providing institutions and processes that will lead
new immigrants to embrace the moral culture of their new homeland,
even if the culture is changed somewhat in the process. The patriotic
movement would do best to recognize that assimilation is unnecessary
and unduly taxing while unbounded pluralism is insufficiently inte-
grative. Sorting out which elements of the new homeland's values and
norms the immigrants must absorb and in which areas they are free to
affirm diversity is the basis of the model the movement ought to adopt—
Diversity within Unity.

8

THE NEED FOR SELF-RESTRAINT

The patriotic movement may well be able to find policy consensus on many issues, including immigration and free trade. This consensus need not, nor should it aspire to, resolve all differences. In several matters the main goal may be to contain differences by explicating a core of shared values. However, the patriotic movement faces a major challenge when it must sort out its positions with regard to what has been called culture war issues, such as abortion, same-sex marriage, and transgender rights.

When deliberating culturally sensitive topics, both sides feel that they are concerned with absolutes and tend to hold that the other side has neither a moral nor a legal foot to stand on. The question arises, How can one contain conflicts when core values are at stake? Part of the answer lies in leaving some contested matters out of the public realm. Indeed, some advocate that marriage, for instance, should not be defined by the state, that each couple be left free to form their own marriage contract.

Some issues, however, the state cannot avoid—whether abortion should be legal, whether LGBTQ people have the same rights as heterosexual citizens, and what constitutes discrimination. I believe that if the opposing sides have a strong sense of community on other grounds, this will help people deal with these differences, but I grant that culture war topics will remain divisive even when all parties are strong patriots. The answer might be found in leaving these matters to the courts, which in the past worked out middle grounds that most citizens learned to live with. Others, though, hold that leaving these matters to the courts exacerbates rather than lessens the divisions, as the "losing" side feels the courts' adjudication ("legislation from the bench") foists its decisions without genuine public debate and consensus.[1] However, as I see it, the courts may often be the only place these issues can be worked out. In either case, I suggest, all parties involved should show a measure of self-restraint.

Legal Rights vs. Morally Right

The American law allows landlords to evict tenants who do not pay rent for a few months on any day, including Christmas Eve, as long as proper eviction notices have been served. However, our moral values hold that an eviction on such a holiday would be indecent, would be morally inappropriate. Indeed, in a considerable category of situations our values teach us the enforcement of legal rights to the full limit is morally wrong. Such legal self-restraint is often fostered by intangible moral forces.

The basic moral idea before us has been captured in the phrase "a pound of flesh," signifying conditions where one should not extract what one is due even if one is fully entitled to do so. The expression comes from Shakespeare's *Merchant of Venice* (circa 1599), in which a merchant, Antonio, borrows money from Shylock. The terms of repayment hold that the loan will be interest-free under the condition that if Antonio does not meet his commitment, he will have to pay a pound of his own flesh to Shylock. Antonio's maritime business goes under, and he is forced to default on the loan. In response, Shylock, motivated by mutual enmity, sets out to collect his pound of flesh: "The pound of flesh which I demand of him is dearly bought, 'tis mine, and I will have it." Shylock is depicted not as someone who made a fair deal and intends to claim what is rightfully his but as a heartless, cruel banker.

In the eighteenth century, the phrase started to take on its modern, figurative meaning: to take a pound of flesh is to demand of someone recompense that is legal, yet unreasonable, merciless, or inhumane.[2] For instance, an 1887 newspaper article read, "All the other Great Powers want their pound of flesh from Turkey." A French romantic novel from 1905 used it similarly: "That relentless and stern France which was exacting her pound of flesh, the blood-tax from the noblest of her sons."[3]

The same basic concept is reflected in a court case concerning Walker-Thomas Furniture, a rent-to-own furniture store. Its contracts stipulated that none of the furniture was owned by customers until all of the items purchased were paid for. When a customer defaulted on payment for one item, the store tried to repossess all of their previous purchases that had been paid for in full. The District of Columbia Court of Appeals ruled that courts could refuse to enforce contracts deemed unconscionable and sent the case back to the trial court for such a determination.[4]

Although the term has historically been employed to characterize interpersonal relations, it also has a profound communal implication. It suggests that when community members deal with one another, they ought to make some concessions to each other, because they are dealing with people with whom they have bonds of affection and commitments, as well as people they will need to work with, indeed live with, another day. This holds not only for workplaces, neighborhoods, or towns, but even for nations. Nations serve as imagined communities that forge deep bonds, indicated by how strongly people feel when national sports teams win or lose and when their nation is celebrated or demeaned—and by their willingness to die for their country.

The chapter moves next to examine two situations in which this concept applies on the national level. One concerns free speech and the other, discrimination.

Free Speech: A Right Does Not Make It Right

A crucial difference exists between the *right* to say highly offensive things—to use the n-word, to employ ethnic slurs, to argue that soldiers died in battle because their nation tolerates homosexuality—and the right*ness* of saying these things. It is the difference between a legal right to free speech and what we consider morally appropriate speech. All of us are not only citizens with a whole array of rights but also members of various communities comprised of people with whom we reside, work, play, pray, take civic action, and socialize. These communities, in effect, inform one that if someone engages in offensive speech—which, granted, is one's right—that person had better have a sound reason to so express themselves. For instance, offensive speech may be essential for an artistic work that depicts the perspective of the oppressed. Otherwise, people who engage in offensive speech without a cause are considered morally flawed.

Many democracies deal with this dilemma by enacting laws that limit free speech; for example, they ban hate speech. In the US, however, we have, in effect, decided to rely on our communitarian sensibilities to prevent—and, as I show next, informally curb—hate speech rather than to legally prohibit it.

In many situations, the notion that one should not engage in offensive speech unless there is a particular reason to do so is supported by informal social mechanisms. Those who express their right to free speech to the full limit by wantonly offending other community members are subject to social pressure, condemnation, suspensions, and even job loss. For example, Lawrence Summers, serving as the president of Harvard University, resigned after the public outcry following his remarks that women's underrepresentation in the sciences may reflect their intellectual shortcomings.

In 2017, June Chu, a dean at Yale University, was placed on leave for writing demeaning Yelp reviews, and later left her position. "If you are white trash, this is the perfect night out for you!" Chu wrote in a review of a restaurant.[5] In a review of a movie theater, she described employees as "barely educated morons trying to manage snack orders for the obese and also try to add $7 plus $7."[6] Chu apologized, saying her comments had been "wrong" and "insensitive."[7] Kenneth Storey, a visiting assistant professor, was fired from the University of Tampa after he tweeted, in reference to the destruction caused by Hurricane Harvey in 2017: "I don't believe in instant karma but this kinda feels like it for Texas. Hopefully this will help them realize the GOP doesn't care about them."[8] After receiving a chorus of condemnation, he deleted the tweet and issued an apology

In 2014, Elizabeth Lauten, communications director for former US representative Stephen Fincher (R-TN), resigned after the critical remarks she made on Facebook about Malia and Sasha Obama went viral and prompted a backlash. "Act like being in the White House matters to you. Dress like you deserve respect, not a spot at a bar,"[9] wrote Lauten of the first daughters, then sixteen and thirteen years old. She quickly apologized and admitted she "judged the two young ladies in a way that I would never have wanted to be judged myself as a teenager."[10]

When faced with a community's pushback, free speech advocates sometimes complain, calling it soft or outright censorship. For example, some users of the social media site Reddit wanted its CEO fired for censorship after five forums (out of thousands) were deleted for racial or other forms of harassment. Facebook has been criticized and even sued for censorship because it bans users who display pictures of women's breasts. Twitter was criticized for introducing content filters and temporary account suspensions for abusive messages and "indirect threats of violence,"[11] in what one user said "can only be described as heavy-handed censorship." And in response to a Harris Poll showing that 71 percent of Americans want a rating system for books to protect children from inappropriate content, like those that exist for movies and games, free speech advocates argued that such a proposal would "raise serious concerns about censorship."[12]

These champions of free speech, unwittingly or deliberately, use the horror that the term "censorship" evokes to object to social reactions to offensive speech. In doing so, they attempt to delegitimize social pressure, which is a fundamental element of all communities. Censorship, by definition, takes place when the government exercises its coercive powers to prevent speech by jailing dissenters, closing newspapers, taking over TV stations, and so on. Social pressure merely ensures that before one speaks, one asks whether what one has to say justifies the hurt it will cause, often to people who have already been hurt greatly.

One can readily imagine communities in which the social pressure to limit speech is much too high. However, in the US and other liberal democracies, excessive moral fostering of self-restraint is relatively rare, while instances of exercising free speech with very little concern for others seem quite common. The Supreme Court has ruled that the Westboro Baptist Church (which believes that God is punishing the US for its acceptance of homosexuality) is allowed to picket the funerals of military service members, displaying signs with statements such as "Thank God for dead soldiers" and "You're Going to Hell."[13] The Supreme Court also struck down a Massachusetts law that created a thirty-five-foot buffer zone around abortion clinics that protesters were not allowed to enter.[14] Protesters often follow patients to the doors of clinics, shout phrases such as "baby killers," and even threaten patients and physicians.[15] These legal rights are morally beyond the pale—and a decent human being will not exercise such rights.

One may argue that there is no clear line between speech that is offensive and vital for a thriving democracy, and speech that is merely hurtful and advances no cause other than hate and humiliation. Indeed, there is a continuous debate over whether the social mechanisms that curb abusive speech are too powerful or not powerful enough (for instance, there are often debates on college campuses on whether certain speakers should be invited, or if "safe zones" and trigger warnings should be provided). True, societies may oversteer in one direction or the other (a common failing of all societies, which are driven like cars whose steering wheels are very loose, tending to overshoot in one direction and then overcorrect in the opposite one). However, these valid observations do not invalidate our basic moral sense that not all legally entitled speech is morally appropriate. We argue about where the boundaries lie and grant that the lack of clarity may lead people to cross the line—however, in the process we, in effect, acknowledge the premise that some self-restraint is morally commendable.

Gay Rights: Cakes, Flower Arrangements, and Makeup Artists

The question of whether a devout Christian baker can legally refuse to make a wedding cake for a gay couple, especially with such an inscription as "For the marriage of Jim and John," provides an illuminating example of the issue at hand.

In 2012, Jack Phillips, the owner of Masterpiece Cakeshop, declined on religious grounds to bake a wedding cake for Dave Mullins and Charlie Craig's wedding reception in Colorado before their marriage in Massachusetts. According to Phillips, he told the couple he would make them other baked goods, but he "just can't make a cake for a same-sex wedding."[16] Although Colorado did not recognize same-sex marriage at the time, the Colorado Anti-Discrimination Act (CADA) was in place, which includes discrimination based on sexual orientation. An administrative law judge ruled in favor of Mullins and Craig, and in 2014 the Colorado Court of Appeals also sided with the couple. After Phillips's appeal was denied by the Colorado Supreme Court, Phillips petitioned the US Supreme Court, which agreed to hear the case in 2017. In the meantime, rather than make cakes for both same-sex and opposite-sex couples, Phillips stopped making wedding cakes entirely, losing 40 percent of his business. In June 2018 the Supreme Court ruled 7–2 in favor of Phillips. However, the decision was narrowly based and did not clearly address whether First Amendment rights allow businesses to refuse service to gay couples on religious grounds. Instead, the Court offered a largely procedural, case-specific ruling by finding that a member of the Colorado Court of Appeals expressed religious hostility toward Phillips.[17]

One should note that Phillips's refusal of service was not an isolated incident. Aside from Phillips himself admitting that he had refused service to other gay couples in the past,[18] there was another nationally recognized case regarding an Oregon bakery whose owner refused to make a cake for a same-sex couple. The couple owning the bakery was ordered to pay $135,000 in damages, to be collected when the ongoing appeals process is over.[19]

Furthermore, the issue at hand is actually broader. For example, the

Supreme Court in Washington state heard a case in which a florist re-fused to make floral arrangements—regardless of whether the designs were hers—for a gay couple's wedding because it went against her religious beliefs. According to the florist, Baronelle Stutzman, making floral arrangements for a same-sex wedding, or allowing employees of her store to do so, amounts to participation in, and therefore endorsement of, same-sex marriage. She would, however, be willing to sell gay people bulk flowers and raw materials.[20] The case has similarities to that of Jack Phillips—just as Phillips offered other baked goods, the florist offered to sell individual or prearranged flowers to the couple.[21] Also, like Phillips, since the lawsuit began, she has stopped selling flowers for all weddings.[22]

As I see it, many who read about these cases have conflicting judgments. On the one hand, they realize that law prohibits people who serve the public from discriminating on the basis of race, religion, and—most agree—sexual orientation. On the other hand, they sense that compelling behavior that violates someone's religious conscience is not a matter one should consider lightly. Moreover, they wonder why gay people would wish to force someone who treats them as abject sinners to make them a wedding cake. Would a gay couple truly want flowers at their wedding from someone they feel hates them? Why give their business to such people? Various attempts have been made to resolve this conflict between the legal and the social/moral intuition. Those are next briefly reviewed and my suggestion added.

Religious Exception?

We allow people to discriminate (or do not consider it discrimination) if the differences made are essential for religious expression. Thus, the law allows synagogues to retain only Jews as rabbis. With respect to the Masterpiece Cakeshop case, the Colorado Court of Appeals points out that although CADA has an exemption for "places primarily used for religious purposes," the primary function of Masterpiece is not for religious purposes, and therefore it is not exempt.[23] The appeals court also draws a parallel between the case at hand and a challenge to the Civil Rights Act of 1964 in which a district court ruled that religious beliefs do not give someone the right to discriminate on the basis of race: "Undoubtedly [the] defendant . . . has a constitutional right to espouse the religious beliefs of his own choosing, however, he does not have the absolute right to exercise and practice such beliefs in utter disregard of the clear constitutional rights of other citizens. This Court refuses to lend credence or support to his position that he has a constitutional right to refuse to serve members of the Negro race in his business establishment upon the ground that to do so would violate his sacred religious beliefs."[24]

According to the Colorado Court of Appeals: "CADA does not compel Masterpiece to support or endorse any particular religious views. The law merely prohibits Masterpiece from discriminating against potential customers on account of their sexual orientation."[25] It further noted that "CADA does not prevent Masterpiece from posting a disclaimer in the store or on the internet, indicating that the provision of its services does not constitute an endorsement or approval of conduct protected by CADA."[26] In the terms used here, making a business owner serve people in ways that he considers a gross violation of his faith is not exacting a pound of flesh; violating his strongly held beliefs is trumped by the commitment to equality and justice. To yield on these matters would amount to giving up a whole lot more than a pound; it would compromise basic rights and principles.[27]

On the other hand, some are concerned about protection of religious beliefs and practices. Kerri Kupec, one of the florist's lawyers, posited that "Under this kind of rationale, that's happening in Washington state, a gay singer could be forced by the government to perform at a religious conference that is promoting marriage as a man-woman union."[28] Richard Epstein, a law professor at New York University, maintains that it is the American Left that is intolerant: "The people who are bigots are on the other side."[29] Epstein supports a religious exemption for business owners in cases like these and believes that the free market takes care of the problem of discrimination against gay individuals.[30] Viewed this way, the issue of exacting a pound of flesh does not arise, because those who seek to force service on those who hold that such service violates their beliefs do not have a case to begin with.

A Form of Speech?

According to Phillips, wedding cakes have an inherent "communicative nature," which conveys celebration.[31] If forced to make a cake for a gay couple's wedding celebration, he would be compelled to make a statement, or speech, he does not feel comfortable making.[32] According to Phillips's lawyers: "The wedding cakes that Jack designs and creates . . .

are very clearly a method of communication. . . . Jack could not just bake a cake and pretend it did not mean anything."[33] The appeals court recognized that "a wedding cake, in some circumstances, may convey a particularized message celebrating same-sex marriage and, in such cases, First Amendment speech protections may be implicated."[34] However, this was a nonissue for the court because Phillips refused to serve the couple without discussing the design of the cake or any written inscriptions the couple may have wanted. There was no communicative content.[35]

In contrast to this opinion, the Department of Justice (DOJ) stated in a 2017 amicus brief on behalf of Jack Phillips that "A custom wedding cake is a form of expression,"[36] and "Forcing Phillips to create expression for and participate in a ceremony that violates his sincerely held religious beliefs invades his First Amendment rights."[37]

The DOJ's opinion is thus in line with the arguments of Phillips's lawyers, who insist that the Colorado Court of Appeals "considered the wrong question"[38] when it determined that "designing and selling a wedding cake to all customers free of discrimination does not convey a celebratory message about same-sex weddings."[39] They contend that the proper question is whether the wedding cakes made by Phillips qualify as "expressive conduct," whereas the Colorado Court of Appeals "looked for expression only in Phillips's *decision* not to create a wedding cake celebrating a same-sex marriage"[40] (emphasis added). The DOJ holds that Phillips's cakes do qualify as expressive conduct and thus the Free Speech clause applies in this case. One could limit this claim to customers' requests to add a specific inscription that could be read as an explicit endorsement of gay marriage; this might be considered a pound of flesh—but not just making cakes or otherwise serving people. In other words, requiring a cake maker to bake a blank cake is acceptable, but requiring one to write an inscription supportive of the marriage is not. I will show below more compelling ways to discern what constitutes a fair demand and when making such demands becomes analogous to exacting a pound of flesh.

Fair Warning?

Still another way out of the box is for businesses to post their religious preferences and thus avoid the conflict altogether. According to Andrew Koppelman, law professor at Northwestern University, "The most sensible reconciliation of the tension would permit business owners to present their views to the world, but forbid them either to threaten to discriminate or to treat any individual customer worse than others."[41] He elaborates, asserting: "If proprietors who object to same-sex marriage could make their views known, then even if they have no statutory right to refuse to facilitate ceremonies they regard as immoral, they are unlikely to be asked to participate in those ceremonies. On the contrary, same-sex couples will almost all want nothing to do with them. Announcements of the proprietor's views will not absolutely guarantee that service will not be demanded, but it will make such demands rare."[42] The issue with Koppelman's solution is that several states prohibit businesses from displaying announcements that, in effect, assert that a protected class is unwelcome. In the case of Jack Phillips, the Colorado Court of Appeals stated that a business cannot post a notice stating intent to refuse service to those who participate in a same-sex marriage or stating that those who participate in a same-sex marriage are not welcome. On the other hand, in the case of a photographer in New Mexico, the New Mexico Supreme Court held: "Businesses retain their First Amendment rights to express their religious or political beliefs. They may, for example, post a disclaimer on their website or in their studio advertising that they oppose same-sex marriage but that they comply with applicable antidiscrimination laws."[43] Koppelman himself is doubtful that the Supreme Court would allow such a solution to stand, as it may be understood as an explicit form of discrimination.

Notching the Slope

A good part of the give-and-take on the issues at hand, including the line of questioning the Supreme Court judges engaged in when they heard the case of *Masterpiece Cakeshop v. Colorado Civil Rights Commission* in 2017, included weighing in on what constitutes a pound of flesh versus a fair demand. The questions of some judges seem to indicate that while they thought allowing refusal of services might be acceptable under some limited conditions, they feared such exceptions would open the floodgates to widespread discrimination. The issue hence is, How can one ensure that such an opening will not be excessive?

This challenge is a very familiar one, often referred to as the slippery slope. One recognizes that some limited change might well be called for, but one fears that a shift from the status quo will lead to the lower—wrong—end of a deep slope. The argument in the case at hand takes two major forms. One, if bakers can refuse to make cakes, should other business owners be allowed to refuse their services? As Washington Supreme Court justice Mary Yu asked, "Is it the landscape architect next? The barber?"[44] According to James Oleske, "proposed exemptions would not only allow businesses to withhold wedding-day services, but would also 'threaten to subject same-sex couples to discrimination in employment, public accommodations, and housing across time and in situations far removed from the marriage celebration.'"[45]

The second slope concerns the implications of refusing service to gay people on potential discrimination against other groups of people, such as African Americans. According to Washington attorney general Bob Ferguson, "once you go down the road of allowing this exception . . . you can refuse service to an interracial couple based on your religious beliefs."[46]

As I have suggested previously, if one adheres to this position, then any changes, however justified, must be avoided. I hold that instead one needs to find places to notch the slope, to ensure that one can move to a limited extent but not beyond a point clearly marked. What are the appropriate markers? One possible criterion that courts often use in other contexts concerns the scope of the harm. If a refusal to sell cakes by one shop inflicts very limited harm, it should be tolerated. This might be said to be the case as cakes are readily available from other sources, especially in this era of e-commerce. Wedding cakes are ordered way ahead of time and hence differ, say, from an immediate need like medication. Also, the cakes are merely one marginal feature of wedding ceremonies compared to that of exchanging vows, wedding bands, and so on. The same holds for the services of the florist and makeup artists—but not for those of lodging, catering, employment, credit, transportation, not to mention medical treatment. One may say that there are plenty of eateries and hence there is no harm in rejecting food service. However, there are many conditions under which this is not the case—for instance, when seeking food late at night or in isolated areas or when one has special dietary requirements such as halal, kosher, vegan, gluten free, diabetic, or infant-friendly. If service is refused in the one place in town that provides these foods at a particular time of day, one may well have difficulties finding another. The same holds for lodging; denial of service late in the day, on a holiday eve, at a major sports or musical event, and so on may impose considerable harm on a person seeking to find an alternative.

The US Supreme Court declined to hear a challenge to the Protecting Freedom of Conscience from Government Discrimination Act, a Mississippi law that critics argue "lets government clerks refuse to issue same-sex marriage licenses and lets adoption and foster-care organizations decline to place children with LGBT families."[47] As I see it, this clearly is on the wrong side of the "notch."

A counterargument is that at issue is not the provision of service per se but the normative principle regulating the provision. The harm, one may well argue, is not to the supply of cakes but to the principle that all people are to be treated equally. To push the point: a gay couple may well not want a wedding cake from someone who strongly disapproves of their conduct—and may even think that a service obtained through coercive measures of the law would mar their happy celebration and that they may as well feed the cake to the dogs—but still insist on the service, to uphold the nondiscrimination principle and to stave off pernicious precedents. I refer to such concerns as "symbolic," by which I mean that the issue is not the object at hand but what it stands for.

If one believes that to compromise even at the margin weakens the legal principle, then the moral precept of not asking for a pound of flesh does not apply because to allow for exceptions, even if they cause little or no substantive harm, violates the principle involved. However, if one holds that insisting on the pound of flesh undermines support for the legal principle, because it makes its advocates look like rabid ideologues lacking in sympathy, one would favor making exceptions when the refusal causes little or no substantive harm.

The following case, discussed in the *Washington Post*,[48] provides an example of how North Carolina reached a middle-ground solution that tries to respect both religious and LGBT rights. In 2014, Gayle Myrick resigned as a magistrate in North Carolina because she was unwilling to perform civil marriages for same-sex couples. Myrick's supervisor suggested that Myrick could be excused from performing marriages, but someone higher up said that Myrick's schedule could not accommodate such a change. Myrick says she "didn't want to stop anyone from getting married" but knew her "religious convictions would not allow [her] to perform [same-sex] marriages personally."[49] She reached a settlement with the government after a federal judge sided with her. North Carolina has since passed a law that allows magistrates to excuse themselves from performing marriages if they have religious objections but at the same time stipulates that other magistrates—willing to perform marriages for same-sex couples—be available in such a case.[50]

One should recognize the cardinal communitarian observation that we are not just rights-bearing individuals, out to carry those individual rights wherever they will take us, but also members of communities. And that such membership entails a measure of sympathy for people whose profound beliefs we strongly disagree with. We should recognize that they hold their beliefs just as strongly as we hold ours. This is *not* to suggest moral equivalency but to help appreciate that those who hold values we consider morally flawed did not choose these values but were brought up to believe in them, and that those values were reinforced by their religious leaders and those they personally know and, until very recently, were reaffirmed in the law of the land! One ought to recall that it was President Bill Clinton who, in 1996, signed the Defense of Marriage Act, which defined marriage as the union of a man and woman. And that even when President Barack Obama came to office in 2009, he was reluctant to support gay marriage. Our fellow community members need to be helped to transition and given some time to adapt—as long as the harm to those who grant them some leeway is minimal or basically symbolic and does not undermine the legal principle involved, because clearly delineated exceptions are carved out.

David Brooks takes this communitarian approach to a much higher level and suggests that the gay couple should have said to the baker: "Fine, we won't compel you to do something you believe violates your sacred principles. But we would like to hire you to bake other cakes for us. We would like to invite you into our home for dinner and bake with you, so you can see our marital love, and so we can understand your values. You still may not agree with us, after all this, but at least we'll understand each other better and we can live more fully in our community."[51] Although Brooks carries the communitarian idea several steps further than I do, the thesis he draws on is the same. Confronting and exercising all the legal rights one may be entitled to is not always the preferred way to conduct oneself, especially if one cares about the other and the community.

In Conclusion

A challenge the patriotic movement faces is how to deal with people with conflicting core values. The more the movement is able to shore up the sense of overarching community, and the sharing of core values in areas other than those in conflict, the more one must expect that cultural wars will be contained. Privatizing some issues will limit the realm of conflict. Nevertheless, culture wars remain an important challenge to the patriotic movement. Calling on all sides to impose a measure of self-restraint and not to push their claims to the point they undermine the common good will mitigate the cultural wars.

9
CURBING SPECIAL INTEREST GROUPS

I have stressed throughout this volume that a patriotic movement should not, and need not, seek harmony and conformity, let alone suppress conflicts and differences in the name of unity. It "merely" needs to formulate and promote core values that can contain conflicts and provide criteria for their resolution. Jean-Jacques Rousseau refers to this challenge as a continual contest between the general will and "the particular and often contradictory wills of individuals in groups."[1]

In most democratic societies, the national community and its core values have weakened as libertarian ideologies and narrowly based special interests have gained more power. The common good has been eroding. Assets intended to serve the whole community, or those most in need, have been increasingly diverted to the wealthy and the powerful. While this is true for most democracies, this is particularly the case in the US. Hence, this chapter focuses on the ways the common good is undermined in the US.

Democracy is premised on the separation of economic (and social) power from political power. Democracy can tolerate a fair amount of difference in the accumulation of economic power (although the current levels of inequality may pose a danger to democracy all of their own), but it requires that economic power will not be converted into political power—that in civic life equality will reign, that each person will have just one vote. In many democracies, especially in the US following several Supreme Court resolutions (discussed below), those who have amassed economic power are also concentrating political power. Concentration of political power undermines the social contract that is at the foundation of democratic regimes, rendering them less legitimate.

Among the factors that engender populism, few are as important as the failure of representation. America's Founding Fathers were correctly worried about what they called the mobs, the masses, whose initial raw reactions to a national challenge can be very troubling. The Founders hence sought to set up political institutions that will absorb these raw expressions and—through deliberations in legislative bodies and the accompanying moral dialogues—transform these expressions into more reasoned and responsible positions.

However, as elected officials increasingly heed narrowly based special interests, the outcomes of their deliberations no longer serve to absorb raw protest and convert it into sensible policies. The masses may not always fully understand why and how the representation system is corrupted, but they sense that their values and interests are no longer heeded. As a result they have become prey to demagogues who use social media to give voice to the raw, unprocessed feelings of the masses. It takes years before people realize that these demagogues give voice but do not deliver. The people then turn to other such demagogues, maintaining populism. As the patriotic movement seeks to rejuvenate democracy, it must work to ensure that elected officials represent the people and not narrowly based special interests.

Deep Pockets

By far the most important tool that special interest groups use is providing large amounts of money to elected officials and those who seek public office. These payments very often amount to legalized bribery. A patriotic movement cannot succeed unless it seeks to limit the influence of economic power in shaping public policy and laws as a major part of its agenda.

Campaign finance reforms are said to be unappealing to the public, either because people are more interested in substantive than in procedural issues or because they believe politics cannot be cleaned. Given the massive harm caused by legalized bribery by special interests, however, the patriotic movement has no choice. It will either find a way to address this issue, and profoundly rather than at the margin, or it will be unable to protect the common good.

Many suggestions have been made on ways to limit the contributions donors can *give*. This chapter takes into account the Supreme Court's rulings that these limitations tend to violate freedom of speech (roughly summed up in the phrase "money is speech").[2] Hence I suggest that instead of limiting what people can give, the law should limit what donors can *get* in return for their contributions. Many donors would not be motivated to make campaign contributions if they could no longer gain substantial material benefits unavailable to other parties with the same attributes. In effect, if contributors get benefits—denied to others with the same qualifications—in exchange for their contributions, they should be treated as if they had violated the law by giving a bribe. (The issues that arise in proving that indeed there was a quid pro quo are discussed below.)

At the same time, those who make contributions because they support the moral, philosophical, or ideological positions of elected officials, or strive to promote the common good—and hence neither seek nor gain any substantial material benefits for themselves in return—would continue to be free to make contributions.

Discriminatory Benefits

To curb the corrupting effects of campaign contributions, Congress should enact a law, and/or the courts should interpret existing law, that would treat as a bribe those campaign contributions in which the contributors gain a substantial material benefit not granted to others under comparable circumstances. The text should state something along the lines of the following: anyone who "directly or indirectly gives, offers, or promises anything of value to any member of Congress or a person seeking to be elected as a member of Congress, for or because of any act performed or to be performed by such person, who in return modifies Congressional acts to provide a special substantial benefit to the contributor himself/herself or a corporation, will be charged with having offered a bribe."[3] The penalty for such a violation of the law ought to be the same as for bribes offered to those in the executive branch or to judges.

The benefits, under discussion, may include appropriation of public funds (as when Congress votes that public funds will be granted to a particular person or corporation, e.g., available only to car companies operating in Michigan); tax reductions (e.g., available only to managers of hedge funds); granting credit at favorable terms (e.g., below the market value); exclusive rights to provide a service or product (e.g., supplying food to troops in noncompetitive bidding); according exclusive access to valuable resources (e.g., rights to use a former military base in the heart of San Francisco); or otherwise ensuring substantial material benefit to some while not making these same benefits available to others with the same attributes.

The qualification "substantial" material benefits serves to prevent zealous prosecutors from going after people receiving minor benefits, for instance, free school lunches to children who are not entitled to get them. The qualification "material" benefits is included to avoid criminalizing contributions made in exchange for supportive speech, for example, a member of Congress from Indiana praising the Hoosiers. However, if the praise leads to considerable material gains, for instance, the elected official praises a product of the contributor—within a defined period before or after the donation was made—and the praise results in substantially increased sales, it would be considered a bribe. (These distinctions are important as similar concerns were raised by the Supreme Court in *United States v. Sun-Diamond*, which maintained that an overly broad interpretation of the federal bribery and gratuities statute "would criminalize, for example, token gifts to the President based on his official position and not linked to any identifiable act—such as the replica jerseys given by championship sports teams each year during ceremonial White House visits.")[4] From here on, the term "benefits" is used to refer to substantial material benefits.

All special benefits should be banned preceding or following contributions for two years for members of the House and three for members of the Senate. One may wonder how members of Congress are to know whether they will be rewarded with contributions upon granting a benefit to a given person or corporation. They may well not. The clause is still needed to prevent contributors from promising elected officials contributions after enactment of special favors. The onus is on the contributor, not on the member of Congress.

Some contributors argue that they give because they share the philosophical positions of the candidates. However, if they do not donate to other political candidates with similar views but only to those who reciprocate with special benefits, this defense should not stand. This argument is particularly indefensible when benefits follow contributions to elected officials with opposing philosophies. This nonpartisan opportunism is not uncommon. As Donald Trump revealed: "I give to everybody. When they call, I give. And you know what, when I need something from them two years later, three years later, I call them. They are there for me."[5]

To illustrate: Senators Orrin Hatch and Tom Harkin cosponsored the Dietary Supplement Health and Education Act of 1994, which defined supplements as food rather than drugs, allowing the supplements to be marketed and sold without appropriate oversight and safety testing. Since that time, they have continued to mobilize senators to vote against legislation to regulate the supplements industry. They pressured the Senate to vote down Senator Dick Durbin's amendment to the 2012 FDA Safety and Innovation Act, which would have required supplements with potentially serious side effects to be labeled, and Senator John McCain's 2010 Dietary Supplement Safety Act, which would have required "manufacturers to register with the FDA and fully disclose the ingredients." They also pressured FDA officials to weaken their draft "Dietary Ingredient Guidance."

Harkin and Hatch's efforts are a major reason that unregulated supplements suffer from poor quality control and inspection. A 2013 study found that herbal supplements often contain unlabeled fillers or contaminants and that fully a third showed "no trace of the plant advertised on the bottle."[6] The two senators have been the top recipients of donations from this industry for decades.[7] There are numerous cases of such quid pro quo. One can argue that Senator Hatch, a conservative Republican, voted that way because he is opposed to regulation on ideological grounds. The same cannot be said about Senator Harkin, a liberal Democrat.

How is one to determine that the benefits elected officials grant, which follow or precede contributions within the defined period, are preferential to the contributor? Part of the answer is found in the defining attributes of the legislation. If the attribute is not impartial to the relevant constituency receiving the benefits (say, targeting all children, all farmers, or all exporters) but focuses only on the group related to the contributor (say, only children in private schools if the donor is an association of private schools), a bribe may be suspected.

Sometimes Congress members can and do define attributes of various benefits in impartial terms, but on closer examination, only one or a small number of chosen beneficiaries is found to qualify; for example, funds for a stadium are to be provided to a city a mile high and with a population of at least one million people. While the text does not single out a particular city, in effect only one city meets these criteria, Denver. The test lies in determining the relevance of the attribute. If it is true, in the case at hand, that football players cannot play in a smaller city at a lower altitude, then no bribe may be suspected. If not, red flags should be raised. One may argue that sorting out various attributes to determine whether specific benefits are related to specific contributions in partial terms is a messy and subjective task. However, there is considerable evidence from other areas of law to determine when the attributes are justified and when they are merely rationalizations for special treatment.

Thus, US employment law allows preferential criteria, that is, discrimination, based on bona fide occupational qualifications that encompass national origin, sex, and religion. Employers may use such criteria when "reasonably necessary to the normal operation of that particular business or enterprise."[8] For example, in *Dothard v. Rawlinson,* the Supreme Court ruled that although Alabama's height and weight requirements for prison guards were unlawful because they disproportionately discriminated against female candidates, the prohibition of women working as prison guards in a male maximum security prison was justified under the bona fide occupational qualification exception out of security concerns. The Court reasoned: "A woman's relative ability to maintain order in a male, maximum security, unclassified penitentiary of the type Alabama now runs could be directly reduced by her womanhood. There is a basis in fact for expecting that sex offenders who have criminally assaulted women in the past would be moved to do so again if access to women were established within the prison."[9]

Age can also fall under the category of bona fide occupational qualifications according to the Age Discrimination in Employment Act.[10] In *Western Air Lines v. Criswell,* the Supreme Court ruled that the bona fide occupational qualification exception allowed for a mandatory retirement age of flight engineers for public safety reasons.[11] In contrast, in *Griggs v. Duke Power Co.,* the Court ruled that the power company's requirement of a high school diploma for employment could not be upheld (i.e., it was not a relevant attribute) because the nature of the job did not require the skills and knowledge associated with such a degree. And the requirement discriminated against African Americans.[12]

One can further illuminate the difference between relevant and discriminatory distribution of benefits by returning to the vitamin supplements act. The question is whether supplements are foods or drugs. The fact is that people do not take them for nutrition and are not concerned about their calories, fats, or sugar. They take them, in small amounts, to improve their health. Classifying supplements as food obfuscates the relevant attribute in favor of an irrelevant, biased attribute in order to provide special benefits to the vitamin supplement industry not available to other drug makers. It is a skewed, unfair definition on the face of it.

If the Sierra Club made contributions to secure "untrampled ski slopes for its members," as it was charged, these contributions would be a violation of the suggested law. On the other hand, contributions intended to protect the environment for everyone are not. If Emily's List made contributions to politicians who secure abortion rights only for its members, it would be in violation of the suggested law; as long as it makes these only to politicians who support these rights for all women, it is not a violation—even if this right is not extended to men, because this discretion is based on a relevant attribute. Scholars tend to consider it a flaw if a definition is not airtight. However, in law there are always fuzzy cases. This does not mean that laws need to be abandoned; borderline cases can be decided by juries.

Note that the suggested approach expands the definition of quid pro quo in two ways. First, it does not require proof for an explicit agreement between the giver (the contributors) and the provider of special benefits (the member of Congress whose campaign received the contribution). That is between the Give and the Get. There are many situations where the connection between the donations and the allotment of benefits is obvious, so that any reasonable person would see that corruption was taking place. A criterion often used by the courts, "reasonable person" is defined as "a hypothetical person in society who exercises average care, skill, and judgment."[13]

This chapter's focus is on the prosecution of contributors and leaves the treatment of Congress members who received contributions deemed illegal to Congress itself. The reforms proposed in this chapter require proof of payment by a donor and the subsequent receipt of an irrelevant benefit. For those who feel that intent needs to be proven, it could be done in a variety of ways, whether through leaked emails, disaffected staff, or whistleblowers.

Additional Considerations

"Getting Only Access"

Some advocates of the prevailing system argue that contributors are merely buying access rather than gaining benefits. The Supreme Court has reinforced this claim in *Citizens United*. According to the opinion delivered by Associate Justice Anthony Kennedy in *Citizens United*, "Ingratiation and access . . . are not corruption."[14]

Gaining access is by itself a very valuable benefit. Members of Congress work under great time constraints. Many, especially House members, spend a significant amount of time each week soliciting funds. According to Representative Rick Nolan, new members were told to fund-raise for thirty hours each week in 2016.[15] Newly elected House

Democrats were advised to spend at least twenty hours per week fundraising in 2013.[16] They vote hundreds of times a year.[17] They are expected to attend staff briefings on bills' contents, as well as committee meetings of Congress and of their party. They also need to visit their constituents and travel back and forth between their home and DC. And they have, of course, personal needs, ranging from family matters to friendships and hobbies. For a person representing a special interest, gaining even fifteen minutes of a Congress member's time is a valuable benefit simply due to scarcity. Congress members have limited time to give, and any time granted to one lobbyist cannot be granted to others, who might have opposing views. Moreover, for many lobbyists of special interests, merely demonstrating privileged access to political power allows them to be rewarded by the special interest they represent.

In many situations, though, contributions lead to, or are followed by, very concrete benefits well beyond access. Leading up to the congressional repeal of the US oil export ban, some of the largest oil and gas companies contributed millions of dollars to the Senate Leadership Fund, a super PAC for Senate Republicans run by former aides to Senator Mitch McConnell. Specifically, "In the second half of 2015, Senate Leadership Fund received $1 million from Chevron, $1 million from Petrodome Energy, $750,000 from Devon Energy Corporation and $500,000 from Freeport LNG CEO Michael Smith."[18] Congress passed the repeal of the oil export ban as part of a spending bill designed to prevent a government shutdown, and it was subsequently signed by President Obama.[19] "For oil executives," Clifford Krauss and Diane Cardwell reported, "[this] was the culmination of a long-sought goal."[20] The sixty-two senators who voted for the Keystone XL Pipeline collectively received $31,754,343 from fossil fuel companies, compared to the combined total of $2,672,091 given to the thirty-six who voted against it.[21]

The fact that campaign contributions flow much more to committees that can dish out benefits, especially appropriations committees, and much less to committees unable to do so (e.g., foreign policy), and much more to chairs rather than their members, is indirect evidence of the connection between Give and Get.

Nonconstituent Donations Are Particularly Suspect

Particularly suspect are benefits granted to contributors, individuals, or corporations outside Congress members' districts. This is far from a rare phenomenon. According to Anne Baker, between 2006 and 2012,

"The average member of the House received just 11 percent of all campaign funds from donors inside the district."[22] *McCutcheon* is a case that highlights nonconstituent contributions: Shaun McCutcheon, who had contributed to sixteen federal candidates, filed a complaint because of his inability to contribute to twelve other federal candidates, as well as various political committees, because of aggregate limits. McCutcheon was a resident of Alabama and had contributed to congressional candidates across the country.[23] None of the twelve candidates to whom he intended to contribute was running for election from Alabama.[24] As Richard Briffault explains: "By preserving the base limits while striking down the aggregate limits, *McCutcheon* enables an individual to give much more money but—not any more money to any one candidate. . . . Unless the donor wants to give money to many more candidates campaigning against each other in the same electoral contest—which seems unlikely—the donor will give to more candidates in many different states and districts. By striking down the aggregate limits, *McCutcheon* directly promotes contributions by non-constituents."[25] Briffault then tackles the Court's rhetoric in *McCutcheon* with regard to responsiveness, asserting that despite Chief Justice John Roberts's "contention that striking down the aggregate donation cap will *promote* the accountability of representatives to their constituents," in fact it does no such thing. As Briffault points out, representatives may be responsive to contributors, but when these contributors are not constituents, it "undermin[es] the very responsiveness to the people that the Chief Justice rightly celebrates as 'key to the concept of self-governance.'"[26] In short, campaign contributions from nonconstituents should face a higher level of scrutiny than those from constituents. They are particularly likely to lead to inappropriate benefits because interests served do not stem from the constituency that the given member of Congress has a duty to serve—and may well disadvantage them when the benefits flow to others.

Acts Are Not Speech

Courts have limited admissible evidence in the bribery prosecution of Congress members in light of the US Constitution's Speech or Debate Clause, which states that "for any Speech or Debate in either House, they [senators and representatives] shall not be questioned in any other place."[27] For example, in *United States v. Helstoski,* a congressman is charged with accepting bribes to introduce private bills. The Court ruled that past legislative acts could not be used in trial due to the Speech or

Debate Clause, though the Court explicitly recognized that this ruling would have a major impact on prosecuting bribery. In its opinion, the Court stated: "The Government . . . argues that exclusion of references to past legislative acts will make prosecutions more difficult because such references are essential to show the motive for taking money. . . . We do not accept the Government's arguments; without doubt the exclusion of such evidence will make prosecutions more difficult. Indeed, the Speech or Debate Clause was designed to preclude prosecution of Members for legislative acts. We therefore agree with the Court of Appeals that references to past legislative acts of a Member cannot be admitted without undermining the values protected by the Clause."[28] Joseph Weeks wryly but correctly points out that such rulings make it extremely difficult to establish that a member of Congress acts illegally, because "all legislative acts of the defendant at the time of trial are past legislative acts."[29]

A straightforward reading of the Speech or Debate Clause shows that it covers speech that is distinguishable from acts. In effect, a large body of law is based on this distinction. Simply put, talking about illicit conduct is usually treated very differently from acting on those words. In legal practice, there is a world of difference between threatening to kill someone and actually killing someone. The Supreme Court's assertion in *United States v. Apfelbaum* that "in the criminal law, both a culpable *mens rea* and a criminal *actus reus* are generally required for an offense to occur"[30] speaks to this point. The First Amendment protects offensive speech—even hate speech—but not harmful action. When people are threatened, but merely with words, the police often respond that they have no grounds on which to act.

Deliberation and voting on the House or Senate floor should be distinguished along the same lines. The vote should not be construed as speech but as an act. Associate Justice Antonin Scalia provided the following rationale for this distinction: "There are, to be sure, instances where action conveys a symbolic meaning—such as the burning of a flag to convey disagreement with a country's policies. . . . But the act of voting symbolizes nothing. It *discloses,* to be sure, that the legislator wishes (for whatever reason) that the proposition on the floor be adopted, just as a physical assault discloses that the attacker dislikes the victim. But neither the one nor the other is an act of communication."[31] In short, if contributors gain discriminatory benefits from a Congress member to whom they donated funds within the defined period, the Speech or

Debate Clause of the Constitution should not be read as providing them with legal cover.

Independent Expenditures Need to Be Tied In

The Supreme Court has ruled that independent expenditures[32] pose no threat of corruption as they are uncoordinated with the candidate and that imposing limitations amounts to infringing on free speech. In *Citizens United v. Federal Election Commission,* the group Citizens United produced a scathing documentary on then senator Hillary Clinton with the intention of releasing it within thirty days of the primary election. The release of "electioneering communications" paid for by corporations and unions within thirty days of the primary was prohibited at the time. The Court overturned this restriction and opened the door to unlimited independent expenditures. The Court quotes *Buckley* to explain its rationale: "The absence of prearrangement and coordination of an expenditure with the candidate or his agent not only undermines the value of the expenditure to the candidate, but also alleviates the danger that expenditures will be given as a quid pro quo for improper commitments from the candidate."[33] The Court held that because independent expenditures are not coordinated with the candidate, there is no risk for quid pro quo corruption. The ruling in *Citizens United* helped lay the foundation for super PACs to which individuals and corporations can make unlimited contributions.[34]

There are several ways that candidates and the so-called independent PACs sidestep anticoordination regulations. First, Federal Election Commission (FEC) rules allow super PACs and campaigns to communicate directly. They may not discuss a candidate's strategy but may confer on "issue ads" featuring a candidate.[35] Matea Gold writes that "it is now standard practice for candidates to share suggested television ad scripts and video footage online—materials that are then scooped up by outside groups and turned into television spots."[36] Second, it is very easy for those who spend the super PAC monies to note which points their candidate is flagging and run ads to support these points, prepare supportive campaign literature, and so on. Finally, many candidates fundraise for super PACs, and while the candidates themselves cannot ask for contributions of more than five thousand dollars, the FEC issued an advisory opinion that allows campaign aides to raise greater amounts for super PACs.[37] Not surprisingly, super PACs with ties to a specific candidate appear to gain most of the contributions.[38] In the words of Representative David Price (D-NC), "It amounts to a joke that there's no coordination between these individual super PACs and the candidates."[39] As the election law attorney Robert Kelner puts it, "If there's no separation between the campaigns and outside groups, then the logic of the *Citizens United* decision really falls apart."[40]

In determining whether a given party made contributions that led to inappropriate benefits, one must take into account the contributions made to independent groups, which in effect are coordinated with the member of Congress. As a result, if the reforms here suggested are to take effect, gaps in disclosure need to be addressed so that the source of contributions to "independent groups" is not obscured and connections can be made between such contributions and benefits.

"If It Ain't Broke, Don't Fix It"

Arguments against campaign regulation often diminish the role of money in politics by highlighting cases where winners are far outspent by their opponents. In that vein, Bradley Smith writes that higher spending does not necessarily translate into victory. Michael Huffington, Lewis Lehrman, Mark Dayton, John Connally, and Clayton Williams are just a few of the lavish spenders who wound up on the losing end of campaigns. As Michael Malbin, director of the Center for Legislative Studies at the Rockefeller Institute of Government, explains, "Having money means having the ability to be heard; it does not mean that voters will like what they hear."[41]

As many studies show, however, the cases where the highest-spending candidate lost are few and far between. For instance, in 2008, candidates who raised more funds than their opponents won 93 percent of House elections and 94 percent of Senate elections.[42] In the 2012 midterm elections, 93.8 percent of House races and 75.8 percent of Senate races were won by the candidate who spent more. In 2014, these numbers increased to 94.2 percent for the House and 81.8 percent for the Senate.[43]

"Lobbying Is a Constitutionally Protected Right"

Some skeptics of campaign regulation contend that lobbying is protected by the Constitution. The First Amendment accords Americans the right to "petition the government for a redress of grievances."[44] The reforms advocated in this chapter do not aim to ban lobbying; rather, their goal is only to prevent those interests that back up their lobbying with campaign contributions from gaining benefits unavailable to others in similar circumstances. True, the Supreme Court ruled in *Buckley v. Valeo* that "equalizing the financial resources of candidates competing for federal office" is not "a justification for restricting the scope of federal election campaigns."[45] However, the reforms here suggested do not seek to equalize the playing field but merely to ensure that many voices that are currently drowned out will gain a chance to be heard.

"One Cannot Stop Private Monies from Gushing into Politics"

While imperfect, the UK's election system provides a helpful model for emulation and for curbing cynicism that money will find its way into elections one way or another. Parliamentary campaigns in the UK have strict and low spending limits.[46] As of the 2015 general election in the UK, during the months before candidacy has been formally declared, individuals could spend £30,700 (an extra allotment is granted of either 9p or 6p per voter depending on whether they are contesting a county or borough seat, respectively). Once a person became an official candidate, the short campaign limit, about a month, allowed £8,700 to be spent.[47] The spending limits for political parties depend on the number of seats that party contests; the highest limit would be £19.5 million if a party had candidates running in all 650 constituencies.[48] Furthermore, paid political advertising on television and radio is illegal. Instead, political parties are granted a certain amount of free radio and television coverage. Candidates are allowed to send one election communication to every elector in the constituency through the postal system at no cost.[49]

The length of campaigns in the UK is drastically shorter than in the US. In 2015, the duration of the "official" campaign was thirty-seven days, and this was the longest in modern British history.[50] Particularly of note is that party discipline is very strong in the UK, inherent in its parliamentary system. Members of Parliament (MPs) vote on most issues in line with the instructions from their party whip.[51] This rule makes MPs much less corruptible than members of Congress. Making a deal with an MP is of little value because the MP cannot deliver if the deal differs from the party line. The UK system is not perfect. For instance, some members of Parliament were found to receive gifts in return for asking questions during debates of interest to the donor. The differences with the American system, however, are still stark. In the US, distribution of benefits to special interests in exchange for campaign contributions is rampant, whereas in the UK such distributions are rare, as far as individual legislators are concerned. We can aspire to a much cleaner political system.[52]

Limiting Contributions Is More Important Than Limiting Perks

This chapter focuses on contributions of funds, whereas the media often spotlight perks, such as free meals (as long as they do not cost more than two hundred dollars) and some forms of travel.[53] The issue of campaign contributions seems too abstract and "procedural" to many voters rather than pressing and substantive. Such contributions, however, are much more consequential than perks. If a Congress member does not get gifts or junkets, his lifestyle may become less ritzy, but if he loses campaign contributions, he is likely to lose his job in the next election, including his power, income, prestige—as well as the perks. Moreover, members of Congress can draw on their campaign chest to pay for perks.[54] No wonder Congress members have been more amenable to limiting legal perks than capping legal contributions. The latter matter much more and should be the first, second, and third priority of any reform.

Limiting the Give?

Concern over the corrupting influence of campaign contributions has led to a considerable number of reforms to limit what a contributor can give a member of Congress or someone seeking to become one. Many of these reforms have been declared unconstitutional by the Supreme Court; others have failed for different reasons. A few illustrations follow.

The Federal Election Campaign Act (FECA) of 1971 and its 1974 amendments established limits on campaign contributions and expenditures. Contribution limits were set for the amount individuals, groups, and political committees could give a single candidate during an election cycle, in addition to an annual contribution limit for individual contributors. Independent expenditure limits were imposed on individuals and groups that capped the amount each candidate could spend in a given election. Expenditure limits were also placed on the amount of personal funds a candidate can use to finance his or her campaign, as well as on the total amount a campaign can spend on an election. However, in the 1976 case *Buckley v. Valeo*, the Supreme Court ruled that the expenditure limits were unconstitutional on First Amendment grounds, as they directly restrict political expression. (This rationale is often referred to as the Court having ruled that "money is speech.")

Besides noting restriction of political expression, the Court also ruled that the independent expenditure limits conflicted with the freedom of association protected by the First Amendment. It reasoned that "limitation on independent expenditures 'relative to a clearly identified candidate' precludes most associations from effectively amplifying the voice of their adherents, the original basis for the recognition of First Amendment protection of the freedom of association."[55]

The political expression rationale was also used by the Court to rule that limits on millionaires and billionaires using their own funds to finance a campaign were unconstitutional. The Court maintained that "the candidate, no less than any other person, has a First Amendment right to engage in the discussion of public issues and vigorously and tirelessly to advocate his own election."[56] The Court asserted the importance of candidates' "unfettered opportunity" for expressing their position so that voters can form an educated opinion.[57]

The Court indicated it believes that all expenditure limits infringe on First Amendment freedoms and that no corruption risks would stem from their removal.[58] The expenditure limits were judged unconstitutional. The justices did uphold the contribution limits, but as we shall see, the aggregate limit, which set a cap for the annual amount that can be given (as opposed to the amount that can be given directly to each candidate), was later struck down.

The Bipartisan Campaign Reform Act of 2002 (BCRA) had a provision that prevented corporations, non-profits, and labor unions from issuing electioneering communications sixty days before a general election or thirty days before a primary. This act, coupled with prior legislation that banned direct political advocacy by corporations, was overturned by the Supreme Court's 2010 decision in *Citizens United,* which ruled that corporations can engage in direct political advocacy and should face no limitations on their campaign contributions.[59]

In 2014, the Supreme Court in *McCutcheon v. Federal Election Commission* struck down the aggregate limits on campaign contributions to all candidates set by the FECA. The Court ruled that the limits were unconstitutional and violated the First Amendment. As a result, there are no limits on the number of candidates to whom an individual may contribute.[60]

Various constitutional amendments have been proposed to address campaign finance regulation. However, in 1997 and in 2014, the Senate rejected proposed amendments to allow Congress to determine campaign spending limits in federal elections.[61] The other avenue for an amendment to the Constitution, which relies on an introduction by two-thirds of the state legislatures, is a very hard row to hoe, and little progress has been made.

That almost all attempts to limit the flood of private monies into the hands of public officials have failed is evident in the continued growth of election expenditures. (They have grown increasingly quickly even if accounting for inflation and population growth.)[62] In 1998, congressional races cost approximately $1.6 billion ($2.4 billion adjusted for inflation); by 2014, they cost $3.8 billion.[63] While total money spent on the 2016 presidential election was slightly lower than during the prior two elections ($2.4 billion compared to $2.8 billion in 2008 and $2.6 billion in 2012), money spent on 2016 congressional races reached a new high, costing more than $4 billion.[64]

All this suggests the merit of focusing on what contributors can *get* rather than on what they can *give*. This does not mean that campaign contributions should not be regulated; rather, targeting unscrupulous benefits seems a much more promising approach for reformers. Limiting the Get has one other merit. Limiting the Give means limiting even those who do not seek special benefits, those who may support a candidate for philosophical or moral reasons. This is not the case if one limits only self-seeking benefits.

Transparency Is Woefully Insufficient

Courts have held that corruption can be deterred through transparency and disclosure requirements. In *McCutcheon v. Federal Election Commission* (2014), the Supreme Court stated that "disclosure of contributions minimizes the potential for abuse of the campaign finance system [and] . . . may also 'deter actual corruption and avoid the appearance of corruption by exposing large contributions and expenditures to the light of publicity.'"[65]

While often discussed as an alternative to regulation, transparency is, in effect, a form of government regulation. Unlike other forms of regulation, however, transparency has a major disadvantage: it assumes that the public has the requisite resources to interpret the findings and translate them into effective political action, above all in voting choices.[66] Substantial behavioral economics research says otherwise: the public is unable to properly process and act on even simple information because of "wired in," congenital, systematic cognitive biases.[67] Numerous books, studies, and TV reports by *60 Minutes* and *Frontline,* among others, have not convinced the public to grant high priority to campaign financing reforms.

Further, while in principle super PACs are required to disclose their contributions, many of their donors can remain anonymous. The Sunlight Foundation provides a revealing example: "In 2010, a super PAC that was active in one of that year's marquee House races listed a single donor: a 501(c)(4) organization that does not have to disclose its donors. This is what is known among some campaign finance lawyers as 'the Russian doll problem.'"[68]

The 501(c)(4) and 501(c)(6) organizations fall in the category of politically active non-profits, which can accept unlimited contributions and are typically under no obligation to disclose their contributors. In theory their political activity is limited, but in practice these limits are often unenforced. The prevalence of these organizations in federal elections has increased. They are considered to provide "dark money" because their funding sources are obscured.[69] As part of the reforms here suggested, disclosure should be mandatory for all organizations that spend in one way or another on political campaigns.

Many super PACs also have misleading or vague names that make it impossible to know which interests they are seeking to promote. How is one to tell that Americans for Progressive Action was started by a Republican and never supported any Democrat or that American Bridge 21st Century supports Democrats, while America Rising supports Republicans?[70]

In *Buckley,* the Court did recognize that disclosure may not be sufficient to prevent corruption, stating that "Congress was surely entitled to conclude that disclosure was only a partial measure, and that contribution ceilings were a necessary legislative concomitant to deal with the reality or appearance of corruption."[71] However, when Congress did act, the Court struck down practically all the limits Congress had set on making contributions.

The Ground for What Constitutes Bribery

The reforms here suggested entail treating as bribery any material campaign contributions that result in special benefits not available to others with the same attributes, unless the difference is relevant. For these reforms to be implemented, Congress or the Court needs to revisit the way quid pro quo is determined.[72]

In the 1999 Supreme Court case *Sun-Diamond,* an agricultural trade association was charged with giving illegal gifts to Michael Spy, secretary of the Department of Agriculture, in which Sun-Diamond's member cooperatives had vested interests. Sun-Diamond objected to the charges because the indictment did not show a link between the gifts and the issues of interests. The Supreme Court agreed and held that "in order to establish a violation of 18 U.S.C. § 201(c)(1)(A), the Government must prove a link between a thing of value conferred upon a public official and a specific 'official act' for or because of which it was given."[73] According to the Supreme Court, prosecuting federal bribery and gratuities required explicit proof of a quid pro quo arrangement.[74]

In a private meeting, a high-ranking official of the US Department of Justice pointed out that the department understands quid pro quo to have taken place only when the donor explicitly conditions the donation to some benefit. If a congressional committee is about to vote on whether to grant a special favor tailored to match only a single donor, and that donor indicates that he will make a major donation after the vote, or half before and half after, and members of the committee then vote in line with the interests of the donor, such practice does not qualify as quid pro quo under current law.

For the suggested reforms here outlined to be effective, the bar must be lowered for what classifies as quid pro quo. The Supreme Court's very narrow interpretation of quid pro quo is precluding the prosecution of many corrupt acts. This interpretive trend must be overturned, either by Congress or the Court itself.

In Conclusion

Under the current system, a lobbyist can visit a member of Congress on the eve of a vote on a bill that would grant his special interest group a multimillion-dollar benefit (in the case of oil companies, it could be measured in billions) and inform the member that his group just made a major donation to his election campaign (PAC or a related super PAC). The lobbyist could also state that his group is considering tripling this amount and that he will be back next week (after the vote) to let the member of Congress know the result of his group's deliberations. By current law, such statements are not considered an attempt to bribe a public official because no quid pro quo was explicitly mentioned. That is, the US employs an extremely limited definition of quid pro quo. The definition should be expanded to account for benefits clearly favoring the interests of those who made contributions before or after the vote, within a defined period.

One may prefer other ways to stop what is, in effect, widespread, systematic legalized bribery. However, no one concerned about shoring up democracy, functional governance, and the common good—the agenda of the patriotic movement—can ignore the importance of curbing the ways private money floods into the hands of public officials.

10

THE RISING (MORE) NATION-CENTERED WORLD ORDER

That the nation remains the principal political community in democracies has two basic implications. Domestically, national commitments help stem globalist encroachments on essential attachments (see chapter 3). Many lament this and yearn for a world without borders, some fearing that nationalism spawns xenophobia and jingoism, and others envisioning universal fellowship as a high human good. Whatever concerns and aspirations critics of nationalism may have, the response in the near term should not be to reject nationalism but instead to embrace "good" nationalism, as Canadians, Norwegians, Swiss, and Costa Ricans do, among others. Attempts to override nationalism will continue breeding alienation and populism in the foreseeable future.

The same is true of international relations. Attempts to shape global security and development without respecting national sovereignty and national core values are bound to fail. Patriotic foreign policy needs to accept that for now international institutions and collaborations can be stable and effective only if they accommodate national loyalties.[1]

The Liberal International Order (LIO) is being challenged by populism in nations that built and have long supported that order (especially in the US). The LIO is also being tested by rising powers, particularly China, and those seeking to restore their prominence, especially Russia. Many hold that the LIO is in crisis.[2] Robert Kagan, for example, writes about "the twilight of the liberal world order," which is starting "to weaken and fracture at the core" and may be a harbinger of a major global conflict.[3]

This chapter acknowledges these cautionary observations about the LIO but points to a new international order that is already evolving. I will refer to it as a Nation-Centered System (NCS) because it is more nationalist and less multilateral (and much less supranational) than the LIO. I cannot stress enough that the transition is a relative one. Nations have long played a key role in the LIO, and multilateralism will remain important in the NCS—only considerably less so than in the recent past.

The NCS accords higher value to national sovereignty than does the LIO and is based more on agreements among nations than on collective decision-making. It is also less focused on the promotion of individual rights, democratization, free movement of people and goods, and the quest for democratic global governance—and more on stability and peace. In this way, the NCS is more similar to the preliberal world order that existed before 1945 than it is to the order formed, mainly by the US, in the wake of World War II. As we shall see, this scaling back, which the patriotic movement ought to recognize, is necessary to facilitate higher levels of global governance. To put it in popular terms, we need to take one step back in order to be able to take two steps forward.

The transition from the LIO to the NCS is a response to a widening gulf between institutional and normative developments on the one hand and community building on the other hand (from here on referred to as the communitarian gap). In other contexts, scholars have studied institutional and normative lag.[4] Here, the opposite developments are examined. For lack of a better term, I refer to them as premature advancements.[5] Today, there are indications that premature advancements at the institutional and normative level are being scaled back because supranational community building is lagging. This trend helps reduce the communitarian gap, thereby laying the foundation for firmer progress in the future. Reducing the gap should be a cornerstone of patriotic foreign policy.

In other words, on the international level power has been transferred, especially in the EU, to supranational governing bodies without significant supranational community building. Theoretically, this communitarian gap could be closed by rushing to build the supranational community. Such social construction, however, is unrealistic in the foreseeable future given the fierce commitments to national communities that are being expressed in many countries. Consequently, the supranational powers for a transitional period must be scaled back. Like it or not, many nations must face the fact that their foreign policy will be driven more by national values and interests and less by multilateral commitments and especially not by supranational ones. I will show next that to make progress, some scaling back of internationalism is now needed. This is a thesis that the patriotic movements of different nations should all come to embrace.

Excessive Supranationalism?

I used the term "progress," which implies a specific preferred direction for the future trajectory of the international order. This direction is prescribed by the need for more effective and legitimate global governance. Such governance is called for because the world is facing a growing number of global challenges that cannot be managed effectively by national governments alone.

Nations can cooperate on shared goals in two ways. One is through the inter-nation model, in which nations enter into mutually beneficial policy agreements that preserve their sovereignty. NAFTA, NPT, and NATO are useful examples. Because each nation must consent to all significant changes in policy, a cumbersome process that often requires months if not years of negotiations before a major change can be introduced—and each nation in effect holds veto power—this model is limited in the scope of international work it can accomplish.[6]

The second way for nations to cooperate is through the "supranational" model. Here unanimous consensus is not required. Once an international organization adopts democratic procedures, recalcitrant countries can be ignored. And once the states involved yield some authority to the governing body, which supranationality entails by definition, decisions can be made in short order by a central body. A key example is the institutions of the European Union, especially the Commission.

John B. Judis, in his book *The Nationalist Revival*, draws a distinction between globalism and internationalism.[7] The latter requires that nations cede some of their sovereignty to international organizations—but not throw their borders open to trade and immigration, or allow rulings by international institutions and international laws to trump national ones. As I see it, a lot depends on what "some of their sovereignty" means. If the concessions are significant, they require communitarian preparation, the kind of community building this book suggests is essential for moving beyond an international order based on independent nations. A little internationalism may not give one indigestion, but it's best to avoid gobbling the stuff down. I will show below how the LIO involved an increase in the number of supranational institutions and show that this increase has outpaced supranational community building and, consequently, public support.

A parallel development is occurring on the normative level. The liberal elements of the LIO entail global norms and normative principles that supersede national ones.[8] The advance of *human* rights is the most potent illustration. Failure to abide by the various treaties of the United Nations Universal Declaration of Human Rights leads to all kinds of symbolic condemnations and material sanctions.

Both developments presume that most citizens of nations of the world will embrace the attendant loss of national sovereignty and consider it to be legitimate. However, for this to occur requires a measure of supranational community building because most citizens in the modern world, in effect, continue to view their state as their community, albeit an imagined one.[9] For many, their very definition of self includes particular national traditions and loyalties. Unless supranational institutions can cultivate some of this sense of shared community and extend it to the relevant supranational governing bodies, reducing national particularity and sovereignty will continue to result in alienation and pushback.

The essentiality of community building in supranational governance is contested by neofunctionalists like Ernst B. Haas, who theorized that economic and administrative integration is sufficient to engender community building. In his analysis, as more decisions affecting more interests are moved to the supranational governing bodies, the more citizens' allegiances will shift from the national to the supranational level.[10] If true, there would be no need for engaging in community building per se, as the formation of a supranational community would be the *result* of successful economic and administrative integration. I have shown in the past that the neofunctionalists underestimate the import of national identity and emotive group attachments in citizens' perceptions of political legitimacy.[11]

Hedley Bull famously distinguished between a system of states and a society of states—the latter being akin to what is often referred to as an international community—and he suggested that such a community exists. In contrast, I hold that to the extent that such a community exists, it is insufficient to support the rise in supranational governance and its normative design. In the following section, I will defend this thesis by examining recent developments in the EU and globalist structures that face a retreat to nationalism. Measures to move forward again are not yet evident.

The EU: Supranational Institutions, but National Communities

Founded in 1957, the EU's precursor, the European Economic Community, was primarily a trade association encompassing six nations.

Over the decades following its establishment, the EU added members and expanded its missions. Initially, its focus was on administrative and regulatory matters intended to facilitate trade, travel, and commerce among the member nations. These changes were low-key, aiming to increase efficiency, but largely did not challenge citizens' sense of national identity.[12] The EU Commission also invented a sage way to manage missions across borders by not forcing all nations to adhere to the same standards, instead setting minimal standards for all nations to follow. Further, many small measures were introduced "under the radar"—by being buried in complex legal documents, for instance.[13]

Over time, the level and scope of integrated activities expanded, as did the number of countries involved. In 1985, several member states signed the Schengen Agreement, which lifted border checks and allowed for the free movement of people among member states. The introduction of the European Economic and Monetary Union (EMU) in the early 1990s marked another significant expansion of EU-wide governance. Under the EMU, twelve of the member states adopted a common currency and monetary policy, establishing the European Central Bank, and set new regulations on national budgets, such as setting permissible deficit levels and minimum budget allocations to R&D and defense. Further, since 2005, following massive immigration from Asia and Africa, the EU formed a policy that required each member nation to accept a given number of refugees.

As a result of expanding its missions, the EU involved itself in matters of much higher emotive and normative content—engaging the core values of the citizens of the member nations, people's sense of identity, and communal self-governance. The flip side of this rise in supranationalism was a sense of loss of national sovereignty.

Furthermore, the EU, in effect, required some nations to decelerate their economy's growth to offset that of nations whose economies were overheating. Even more contentiously, the absence of border controls facilitated large population flows both within and into the EU. The French were upset by the influx of Polish workers into France—popularly known as the Polish Plumber problem—after 1985. The British were still troubled by the stream of workers from Baltic countries as well as new immigrants and asylum seekers. Anger directed at immigrants animated the push for Brexit by the nationalists of the UK Independence Party (UKIP). The UKIP spokesperson Nigel Farage campaigned with a poster depicting an endless line of refugees and the words "Breaking Point." Brexit advocates found themselves unified under the banner of "Leave: we want our country back." Several EU member nations restored border controls.

While the EU was founded like a typical intergovernmental organization by a treaty requiring unanimous agreement among all members, thus protecting their sovereignty, successor treaties replaced unanimous decision-making with qualified majority voting (QMV) in more and more areas of EU governance. The Treaties of Amsterdam (1999), Nice (2003), and Lisbon (2009) extended QMV into border security standards, immigration, public health, financial assistance, and dozens of other areas.[14] These changes contributed to the sense of loss of national sovereignty.

In addition to challenges posed by the EU itself, rulings by European courts made millions of EU citizens feel that their moral sensibilities and national independence were being violated. To give but one example: a 2013 decision by the European Court of Human Rights (ECHR) on UK prison sentences culminated in a widely held sense that the court had encroached on the nation's right to decide how to protect its citizens. In *Vinter and Others v. The United Kingdom,* the ECHR declared the practice of mandatory life sentences for convicted murderers a human rights violation because to deny opportunity for release constitutes inhumane treatment.[15] Without recourse to an appeals process, the UK was compelled to comply with the decision. Conservative and Labour MPs alike felt the court had usurped Parliament's legislative powers.[16]

These developments have bred growing disaffection, with Brexit being its most forceful manifestation. Other nations actively contemplating EU departure included, at one point or another, Greece, France, the Netherlands, and Denmark. Populist nationalism rose in many member nations. In Austria, Norbert Hofer nearly won the 2016 presidential election under the banner of the FPÖ (Freedom Party of Austria), a party whose first leaders were former SS officers. In the 2017 Austrian parliamentary elections, the FPÖ came in third, receiving 51 of the 183 seats in the National Council. Also in 2017, a far-right party in Germany (the AfD, or Alternative for Germany) won seats in Parliament for the first time in more than fifty years, declaring its intent to "take back our country and our people."[17] Two Eurosceptic parties garnered more than half of all votes in the 2018 Italian general election. One of these parties, the League, uses the slogan "Italians First."[18] In Poland and Hungary, right-wing populists did ascend to power, with Andrzej Duda winning the Polish presidency in 2015 and Viktor Orbán's Fidesz party ruling Budapest since 2010.

While right-wing populist candidates were fended off in the recent presidential elections of France and the Netherlands, the parties of those candidates (National Front and Dutch Party for Freedom) saw gains in their share of legislative seats on the national and European levels. Other nationalist populist parties like Alternative for Germany, Sweden Democrats, and Golden Dawn (Greece) have similarly gained steam in their respective countries in the past decade, supported by voters who seem to view them as the defenders of national sovereignty.[19]

I have noted that there is a growing need for supranational governance as many challenges ahead cannot be managed by each nation on its own or by inter-nation governance, which is slow and cumbersome. Given that the EU provides by far the most advanced form of supranational government, the critical question is, Why does it face such vehement populist pushback? In my judgment, to reiterate, supranational government can endure and flourish only if it is accompanied by supranational community building, where national bonds and values are expanded to include the new governing body. The EU failed to build such a community as it transferred over more power to "Brussels."

The West Germans granted the equivalent of a trillion dollars to the East Germans during the decade that followed reunification with little hesitation. "They are fellow Germans" was the only explanation needed. The same Germans resisted granting much smaller amounts to Greece and other EU nations in trouble. They were not members of "our tribe." The power of communal bonds at the national level is most clearly seen in that while millions of people are willing to die for their nation, few are willing to sacrifice much of anything for the EU.

If I am correct that the EU cannot maintain its current level of policy integration, let alone expand its scope, as French president Emmanuel Macron and German chancellor Angela Merkel have been calling for, then the EU has two options: building the supranational community or shrinking its missions. Given that no signs of major community building are in the offing, shrinking is, in effect, the only option. In effect, this scaling back is already happening.

In a significant manifestation of the EU scaling back, many EU members are restoring their own control over their borders to limit the movement of EU citizens and immigrants. New border checks have been erected in Germany, Denmark, Sweden, Norway, and Austria. Governments in Greece, Italy, France, and Portugal have defied the EU's budget deficit and GDP-to-debt ratio constraints. Furthermore, the Czech Republic, Hungary, and Poland have refused to accept the number of immigrants they are supposed to absorb according to EU policy.

Steps taken to foster an EU-wide community include promoting shared symbols (e.g., an EU flag), student exchanges (e.g., Socrates), and an EU anthem ("Ode to Joy"). These steps have only resulted in a rather thin sense of community, as indicated by various public opinion polls and by the moves to curtail the scope and level of integrated activities. A much stronger effort at community building will be needed before the EU can expand its missions again without causing ever-more backlash. The steps that must be taken to build such a community are far from clear, given the powerful hold that national ideals have on most EU citizens.[20]

Globalists Encounter Nationalists

Premature supranational advancements and the need to scale them back to prepare the ground for more sustainable ones are also evident on the global level. The communitarian gap internationally is much less severe than in the EU, but not because there is more international community building, far from it, but because supranationalism is much more limited and found largely in the normative rather than the institutional realm.

In recent years, those who favor postnational or supranational positions (although they do not use these terms) have been called, quite appropriately, "globalists," and those who oppose such developments have been referred to as "nationalists." The rise of populism in many democratic polities in the 2010s is often attributed to a nationalistic reaction to the ascent of globalization.

Specifically, some find that globalization undermines both local and national communities. The argument runs as follows: As people moved from villages to cities, they lost many of the social bonds that provided them with emotional security.[21] These bonds also had protected them from the siren calls of would-be demagogues. Once the society of communities turned into a mass society of individuals bereft of social moorings,[22] demagogues gained more sway over the public, particularly when economic conditions deteriorated. The conditions in pre–Nazi Germany are often cited to illustrate these developments. When this analysis is applied to contemporary populism in the terms already introduced, we are said to be witnessing the rise of globalization undermining communities, and thus leading to nationalist populism.

In addition, large segments of the population in liberal democracies are reported to have lost employment because freer trade led to jobs moving to developing countries; most of those who are employed gained little increase in real income and experienced growing income insecurity and inequality, as well as a loss of dignity (associated with the loss of traditional jobs like coal mining). The same people are also found to be reacting to expanding diversity due to immigration, and to cultural changes resulting from extensions of individual rights (e.g., legalization of gay marriage). The affected people view the rise of diversity as undermining both their social standing and their shared core values and customs.[23] Additionally, they feel snubbed and despised by globalist elites.[24] As Arlie Russell Hochschild points out: "For the Tea Party around the country, the shifting moral qualifications for the American Dream had turned them into strangers in their own land, afraid, resentful, displaced, and dismissed by the very people who were, they felt, cutting in line. . . . Liberals were asking them to feel compassion for the downtrodden in the back of the line, the 'slaves' of society. They didn't want to; they felt downtrodden themselves."[25] Globalists do not ignore these causes of populism; however, they tend to view them as pathological reactions to the unstoppable march of future trends. They tend to see nationalists as misinformed, misled, or captured by the emotive appeals of demagogues. Moreover, globalists often view the weakening of particularistic bonds—the weakening of commitments to local or national communities—as liberating. History is seen as a march from particularism to universalism, from close local and national communities toward a global one.

Globalists have little room for communities in their moral and philosophical vocabulary. True, some associate these bonds and values with an elusive global community. Most see people as freestanding individuals, endowed with rights by the mere fact that they are human and not because they are members of this or that community or nation. One can fully subscribe to the fact that human rights are inalienable, but one must also take into account that these are best combined with particularistic social responsibilities, including to family members, friends, community members, and fellow citizens.

Globalists have made progress on both the institutional and normative level. One can debate how far they have progressed but not that these developments greatly exceeded what the very meager global community building can support. Several scholars, for instance, Anne-Marie Slaughter, suggest that informal transnational networks provide a measure of the needed community.[26] (David Singh Grewal takes a more critical view of these networks.)[27] However, rising nationalism in many parts of the world suggests that these networks provide only for a thin community and that curbing nationalism will require a much thicker global community—that is, one in which people will tie their identity, sense of belonging, and loyalties in part to the global community. Amartya Sen[28] and Kwame Anthony Appiah[29] point out that people have complex, multilayered identities, acting, for instance, sometimes as nationalists and sometimes as globalists, depending on the context. However, when these identities clash, for large segments of the population national identity reigns supreme. The patriotic movement can work to ensure that the content of the national identities be constructive and change over the longer run to make more room for supranationalism. It would be highly unrealistic, however, to ignore the current primacy of national identities.

Next, I examine key elements of the LIO and outline ways they are or can be scaled back as the NCS is developed. To reiterate, the changes are in degree, not absolutes. For example, there is some reduction in support for the UN, but few call for its termination.

The Elements of the LIO and NCS

The High Normative Standing of Sovereignty

LIO advocates offer considerably different accounts of its normative principles and their priorities. G. John Ikenberry, whose work on the LIO is often cited, spotlights the Westphalian normative principle[30] for the LIO, delineating it as "foundational" to the whole framework.[31] The principle has two components: that no nation may interfere in the internal affairs of another nation[32] and that no nation may alter borders by force.

One ought to note that the Westphalian norm sanctifies the state and not the individual. Indeed, for centuries, until the Responsibility to Protect (RtoP) modification was introduced, and significantly even after that watershed, the Westphalian norm left citizens at the mercy of the state. Given that both globalists and LIO advocates stress the promotion of human rights, their liberal idealism directly conflicts with the

Westphalian norm. In other words, this key element of the LIO is not liberal at all.

The US and its allies sought to weaken national sovereignty by promoting the Responsibility to Protect (RtoP), which defined legitimate conditions for armed international intervention in the internal affairs of other nations—for the sake of endangered individuals.[33] (Most nations, including China and Russia, agreed to this change in the rules of world order.)[34] RtoP should be seen as a liberal correction precisely because it seeks to protect people from states rather than protecting states from each other, or those in power in each state from internal challenges.

Many nations (and even liberals in the West), however, soured on RtoP after the US and its allies used it to try to legitimate coercive regime changes, notably in Libya, where democracy-building ambitions (and not the protection of endangered individuals) were a factor in extending a devastating civil war and creating a new breeding ground for ISIS. In the Syrian civil war, the US insisted for the first four years that Bashar al-Assad had to go—to open the way for regime change—as a *precondition to any negotiation on ending the conflict. (One could say that Assad could have been replaced without changing the regime. However, this is not what the US wanted, for good reason. There was little to be gained by replacing one tyrant with another. One could argue that US demands did not involve coercion, but the US greatly ramped up its armed support for anti-Assad forces when he refused to give up power.)

While China supports RtoP as it pertains to "genocide, war crimes, ethnic cleansing and crimes against humanity," it insists that "it is not appropriate to expand, willfully to interpret or even abuse this concept."[35] The fact that RtoP lost a good part of its legitimacy is one indication of the transition from the LIO to NCS. That is, a regime that was not very liberal to begin with and has become less so after an attempt to liberalize it largely failed when the new liberal principle was abused by those who advanced it.

To restore this liberal element, in the future RtoP will have to be employed only to prevent flagrant humanitarian atrocities and not to promote regime change.[36] Even though more expansive ideas of international responsibility—such as my call for a responsibility to contain transnational terrorists[37] and Richard Haass's recasting of sovereignty as transnational responsibility[38]—have merit, the current international community is too weak to sustain them.[39]

Abuse of RtoP is not the only consequence of the US and its allies' departure from Westphalian norms of national sovereignty in the name of liberal causes. After the collapse of the USSR, Francis Fukuyama theorized that the whole world was on its way to embrace liberal democratic regimes, leading to the "end of history" in the sense that once all nations had such a regime, no more regime changes would be sought or needed.[40] He also suggested that some nations are "stuck in history" and needed a push to make the change. Indeed, the 2003 invasion of Iraq was partly justified on such grounds. Building a liberal democratic regime was used to defend the US presence in Iraq—long after Saddam Hussein was captured, his regime unraveled, and no nuclear weapons were found.[41] The same rationalizations were at play in interventions in Afghanistan and Libya.

In several of these nations, coercive regime change led to civil wars, high levels of both civilian and military casualties, and mass displacement. Hundreds of billions of US dollars have been squandered. One might argue that these are the inevitable labor pains of the birth of liberal democracy. However, by and large the result of US intervention was either anarchy or a new authoritarian government. (In some cases, the new regimes are labeled "developing democracies," although they hardly qualify.[42] Both Iraq and Afghanistan are losing many of the democratic features they acquired under American tutelage.)

The transition toward an NCS would benefit if the US gave up on the promotion of liberal democracy by coercive means. This policy shift would be highly justified on moral grounds (sparing hundreds of thousands of casualties; priority of the right to live);[43] prudential grounds (the sacrifices do not lead to the desired results);[44] and the grounds of sustainability (such a move would help mitigate opposition from rising powers and nationalists). At the same time, the promotion of liberal democracy can continue by using nonlethal means. These include public diplomacy, leadership training, cultural and educational exchanges, and increased contacts with democratic nations (through travel and trade).

Yoram Hazony's *The Virtue of Nationalism* is highly relevant to this discussion.[45] He astutely advocates for what I call the communitarian virtues of the national state, its value as a community that provides for human flourishing. Arguing that the best global order is based on independent nation-states, he views all attempts to build more encompassing communities as dangerous utopias. Here we differ. As I see it, in the longer run most of the challenges humanity faces will have to be addressed through some form of global governance. And such governance will be possible only if there is a significant transfer of loyalty from nation-states (themselves imagined) to an imagined global community.

Aspiration vs. Reality of World Governance

The UN is treated as a (if not the) major institutional element of the LIO.[46] G. John Ikenberry writes that one of the hallmarks of liberal internationalism is "rule-based relations enshrined in institutions such as the United Nations."[47] Jeff Colgan and Robert Keohane note that the UN is a "key feature of the liberal order."[48] When nations do not abide by UN resolutions, many liberals chastise them as if they have broken the law. They, in effect, assume that the UN is akin to a democratic government whose representatives speak for the electorate, whom, in return, they expect to comply with enacted laws.

This view of the UN is based on what many hope the UN could be, not on what it is.[49] The UN Security Council is neither democratic nor liberal. Its veto power is wielded by the winners of World War II, whereas large parts of the world—including India, Brazil, Japan, Indonesia, Germany, and Nigeria—have, in effect, no say. It is as if the US were governed by New York, Texas, Louisiana, Rhode Island, and Delaware! A handful of nations can impose UN-authorized sanctions on any nation or group of nations while having immunity to any unwanted counterclaims. At the UN, even if all the nations of the world chose to act together, they could not impose such sanctions on any of the five, who immunize themselves by their veto power.

Further, it takes a considerable suspension of disbelief to call the UN General Assembly "the most democratic and representative body."[50] In it, India and Luxembourg, Nigeria and East Timor, Brazil and St. Lucia have one vote each. The assembly feels it is free to pass all kinds of resolutions because its members are aware that they are backed by no credible enforcement mechanism. There is little that is democratic about a majority vote when the votes that are cast are by representatives of authoritarian regimes that are indifferent to the preferences of their people. And the UN can hardly be viewed as liberal when for decades the most brazen violators of human rights have served on and headed the UN Commission on Human Rights as well as the UN Human Rights Council that replaced it.[51]

It follows that unless there are major reforms in the ways the UN is composed and acts, it ought to be viewed as an aspirational ideal rather than an institution with binding legitimacy. Nationalists have a case when they argue that the UN violates national sovereignty. There is room for legitimate questioning about the extent to which nations should mind UN resolutions until it is much more representative. It has less of a role to play in the NCS than liberals assume it played in the LIO.

A great deal of international governance is carried out through a large variety of international organizations, such as the International Labor Organization, the International Red Cross, the World Health Organization, as well as informal bodies, such as the G7, G8, and G20. They mainly work by reaching consensus among member nations—or their decisions are not binding on those nations that dissent—but not on Wilsonian principles. They could therefore find their place in the NCS without difficulty.

The world needs much stronger forms of global governance based on liberal democratic principles. However, it is sociologically not ready to be governed the way liberal democracies are, as very little global community building has taken place. Until such community building is much more advanced, treating aspirations as if they were actualized, or as normative ramming rods, does not make for a more liberal LIO but engenders cynicism and opposition. One way to correct this gap is to scale back these claims. This is a distinctive mark of the NCS.

Free Trade

In spelling out the elements of the LIO, several scholars have emphasized free trade. Robin Niblett writes: "At the heart of the [liberal international] order were the Bretton Woods institutions—the International Monetary Fund and the World Bank—and the General Agreement on Tariffs and Trade, which became the World Trade Organization in 1995. Underpinning all these institutions was the belief that open and transparent markets with minimal government intervention—the so-called Washington consensus—would lay the foundation for economic growth."[52]

Globalists hold that trade increases the efficiency of all economies and hence the wealth of nations. They tend to see nationalist populists opposing free trade as ignoramuses, oblivious to the grand benefits of free trade as it reduces the costs of consumer goods. Globalists point out that most jobs are lost due to automation and not trade. However, between 2000 and 2015, the US lost five million largely manufacturing (well-paying and meaningful) jobs to trade.[53] These job losses are an important source of nationalist populism. Nationalist populists call for protecting their nations' workers from the ill effects of free trade by imposing high tariffs on imports, among other measures, and they tend to frame advocates of free trade as unpatriotic. Both sides use the arguments for and against free trade as ideological ramming rods.

The scaling back that is necessary regarding trade is mainly a rhetorical one. Both boosters and knockers of free trade argue about a practice that does not exist. To support this proposition, I will quickly review points others have made. First, there never was free trade because there are strong national barriers on the movement of labor, highlighted by the reactions to mass immigration.

Second, the flow of trade is affected by numerous actions of national governments, even if they are not controlling the flow of capital, directly setting exchange rates, or imposing tariffs. Changes in taxation levels, deficit size, investment in research and development, subsidies, and terms of credit provided by the government, all affect trade. Trade is also limited to protect national security (e.g., bans on the sale of certain high-tech items and many weapons), to ensure food and drug safety, to pressure nations to democratize (e.g., the embargo against Cuba), to prevent the development of nuclear weapons (e.g., sanctions against trade with North Korea and Iran), to protect endangered species and archaeological sites, and to discourage child labor. A side agreement of the North American Agreement on Labor Cooperation (NAALC), often referred to as a free trade agreement, required the three countries to enforce labor protections, including the rights of association, organization, collective bargaining, to strike, and certain "technical labor standards," such as compensation in cases of illness.

To avoid being misled by ideological claims, one should refer to less versus more managed trade—"freer" trade, as responsible economists do—but not to "free trade." Most importantly, it follows that calls for making some changes in the ways and the extent to which trade is managed can be considered and be part of the patriotic movement agenda.[54] Indeed, such changes were often made in the past during the period considered the golden days of the LIO. In this way, the populist opposition to transnational trade may be mitigated.

The extent to which trade needs to be managed depends to a great extent on measures such as Trade Adjustment Assistance, though it may have to be expanded to become Technology Adjustment Assistance, given that automation is a major source of disruptive change. The more we can ensure that those displaced by trade or automation are either retrained for different jobs (jobs that pay and provide benefits and meaning similar to those they lost) or hired to carry out public jobs, the less additional trade management will be needed.[55]

In short, trade was never as liberal as globalists often suggest. Managing it somewhat more (if TSA is not adequate) as part of the transition to an NCS should help mitigate nationalist populism.

Free Movement of People

Globalists favor the free movement of people across national borders. They strongly support the Schengen Agreement, which removes border controls between many European nations. They strongly supported Angela Merkel, the German chancellor, when she opened the doors to more than a million immigrants. And they view restriction on immigration as typical right-wing, xenophobic, reactionary, nationalist policies.[56] Such sweeping affirmations of open borders often do not recognize a tension between open-ended immigration, especially of people from different cultures, and sustaining communities. Communities benefit from a measure of stability, continuity, and a core of shared values. A truly free flow of people across borders is endangering national values and communities and is politically unsustainable.[57]

In effect, scaling back the liberal flow of people, as part of the transition to an NCS, is already taking place. All the countries involved—even those highly supportive of immigration, such as Australia and Canada— limit the number of immigrants they receive each year and favor some kinds of immigrants over others. We have already seen that all the European nations involved have limited immigration, some very drastically. I am not arguing that these limitations are just, set at the right level, or grant morally appropriate preference to some immigrants over others. I simply note that the communitarian gap undermined the previous higher levels of immigration. Accelerating the integration of immigrants into the host societies may allow another increase in immigration in the future. Meanwhile, nationalist populism is forcing immigration to be scaled back.

Freedom of Navigation: Liberal and Consensual

In many ways, freedom of navigation is a quintessential liberal element of the LIO. It seeks to ensure that people of all nations are able to move about freely on the seven seas. The US undergirded this freedom frequently and pushed back against limitations on travel on the seas by friend and foe alike.[58] There seems to be no reason that this element could not be readily incorporated into the NCS.

Various concerns have been voiced about China seeking to limit freedom of navigation. To the extent that these refer to China's call for an Air Defense Identification Zone over the South China Sea, many other nations have similar zones, and no plane can approach within several hundred miles of the US without identifying itself.[59] Above all, China would suffer much more than the US if the flow of goods were interrupted, because China is much more dependent on such flows than the US or its allies. Populists have shown little interest in this subject. In short, one should expect smooth sailing for freedom of navigation in the NCS.

In Conclusion

The Liberal International Order (LIO), forged by the US at the end of World War II, is challenged by nationalist populism and rising powers, prompting concerns that anarchy may follow and that liberal values such as free trade, free movement of people, and freedom of navigation will be undermined. I have tried to show in this chapter that the LIO is being transformed rather than ending. One adaptation involves some sharing of power, as the US is no longer as hegemonic as it was in 1945, when the foundations for this order were first laid. In other areas, the LIO has prematurely advanced in the much-needed direction of more supranational governance. As long as people hold their nation to be their main political community—until supranational communities develop on a regional and one day global level—high respect for national sovereignty will need to underpin international order and serve as a basis for the patriotic movement's foreign policy.[60]

This, in turn, requires some limits on the movement of goods and people, though not on navigation. Another important adaptation entails promoting human rights and democratic regimes only by nonlethal means, steering clear of coercive regime change (a rather illiberal form of action). The transition from an LIO to NCS and its consecutive adaptation to the sociological reality has already begun.

This chapter has a subtext that should be openly addressed. It assumes that in revising the existing world order, the preferences of national populists and rising powers should be taken into account by the patriotic movement. The movement should not ignore that the world-wide distribution of power has changed since 1945 or that premature globalist advancements are one reason national populism is rising and endangering liberalism. Moreover, as long as the future promotion of liberal values is limited to nonlethal means, respect for national sovereignty and the promotion of liberalism can both find a place in the new international order—one more centered on nation-states, until transnational community building allows for an expansion of globalism.

II

THE NEW ATHENS, A POST-AFFLUENCE LEGITIMACY

The patriotic movement, as it sorts out what are the core values the nation is to share and dedicate itself to, must also determine which economic system best serves these values. Over recent decades, as even former communist countries have adopted capitalism as their main economic system, it seems as if the debate has ended. While some nations combine capitalism with authoritarian forms of government and others with democratic ones, very few states now still seek the planned economic systems. Even North Korea and Cuba are beginning to relent. Most nations act as if they consider an affluent life, working hard to gain higher levels of consumption—even if it entails sacrificing some other goods (e.g., more time with the family)—as the good life the national government should help promote.[1] In effect, a good part of the legitimacy of many regimes is that they are or are about to provide material affluence.

This consensus needs to be subjected to critical evaluation. There are major reasons to doubt that a world in which ever-more people are seeking ever-more affluence is sustainable. Sustainability is a term so often used that one tends to gloss over it. However, there are strong reasons to doubt the environment can tolerate ever-higher levels of resource extraction to meet ever-rising global market demands for goods and services. Also, rising automation may well kill more jobs than it creates, leaving tens of millions of people—many of them young and educated—without a meaningful occupation. The same holds for the ever-higher social burdens capitalism engenders as it externalizes the social costs it imposes. All these developments call for a reexamination of the legitimacy of capitalism and the legitimacy of material affluence.

Equally important is that even if one could keep the world on a pathway of ever-higher economic grown (and materialism), there are reasons to doubt that this would make people flourish and be content. This chapter hence focuses on addressing the question, What makes a good society and what constitutes a life well lived for those whose basic economic needs have been met?[2]

Income and Happiness

Data suggest that once a certain threshold of income is reached, additional accumulation of income creates little additional contentment. On the whole, social science findings, despite their well-known limitations and sometimes conflicting conclusions, seem to confirm the weak link between happiness and income—with the notable exception of the poor. Frank M. Andrews and Stephen B. Withey found that socioeconomic status has a meager effect on the "sense of well-being" and no significant effect on life satisfaction.[3] A survey of more than one thousand participants, who rated their sense of satisfaction and happiness on a 7-point scale and a 3-point scale, noted no correlation between socioeconomic status and happiness; in fact, the second-highest socioeconomic group was consistently among the least happy of all seven brackets measured. Further, Jonathan Freedman discovered that levels of reported happiness do not vary greatly among different economic classes, apart from the poor, who tend to be less happy than others.[4]

Additional evidence suggests that economic growth does not significantly affect happiness (though at any given time the people of poor countries are generally less happy than those of wealthy ones). David G. Myers and Ed Diener reported that while per-capita disposable (after-tax) income in inflation-adjusted dollars almost exactly doubled between 1960 and 1990, virtually the same proportion of Americans reported that they were "very happy" in 1993 (32 percent) as they did in 1957 (35 percent).[5] Although economic growth has slowed since the mid-1970s, Americans' reported happiness has been remarkably stable (nearly always between 30 and 35 percent) across both high-growth and low-growth periods.[6] Moreover, in the same period (1960–90), rates of depression, violent crime, divorce, and teen suicide all rose dramatically.[7]

In a 1973 study, Richard Easterlin reported on a phenomenon that has since been labeled the "Easterlin Paradox."[8] At any given time, higher income generates more happiness, though over the longer run (ten years or more), happiness fails to increase alongside national income. In other words, long-term economic growth does not improve the overall happiness of citizens. Japan is an often-cited example of the Easterlin Paradox.

Between 1962 and 1987, the Japanese economy grew at an unprecedented rate, more than tripling its GNP per capita; yet Japan's overall happiness remained constant over that period.[9] Similarly, in 1970, while the average American income could buy over 60 percent more than it could in the 1940s, average happiness did not increase.[10] Another survey found that people whose income had increased over a ten-year period were no happier than those whose incomes had stagnated.[11]

Interest in the Easterlin Paradox was revived in the late 1990s and early 2000s, as several scholars called into question Easterlin's findings. A 2006 paper by Ruut Veenhoven and Michael Hagerty explained some of the reasons for the discrepancy among happiness researchers.[12] First, changes in happiness tend to be small and must be aggregated over long periods of time. As very little data spans more than a few decades, its significance is open to different interpretation. Also, average happiness tends to fluctuate, making it difficult to separate the overall trend from the statistical noise. Further, happiness surveys lack uniformity; methodologies and questions have changed over time, possibly skewing results. Social scientists may choose to limit their data to only identical surveys (as Easterlin did) or to draw on a variety of surveys (as Veenhoven and Hagerty did), which may lead to different conclusions.

While such issues can be raised about most social science studies of this kind (especially longitudinal studies), a more serious challenge is Veenhoven and Hagerty's finding that both happiness and income increased in the second half of the twentieth century, indicating a correlation between the two.[13] Ruut Veenhoven and Floris Vergunst's more recent paper contests Easterlin's empirical findings, arguing that data taken from the World Database of Happiness reveals a positive correlation between GDP growth and affective well-being.[14] Similarly, a 2008 study by Betsey Stevenson and Justin Wolfers noted a similar correlation between income growth and happiness.[15]

In December 2010, Easterlin and his associates challenged Stevenson and Wolfers's study.[16] Showing that much of the study's data focused on a short period (six years instead of ten), they argued that longer-term trends were attributable to factors other than economic growth. They also added data from a number of non-Western, developing countries, including China, South Korea, and Chile, and found further support for the Easterlin Paradox. Although China's growth rate doubled per-capita income in less than ten years, South Korea's in thirteen, and Chile's in eighteen years, none of these countries showed a statistically significant increase in happiness. The authors wrote: "With incomes rising so rapidly in these three different countries, it seems extraordinary that there are no surveys that register the marked improvement in subjective well-being that mainstream economists and policy makers worldwide would expect to find."[17]

As already noted, there is one important exception to these findings—when incomes of the poor are increased, happiness is significantly enhanced. This observation is important because some may use the data I cited to argue for the futility of reforms seeking to improve the lot of the poor. Thus, as Richard Layard's 2005 book *Happiness: Lessons from a New Science* shows, when a country's average income exceeds $20,000 a year per person, contentment also rises considerably.[18] Layard used happiness data from three major long-term public opinion surveys (the Euro-barometer for western Europe, the General Social Survey for the United States, and the World Values Survey for eastern Europe and developing nations) to calculate an average happiness measure for each country, which was compared to average income per capita. (Critics of this data argue that it used absolute rather than proportional measurements.)[19]

A 2010 study identified $75,000 as the threshold after which additional income produces little additional happiness.[20] The study's authors found that while high income improved individuals' life evaluation (their thoughts about their life), it did not improve emotional well-being, defined as "the frequency and intensity of experiences of joy, stress, sadness, anger, and affection that make one's life pleasant or unpleasant."[21] Hence, whereas life evaluation rises steadily with increases in income, emotional well-being does not progress once an annual income of $75,000 is reached.[22] A 2018 study found that "satiation occurs at $95,000 for life evaluation and $60,000 to $75,000 for emotional well-being. However, there is substantial variation across world regions, with satiation occurring later in wealthier regions. We also find that in certain parts of the world, incomes beyond satiation are associated with lower life evaluations."[23]

In short, although the data does not all point in one direction, the preponderance of the evidence suggests that, at the very least, high levels of income do not buy much happiness. Thus, the legitimacy bestowed by affluence is questionable, regardless of whether or not a high-growth pathway is achievable and sustainable.

The Sisyphean Nature of Affluence

One reason high wage-earners derive less happiness from additional income is that material goods are judged *relative* to goods available to others rather than in terms of their intrinsic worth. Indeed, Easterlin himself observed that individuals tend to evaluate their earnings and satisfaction on a comparative rather than absolute scale. The familiar expression "keeping up with the Joneses" captures well this competitive character of contentment in social life where goods are used as visible markers of rank in a never-ending race.

Different studies have shown how contextual judgments affect reported subjective well-being. For example, people taking happiness surveys in the presence of someone in a wheelchair rate themselves as 20 percent happier on average than those in a control group.[24] Given this, increasing the total wealth of a given society would not necessarily increase the happiness of its members, as more or "better" consumer goods would merely raise the bar for what people judged to be "good"— leaving people perpetually dissatisfied with their material objects despite their higher quality and quantity. At the same time, improving the material plight of the poor *would* enhance their reported well-being, as their possessions would move closer to the societal standard.

The same social factor seems to help explain why small-towners are happier than big-city dwellers.[25] Daniel Gilbert notes: "Now, if you live in Hallelujah, Arkansas, the odds are good that most of the people you know do something like you do and earn something like you earn and live in houses something like yours. New York, on the other hand, is the most varied, most heterogeneous place on earth. No matter how hard you try, you really can't avoid walking by restaurants where people drop your monthly rent on a bottle of wine and store windows where shoes sit like museum pieces on gold pedestals. You can't help but feel trumped."[26] Another explanation for the disconnect between increased income and happiness draws on the adaptivity of human satisfaction to varying conditions known as the "hedonic treadmill" theory.[27] There are different accounts of what constitutes the hedonic treadmill.[28] One account suggests that people psychologically acclimatize to changes in well-being, gravitating to a set level of happiness regardless of external stimulus. In a seminal study that coined the term, Philip Brickman, Dan Coates, and Ronnie Janoff-Bulman observed that lottery winners were no happier than a control group of nonwinners.[29] Another survey found that the one hundred wealthiest Americans on the Forbes List were only "modestly" happier than a control group selected at random from the same geographic areas.[30]

The hedonic treadmill is also construed through rising expectations in the wake of improvements in material well-being. Thus, a study of rural Chinese found that while rising incomes improved subjective well-being, income aspirations also grew and quickly offset satisfaction gains.[31] According to the authors, this "partial hedonic treadmill" explains why China's rapid economic growth has not elevated subjective well-being.[32] It would also explain Amartya Sen's findings that subjective well-being is often higher among citizens of poor than of rich countries, as the former may be more resourceful in adjusting their expectations to match their circumstances, whereas the latter tend to covet a higher quality of life than they can realistically attain.[33]

In whatever way the hedonic treadmill is understood, the basic insight holds: there is no way to find contentment in the high-growth, high-consumption way of life because well-being is pinned to runaway desire and external validations.

Historical Precedents for Non-Affluence-Based Contentment

In seeking alternatives to material affluence as the source of happiness, one can turn to historical movements and previous cultures and modes of legitimacy that defined the good life by drawing on core values other than affluence. As Jeffrey Sachs notes: "The essence of traditional virtue ethics—whether in Buddhism, Aristotelianism, or Roman Catholicism—is that happiness is achieved by harnessing the will and the passions to live the right kind of life. Individuals become virtuous through rational thought, instruction, mind training, and habits of virtuous behavior."[34] Consider the Buddhist tradition where happiness is understood not as self-aggrandizement or gratification but rather as self-enlightenment and transformation; being happy demands attaining a new way of experiencing and partaking in the world, and as such is more akin to a skill or ability than a sensation.[35]

For centuries the literati of imperial China came to prominence not through acquisition of wealth but through pursuit of knowledge and cultivation of the arts. This group of scholar-bureaucrats dedicated their early lives to rigorous study, in preparation for the exams required for government service. They spent years memorizing the Confucian classics. The literati, having passed the imperial exams, were qualified for government service but instead elected to dedicate their lives to the arts or retired early in order to follow artistic pursuits. They played music and composed poetry, learned calligraphy, and gathered with like-minded friends to share ideas and discuss great works of the past.

Reinhard Bendix writes that in keeping with Confucian teachings, "the educated man must stay away from the pursuit of wealth . . . because acquisitiveness is a source of social and personal unrest. To be sure, this would not be the case if the success of economic pursuits was guaranteed, but in the absence of such a guarantee the poise and harmony of the soul are jeopardized by the risks involved. . . . The cultured man strives for the perfection of the self, whereas all occupations that involve the pursuit of riches require a one-sided specialization that acts against the universality of the gentleman."[36]

The Ancient Greeks—aside from the Epicureans[37]—generally took "happiness" to be the pursuit of excellence rather than pleasure. For example, Aristotle conceived "happiness" (*eudaimonia*) as the exercise of human faculties in accordance with various practical and intellectual virtues, such as prudence, justice, courage, or temperance. To be happy is to realize your full potential in diverse practices as parent, friend, worker, and citizen.[38] Aristotle's happiness, best translated as flourishing, is a way of being that requires cultivation and involves finding a balance between "excess and deficiency," experiencing "emotions at the right times and on the right occasions and towards the right persons and for the right causes and in the right manner."[39] Aristotle's conception of happiness is much broader than that of many contemporary thinkers, amounting to "a kind of living that is active, inclusive of all that has intrinsic value, and complete, meaning lacking in nothing that would make it richer or better."[40] It thus stands in contrast to the idea of welfare used by most contemporary economists, which lines up much more with Bentham's account of happiness.[41]

St. Thomas Aquinas sought to synthesize an Aristotelean conception of happiness with Christian teachings. He redefined Aristotle's everyday virtues with a view of human beings' ultimate destiny. For Aquinas, true happiness cannot attach to worldly honors and riches; attaining it is nothing short of attaining one's final good, which is fellowship with God alongside other saints.[42] Earthly life is but a formidable training of the soul for eternal life.[43] Whatever intermittent fulfillment is experienced in the course of completing daily responsibilities, it is full of conflicts and ordeals that will be set aright in the Kingdom to come.[44]

During the Middle Ages, knights were expected to adhere to an exacting code of chivalry. The tenets they were to live by are well captured in the "Song of Roland," an eleventh-century poem. Throughout the poem, the worthy knight is shown to gladly and faithfully serve his liege lord, to protect the weak and the defenseless, to show proper reverence for God, to respect and honor women, to be truthful and steadfast, and to view financial reward with revulsion and disdain. In traditional Jewish communities, studying the Torah was considered the preferred way of life.

In recent ages, numerous social movements and communities advocated consumerism-resistant forms of the good life within capitalist societies. The Shakers, who left Manchester for America in the 1770s, founded religious communities characterized by a simple ascetic lifestyle.[45] Other such communities (some secular, some religious) include the Brook Farm Institute, the Harmony Society, the Amana Colonies, and the Amish. In Britain, John Ruskin founded the Guild of St. George in the 1870s to help form agrarian communities whose members would lead a simple and modest life. Jewish refugees to Palestine in the early twentieth century established kibbutzim, in which austerity was considered virtuous, consumption restrained, communal life promoted, and socialist and Zionist agendas advanced.

In the 1960s, a counterculture (hippie) movement rose on both sides of the Atlantic. Its core values were anticonsumerism, communal living, equality, environmentalism, free love, and pacifism. Timothy Leary encapsulated the hippie ethos when he advised a crowd to "turn on, tune in, and drop out."[46] The British iteration of the hippie movement manifested itself in London's underground culture, a "community of like-minded anti-establishment, anti-war, pro-rock'n'roll individuals, most of whom had a common interest in recreational drugs," and many of whom opted out of mainstream consumerist culture.[47] Many of these movements and communities sought to renounce both consumerism and work structures while fostering an alternative universe committed to asceticism and various transcendental practices drawing on eclectic spiritual, religious, and social ideas. The underlying goal was to replace rather than limit capitalism.

Most important, these various movements and communities failed to lay a foundation for a new contemporary society—and practically all of them either disintegrated, shriveled, or lost their defining features. It seems that most people cannot abide an austere, ascetic lifestyle in the longer run. Hence if the patriotic movement intends to form a society less centered around consumption, it should not seek to displace consumption but to limit it and channel some of its resources and energy to other pursuits. If one questions whether consumption can be curbed without frustrating basic human needs, Maslow's work provides an answer, albeit not a fully satisfactory one.

The Maslowian Exit

Abraham Maslow's "A Theory of Human Motivation," though published in 1943, speaks directly to our current predicament. Maslow argued that humans have a hierarchy of needs. At the bottom are the basic human necessities of safety, food, shelter, clothing, and health; once these needs are met, affection and self-esteem are next in line; and, finally, the pinnacle of satisfaction is achieved by attending to what he calls "self-actualization." So long as basic creature comforts are satisfied, rising wealth facilitates genuine contentment. However, once consumption is used to satisfy the higher needs, it runs the risk of morphing into consumerism and spawning varied social malaises.

One might object that economic growth is necessary for satisfying not just basic necessities but higher-order needs as well. It might be suggested, for example, that the goods of self-esteem and self-actualization often require material support well beyond what a low-growth economy can provide.

In response, one might observe that a game of chess can be enjoyed whether played with plastic or mahogany pieces, a reading of *Hamlet* whether it is printed in a cheap paperback or leather-bound edition; and bonding with children whether one builds a toy together or buys an expensive one. In a similar vein, one might note that God answers prayers irrespective of whether someone wears the most recent designer garments or regular blue jeans.

In historical terms, in the US a turning point for people with incomes well above the poverty line came in the decades following World War II. Around the time of World War II, economists held that individuals have fixed needs. Once those needs are satisfied, people would allocate additional income toward savings rather than consumption. During the war, however, as the American productive capacity greatly expanded, the economists feared that, once the conflicts ended and war-related materials would be no longer needed, there would be massive unemployment and economic depression, comparable to that of the 1930s. Why produce more when fixed, peacetime needs are sated? In this context, David Riesman published a widely discussed essay called "Abundance for What?"[48] He suggested that the "surplus" be used for public projects, such as maintaining the 1955 lifestyle of New Orleans so future generations could visit this sociological Disneyland to appreciate life in earlier ages, much as we do today in Colonial Williamsburg.[49] John Kenneth Galbraith suggested that, given that private needs were met, excess productive capacities could be used for public goods such as schools and parks.[50] These ideas, however, were soon set aside when Vance Packard's *The Status Seekers* called attention to the fact that large-scale advertising is able to produce artificial, unbounded private wants.[51] The notion that people can be sated by buying a given amount of goods and services, any amount, went out the window. Capitalism banks on people wanting ever more, whether or not they need more.

In the decades that followed World War II, industrial corporations discovered that they could manufacture artificial needs for whatever products they were selling. For instance, first women and then men were taught that they smelled bad and needed to purchase deodorants. Men who used to wear white shirts and gray flannel suits learned that they "had to" purchase a variety of shirts and suits and that last year's style was not proper in the year that followed. Soon, it was not just suits but also cars, ties, handbags, sunglasses, watches, and numerous other products that had to be constantly replaced to keep up with the latest trends. More recently, people have been convinced that they have various illnesses (such as restless leg syndrome) requiring medications.

One cannot stress enough that the quest for a new definition of the good life is a project for those whose creature comforts have been well and securely met. Urging such a project on individuals, classes, or societies that have not reached that stage of economic development is to promote what sociologists call "status acceptance," to urge the "have-nots" to love their misery. It is to provide a rationale to those who "have" all they need and more—and who deny such basics to others. Such a position hardly comports with a definition of a good life.

To reiterate, material consumption per se is not the issue. Maslow does not suggest an austere life of sacks and ashes or of making a virtue out of poverty. Rather, his theory holds that securing basic creature comforts is fully legitimate. However, material consumption turns into an obsession when—after necessities are provided—people use the means suitable for attending to creature comforts to try to buy affection, esteem, and even self-actualization. This point is the subject of a considerable number of plays and novels, most dramatically *Death of a Salesman*. In the play, the husband (the context is of earlier generations where breadwinners were typically men) neglects his spouse, children, and community by investing his time and energy in "bringing home the bacon." In the process, both he and his family are shortchanged.

Maslow's conception of the good life falls short, however, in its characterization of self-actualization as the highest good. It is far from clear what he means by this concept, although leading with the "self" serves as a warning signal. Maslow does not find that self-actualization is best achieved by finding meaning in or serving anything greater than self. Any and all forms of self-expression seem equally valued. As implied by its name, self-actualization is highly individualistic and reflects Maslow's premise that the self is "*sovereign and inviolable*" and entitled to "*his or her own tastes, opinions, values, etc.*"[52] That is, self-actualization refers to an individual need for fulfillment.[53] The particular form self-actualization takes varies greatly from person to person. In some individuals, "it may take the form of the desire to be an ideal mother, in another it may be expressed athletically, and in still another it may be expressed in painting pictures or in inventions."[54] Indeed, some have characterized Maslow's self-actualization as "healthy narcissism."[55]

Contributions to Sustainability and Social Justice

If postmodern societies could develop a culture of moderation where everyone could attain sufficient income to secure basic creature needs and cultivate nonmaterialistic values, that culture would provide one obvious and one less obvious additional major contribution to higher levels of contentment as well as less alienation and populism.

Obviously, a good life that moderates material consumption and fosters nonmaterialistic pursuits is much less taxing on the environment than is consumerism. Practices centering on transcendental, nonmaterialistic values usually require relatively few resources, fossil fuels, or other sources of energy. Social activities (such as spending more time with children) demand time and personal energy but not large material or financial outlays (often those who spend large amounts of money on their kids' toys or entertainment bond less with them than those whose relations are less mediated by objects). The same holds for cultural and spiritual activities such as prayer, meditation, enjoying and making music, art, sports, and adult education. True, consumerism has turned many of these pursuits into expensive endeavors. However, one can break out of this mentality and find that it is possible to engage in most nonmaterialistic activities quite profoundly using a moderate number of goods and services. One does not need designer clothes to enjoy the sunset or shoes with fancy labels to benefit from a hike. In short, the transcendental society is much more sustainable than consumeristic capitalism.

Much less obvious are the ways a culture of moderation serves social justice. Social justice demands fair distribution of material resources among different social groups. This entails reallocation of wealth from those disproportionally endowed to those who are underprivileged. A major reason such reallocation of wealth has been surprisingly limited in free societies is that the wealthy also tend to be politically powerful. Promoting social justice by organizing those with less, and forcing those in power to yield, has had limited success in democratic countries and led to massive bloodshed in others. If, however, those wielding power would embrace a culture of moderation, they would be much more ready to share their assets. This thesis is supported by the behavior of middle-class people committed to the values of giving and attending to the least among us—values prescribed by many religions and by left liberalism. This important thesis requires a whole distinct study and is included here merely to mention a major side benefit of the new culture, rather than document it.

There are three major sources of nonmaterialistic contentment that provide for a life reaching beyond the self. While all are compatible with the Maslowian hierarchy of human needs, they also add a new dimension or requirement to the way these needs are to be understood and pursued. Because these sources of contentment are very familiar, they are only briefly listed below.

The Contentment of Mutuality

Spending time with those with whom one shares bonds of affinity—children, spouses, friends, members of one's community—has often been shown to make people content.[56] Indeed, approval by intimate others is a main source of affection and esteem, Maslow's second layer of human needs. However, social relations are about more than making the ego happy. These relationships are based on mutuality, in which two people "give" and "receive" in one and the same act. Those who engage in lasting, meaningful, and effective relationships find them to be a major source of mutual enrichment, which can be achieved with very little expenditure or material costs. (Note that much of the literature contrasts ego-centered activities with altruistic ones.[57] Much more attention should be paid to mutuality, because it is much more common and more stable than altruism.)

Both introverts and extroverts report feeling happier when they are with other people.[58] Derek Bok writes that "several researchers have concluded that human relationships and connections of all kinds contribute more to happiness than anything else."[59] Conversely, people who are socially isolated are less happy than those who have strong social relationships. As one study put it, "Adults who feel socially isolated are also characterized by higher levels of anxiety, negative mood, dejection, hostility, fear of negative evaluation, and perceived stress, and by lower levels of optimism, happiness, and life satisfaction."[60] Research shows that married people are happier than those who are single, divorced, widowed, separated, or cohabiting.[61] In addition, the presence of close friendships can have nearly as strong an impact on contentment as a successful marriage.[62]

Contentment from Community Involvement

Researchers who examined the effect of community involvement (as opposed to merely socializing with friends or family) also found a strong correlation with happiness. One study, which evaluated survey data from forty-nine countries, noted that membership in nonchurch organizations has a significant positive correlation with happiness.[63] Bok notes, "Some researchers have found that merely attending monthly club meetings or volunteering once a month is associated with a change in well-being equivalent to a doubling of income."[64] Other studies have observed that individuals who devote substantial amounts of time to volunteer work have greater life satisfaction than all others.[65]

Political participation, too, can yield the fruits of bonding and meaningful activities. As one scholar notes, using the terms of an economist, "Citizens do not only gain utility from the outcome of the political process and its material consequences but also from the democratic process itself."[66] This is particularly true when the political culture and processes are perceived as fair and, thus, even those whose preferred candidates are defeated feel that they had their day in court.[67] Also, research shows that adolescents who have a greater commitment to society or pursue some meaningful social cause are more content than their less engaged peers.[68] (This promotion of community involvement is reminiscent of Robert Putnam's notion of social capital, i.e., the sort of close community bonds he suggests ward off a variety of social ills.)[69]

Some scholars have been more critical of community involvement. Pierre Bourdieu suggests that the social capital associated with communal bonds is possessed not by the community but by individuals who then deploy it in social struggles with others in their community.[70] Thus, where Putnam might prize a social club like the Elks for cultivating social stability and trust, Bourdieu might see a small in-group whose members seek to outmaneuver communal competitors.

As I see it,[71] smaller communities are best integrated into more encompassing communities—families into neighborhoods, neighborhoods into regional communities, and these into national, and, best, supranational ones.[72] The more encompassing loyalties help mitigate the tendency of smaller communities to maximize their well-being at the expense of others. When such loyalties are absent, the correct move is to add commitments to the more encompassing communities rather than give up on the rich fruits of the smaller ones.

Transcendental (Religious, Spiritual, and Intellectual) Pursuits

Extensive evidence indicates that people who consider themselves religious, express a belief in God, or regularly attend religious services are more content than those who do not. According to one study, agreement with the statement "God is important in my life" was associated with a gain of 3.5 points on a 100-point scale of happiness.[73] (For comparison, unemployment is associated with a 6-point drop on the same scale.) Other studies show that those with a deep religious faith are healthier, live longer, and have lower rates of divorce, crime, and suicide.[74] Robert Putnam and David Campbell reported that "a common finding [of happiness researchers] is that religiosity is among the closest correlates of life satisfaction, at least as strong as income."[75] They found that the difference in happiness between a person who goes to church once a week and someone who does not attend church was "slightly larger than the difference between someone who earns $10,000 a year and his demographic twin who earns $100,000 a year."[76]

There is some debate as to whether the effect of religiosity on happiness is attributable to participation in religious activities (attending church services, involvement with a religious community) or religious belief. Layard characterizes the correlation between belief in God and life satisfaction as "one of the most robust findings of happiness research,"[77] whereas Putnam and Campbell argue, "The religious edge in life satisfaction has less to do with faith itself than with communities of faith."[78] Whoever is correct, one still learns that religious life is positively correlated with happiness.

There seems to be less research on transcendental activities other than religious pursuits. However, the existing evidence indicates that participation in activities of profound meaning to the individual is associated with happiness. For example, "two studies that examined groups that chose to change their lifestyle to achieve personal values such as 'environmental friendliness' and 'voluntary simplicity' found that both experienced higher levels of well-being."[79] A study used survey data from more than five hundred subscribers of a back-to-the-land magazine to measure participants' sense of well-being and determine whether they lived up to their sustainability values. The researchers found that those who were able to put their values into practice (live in a sustainable, ecologically friendly manner) were more satisfied with their lives than those who did not.[80]

Much like social activities, volunteering, and political action, transcendental activities also provide nonconsumerist sources of contentment. Although some can be isolating and self-centered, many also serve community building.

In Conclusion

The patriotic movement must ask which economic system will best serve the renewed national purpose. Most nations act as if they consider the affluent life as the good life that the national government should help promote. However, it is far from clear that all nations can find a high growth pathway or, even if they could, whether a world in which ever-more billions of people each consume ever more is sustainable. Most importantly, this chapter shows that even if such consumption were possible, ever-higher income and material consumption do not provide for ever-higher levels of contentment. Instead, the patriotic movement ought to favor an economy that ensures that everyone has their basic needs well met. Once this has been achieved, people will limit their further consumption and use the freed time and resources to gain contentment from other sources. Namely, contentment will be derived from sources that are neither labor- nor capital-intensive, ones that are sustainable and more amenable to redistribution. These include cultivating intimate relations, public service (e.g., volunteering), and transcendental activities.

I started this book by pointing out that moral dialogues are needed for the moral agenda of the patriotic movement to percolate up, not to be dictated down. I provide several topics that such dialogues will have to cover if the patriotic movement is to provide a solid foundation for liberal democracy, such as the proper level and kind of trade and immigration, and the need to balance individual rights and the common good. At the top of the list of these topics is the question, What values should we gear the economy to serve?

More generally, the patriotic movement needs to achieve more than merely reuniting us by reinforcing the national community to contain—but not suppress!—differences. It must figure out what we are all seeking to accomplish together, above and beyond our varying personal and subgroup pursuits, and what kind of future we envision for the nation—aside from what we labor to gain for our families, local communities, and various identity groups. It is not enough to stress that we are, all of us, in this boat together and should be sure to keep it afloat. We would do best to concern ourselves with where it is destined to sail and how it has to be reconstructed to travel to wherever we are seeking to reach.

ACKNOWLEDGMENTS

I am indebted for comments on previous drafts to Oleg Makariev, Rory Donnelly, and Kevin Hudson. Jeffrey Hallock worked diligently to help me put this book together.

Some of the chapters of this book draw on previously published material. These have been much modified. Chapter 1, "National Moral Dialogues," draws on the article "Moral Dialogues," published in the *Social Science Journal;* chapter 6, "Privacy vs. the Common Good: A Case Study," draws on "Apple: Good Business, Poor Citizen?," published in the *Journal of Business Ethics;* chapter 7, "Diversity within Unity," draws on "Immigration: Europe's Normative Challenge," published in the *Journal of International Migration and Integration;* and chapter 10, "Curbing Special Interest Groups," draws on "The Rising (More) Nation-Centered World Order," published in the *Fletcher Forum of World Affairs.* Material is used with the permission of the publishers.

NOTES

Introduction

1. See David Runciman, *How Democracy Ends* (London: Profile, 2018).

2. See Kevin M. Kruse and Julian E. Zelizer, *Fault Lines: A History of the United States since 1974* (New York: Norton, 2019).

3. Pew Research Center, *Partisanship and Animosity in 2016* (Washington, DC: Pew Research Center, June 22, 2016), 27, http://assets.pewresearch.org/wp-content/uploads/sites/5/2016/06/06-22-16-Partisanship-and-animosity-release.pdf.

4. Pew Research Center, *The Partisan Divide on Political Values Grows Even Wider* (Washington, DC: Pew Research Center, October 5, 2017), 66, http://assets.pewresearch.org/wp-content/uploads/sites/5/2017/10/05162647/10-05-2017-Political-landscape-release.pdf.

5. Wakefield Research, "New Wakefield Research Study: The Trump Effect on American Relationships," news release, May 10, 2017, https://www.wakefieldresearch.com/blog/2017/05/10/new-wakefield-research-study-trump-effect-american-relationships.

6. Michael R. Bloomberg, "Here's Your Degree: Now Go Defeat Demagogues," *Bloomberg*, April 30, 2016, https://www.bloomberg.com/view/articles/2016-04-30/here-s-your-degree-now-go-defeat-demagogues.

7. Isaac Stanley-Becker, "The Center in British Politics Has All but Disappeared, Leaving the Country as Polarized as the U.S.," *Washington Post*, June 8, 2017, https://www.washingtonpost.com/world/europe/the-center-in-british-politics-has-all-but-disappeared-leaving-the-country-as-polarized-as-the-us/2017/06/07/045b0554-4afa-11e7-987c-42ab5745db2e_story.html?utm_term=.72dd4a2e0fb3; "French More Polarized, Extreme Than Other Europeans, Poll Suggests," Reuters, May 5, 2017, https://www.reuters.com/article/us-france-election-polarisation-poll-idUSKBN1810MT; Anne Applebaum, "A Warning from Europe: The Worst Is Yet to Come," *Atlantic*, October 2018, https://www.theatlantic.com/magazine/archive/2018/10/poland-polarization/568324/.

8. See Ben Sasse, *Them: Why We Hate Each Other—and How to Heal* (New York: St. Martin's, 2018); William Egginton, *The Splintering of the American Mind: Identity Politics, Inequality, and Community on Today's College Campuses* (London: Bloomsbury, 2018); Steve Kornacki, *The Red and the Blue: The 1990s and the Birth of Political Tribalism* (New York: Ecco, 2018); and Stephen Hawkins, Daniel Yudkin, Míriam Juan-Torres, and Tim Dixon, *Hidden Tribes: A Study of America's Polarized Landscape* (New York: More in Common, 2018).

9. Hanno Scholtz, "Idea, Background, and Conditions for the Implementa-

tion of Network-Based Collective Decision-Making," working paper, 2018, https://www.researchgate.net/publication/324248883_Idea_background_and_conditions _for_the_implementation_of_network-based_collective_decision-making ?isFromSharing=1.

10. Gretchen Livingston and Anna Brown, *Intermarriage in the U.S. 50 Years after "Loving v. Virginia"* (Washington, DC: Pew Research Center, May 18, 2017), 5.

11. *Merriam-Webster Unabridged Online*, s.v. "loyal opposition," https://www .merriam-webster.com/dictionary/loyalopposition.

12. *Oxford English Dictionary Online*, s.v. "opposition," http://www.oed.com /view/ Entry/131990?redirectedFrom=loyal+opposition#eid33197504.

13. For a review of the literature on US demographics and perceptions of "the white minority," see Thomas B. Edsall, "Who's Afraid of a White Minority?," *New York Times,* August 30, 2018. Amanda Taub wrote in the *New York Times:* "The mantra is not all about bigotry. Rather, being part of a culture designed around people's own community and customs is a constant background hum of reassurance, of belonging. The loss of that comforting has accelerated a phenomenon that Robin DiAngelo, a lecturer and author, calls 'white fragility'—the stress white people feel when they confront the knowledge that they are neither special nor the default; that whiteness is just a race like any other." And, "Even some conservative analysts who support a multiethnic 'melting pot' national identity, such as the editor of *National Review,* Reihan Salam, worry that unassimilated immigrants could threaten core national values and cultural cohesion" (Amanda Taub, "Behind 2016's Turmoil, a Crisis of White Identity," *New York Times,* November 1, 2016, https://www.nytimes .com/2016/11/02/world/americas/ brexit-donald-trump-whites.html).

14. Amitai Etzioni, "Inventing Hispanics: A Diverse Minority Resists Being Labeled," Brookings Institution, December 1, 2002, https://www.brookings.edu /articles/inventing-hispanics-a-diverse-minority-resists-being-labeled/.

15. Don Gonyea, "Majority of White Americans Say They Believe Whites Face Discrimination," National Public Radio, October 24, 2017, https://www.npr.org/2017/10 /24/559604836/majority-of-white-americans-think-theyre-discriminated-against.

16. Kwame Anthony Appiah, *The Lies That Bind: Rethinking Identity* (New York: Norton, 2018).

17. John Sides, Michael Tesler, and Lynn Vavreck, *Identity Crisis: The 2016 Presidential Campaign and the Meaning of America* (Princeton, NJ: Princeton University Press, 2018).

18. "*The Economist* at 175," *Economist,* September 13, 2018, https://www.economist .com/essay/2018/09/13/the-economist-at-175.

19. Virginia A. Rauh et al., "Brain Anomalies in Children Exposed Prenatally to a Common Organophosphate Pesticide," *Proceedings of the National Academy of Sciences in the United States* 109, no. 20 (2012), http://www.pnas.org/content/pnas /early/2012/04/25/1203396109.full.pdf.

20. Barry Meier, "Origins of an Epidemic: Purdue Pharma Knew Its Opioids Were Widely Abused," *New York Times,* May 29, 2018, https://www.nytimes.com /2018/05/29/ health/purdue-opioids-oxycontin.html.

21. Art Van Zee, "The Promotion and Marketing of OxyContin: Commer-

cial Triumph, Public Health Tragedy," *American Journal of Public Health* 99, no. 2 (2009), https://www.ncbi.nlm.nih.gov/pmc/articles/PMC2622774/.

22. National Safety Council, "NSC Poll: 99% of Doctors Prescribe Highly-Addictive Opioids Longer than CDC Recommends," news release, March 24, 2016, https://www.nsc.org/in-the-newsroom/nsc-poll-99-of-doctors-prescribe-highly-addictive-opioids-longer-than-cdc-recommends; Anupam B. Jena, Michael Barnett, and Dana Goldman, "How Health Care Providers Can Help End the Overprescription of Opioids," *Harvard Business Review,* October 24, 2017, https://hbr.org/2017/10/how-health-care-providers-can-help-end-the-overprescription-of-opioids; "Prescription Opioid Data: Prescribing Practices," Center for Disease Control, 2017, https://www.cdc.gov/drugoverdose/data/prescribing.html.

23. Center for Disease Control, "U.S. Drug Overdose Deaths Continue to Rise: Increase Fueled by Synthetic Opioids," news release, March 29, 2018, https://www.cdc.gov/media/releases/2018/p0329-drug-overdose-deaths.html.

24. "Prescription Opioid Data: Key Messages," Center for Disease Control, 2017, https://www.cdc.gov/drugoverdose/data/prescribing.html.

25. Edward Wyatt, "Promises Made, and Remade, by Firms in S.E.C. Fraud Cases," *New York Times,* November 7, 2011, https://www.nytimes.com/2011/11/08/business/in-sec-fraud-cases-banks-make-and-break-promises.html?pagewanted=all.

26. Carlos Lozada, "Let's See Some I.D.," *Washington Post,* October 21, 2018, B1.

27. Amitai Etzioni, "My Kingdom for a Wave," *American Scholar,* December 6, 2013, https://theamericanscholar.org/my-kingdom-for-a-wave/#.W4lhvy7wbcs.

28. For other notable texts on patriotism, see John Kleinig, Simon Keller, and Igor Primoratz, *The Ethics of Patriotism: A Debate* (Oxford, UK: Wiley-Blackwell, 2015); Igor Primoratz and Aleksander Pavkovic, eds., *Patriotism: Philosophical and Political Perspectives* (Farnham, UK: Ashgate, 2008); Omar Swartz, *Against the New Patriotism and Other Essays on Social Justice, 2001–2009* (Leicester, UK: Troubador, 2014); and Anne Applebaum, "Don't Let the Nationalists Steal Patriotism," *Washington Post,* December 29, 2018, https://www.washingtonpost.com/opinions/global-opinions/dont-let-the-nationalists-steal-patriotism/2018/12/28/d78b310e-0a0e-11e9-85b6-41c0feoc5b8f_story.html?utm_term=.9944c8730bc7.

29. Lawrence Summers, "Voters Deserve Responsible Nationalism Not Reflex Globalism," *Financial Times,* July 10, 2016, https://www.ft.com/content/15598db8-4456-11e6-9b66-0712b3873ae1.

30. David Brooks, "The Nationalist Solution," *New York Times,* February 20, 2015, https://www.nytimes.com/2015/02/20/opinion/david-brooks-the-nationalist-solution.html.

31. Barton Swaim, "The Right Way to Defend Democracy," *Wall Street Journal,* March 9, 2018.

32. William A. Galston, "In Defense of a Reasonable Patriotism," Brookings Institution, July 23, 2018, https://www.brookings.edu/research/in-defense-of-a-reasonable-patriotism/.

33. George Orwell, "Notes on Nationalism," *Polemic,* May 1945, http://www.orwell.ru/library/essays/nationalism/english/e_nat.

34. For additional discussion, see Amitai Etzioni, *Security First: For a Muscular,*

Moral Foreign Policy (New Haven, CT: Yale University Press, 2007); Robert Dahl, *Polyarchy: Participation and Opposition* (New Haven, CT: Yale University Press, 1972); and S. M. Lipset and Jason M. Lakin, *The Democratic Century* (Norman: University of Oklahoma Press, 2004).

35. Charles Taylor, "Why Democracy Needs Patriotism," in *For Love of Country: Debating the Limits of Patriotism,* ed. Joshua Cohen (Boston: Beacon, 1996), 120.

36. Larry Siedentop questions where the idea of liberalism has come from and the historical development of liberalism in *Inventing the Individual: The Origins of Western Liberalism* (Cambridge: Belknap Press of Harvard University Press, 2014).

37. See Susan Wolf, "Moral Obligations and Social Commands," in *Metaphysics and the Good: Themes from the Philosophy of Robert Merrihew Adams,* ed. Samuel. Newlands and Larry M. Jorgensen (Oxford: Oxford University Press, 2009).

I. National Moral Dialogues

1. In fact, some communitarians (e.g., MacIntyre and Hauerwas) evaluate communal bonds to question not only globalism but also nationalism, arguing that meaningful bonds and values can develop only in small, tightly knit communities of associations, clubs, churches, neighborhoods, small towns, etc. among people who share the same narrative of the good life (see Alasdair MacIntyre, *After Virtue* [Notre Dame, IN: University of Notre Dame Press, 1981], 256–63).

2. For an evaluation of core values in communities across the globe, see Michael Ignatieff, *The Ordinary Virtues: Moral Order in a Divided World* (Cambridge: Harvard University Press, 2017).

3. *Encyclopædia Britannica Online,* s.v. "ideal type," http://www.britannica.com /topic/ideal-type.

4. In 2015, Israeli president Reuven Rivlin called for a dialogue among the four tribes of Israel—secular Jews, Haredim (ultra-Orthodox), national religious groups, and Israeli Arabs—to formulate a new concept of partnership. Amitai Etzioni provided a map of how to accomplish this goal in his 2016 presentation for the Herzliya Conference, "From Partnership to Community," https://papers.ssrn.com /sol3/papers.cfm?abstract_id=2825302.

5. H. D. Wu and Renita Coleman, "Advancing Agenda-Setting Theory: The Comparative Strength and New Contingent Conditions of the Two Levels of Agenda-Setting," *Journalism and Mass Communication Quarterly* 86, no. 4 (2009): 775–89, http://proxygw.wrlc.org/login?url=http://search.proquest.com/docview /216940500?accountid=11243.

6. Amitai Etzioni, "COIN: A Study of Strategic Illusion," *Small Wars & Insurgencies* 26, no. 3 (2015): 345–76.

7. Aldon D. Morris, "A Retrospective on the Civil Rights Movement: Political and Intellectual Landmarks," *Annual Review of Sociology* 25 (1999): 535.

8. Data Source: Google Trends, "social inequality," www.google.com/trends.

9. World Movement for World Federal Government, *Montreux Declaration* (Switzerland: Secretariat for World Movement for World Federal Government, August 23, 1947), http://www.cvce.eu/content/publication/1999/1/1/adf279f7-80a4 -4855-9215-48a5184328aa/publishable_en.pdf.

10. Data Source: Google Trends, "transgender bathrooms," www.google.com /trends.

11. George Stigler and Gary Becker, "De gustibus non est disputandum," *American Economic Review* 67, no. 2 (1977): 76.

12. See Amartya K. Sen, "Rational Fools: A Critique of the Behavioral Foundations of Economic Theory," *Philosophy & Public Affairs* 6, no. 4 (1977): 317–44; Richard H. Thaler, *Misbehaving: The Making of Behavioral Economics* (New York: Norton, 2015); Daniel Kahneman, *Thinking, Fast and Slow* (New York: Farrar, Straus and Giroux, 2011); and Herbert A. Simon, *Administrative Behavior: A Study of Decision-Making Processes in Administrative Organizations* (New York: Free Press, 1997).

13. Bernard Cohen, *The Press and Foreign Policy* (Princeton, NJ: Princeton University Press, 2016), 13.

14. Robert E. Goodin, *No Smoking: The Ethical Issues* (Chicago: University of Chicago Press, 1989).

15. See Michael Lerner and Cornel West, *Jews and Blacks: Let the Healing Begin* (New York: G. P. Putnam's Sons, 1995).

16. For additional examples, see Michael LaBossiere, *Moral Methods* (self-pub., 2012).

17. *Oxford English Dictionary Online*, s.v. "culture," http://www.oed.com/view /Entry/45746?rskey=WuBW7i&result=1&isAdvanced=false#eid.

18. Stephen Prothero, *Why Liberals Win the Culture Wars (Even When They Lose Elections): The Battles That Define America from Jefferson's Heresies to Gay Marriage* (New York: HarperCollins, 2016).

19. Amitai Etzioni, *A Comparative Analysis of Complex Organizations* (New York: Free Press of Glencoe, 1961).

20. Ibid.

21. Dennis Hume Wrong, *The Problem of Order: What Unites and Divides Society* (New York: Free Press, 1994).

22. Alan Lewis, *The Psychology of Taxation* (New York: St. Martin's, 1982), 5–6.

23. Amitai Etzioni, *The New Golden Rule: Community and Morality in a Democratic Society* (New York: Basic, 1996), 146.

24. Ibid., 143.

25. Bowers v. Hardwick, 478 US 186 (1986).

26. The Defense of Marriage Act, HR 3396, 104th Cong., 2nd sess., Cong. Rec. 142 (July 11–12, 1996) H104–664, https://www.govtrack.us/congress/votes/104-1996 /h316.

27. The Defense of Marriage Act, HR 3396, 104th Cong., 2nd sess., Cong. Rec. 142 (September 10, 1996) S280, https://www.govtrack.us/congress/votes/104-1996 /s280.

28. David Cole, *Engines of Liberty: The Power of Citizen Activists to Make Constitutional Law* (New York: Basic, 2016), 28.

29. William J. Clinton, *Public Papers of the President of the United States, William J. Clinton, in Book 2, July 1 to December 31, 1996* (Washington, DC: Government Printing Office, 1998), 1635.

30. "Marriage," Gallup, 2016, http://www.gallup.com/poll/117328/marriage.aspx.

31. "Growing Public Support for Same-Sex Marriage," Pew Research Center, February 7, 2012, http://www.pewresearch.org/data-trend/domestic-issues /attitudes-on-gay-marriage/.

32. Jeffrey Schmalz, "In Hawaii, Step toward Legalized Gay Marriage," *New York Times*, May 7, 1993, http://www.nytimes.com/1993/05/07/us/in-hawaii-step-toward -legalized-gay-marriage.html.

33. Cole, *Engines of Liberty*, 28.

34. Pam Belluck, "Massachusetts Arrives at Moment for Same-Sex Marriage," *New York Times*, May 17, 2004, http://www.nytimes.com/2004/05/17/us /massachusetts-arrives-at-moment-for-same-sex-marriage.html?_r=0.

35. Cole. *Engines of Liberty*, 82.

36. Ibid., 49.

37. Ibid., 51.

38. Ibid., 48–49.

39. Ibid., 70.

40. Ibid., 68–70.

41. Ibid., 74.

42. Associated Press, "Number of Gay and Lesbian TV Characters Growing, says GLAAD," CBS News, October 1, 2014, http://www.cbsnews.com/news/number -of-gay-and-lesbian-tv-characters-growing-says-glaad/.

43. Eliana Dockterman, "These Shows Helped Shape America's Attitudes about Gay Relationships," *Time*, June 26, 2015, http://time.com/3937496/gay-marriage -supreme-court-ruling-tv-shows-changed-america/.

44. Paul Hitlin and Sovini Tan, "In Social Media, Support for Same-Sex Marriage," Pew Research Center, May 17, 2012, http://www.journalism.org/2012/05/17 /social-media-support-samesex-marriage/.

45. Ibid.

46. Ibid.

47. Alexis Kleinman, "How the Red Equal Sign Took over Facebook, According to Facebook's Own Data," *Huffington Post*, March 29, 2013, http://www .huffingtonpost.com/2013/03/29/red-equal-sign-facebook_n_2980489.html.

48. Maureen McCarty, "One Year Out, the Little Red Logo That Transformed the Marriage Equality Narrative," March 25, 2014, Human Rights Campaign, http://www.hrc.org/blog/one-year-out-the-little-red-logo-that-transformed-the -marriage-equality-nar.

49. Paul Hitlin, Mark Jurkowitz, and Amy Mitchell, "News Coverage Conveys Strong Momentum for Same-Sex Marriage," Pew Research Center, June 17, 2013, http://www.journalism.org/2013/06/17/news-coverage-conveys-strong -momentum/.

50. Ibid.

51. Associated Press, "In California, Protests over Gay Marriage Vote," *New York Times*, November 9, 2008, http://www.nytimes.com/2008/11/10/us/10protest.html.

52. Ibid.

53. United States v. Windsor, 133 S. Ct. 2675 (2013).

54. Obergefell v. Hodges, 135 S. Ct. 2584 (2015).

55. "Marriage," Gallup, 2016, http://www.gallup.com/poll/117328/marriage.aspx.

56. Cole, *Engines of Liberty*, 92.

57. Ferdinand Tönnies, *Community and Society (Gemeinschaft und Gesellschaft)*, trans. and ed. Charles P. Loomis (East Lansing: Michigan State University Press, 1957).

58. Edward Blakely, "In Gated Communities, Such as Where Trayvon Martin Died, a Dangerous Mind-Set," *Washington Post*, April 6, 2012, https://www.washingtonpost.com/opinions/in-gated-communities-such-as-where-trayvon-martin-died-a-dangerous-mind-set/2012/04/06/gIQAwWG8zS_story.html.

59. "Communitarian critics want us to live in Salem, but not believe in witches" (quote from Amy Gutmann, "Communitarian Critics of Liberalism," *Philosophy and Public Affairs* 14, no. 3 [1985]: 319).

60. Amitai Etzioni, "On Communitarian and Global Sources of Legitimacy," *Review of Politics* 73, no. 1 (2011): 105.

2. Communities Are Essential but Suspect Building Blocks

1. Yoram Hazony, "The Liberty of Nations," *Wall Street Journal*, August 24, 2018, https://www.wsj.com/articles/the-liberty-of-nations-1535120837.

2. See Robert E. Park, *Race and Culture* (New York: Free Press, 1950).

3. Carolyn Y. Johnson, "Talking to the Other Side Can Stoke Polarization," *Washington Post*, September 8, 2018.

4. See Hugo Mercier and Dan Sperber, *The Enigma of Reason* (Cambridge: Harvard University Press, 2017).

5. National Fire Administration, "National Fire Department Registry Quick Facts," news release, October 5, 2018, https://apps.usfa.fema.gov/registry/summary.

6. Richard Rorty, "The Unpatriotic Academy," *New York Times*, February 13, 1994, https://www.nytimes.com/1994/02/13/opinion/the-unpatriotic-academy.html.

7. Jean Baldwin Grossman, Joseph P. Tierney, and Nancy Resch, *Making a Difference: An Impact Study of Big Brothers/Big Sisters* (Philadelphia: Public/Private Ventures, 2000); Leonard LoSciuto, Amy K. Rajala, Tara N. Townsend, and Andrea S. Taylor, "An Outcome Evaluation of 'Across Ages': An Intergenerational Mentoring Approach to Drug Prevention," *Journal of Adolescent Research* 11, no. 1 (1996): 116–29, https://journals.sagepub.com/doi/10.1177/0743554896111007; Robert Aseltine, Mathew Dupre, and Pamela Lamlein, "Mentoring as a Drug Prevention Strategy: An Evaluation of 'Across Ages,'" *Adolescent and Family Health* 1 (2000): 11–20.

8. Patrick T. Terenzini, Ernest T. Pascarella, and Gregory S. Blimling, "Students' Out-of-Class Experiences and the Influence of Learning and Cognitive Development: A Literature Review," *Journal of College Students Development* 37 (1996): 149–61; Toni A. Campbell and David E. Campbell, "Faculty/Student Mentor Program: Effects on Academic Performance and Retention," *Research in Higher Education* 38, no. 6 (1997): 727–42, https://www.jstor.org/stable/40196285.

9. Grossman, Tierney, and Resch, *Making a Difference: An Impact Study of Big Brothers/Big Sisters;* Aseltine, Dupre, and Lamlein, "Mentoring as a Drug Prevention Strategy: An Evaluation of 'Across Ages.'"

10. Rajashi Ghosh and Thomas G. Reio Jr., "Career Benefits Associated with Mentoring for Mentors: A Meta-analysis," *Journal of Vocational Behavior* 83, no. 1 (2013), https://www.sciencedirect.com/science/article/pii/S0001879113001012.

11. Martin West, "Testing, Learning, and Teaching: The Effects of Test-Based Accountability on Student Achievement and Instructional Time in Core Academic Subjects," in *Beyond the Basics: Achieving a Liberal Education for All Children,* ed. C. E. Finn Jr. and D. Ravitch (Washington, DC: Thomas B. Fordham Institute, 2007), 45–62.

12. Sarah Shapiro and Catherine Brown, "The State of Civics Education," Center for American Progress, February 21, 2018, https://www.americanprogress.org/issues/education-k-12/reports/2018/02/21/446857/state-civics-education/.

13. Matthew Shaw, "Civic Illiteracy in America," *Harvard Political Review,* May 25, 2017, http://harvardpolitics.com/culture/civic-illiteracy-in-america/.

14. Ibid.

15. Yascha Mounk, *The People vs. Democracy* (Cambridge: Harvard University Press, 2018), 251.

16. E. J. Dionne Jr., *Our Divided Political Heart: The Battle for the American Idea in an Age of Discontent* (New York: Bloomsbury, 2012), 4.

17. Ibid., 21

18. Amitai Etzioni, *The Spirit of Community: Rights, Responsibilities, and the Communitarian Agenda* (New York: Touchstone, 1993).

19. Stanley McChrystal, "Stanley McChrystal: Every American Should Serve for One Year," *Time,* June 20, 2017, http://time.com/4824366/year-national-service-americorps-peace-corps/.

20. Stanley McChrystal, "How a National Service Year Can Repair America," *Washington Post,* November 14, 2014, https://www.washingtonpost.com/opinions/mcchrystal-americans-face-a-gap-of-shared-experience-and-common-purpose/2014/11/14/a51ad4fa-6b6a-11e4-a31c-77759fc1eacc_story.html?utm_term=.cd6f236f70a7.

21. Isabel V. Sawhill, "It's Time to Make National Service a Universal Commitment," Brookings Institution, November 30, 2017, https://www.brookings.edu/blog/up-front/2017/11/30/its-time-to-make-national-service-a-universal-commitment/.

22. *Dictionary.com,* s.v. "globalism," https://www.dictionary.com/browse/globalism.

23. Greg Ip, "We Are Not the World," *Wall Street Journal,* January 6, 2017, https://www.wsj.com/articles/we-arent-the-world-1483728161.

24. See Ian Bremmer, *Us vs. Them: The Failure of Globalism* (New York: Penguin Random House, 2018).

25. Anand Giridharadas, *Winners Take All: The Elite Charade of Changing the World* (New York: Knopf, 2018), 146–47.

26. Dani Rodrik, *The Globalization Paradox* (New York: Norton, 2012), 88. Michael Lind has written at length about free trade, with particular emphasis on

disagreements among economists skeptical of free trade such as Rodrik, Ha-Joon Chang, and Paul Bairoch, and free-trade advocates such as Jeffrey Sachs, Jagdish Bhagwati, and Paul Krugman (see Michael Lind, "Free Trade Fallacy," *Prospect Magazine,* January 20, 2003, https://www.prospectmagazine.co.uk/magazine /freetradefallacy). Joseph Stiglitz has also examined flaws in the global economic system, as currently constructed, in his books *Globalism and Its Discontents* (2002) and *Fair Trade for All* (2005).

27. See Woodrow Wilson's "Fourteen Points," January 8, 1918, http://avalon.law .yale.edu/20th_century/wilson14.asp.

28. Milton Friedman and Rose D. Friedman, "The Case for Free Trade," Hoover Institution, October 30, 1997, https://www.hoover.org/research/case-free-trade.

29. Sam Bowman, "Coming out as Neoliberals," Adam Smith Institute, October 11, 2016, https://www.adamsmith.org/blog/coming-out-as-neoliberals.

30. Adam Smith Institute, 2018, https://www.adamsmith.org/#.

31. Alex Tabarrok, "The Case for Getting Rid of Borders—Completely," *Atlantic,* October 10, 2015, https://www.theatlantic.com/business/archive/2015/10/get-rid -borders-completely/409501/.

32. Joseph H. Carens, "Aliens and Citizens: The Case for Open Borders," *Review of Politics* 49, no. 2 (1987): 251–73, https://www.jstor.org/stable/pdf/1407506.pdf.

33. Jacob Hornberger, "There Is Only One Libertarian Position on Immigration," Future of Freedom Foundation, August 25, 2016, http://www.fff.org/2015/08/25/one -libertarian-position-immigration/.

34. Samuel Huntington, "Dead Souls: The Denationalization of the American Elite," *National Interest,* March 1, 2004, https://nationalinterest.org/article/dead -souls-the-denationalization-of-the-american-elite-620.

35. Johnathan Haidt, "The Ethics of Globalism, Nationalism, and Patriotism," *Minding Nature* 9, no. 3 (2016), https://www.humansandnature.org/the-ethics-of -globalism-nationalism-and-patriotism.

36. Johnathan Haidt, "When and Why Nationalism Beats Globalism," *American Interest* 12, no. 1 (2016), https://www.the-american-interest.com/2016/07/10/when -and-why-nationalism-beats-globalism/.

37. Theresa May, "2016 Conservative Party Conference" (speech, Birmingham, UK, October 5, 2016), https://www.mirror.co.uk/news/uk-news/theresa-mays -speech-conservative-party-8983265.

38. Martha Nussbaum, "Patriotism and Cosmopolitanism," in *For Love of Country: Debating the Limits of Patriotism,* ed. Joshua Cohen (Boston: Beacon, 1996), 5.

39. Ibid., 6.

40. "Yuval Noah Harari: Nationalism vs. Globalism: The New Political Divide," Tiny TED, n.d., https://en.tiny.ted.com/talks/yuval_noah_harari_nationalism_vs _globalism_the_new_political_divide.

41. Ibid.

42. Jamie Mayerfeld, "The Myth of Benign Group Identity: A Critique of Liberal Nationalism," *Polity* 30, no. 4 (1998): 576, https://www.jstor.org/stable/pdf/3235255 .pdf?refreqid=excelsior%3A948d33ac025aa5bf5d2f3437df3c81c6.

43. James S. House, Karl R. Landis, and Debra Umberson, "Social Relationships and Health," *Science* 241 (July 1988): 540.

44. John T. Cacioppo and Louise C. Hawkley, "Social Isolation and Health, with an Emphasis on Underlying Mechanisms," *Perspectives in Biology and Medicine* 46, no. 3 (2003): S39–S52.

45. John T. Cacioppo and Louise C. Hawkley, "Loneliness Matters: A Theoretical and Empirical Review of Consequences and Mechanisms," *Annals of Behavioral Medicine* 40, no. 2 (2010): 218.

46. Steven Stack and J. Ross Eshleman, "Marital Status and Happiness: A 17-Nation Study," *Journal of Marriage and Family* 60, no. 2 (May 1998): 527–36; see also Richard A. Easterlin, "Explaining Happiness," *Proceedings of the National Academy of Sciences of the United States of America* 100, no. 19 (2003): 11176–83.

47. See Erich Fromm, *Escape from Freedom* (New York: Henry Holt, 1941); and William Kornhauser, *The Politics of Mass Society* (Glencoe, IL: Free Press, 1959).

48. Robert A. Kagan and Jerome H. Skolnick, "Banning Smoking: Compliance without Enforcement," in *Smoking Policy: Law, Politics, and Culture*, ed. Robert L. Rabin and Stephen D. Sugarman (New York: Oxford University Press, 1993).

49. See T. R. Reid, *Confucius Lives Next Door: What Living in the East Teaches Us about Living in the West* (New York: Random House, 1999).

50. Amy Gutmann, "Review: Communitarian Critics of Liberalism," *Philosophy and Public Affairs* 14, no. 3 (1985): 319.

51. David Brooks, "Yes, I'm an American Nationalist," *New York Times,* October 25, 2018, A23.

52. Ernest Renan, "What Is a Nation?," trans. Ethan Rundell, in "Qu'est-ce qu'une nation?," by Renan (text of a conference, Sorbonne, Paris, March 11, 1882).

53. For a book very critical of tribes in Europe, see Akbar Ahmed, *Journey into Europe: Islam, Immigration, and Identity* (Washington, DC: Brookings Institution Press, 2018).

54. Amy Chua, *Political Tribes: Group Instinct and the Fate of Nations* (New York: Penguin, 2018): 54.

55. Ibid., 79.

56. Steven Pinker, *Enlightenment Now: The Case for Reason, Science, Humanism, and Progress* (New York: Penguin, 2018).

57. See Amitai Etzioni, "The Moral Voice," in *The New Golden Rule* (New York: Basic, 1996), 119–59.

58. See Jennifer Welsh, *The Return of History: Conflict, Migration, and Geopolitics in the Twenty-First Century* (Toronto: House of Anansi, 2016).

59. See Kenneth F. Scheve and Matthew J. Slaughter, "How to Save Globalism," *Foreign Affairs* 97, no. 6 (2018).

60. Benjamin Friedman, "The Moral Consequences of Economic Growth," *Society* 43 (2006): 15.

61. Elizabeth Warren and Bill de Blasio wrote a piece for the *Washington Post* in 2015 titled "A New Agenda for Prosperity," in which they outlined policy proposals to rebuild the middle class and "Strengthen the American Dream." All nine proposals of their class-centric approach focus on economics.

62. William A. Galston, "Populism's Challenge to Democracy," *Wall Street Journal,* March 17, 2018.

63. Paul Collier, *The Future of Capitalism: Facing the New Anxieties* (New York: HarperCollins, 2018).

64. Isabel Sawhill, *The Forgotten Americans: An Economic Agenda for a Divided Nation* (New Haven, CT: Yale University Press, 2018).

65. Arlie Russell Hochschild's *Strangers in Their Own Land* (2016) provides much insight and data on these voters, though the book was written before the 2016 election.

66. Jordan Kyle and Yascha Mounk, "Why Populism Refuses to Die," *Washington Post,* March 11, 2018.

67. Barack Obama, "Keynote Address: Democratic National Conference," speech, Boston, July 27, 2004, http://www.washingtonpost.com/wp-dyn/articles /A19751-2004Jul27.html?tid=a_mcntx.

68. Gordon W. Allport, *The Nature of Prejudice* (Cambridge, MA: Addison-Wesley, 1954).

69. Chua, *Political Tribes,* 201.

70. See Rupert Nacoste, "Self-Segregation on College Campuses," *Utne Reader,* April 2015, https://www.utne.com/community/self-segregation-on-college -campuses-zeoz1504zdeh.

71. Chua, *Political Tribes.*

72. Ibid., 189.

73. Ibid., 203.

74. Mark Lilla, *The Once and Future Liberal* (New York: HarperCollins, 2017), 67. Lilla seems unaware that this point is a central thesis of Robert N. Bellah et al. in their book *Habits of the Heart* (1985), and Amitai Etzioni, in *The Spirit of Community* (1993). Indeed, he uses the same notation. The same holds for his assertion that rights presume duties, though previous authors used the term "responsibilities" to make the same point.

75. Mark Lilla, *The Once and Future Liberal,* 129.

76. Ibid., 133.

77. Ibid.

78. Yascha Mounk, "How Liberals Can Reclaim Nationalism," *New York Times,* March 3, 2018.

79. Yascha Mounk, *The People vs. Democracy: Why Our Freedom Is in Danger & How to Save It* (Cambridge: Harvard University Press, 2018), 210.

80. Barack Obama, "50th Anniversary of the Selma to Montgomery Marches" (speech, Selma, AL, March 7, 2015), https://obamawhitehouse.archives.gov/the -press-office/2015/03/07/remarks-president-50th-anniversary-selma-montgomery -marches.

81. Yascha Mounk, *The People vs. Democracy.*

82. Francis Fukuyama, "The End of History," *National Interest* 16 (1989).

83. See Amitai Etzioni, "Benefits for Gig Workers," *Challenge* (2018): 1–14.

84. Paul Fain, "Helping Career Education Become a First Choice," *Inside Higher Ed,* July 5, 2017, https://www.insidehighered.com/news/2017/07/05/california -community-colleges-seek-rebrand-cte-state-kicks-new-money.

85. Sasse, *Them: Why We Hate Each Other—And How to Heal*, 252.

86. Norman Ornstein and Thomas E. Mann, "The Broken Branch: How Congress Is Failing America and How to Get It Back on Track," *Brookings Institution*, June 27, 2006.

87. Gottman and Silver, *The Seven Principles for Making Marriage Work*, 235.

88. One proposal has been to cultivate grassroots drives that rally citizens to tackle a variety of problems that cut across political lines. Jeffrey Stout details in *Blessed Are the Organized: Grassroots Democracy in America* how community-based organizing mobilizes people to confront issues as simple as improving neighborhood signage to as complex as disaster preparedness. A separate account of community-based activism in America comes from James Fallows and Deborah Fallows in *Our Towns: A 100,000-Mile Journey into the Heart of America*. The couple details how activists across what is considered "flyover country" in America are providing practical solutions to local problems through civic engagement and grassroots organizing.

89. Michael Kazin, "America's Never-Ending Culture War," *New York Times*, August 24, 2018, https://www.nytimes.com/2018/08/24/opinion/sunday/chicago-protests-1968-culture-war.html.

90. Barack Obama, "Victory Speech" speech, Chicago, November 7, 2012, https://www.npr.org/2012/11/06/164540079/transcript-president-obamas-victory-speech.

91. Trip Gabriel, "Patriotism: An American Puzzle," *New York Times*, November 6, 2018, https://www.nytimes.com/2018/11/06/us/politics/patriotism-midterms-trump.html.

92. See Amitai Etzioni, *The Spirit of Community: Rights, Responsibilities, and the Communitarian Agenda* (New York: Touchstone, 1993); Amitai Etzioni, *The New Golden Rule: Community and Morality in a Democratic Society* (New York: Basic, 1996); and Nikolas K. Gvosdev, *Communitarian Foreign Policy: Amitai Etzioni's Vision* (Piscataway, NJ: Transaction, 2015).

3. Topics for National Dialogues

1. Pankaj Mishra, "How Rousseau Predicted Trump," *New Yorker*, August 1, 2016.

2. For an evaluation of Hume's philosophical views of religion, see section 8 of William Edward Morris and Charlotte R. Brown, *The Stanford Encyclopedia of Philosophy*, ed. Edward N. Zalta (2017), s.v. "David Hume," https://plato.stanford.edu/archives/spr2017/entries/hume/.

3. David Hume, *The Natural History of Religion* (1757; London: A. and H. Bradlaugh Bonner, 1889), 61.

4. Yoram Hazony, "The Dark Side of the Enlightenment," *Wall Street Journal*, April 7–8, 2018.

5. "Russians Return to Religion, but Not to Church," Pew Research Center, February 10, 2014, http://www.pewforum.org/2014/02/10/russians-return-to-religion-but-not-to-church/.

6. Eleanor Albert, "Christianity in China," Council on Foreign Relations, March 9, 2018, https://www.cfr.org/backgrounder/christianity-china.

7. David Masci, "Why Has Pentecostalism Grown So Dramatically in Latin America?" Pew Research Center, November 14, 2014, http://www.pewresearch.org

/fact-tank/2014/11/14/why-has-pentecostalism-grown-so-dramatically-in-latin
-america/.

8. "Most Muslims Want Democracy, Personal Freedoms, and Islam in Political Life," Pew Research Center, July 10, 2012, http://www.pewglobal.org/2012/07/10
/chapter-3-role-of-islam-in-politics/.

9. Robert Bartley, "The Future of Economic Freedom," Heritage Foundation, October 16, 2000, https://www.heritage.org/trade/report/the-future-economic
-freedom.

10. Bruce Stokes, "Most of the World Supports Globalization in Theory, but Many Question It in Practice," Pew Research Center, September 16, 2014, http://www
.pewresearch.org/fact-tank/2014/09/16/most-of-the-world-supports-globalization
-in-theory-but-many-question-it-in-practice/.

11. Alex Tabarrok, "The Case for Getting Rid of Borders—Completely," *Atlantic,* October 10, 2015, https://www.theatlantic.com/business/archive/2015/10/get-rid
-borders-completely/409501/. In a speech transcript released by WikiLeaks, Hillary Clinton is alleged to have said, "My dream is a hemispheric common market, with open trade and open borders, sometime in the future with energy that is as green and sustainable as we can get it, powering growth and opportunity for every person in the hemisphere" (see https://www.businessinsider.com/hillary-clinton-open
-trade-open-border-immigration-policy-for-migrants-2016-10).

12. Johnathan Haidt, "When and Why Nationalism Beats Globalism," *American Interest* 12, no. 1 (2016), https://www.the-american-interest.com/2016/07/10/when
-and-why-nationalism-beats-globalism/.

4. What Is the Common Good?

1. Jeremy Bentham, *Principles of Morals and Legislation* (1789; London: W. Pickering, 1823), 4: "The community is a fictitious body composed of the individuals who are thought of as being as it were its members. Then what is the interest of the community? It is the sum of the interests of the members who compose it."

2. See Margaret Thatcher, "No Such Thing as Society" (interview, London, September 23, 1987), https://www.margaretthatcher.org/document/106689: "I think we have gone through a period when too many children and people have been given to understand 'I have a problem, it is the Government's job to cope with it!' or 'I have a problem, I will go and get a grant to cope with it!' 'I am homeless, the Government must house me!' and so they are casting their problems on society and who is society? There is no such thing! There are individual men and women and there are families and no government can do anything except through people and people look to themselves first."

3. Amitai Etzioni, *The New Golden Rule: Community and Morality in a Democratic Society* (New York: Basic, 1996); Amitai Etzioni, *The Spirit of Community: Rights, Responsibilities, and the Communitarian Agenda* (New York: Touchstone, 1993).

4. Sebastian Reyes, "Singapore's Stubborn Authoritarianism," *Harvard Political Review,* September 29, 2015, http://harvardpolitics.com/world/singapores-stubborn
-authoritarianism/.

5. T. R. Reid, *Confucius Lives Next Door: What Living in the East Teaches Us about Living in the West* (New York: Random House, 1999).

6. See Lawrence H. Summers, "Morning Prayers Address" (speech, Cambridge, MA, September 15, 2003), http://www.harvard.edu/president/speeches/summers _2003/prayer.php: "It is the basis of much economic analysis that the good is an aggregation of many individuals' assessments of their own well-being."

7. See Friedrich A. Hayek, *The Road to Serfdom* (Chicago: University of Chicago Press, 1994), 95.

8. Ayn Rand, *The Virtue of Selfishness* (New York: New American Library, 1964).

9. This view is advocated particularly by the public choice school of political economy (see William F. Shughart II, *The Concise Encyclopedia of Economics*, 2nd ed. [Indianapolis, IN: Liberty Fund, 2008], s.v. "Public Choice").

10. Martin Gilens and Benjamin I. Page, "Testing Theories of American Politics: Elites, Interest Groups, and Average Citizens," *Perspectives on Politics* 12, no. 3 (2014): 564–81.

11. Erik Baekkeskov, *Encyclopædia Britannica*, s.v. "Market Failure," http://www .britannica.com/EBchecked/topic/1937869/market-failure.

12. Amitai Etzioni, *The Common Good* (Cambridge, UK: Polity, 2004); see also Dinesh Sharma, "A Vaccine Nation," review of *The Vaccine Narrative*, by Jacob Heller (2008), *Health Affairs* 28, no. 2 (2009); and Baekkeskov, "Market Failure."

13. Etzioni, *The Common Good*.

14. Ibid.; see Michael J. Sandel, *Justice: What's the Right Thing to Do?* (New York: Farrar, Straus and Giroux, 2009), 90; see also Charles Taylor, *Philosophical Arguments* (Cambridge: Harvard University Press, 1995), 190–91.

15. See Kevin P. Quinn, "Sandel's Communitarianism and Public Deliberations over Health Care Policy," *Georgetown Law Journal* 85, no. 7 (1997): 2182–83.

16. See Jack B. Sarno, "A Natural Law Defense of *Buckley v. Valeo*," *Fordham Law Review* 66, no. 6 (1998): 2693–737.

17. See *Abrams v. United States*, 250 U.S. 616, 624 (1919).

18. Ibid., 630.

19. "The FCC and Freedom of Speech," Federal Communications Commission, September 13, 2017, http://www.fcc.gov/guides/fcc-and-freedom-speech.

20. Scott L. Cummings, Robert Henigson Professor of Legal Ethics, UCLA School of Law, interview, December 9, 2014.

21. See George Anastaplo, "The Constitution at Two Hundred: Explorations," *Texas Tech Law Review* 22 (1991): 1095–96; United Nations, *The Universal Declaration of Human Rights* (Paris, 1948). The declaration does not recognize all common goods as rights.

22. United Nations, *The Universal Declaration of Human Rights*.

23. See Sarno, "A Natural Law Defense of *Buckley v. Valeo*," 2737. Sarno notes that individual rights are part of the common good.

24. See Lee J. Strang, "An Originalist Theory of Precedent: Originalism, Non-originalism Precedent, and the Common Good," *New Mexico Law Review* 36 (2006): 419–86.

25. William Tyler Page, "The American's Creed," 1917, http://www.ushistory.org/documents/creed.htm.

26. Gunnar Myrdal, *American Dilemma* (New York: Harper Brothers, 1944), xlvii.

5. Rights and Responsibilities

1. See Kostas Vlassopoulos, "Free Spaces: Identity, Experience and Democracy in Classical Athens," *Classical Quarterly* 57, no. 1 (2007): 39–47.

2. "Q&A: What Is a Loya Jirga?," BBC News, July 1, 2002, http://news.bbc.co.UK/2/hi/south_asia/1782079.stm.

3. Dylan Matthews, "It's Official: The 112th Congress Was the Most Polarized Ever," *Washington Post,* January 17, 2013, http://www.washingtonpost.com/blogs/wonkblog/wp/2013/01/17/its-official-the-112th-congress-was-the-most-polarized-ever/.

4. Amitai Etzioni, *The Common Good* (Cambridge, UK: Polity, 2004). In contrast, authoritarian and East Asian communitarians tend be concerned with the common good and pay heed to rights mainly insofar as they serve the rulers' aims; Etzioni, "Communitarianism." At the opposite end of the spectrum, contemporary liberals emphasize individual rights and autonomy over societal formulations of the common good.

5. U.S. Const. amend. IV.

6. Amitai Etzioni, "The Standing of the Public Interest," *Barry Law Review* 20, no. 2 (2015): 191–217.

7. Skinner v. Ry. Labor Execs. Ass'n, 489 U.S. 602, 634 (1989).

8. Mich. Dep't of State Police v. Sitz, 496 U.S. 444, 447 (1990).

9. Jacobson v. Massachusetts, 197 U.S. 11, 11 (1905).

10. Ibid.

11. Marshall v. Barlow's, Inc., 436 U.S. 307, 320 (1978).

12. Andy Kessler, "A Better Way to Make Facebook Pay," *Wall Street Journal,* April 8, 2018, https://www.wsj.com/articles/a-better-way-to-make-facebook-pay-1523209483.

13. Ibid.

14. European Parliament and the Council to the European Union, Regulation (EU) 2016/679 of the European Parliament and of the Council of 27 April 2016, *General Data Protection Regulation,* May 5, 2016, https://eur-lex.europa.eu/legal-content/EN/TXT/?qid=1528874672298&uri=CELEX%3A32016R0679.

15. For a critique of Europe's privacy policies, see Alison Cool, "Don't Follow Europe on Privacy," *New York Times,* May 16, 2018.

16. General Data Protection Regulation, Chapter II, Article 5 (b); General Data Protection Regulation, Chapter IX, Article 89 (1–4).

17. Ibid., Chapter III, Article 21.

18. General Data Protection Regulation (52).

19. Ibid. (159).

20. Ibid. (16).

6. Privacy vs. the Common Good

1. Andi Wilson Thompson, Danielle Kehl, and Kevin Bankston, *Doomed to Repeat History? Lessons from the Crypto Wars of the 1990s* (Washington, DC: New America, 2015), https://www.newamerica.org/cybersecurity-initiative/policy-papers/doomed-to-repeat-history-lessons-from-the-crypto-wars-of-the-1990s/.

2. Ibid., 5.

3. Ibid.

4. Ibid.

5. Ibid.

6. Stewart A. Baker, "Don't Worry Be Happy," *Wired*, June 1, 1994, http://archive.wired.com/wired/archive/2.06/nsa.clipper.html?topic=&topic_set=.

7. Ibid.

8. Thompson, Kehl, and Bankston, *Doomed to Repeat History?*, 9.

9. Ibid.

10. Ibid., 10.

11. Ibid.

12. Ibid., 8.

13. Ibid.

14. Ibid., 17.

15. Andy Greenberg, "Hacker Lexicon: What Is End-to-End Encryption?," *Wired*, November 25, 2014, https://www.wired.com/2014/11/hacker-lexicon-end-to-end-encryption/.

16. Apple, "Privacy," Apple, https://www.apple.com/privacy/approach-to-privacy/.

17. Andy Greenberg, "You Can All Finally Encrypt Facebook Messenger, So Do It," *Wired*, October 4, 2016, https://www.wired.com/2016/10/facebook-completely-encrypted-messenger-update-now/.

18. Google Allo, "Allo," Google, https://allo.google.com/.

19. Matthew Taylor, Nick Hopkins, and Jemima Kiss, "NSA Surveillance May Cause Breakup of Internet, Warn Experts," *Guardian* (UK), November 1, 2013, http://www.theguardian.com/world/2013/nov/01/nsa-surveillance-cause-internet-breakup-edward-snowden.

20. Cade Metz, "Forget Apple vs. the FBI: WhatsApp Just Switched on Encryption for a Billion People," *Wired*, April 5, 2016, https://www.wired.com/2016/04/forget-apple-vs-fbi-whatsapp-just-switched-encryption-billion-people/.

21. Andy Greenberg, "After 3 Years, Why Gmail's End-to-End Encryption Is Still Vapor," *Wired*, February 28, 2017, https://www.wired.com/2017/02/3-years-gmails-end-end-encryption-still-vapor/.

22. James Comey, "Going Dark: Are Technology, Privacy, and Public Safety on a Collision Course?" (speech, Brookings Institution, Washington, DC, October 16, 2014), http://www.fbi.gov/news/speeches/going-dark-are-technology-privacy-and-public-safety-on-a-collision-course.

23. Christopher Hope, "Spies Should Be Able to Monitor All Online Messaging, Says David Cameron," *Telegraph* (UK), January 12, 2015, http://www.telegraph.co

.uk/technology/internet-security/11340621/Spies-should-be-able-to-monitor-all
-online-messaging-says-David-Cameron.html.

24. Eric Lichtblau and Katie Benner, "Apple Fights Order to Unlock San Bernardino Gunman's iPhone," *New York Times*, February 17, 2016, http://www.nytimes
.com/2016/02/18/technology/apple-timothy-cook-fbi-san-bernardino.html?_r=0.

25. Laura Sydell, "In Apple Security Case, Obama Calls to Strike a Balance,"
National Public Radio, March 12, 2016, http://www.npr.org/2016/03/12/470194268
/in-apple-security-case-obama-calls-to-strike-a-balance.

26. Andrew Sparrow, "WhatsApp must be accessible to authorities, says Amber
Rudd," *Guardian* (UK), March 26, 2017, https://www.theguardian.com/technology
/2017/mar/26/intelligence-services-access-whatsapp-amber-rudd-westminster
-attack-encrypted-messaging.

27. Jamie Grierson, "Met Chief: Tech Industry Must Put House in Order after Westminster Attack," *Guardian* (UK), March 29, 2017, https://www.theguardian
.com/uk-news/2017/mar/29/acting-met-chief-craig-mackey-tech-industry-house
-in-order-westminster-attack.

28. David Welna, "The Next Encryption Battleground: Congress," National Public Radio, April 14, 2016, http://www.npr.org/sections/alltechconsidered/2016/04
/14/474113249/the-next-encryption-battleground-congress.

29. Tony Romm, "Apple Hires NFL, Biden Veteran for Key Policy Role," *Politico*,
April 14, 2016, http://www.politico.com/story/2016/04/apple-hires-cynthia-hogan
-221937.

30. Cecilia Kang, "Police and Tech Giants Wrangle over Encryption on Capitol
Hill," *New York Times*, May 8, 2016, http://www.nytimes.com/2016/05/09/technology
/police-and-tech-giants-wrangle-over-encryption-on-capitol-hill.html?_r=0.

31. Joe Uchill, "Apple: Security Vulnerabilities Revealed by WikiLeaks No Longer Work," *The Hill*, March 23, 2017, https://thehill.com/business-a-lobbying/325579
-apple-new-wikileaked-vulnerabilities-no-longer-work.

32. Matt Burgess, "WikiLeaks Drops 'Grasshopper' Documents, Part Four of
Its CIA Vault 7 Files," *Wired*, May 7, 2017, http://www.wired.co.uk/article/cia-files
-wikileaks-vault-7.

33. Ibid.

34. Scott Shane, David E. Sanger, and Vindu Goel, "WikiLeaks Will Help Tech
Companies Fix Security Flaws, Assange Says," *New York Times*, March 9, 2017,
https://www.nytimes.com/2017/03/09/us/wikileaks-julian-assange-cia-hacking
.html.

35. Kif Leswing, "Apple Totally Dissed WikiLeaks This Week—Here's Why," *Business Insider*, March 26, 2017, http://www.businessinsider.com/apple-vs-wikileaks
-why-tech-isnt-happy-with-julian-assange-2017-3.

36. Ibid.

37. Dustin Volz and Joseph Menn, "WikiLeaks Offers CIA Hacking Tools to
Tech Companies: Assange," Reuters, March 9, 2017, http://www.reuters.com/article
/us-cia-wikileaks-assange-idUSKBN16G27Y.

38. Thomas Brewster, "Fresh WikiLeaks Dump Shows CIA Was Hacking

iPhones a Year after Launch," *Forbes,* March 23, 2017, https://www.forbes.com
/sites/thomasbrewster/2017/03/23/wikileaks-cia-apple-mac-iphone-hacking/
#bf402381e3b4.

39. Anick Jesdanun and Michael Liedtke, "WikiLeaks' Offer to Help Tech
Companies with CIA Software Holes Could Be Mixed," *Chicago Tribune,* March 9,
2017, http://www.chicagotribune.com/news/nationworld/ct-wikileaks-cia-hacking
-20170309-story.html.

40. Ibid.

41. Ibid.

42. Rhiannon Williams, "Tim Cook Urges FBI Reform to Respect Privacy in
Letter to Staff," *Telegraph* (UK), February 22, 2016, http://www.telegraph.co.uk
/technology/2016/02/22/tim-cook-urges-fbi-reform-to-respect-privacy/.

43. Nancy Gibbs and Lev Grossman, "Here's the Full Transcript of *Time's* Interview with Tim Cook," *Time,* March 17, 2016, http://time.com/4261796/tim-cook
-transcript/.

44. Craig Federighi, "Apple VP: The FBI Wants to Roll Back Safeguards That
Keep Us a Step Ahead of Criminals," *Washington Post,* March 6, 2016, https://www
.washingtonpost.com/opinions/apple-vp-the-fbi-wants-to-roll-back-safeguards
-that-keep-us-a-step-ahead-of-criminals/2016/03/06/cceb0622-e3d1-11e5-a6f3
-21ccdbc5f74e_story.html.

45. Tim Cook, "A Message to Our Customers," Apple, February 16, 2016, http://
www.apple.com/customer-letter/.

46. Steve Bellovin, "Hi Techies!," Institute for Communitarian Policy Studies,
2016, https://icps.gwu.edu/hi-techies-0.

47. Philip A. Schrodt, "Hi Techies!," Institute for Communitarian Policy Studies,
2016, https://icps.gwu.edu/hi-techies-0.

48. David Bantz, "Hi Techies!," Institute for Communitarian Policy Studies,
2016, https://icps.gwu.edu/hi-techies-0.

49. Cyrus R. Vance Jr., "Privacy and Security in a Digital Age" (panel speaker,
Council on Foreign Relations, Washington, DC, May 11, 2016), http://www.cfr.org
/privacy/privacy-security-digital-age/p37845.

50. Ibid.

51. Ibid.

52. Amitai Etzioni, *The New Golden Rule: Community and Morality in a Democratic Society* (New York: Basic, 1996).

53. Beth Stephens, "Are Corporations People? Corporate Personhood under the
Constitution and International Law," *Rutgers Law Journal* 44, no. 1 (2013): 1.

7. Diversity within Unity

1. United Kingdom, Office for National Statistics, *International Migrants in England and Wales: 2011,* December, 11, 2012, https://www.ons.gov.uk
/peoplepopulationandcommunity/populationandmigration/internationalmigration
/articles/internationalmigrantsinenglandandwales/2012-12-11.

2. Thomas Hylland-Eriksen, *Immigration and National Identity in Norway*
(Washington, DC: Migration Policy Institute, March 2013).

3. Joaquín Arango, *Exceptional in Europe? Spain's Experience with Immigration and Integration* (Washington, DC: Migration Policy Institute, March 2013).

4. European Commission, *Standard Eurobarometer 88: Europeans' Opinion of the European Union's Priorities* (2017), https://ec.europa.eu/commfrontoffice/publicopinion/index.cfm/ResultDoc/download/DocumentKy/82875.

5. Rogers Brubaker distinguishes between two different meanings of assimilation: one is general and abstract and refers to increasing similarity. The other is specific and organic and refers to absorption into a system and conversion. In the first sense, the focus of assimilation is a process, not a final state. In the second sense, assimilation is focused on an end state, and thus assimilation is either achieved or it is not; there are no degrees (see Rogers Brubaker, "The Return of Assimilation? Changing Perspectives on Immigration and Its Sequels in France, Germany, and the United States," *Ethnic and Racial Studies* 24, no. 4 [2001]: 531–48).

6. Michèle Tribalat, *De l'immigration à l'assimilation: Enquête sur les populations d'origine étrangère en France* (Paris: La Découverte/INED, 1996); Gérard Noiriel, "Difficulties in French Historical Research on Immigration," *Bulletin of the American Academy of Arts and Sciences* 46, no. 1 (1992): 21–35.

7. Frédéric Mayet, "Laïcité à Montpellier: Des jupes longues font débat au collège des Garrigues," *Midi Libre*, March 31, 2015, https://www.midilibre.fr/2015/03/31/le-college-des-garrigues-est-soucieux-de-sa-laicite,1144142.php; Stephen Snyder, "Sorry, Your Skirt Is Too Long for France," Public Radio International, May 1, 2015, http://www.pri.org/stories/2015-05-01/sorry-your-skirt-too-long-france.

8. Angelique Chrisafis, "Pork or Nothing: How School Dinners Are Dividing France," *Guardian* (UK), October 13, 2015, http://www.theguardian.com/world/2015/oct/13/pork-school-dinners-france-secularism-children-religious-intolerance; see also Shadi Hamid, *Islamic Exceptionalism: How the Struggle over Islam Is Reshaping the World* (New York: St. Martin's, 2016).

9. Bhikhu Parekh, *The Future of Multi-Ethnic Britain: Report of the Commission on the Future of Multi-Ethnic Britain* (London: Profile, 2000).

10. Jamie Mayerfeld, "The Myth of Benign Group Identity: A Critique of Liberal Nationalism," *Polity* 30, no. 4 (1998): 555–78.

11. David Goodhart, "A Postliberal Future?," *Demos Quarterly* 1 (2014), http://quarterly.demos.co.uk/article/issue-1/a-postliberal-future/.

12. Tim King, "Belgium Is a Failed State," *Politico,* December 2, 2015, http://www.politico.eu/article/belgium-failed-state-security-services-molenbeek-terrorism/.

13. Ellie Vasta, "From Ethnic Minorities to Ethnic Majority Policy: Multiculturalism and the Shift to Assimilationism in the Netherlands," *Ethnic and Racial Studies* 30, no. 5 (2007): 713–40.

14. Monique Kremer, *The Netherlands: From National Identity to Plural Identifications* (Washington, DC: Migration Policy Institute, 2013).

15. Melissa Eddy, "Reports of Attacks on Women in Germany Heighten Tension over Migrants," *New York Times,* January 5, 2016, http://www.nytimes.com/2016/01/06/world/europe/coordinated-attacks-on-women-in-cologne-were-unprecedented-germany-says.html.

16. Andrea Nahles, "Ohne Integration werden die Leistungen gekürzt," *Frank-*

furter Allgemeine, January 31, 2016, http://www.faz.net/aktuell/politik/inland/andrea-nahles-fordert-fluechtlinge-auf-sich-zu-integrieren-14044777.html.

17. Germany, Federal Office for Migration and Refugees, *Content and Scheduling,* December 17, 2015, http://www.bamf.de/EN/Willkommen/DeutschLernen/Integrationskurse/InhaltAblauf/inhaltablauf-node.html.

18. The Diversity within Unity platform, which was originally drafted in 2001 with the help of thirty-three scholars and public intellectuals and has since been endorsed by many others, including government ministers (see "The Diversity within Unity Platform," https://communitariannetwork.org/diversity-within-unity).

19. Andreas Tzortzis, "In Europe, Quizzes Probe Values of Potential Citizen," *Christian Science Monitor,* April 10, 2006, https://www.csmonitor.com/2006/0410/p01s04-woeu.html.

20. Hamida Ghafour, "For Dutch Muslims, There's a Chill in the Air," *Globe and Mail* (Canada), March 15, 2005, F3.

21. "Can You Pass a Citizenship Test?," BBC News, June 16, 2005, http://news.bbc.co.uk/2/hi/uk_news/magazine/4099770.stm.

22. I use the term "national ethos" throughout this chapter. The concept is perhaps similar to the "national identity" discussed by Smith or Huntington, but "ethos" better captures the image of a central essence that remains stable even as other elements around it are transformed (see Anthony D. Smith, *National Identity* [Reno: University of Nevada Press, 1991]; and Samuel Huntington, *Who Are We? Challenges to America's National Identity* [New York: Simon and Schuster, 2004]).

23. Kjell Magne Bondevik, "Speech on the Politics of European Values" (speech, The Hague, Netherlands, September 7, 2004), https://www.regjeringen.no/en/aktuelt/the_politics_of_european_values,/id268847/.

24. Cordelia Bonal and Laure Équy, "L'identité nationale selon Sarkozy," *Liberation,* November 2, 2009, http://www.liberation.fr/france/2009/11/02/l-identite-nationale-selon-sarkozy_591481.

25. Jon Stone, "Britain Must Defend Its Christian Values against Terrorism, David Cameron Says," *Independent* (UK), March 27, 2016, http://www.independent.co.uk/news/uk/politics/david-cameron-easter-message-2016-christian-values-christian-country-a6954996.html.

26. Agence France-Presse, "Norway Goes Secular, Removes Lutheran Church as State Religion," *National Post* (Canada), May 24, 2012, http://news.nationalpost.com/holy-post/norway-goes-secular-removes-lutheran-church-as-state-religion.

27. T. R. Reid, "Church of Sweden Is Thriving on Its Own," *Washington Post,* December 29, 2000, https://www.washingtonpost.com/archive/politics/2000/12/29/church-of-sweden-is-thriving-on-its-own/2a52605f-40c4-43f6-b1cd-9c16f7b27a4e/.

28. Anthony Faiola and Stephanie Kirchner, "Germany Is Trying to Teach Asylum Seekers about Its Liberal Attitudes toward Sex," *Washington Post,* May 13, 2016, https://www.washingtonpost.com/news/worldviews/wp/2016/05/13/germany-is-trying-to-teach-refugees-the-right-way-to-have-sex/?utm_term=.1aae49524602.

29. Robert Long and Paul Bolton, "Faith Schools: FAQ," *House of Commons Library, Briefing Paper Number 0697214,* October 14, 2015, http://dera.ioe.ac.uk/24532/2/SN06972_Redacted.pdf.

30. Rabbi Jonathan Romain is a frequent critic of such schools, arguing that having children of different religions learning in separate schools leads to "very poor social cement" (see "Face to Faith," *Guardian* [UK], April 25, 2008, http://www.theguardian.com/commentisfree/2008/apr/26/religion.faithschools).

31. Micahel Wilshaw, "Her Majesty's Chief Inspector, on the Inspection of Schools Previously Inspected by the Bridge Schools Inspectorate" (letter, Office for Standards in Education, Children's Services and Skills, United Kingdom, November 24, 2015), https://www.gov.uk/government/uploads/system/uploads/attachment_data/file/479122/HMCI__advice_note_BSI.pdf.

32. Finnish National Board of Education, "National Curriculum for Upper Secondary Schools 2003," Reg. No. 33/011/2003, August 27, 2003, http://www.oph.fi/download/47678_core_curricula_upper_secondary_education.pdf.

33. Stefan Dege, "German Muslim Groups React to Burkini Ruling," *Deutsche Welle* (Germany), September 12, 2013, http://www.dw.com/en/german-muslim-groups-react-to-burkini-ruling/a-17085656.

34. Adam Taylor, "In Switzerland, Muslim Schoolchildren Who Refuse to Shake Their Teacher's Hand May Be Fined $5,000," *Washington Post*, May 25, 2016, https://www.washingtonpost.com/news/worldviews/wp/2016/05/25/in-switzerland-muslim-schoolchildren-who-refuse-to-shake-their-teachers-hand-may-be-fined-5000/.

35. The Netherlands, Government of the Netherlands, *Dual Nationality*, https://www.government.nl/topics/dutch-nationality/contents/dual-nationality.

36. The Netherlands, Government of the Netherlands, "Language Learning on Social Assistance Benefit," news release, June 27, 2014, https://www.government.nl/latest/news/2014/07/01/language-learning-on-social-assistance-benefit.

37. Soeren Kern, "Austria's Islamic Reforms," *International New York Times*, April 7, 2015, 7.

38. King, "Belgium Is a Failed State."

8. The Need for Self-Restraint

1. See Jeremy Waldron, *Law and Disagreement* (Oxford: Oxford University Press, 2004).

2. *Oxford English Dictionary Online*, s.v. "Pound of flesh," http://www.oed.com/view/Entry/149023?redirectedFrom=%22pound+of+flesh%22#eid29089420.

3. Emma Orczy, *The Scarlet Pimpernel* (Oxford: Oxford University Press, 2018), 50.

4. *Williams v. Walker-Thomas Furniture Company,* 350 F.2d 445 (D.C. Cir. 1965).

5. Christine Hauser, "A Yale Dean Lost Her Job after Calling People 'White Trash' in Yelp Reviews," *New York Times,* June 21, 2017, https://www.nytimes.com/2017/06/21/us/yale-dean-yelp-white-trash.html.

6. Ibid.

7. Ibid.

8. Jeff Weiner, "Winter Park–Based Tampa Professor Fired after Harvey 'Karma' Tweet," *Orlando Sentinel,* August 29, 2017, http://www.orlandosentinel.com/news/politics/political-pulse/os-tweet-harvey-storey-20170829-story.html.

9. Jose A. DelReal and Ed O'Keefe, "Hill Staffer Elizabeth Lauten Resigns after Remarks about Obama Daughters," *Washington Post,* December 1, 2014, https://www.washingtonpost.com/news/post-politics/wp/2014/12/01/embattled-hill-staffer-elizabeth-lauten-reportedly-resigns-after-controversial-remarks/?utm_term=.acoeod1d2f5d.

10. Ibid.

11. Alex Hern, "Twitter Announces Crackdown on Abuse with New Filter and Tighter Rules," *Guardian* (UK), April 21, 2015, https://www.theguardian.com/technology/2015/apr/21/twitter-filter-notifications-for-all-accounts-abuse.

12. Alison Flood, "Are Americans Falling in Love with Censorship?," *Guardian* (UK), August 7, 2015, https://www.theguardian.com/books/2015/aug/07/are-americans-falling-in-love-with-censorship.

13. Snyder v. Phelps, 562 U.S. 443 (2011).

14. McCullen v. Coakley, 134 S. Ct. 2518 (2014).

15. Molly Redden, "12 Horror Stories Show Why Wednesday's Big Supreme Court Abortion Case Matters," *Mother Jones,* January 14, 2014, http://www.motherjones.com/politics/2014/01/abortion-horror-stories-supreme-court-massachusetts-mccullen-coakley/.

16. Adam Liptak, "Cake Is His 'Art': So Can He Deny One to a Gay Couple?," *New York Times,* September 16, 2017, https://www.nytimes.com/2017/09/16/us/supreme-court-baker-same-sex-marriage.html?mcubz=1.

17. Adam Liptak, "In Narrow Decision, Supreme Court Sides with Baker Who Turned Away Gay Couple," *New York Times,* June 4, 2018, https://www.nytimes.com/2018/06/04/us/politics/supreme-court-sides-with-baker-who-turned-away-gay-couple.html.

18. "Bakery Will Stop Making Wedding Cakes after Losing Discrimination Case," CBS Denver, May 30, 2014, http://denver.cbslocal.com/2014/05/30/bakery-will-stop-making-wedding-cakes-after-losing-discrimination-case/.

19. Shelby Sebens, "Oregon Bakery Pays Damages in Lesbian Wedding Cake Case," Reuters, December 29, 2015, http://www.reuters.com/article/us-oregon-gaymarriage-idUSKBN0UC1JV20151229.

20. State of Washington v. Arlene's Flowers, Inc., 389 P.3d 543, 550 (2017).

21. Steven Nelson, "Gay Wedding Flowers Case Heard by State Supreme Court," *U.S. News and World Report,* November 15, 2016, http://www.usnews.com/news/articles/2016-11-15/gay-wedding-flowers-case-heard-by-state-supreme-court.

22. Ibid.

23. Craig v. Masterpiece Cakeshop, Inc., 370 P.3d 272, 89 (Colo. App. 2015).

24. *Id.* at 90 (quoting *Newman v. Piggie Park Enters, Inc.,* 256 F. Supp. 941, 945 (D.S.C. 1966)).

25. *Id.* at 90.

26. *Id.* at 72.

27. This is what James Oleske Jr., associate professor of law, means when he writes, "Even if one were to carve out exemptions that would allow the refusal of service on religious grounds, it would not hold up because people have a constitutional right to equal protection under the laws" (James Oleske, "The Evolution of

Accommodation: Comparing the Unequal Treatment of Religious Objections to Interracial and Same-Sex Marriages," *Harvard Civil Rights-Civil Liberties Law Review* 50 [2015]: 146). Oleske adds: "Although many Americans had religious objections to interracial marriage in the 1960s, and although some still do today, federal and state antidiscrimination laws have not included exemptions that would allow business owners to deny services based on those beliefs. Likewise, although the New Testament quotes Jesus explicitly condemning divorce . . . state laws prohibiting discrimination based on marital status do not contain exemptions allowing commercial businesses to refuse to facilitate the remarriages of divorced people" (ibid., 144).

28. Anna King, "Washington High Court Hears Case of Florist Who Refused to Serve Gay Wedding," National Public Radio, November 15, 2016, http://www.npr.org/2016/11/15/502111408/washington-state-court-case-religious-liberty-versus-anti-discrimination.

29. Nelson, "Gay Wedding Flowers Case Heard by State Supreme Court."

30. Ibid.

31. *Craig v. Masterpiece Cakeshop, Inc.*, 18 (Case No. 2013–0008) (2013). Brief In Opposition to Complainants' Motion for Summary Judgment and in Support of Jack Phillips's Cross Motion for Summary Judgment.

32. *Id.* at 16.

33. *Id.* at 27.

34. *Craig v. Masterpiece Cakeshop, Inc.* at 71 (2015).

35. *Id.*

36. Masterpiece Cakeshop, Ltd. v. Colorado Civil Rights Commission, No. 14CA1351, 8 (Colo. App. 2015), 137 S. Ct. 2290 (No. 16–111). Brief for the United States as Amicus Curiae Supporting Petitioners.

37. *Id.*

38. *Id.*

39. *Id.*

40. *Id.* at 29.

41. Andrew Koppelman, "A Free Speech Response to the Gay Rights/ Religious Liberty Conflict," *Northwestern University Law Review* 110 (2016): 1128.

42. Ibid., 1129.

43. Ibid., 1148.

44. Nelson, "Gay Wedding Flowers Case Heard by State Supreme Court."

45. Oleske, "The Evolution of Accommodation," 102.

46. Nelson, "Gay Wedding Flowers Case Heard by State Supreme Court."

47. Greg Stohr, "U.S. Supreme Court Leaves Intact Mississippi Law Curbing Gay Rights," *Bloomberg,* January 8, 2018, https://www.bloomberg.com/news/articles/2018-01-08/u-s-high-court-leaves-intact-mississippi-law-curbing-gay-rights.

48. Sarah Pulliam Bailey, "Can LGBT Rights and Religious Rights Coexist? Kim Davis-Like Case Tests the Waters," *Washington Post,* February 7, 2018, https://www.washingtonpost.com/news/acts-of-faith/wp/2018/02/07/can-lgbt-rights-and-religious-rights-coexist-kim-davis-like-case-tests-the-waters/?utm_term=.3ad7e74d08e7.

49. Ibid.

50. Ibid.

51. David Brooks, "How Not to Advance Gay Marriage," *New York Times,* December 4, 2007, https://www.nytimes.com/2017/12/04/opinion/gay-marriage-cake -case.html.

9. Curbing Special Interest Groups

1. *Encyclopædia Britannica,* s.v. "General will," https://www.britannica.com /topic/general-will; Christopher Bertram, *The Stanford Encyclopedia of Philosophy,* ed. Edward N. Zalta (2018), s.v. "Jean Jacques Rousseau," https://plato.stanford.edu /archives/fall2018/entries/rousseau/.

2. This concept is derived from the Supreme Court's ruling in *Buckley v. Valeo,* which struck down independent expenditure limits as a violation of the First Amendment, although it was never stated quite that explicitly. The Court reasoned, "The expenditure limitations . . . represent substantial, rather than merely theoretical, restraints on the quantity and diversity of political speech" (424 US 1, 19 [1976]).

3. Bribery of Public Officials and Witnesses, 18 U.S.C. § 201, https://www.gpo .gov/fdsys/pkg/USCODE-2012-title18/html/USCODE-2012-title18-partI-chap11 -sec201.htm.

4. United States v. Sun-Diamond Growers of California, 526 U.S 398, 406–407. This example deals with neither Congress members nor campaign contributions, yet nonetheless gives one an idea of something insubstantial, as well as illustrates the Court's concern about laws that could be construed to criminalize something trivial.

5. Jill Ornitz and Ryan Struyk, "Donald Trump's Surprisingly Honest Lessons about Big Money in Politics," ABC News, August 11, 2015, http://abcnews.go.com /Politics/donald-trumps-surprisingly-honest-lessons-big-money-politics/story?id =32993736.

6. Anahad O'Connor, "Herbal Supplements Are Often Not What They Seem," *New York Times,* November 3, 2013, https://www.nytimes.com/2013/11/05/science /herbal-supplements-are-often-not-what-they-seem.html.

7. Evan Osnos, "Embrace the Irony," *New Yorker,* October 13, 2014.

8. Unlawful Employment Practices, 42 U.S. Code § 2000e–2.

9. Dothard v. Rawlinson, 433 U.S. 321 (1977).

10. Age Discrimination in Employment Act of 1967, Pub. L. 90–202, 29 U.S.C. § 621 (1967).

11. Western Air Lines v. Criswell, 472 U.S. 400 (1985)

12. Griggs v. Duke Power Co., 401 US 424 (1971).

13. *West's Encyclopedia of American Law,* 2nd. ed. (2008), s.v. "Reasonable person," http://legal-dictionary.thefreedictionary.com/Reasonable+Person.

14. Citizens United v. Federal Election Comm'n, 558 U. S. 310, 360 (2010).

15. Cyra Master, "'60 Minutes': Fundraising Demands Turning Lawmakers into Telemarketers," *The Hill,* April 24, 2016, http://thehill.com/blogs/blog-briefing -room/news/277462-60-minutes-fundraising-demands-turning-lawmakers-into.

16. Tracy Jan, "For Freshman in Congress, Focus Is on Raising Money," *Boston Globe,* May 12, 2013, https://www.bostonglobe.com/news/politics/2013/05/11

/freshman-lawmakers-are-introduced-permanent-hunt-for-campaign-money
/YQMMMoqCNxGKh2hotOIF9H/story.html.

17. For example, there were 705 roll call votes in the House and 339 in the Senate during the first session of the 114th Congress.

18. Paul Blumenthal, "Fossil Fuel Company Super PAC Gifts Came before Congress Ended the Oil Export Ban," *Huffington Post,* February 3, 2016, http://www.huffingtonpost.com/entry/fossil-fuel-super-pac-donors_us _56b25c5ae4b04f9b57d82d06.

19. Billy House and Erik Wasson, "Congress Passes U.S. Spending Bill to End Oil Export Ban," *Bloomberg,* December 18, 2015, http://www.bloomberg.com /politics/articles/2015-12-18/house-passes-u-s-spending-bill-that-ends-crude-oil -export-ban.

20. Clifford Krauss and Diane Cardwell, "Expected Repeal of Oil Export Ban Unlikely to Have Immediate Impact," *New York Times,* December 16, 2015, http:// www.nytimes.com/2015/12/17/business/energy-environment/expected-repeal-of -oil-export-ban-unlikely-to-have-immediate-impact.html.

21. Emily Atkin, "Senate Passes Bill to Approve Construction of Keystone XL Pipeline," Think Progress, January 29, 2015, https://thinkprogress.org/senate-passes -bill-to-approve-construction-of-keystone-xl-pipeline-13451fc504a0#.k8ctzrh3h.

22. Anne Baker, "The More Outside Money Politicians Take, the Less Well They Represent Their Constituents," *Washington Post,* August 17, 2016, https://www .washingtonpost.com/news/monkey-cage/wp/2016/08/17/members-of-congress -follow-the-money-not-the-voters-heres-the-evidence/#comments.

23. McCutcheon v. Fed. Elections Comm'n, 893 F. Supp. 2d 133 (D.D.C. 2012), Complaint at 10–11 (No. l:12-cv-01034-JEB).

24. *Id.* at 11–12.

25. Richard Briffault, "Of Constituents and Contributors," *University of Chicago Legal Forum* 3 (2015): 31.

26. Ibid., 34.

27. Joseph Weeks, "Bribes, Gratuities and the Congress: The Institutionalized Corruption of the Political Process, the Impotence of Criminal Law to Reach It, and a Proposal for Change," *Journal of Legislation* 13 (1986): 138.

28. United States v. Helstoski, 442 U.S. 477, 488–489 (1979). The Court later states that "[t]he Speech or Debate Clause was designed neither to assure fair trials nor to avoid coercion. Rather, its purpose was to preserve the constitutional structure of separate, coequal, and independent branches of government" (*Helstoski* at 491).

29. Weeks, "Bribes, Gratuities and the Congress," 141.

30. United States v. Apfelbaum, 445 U.S. 115 (1980).

31. Nevada Commission on Ethics v. Carrigan, 564 U.S. 117, 126–127 (2011).

32. "The term *independent expenditure* means an expenditure by a person for a communication expressly advocating the election or defeat of a clearly identified candidate that is not made in cooperation, consultation, or concert with, or at the request or suggestion of, a candidate, a candidate's authorized committee, or their agents, or a political party committee or its agents" (11 CFR §100.16[a]).

33. *Citizens United v. Federal Election Comm'n*, quoting *Buckley v. Valeo*, 47.

34. Andrew Mayersohn, "Four Years after *Citizens United:* The Fallout," Open Secrets, January 21, 2014, http://www.opensecrets.org/news/2014/01/four-years -after-citizens-united-the-fallout/.

35. Matea Gold, "It's Bold, but Legal: How Campaigns and Their Super PAC Backers Work Together," *Washington Post,* July 6, 2015, https://www.washingtonpost .com/politics/here-are-the-secret-ways-super-pacs-and-campaigns-can-work -together/2015/07/06/bda78210-1539-11e5-89f3-61410da94eb1_story.html.

36. Matea Gold, "Election 2014: A New Level of Collaboration between Candidates and Big-Money Allies," *Washington Post,* November 3, 2014, https:// www.washingtonpost.com/politics/election-2014-a-new-level-of-collaboration -between-candidates-and-big-money-allies/2014/11/03/ec2bda9a-636f-11e4-836c -83bc4f26eb67_story.html.

37. Matea Gold, "Now It's Even Easier for Candidates and Their Aides to Help Super PACs," *Washington Post,* December 24, 2015, https://www.washingtonpost .com/politics/now-its-even-easier-for-candidates-and-their-aides-to-help-super -pacs/2015/12/24/d8d1ff4a-a989-11e5-9b92-dea7cd4b1a4d_story.html.

38. "Strengthen Rules Preventing Candidate Coordination with Super PACs," Brennan Center, February 4, 2016, https://www.brennancenter.org/analysis /strengthen-rules-preventing-candidate-coordination-super-pacs#_ftn3.

39. Gold, "It's Bold but Legal."

40. Gold, "Election 2014."

41. Bradley A. Smith, *Campaign Finance Regulation: Faulty Assumptions and Undemocratic Consequences* (Washington, DC: Cato Institute Policy Analysis 238, 1995), http://www.cato.org/pubs/pas/pa238.html#30.

42. Russ Choma, "Money Won on Tuesday, But Rules of the Game Changed," Open Secrets, November 5, 2014, https://www.opensecrets.org/news/2014/11/ money-won-on-tuesday-but-rules-of-the-game-changed/.

43. Ibid.

44. U.S. Constitution, First Amendment. Zephyr Teachout points out that lobbying was not always viewed as a constitutionally protected right in "The Forgotten Law of Lobbying," *Election Law Journal* 13 (2014): 4. Similarly, Maggie McKinley asserts that people are mistaken when they assume that lobbying is protected by the First Amendment and that the issue has never been decided by the Supreme Court (Maggie McKinley, "Lobbying and the Petition Clause," *Stanford Law Review* 68 [2016]).

45. *Buckley v. Valeo*, at 56.

46. "Campaign Finance: United Kingdom," Library of Congress, https://www .loc.gov/law/help/campaign-finance/uk.php.

47. "2015 Election Campaign Officially Begins on Friday," BBC News, December 18, 2014, http://www.bbc.com/news/uk-politics-30477250.

48. Ibid.

49. "Campaign Finance," Library of Congress.

50. Ian Jones, "Get Ready for the Longest Official Campaign in Modern History,"

Reuters, July 3, 2014, https://ukgeneralelection.com/2014/07/03/get-ready-for-the
-longest-official-campaign-in-modern-history/.

51. Andy Williams, *UK Government & Politics* (Portsmouth, NH: Heinemann, 1998).

52. Richard L. Hasen, "New York City as a Model for Campaign Finance Laws?," *New York Times*, June 27, 2011, https://www.nytimes.com/roomfordebate/2011/06/27/the-court-and-the-future-of-public-financing/new-york-city-as-a-model-for-campaign-finance-laws.

53. Committee on Ethics, "'Widely Attended' Events," U.S. House of Representatives, http://ethics.house.gov/gifts/gift-exceptions-0/widely-attended-events.

54. Weeks, "Bribes, Gratuities and the Congress," 125.

55. *Buckley v. Valeo*, 22.

56. *Id.* at 52.

57. *Id.* at 52–53.

58. *Id.* at 45.

59. *Citizens United v. Federal Election Comm'n*.

60. *McCutcheon v. Fed. Election Comm'n*, 134 S. Ct. 1434 (2014).

61. Eric Schmitt, "Senate Rejects Campaign Finance Amendment," *New York Times*, March 19, 1997, https://www.nytimes.com/1997/03/19/us/senate-rejects-campaign-finance-amendment.html; Associated Press, "Campaign Spending Curb Defeated," *New York Times*, September 11, 2014, http://www.nytimes.com/2014/09/12/us/campaign-spending-curb-defeated.html?_r=0.

62. Derek Willis, "Every Election Is the Most Expensive Election. Or Not," *New York Times*, December 16, 2014, http://www.nytimes.com/2014/12/17/upshot/every-election-is-the-most-expensive-election-or-not.html.

63. "Cost of Election," OpenSecrets, n.d., https://www.opensecrets.org/overview/cost.php?display=T&infl=N.

64. Niv M. Sultan, "Election 2016: Trump's Free Media Helped Keep Cost Down, but Fewer Donors Provided More of the Cash," OpenSecrets, April 13, 2017, https://www.opensecrets.org/news/2017/04/election-2016-trump-fewer-donors-provided-more-of-the-cash/.

65. *McCutcheon v. Fed. Election Comm'n*, 35 (2014).

66. Ann Florini, "Introduction: The Battle of Transparency," in *The Right to Know: Transparency for an Open World*, ed. Ann Florini (New York: Columbia University Press, 2007), 4.

67. Daniel Kahneman, Jack Knetsch, and Richard Thaler, "Anomalies: The Endowment Effect, Loss Aversion, and Status Quo Bias," *Journal of Economic Perspectives* 5 (1991): 193–206; J. Edward Russo and Paul J. H. Shoemaker, *Decision Traps: Ten Barriers to Brilliant Decision-Making and How to Overcome Them* (New York: Simon and Schuster, 1989); Arthur Lefford, "The Influence of Emotional Subject Matter on Logical Reasoning," *Journal of General Psychology* 34 (1946): 127–51; Amos Tversky and Daniel Kahneman, "Judgment under Uncertainty: Heuristics and Biases," *Science* 185 (1974): 1124–31; Marco Cipriani and Antonio Guarino, "Herd Behavior and Contagion in Financial Markets," *B.E. Journal of Theoretical*

Economics 8 (2008); Robert H. Frank, Thomas Gilovich, and Dennis T. Regan, "Does Studying Economics Inhibit Cooperation?," *Journal of Economic Perspectives* 7 (1993): 159–71.

68. Reporting Group, "Nine Things You Need to Know about Super PACs," Sunlight Foundation, January 31, 2012, https://sunlightfoundation.com/blog/2012/01/31/nine-things-you-need-know-about-super-pacs/.

69. Political Nonprofits (Dark Money), OpenSecrets, n.d., https://www.opensecrets.org/outsidespending/nonprof_summ.php.

70. Fredreka Schouten, "Super PACs Hide Their Intentions behind Fuzzy Names," *USA Today,* February 11, 2014, http://www.usatoday.com/story/news/politics/2014/02/11/super-pac-names/5375699/.

71. *Buckley v. Valeo.*

72. See Lawrence Lessig, *America, Compromised* (Chicago: University of Chicago Press, 2018).

73. *United States v. Sun-Diamond Growers of California,* 414.

74. *Id.*

10. The Rising (More) Nation-Centered World Order

1. For a discussion on how American nationalism and foreign policy have evolved in tandem, see Henry R. Nau, "America's International Nationalism," *American Scholar* 12, no. 3 (2017).

2. Robert Kagan, "The Cost of American Retreat," *Wall Street Journal,* September 8–9, 2018; Ivo H. Daadler and James M. Lindsay, *The Empty Throne: America's Abdication of Global Leadership* (New York: Public Affairs, 2018).

3. Robert Kagan, "The Twilight of the Liberal World Order," Brookings Institution, January 24, 2017, https://www.brookings.edu/research/the-twilight-of-the-liberal-world-order/.

4. For more on the concept of "lag," see William F. Ogburn, "Cultural Lag as Theory," *Sociology and Social Research* 41, no. 3 (1957): 167–74.

5. I prefer this term to "multilateral overreach," used to reference similar developments by Jeff Colgan and Robert Keohane because I do consider the setback temporary (see Jeff D. Colgan and Robert O. Keohane, "The Liberal Order Is Rigged," *Foreign Affairs* 96, no. 3 [2017], https://www.foreignaffairs.com/articles/world/2017-04-17/liberal-order-rigged).

6. Further, national governments are overloaded with domestic considerations (see Ian Bremmer, *Us vs. Them: The Failure of Globalism* (New York: Penguin Random House, 2018).

7. John B. Judis. *The Nationalist Revival: Trade, Immigration, and the Revolt against Globalization* (New York: Columbia Global Reports, 2018).

8. Paraphrasing John Mearsheimer: Once you grant individuals in all nations the same rights, you are essentially universalist (John J. Mearsheimer, "Book Launch: The Great Delusion" [speech, Center for Strategic & International Studies, Washington, DC, October 17, 2018], https://www.csis.org/events/book-launch-great-delusion). See also John J. Mearsheimer, *The Great Delusion: Liberal Dreams and International Realities* (New Haven, CT: Yale University Press, 2018).

9. Benedict Anderson, *Imagined Communities: Reflections on the Origin and Spread of Nationalism* (Brooklyn, NY: Verso, 1983).

10. See Ernst B. Haas, "International Integration: The European and the Universal Process," *International Organization* 15, no. 3 (1961): 366–92.

11. Amitai Etzioni addresses Ernst B. Haas and Karl Deutsch on their definition of integration. Haas and Deutsch, according to Etzioni, believe that a common government is a sufficient condition for a union to be deemed highly integrated. Noting the example of the Hapsburg Empire, Etzioni writes, "From our viewpoint, these countries are only partially integrated; they lack at least one central element of integration, that of being the dominant focus of political identification of their citizens" (Amitai Etzioni, *Political Unification Revisited: On Building Supranational Communities* [Lanham, MD: Lexington, 2001], 56). Refers to Karl W. Deutsch, *Political Community and the North American Area* (Princeton, NJ: Princeton University Press, 1957).

12. See James Caporaso, "The European Union and Forms of State: Westphalian, Regulatory or Post-Modern? A Logical and Empirical Assessment," *Journal of Common Market Studies* 34, no. 1 (1996): 29–52.

13. Business Green Staff, "Green Groups Take EU to Court over Biofuels—Again," *Guardian (UK),* May 26, 2011, http://www.guardian.co.uk/environment/2011/may/26/biofuels-energy.

14. For a compendium of areas in which QMV was instated from 1957 to 2004, see Vaughne Miller, *The Extension of Qualified Majority Voting from the Treaty of Rome to the European Constitution,* House of Commons Library, Research Paper No. 04/54, 2004, 10–18.

15. Vinter and Others v. The United Kingdom (European Court of Human Rights, July 9, 2013).

16. "Ministers Angry at European Whole-Life Tariffs Ruling," BBC News, July 9, 2013, http://www.bbc.com/news/uk-23245254.

17. Melissa Eddy, "Far-Right Gains Leave Germans Wondering, What Now?" *New York Times,* September 29, 2017, https://www.nytimes.com/2017/09/29/world/europe/germany-election-far-right.html.

18. John Cassidy, "Why the Center Collapsed in Italy: Recession, Austerity, and Immigration," *New Yorker,* March 5, 2018, https://www.newyorker.com/news/our-columnists/why-the-center-collapsed-in-italy-recession-austerity-and-immigration.

19. "Europe's Rising Far Right: A Guide to the Most Prominent Parties," *New York Times,* December 4, 2016, https://www.nytimes.com/interactive/2016/world/europe/europe-far-right-political-parties-listy.html.

20. For some suggestions, see Amitai Etzioni, *From Empire to Community: A New Approach to International Relations* (New York: Palgrave Macmillan, 2004); Amitai Etzioni, "Nationalism: The Communitarian Block," *Brown Journal of World Affairs* 18, no. 1 (2011): 229–47.

21. Ferdinand Tönnies, *Community and Society (Gemeinschaft und Gesellschaft),* trans. and ed. Charles P. Loomis (East Lansing: Michigan State University Press, 1957).

22. A reviewer of a previous draft noted here that the transition Tönnies points to is not from social relations to atomization but merely a change in the kind of relations people have, from communal to associational. This is indeed the case, but the point is that these are not thick enough.

23. Yuval Levin notes that both conservatives and liberals are nostalgic for a bygone era: liberals miss the 1960s and the Great Society, conservatives miss the 1980s, and both are nostalgic for the 1950s, but for different reasons (see Yuval Levin, *The Fractured Republic: Renewing America's Social Contract in the Age of Individualism* [New York: Basic, 2016]).

24. Amy Goldstein, *Janesville: An American Story* (New York: Simon and Schuster, 2017). In February 2018, the *Economist* ran a piece titled "Meritocracy and Its Discontents" that noted: "Today's meritocrats are not only smug because they think they are intellectually superior. They are smug because they also think that they are morally superior, convinced that people who don't share their cosmopolitan values are simple-minded bigots."

25. Arlie Russell Hochschild, *Strangers in Their Own Land: Anger and Mourning on the American Right* (New York: New Press, 2016).

26. Anne-Marie Slaughter, "The Real New World Order," *Foreign Affairs* 76, no. 5 (September/October 1997): 183–97. See also Anne-Marie Slaughter, *The Chess Board and the Web: Strategies of Connection in a Networked World* (New Haven, CT: Yale University Press, 2017).

27. David Singh Grewal, *Network Power: The Social Dynamics of Globalization* (New Haven, CT: Yale University Press, 2009).

28. Amartya Sen, *Identity and Violence: The Illusion of Destiny* (New York: Norton, 2006).

29. Kwame Anthony Appiah, *Cosmopolitanism: Ethics in a World of Strangers* (New York: Norton, 2006).

30. I refer to it as the Westphalian norm because while it was enshrined in the 1648 Treaty by that name, reference is not to the text of the treaty but to the very wide acceptance of the normative concept reflected in the treaty and supported since.

31. G. John Ikenberry, *Liberal Leviathan: The Origins, Crisis, and Transformation of the American World Order* (Princeton, NJ: Princeton University Press, 2012), 21.

32. Andreas Osiander writes that "Westphalia" is purportedly a narrative about 1648 but is more the product of nineteenth- and twentieth-century fixations on the concept of sovereignty (see Andreas Osiander, "Sovereignty, International Relations, and the Westphalian Myth," *International Organization* 55, no. 2 [2001]: 251–87).

33. Alex Bellamy and Tim Dunne, eds., *The Oxford Handbook of the Responsibility to Protect* (Oxford: Oxford University Press, 2016).

34. For an exchange with Ikenberry on this subject, see G. John Ikenberry and Amitai Etzioni, "Point of Order: Is China More Westphalian Than the West?," *Foreign Affairs* 90, no. 6 (November/December 2011): 172–76.

35. Ramesh Thakur, "Law, Legitimacy and United Nations," *Melbourne Journal of International Law* 11 (2010): 1.

36. Georg Sørensen, *A Liberal World Order in Crisis: Choosing between Imposition and Restraint* (Ithaca, NY: Cornell University Press, 2011).

37. Amitai Etzioni, "Defining down Sovereignty," *Ethics & International Affairs* 30, no. 1 (2016).

38. Richard Haass, "World Order 2.0," *Foreign Affairs* 96, no. 1 (January/February 2017).

39. For an alternative perspective, see the most recent book by Robert Kagan of Brookings, *The Jungle Grows Back: America and Our Imperiled World*. In Kagan's view, weakening grounds for enforcement of international norms through sanctions and intervention create a less stable world order in the long run (Robert Kagan, *The Jungle Grows Back: America and Our Imperiled World* [New York: Knopf, 2018]).

40. Francis Fukuyama, "The End of History," *National Interest* 16 (1989): 3–18.

41. See Stephen M. Walt, *The Hell of Good Intentions: America's Foreign Policy Elite and the Decline of U.S. Primacy* (New York: Farrar, Straus and Giroux, 2018).

42. See Nils Petter Gleditsch, Lene Siljeholm Christiansen, and Håvard Hegre, "Democratic Jihad? Military Intervention and Democracy," World Bank Policy Research Working Paper no. 4242 (2007), http://siteresources.worldbank.org /INTCONFLICT/Resources/DemocraticJihadFinal.pdf.

43. Amitai Etzioni, *Security First: For a Muscular, Moral Foreign Policy* (New Haven, CT: Yale University Press, 2007).

44. An empirical study by Dursun Peksen found that military intervention actually encourages repressive state behavior and that the involvement of an intergovernmental organization or a liberal democracy as an intervener is unlikely to make any major difference on the negative impact of intervention (see Dursun Peksen, "Does Foreign Military Intervention Help Human Rights?," *Political Research Quarterly* 65, no. 3 [2012]: 558–71.

45. Yoram Hazony, *The Virtue of Nationalism* (New York: Basic, 2018).

46. G. John Ikenberry, "The Liberal International Order and Its Discontents," *Millennium: Journal of International Studies* 30, no. 3 (2010).

47. G. John Ikenberry, "The Future of the Liberal World Order: Internationalism after America," *Foreign Affairs* 90, no. 3 (May/June 2011): 56, http://www.jstor.org /stable/23039408.

48. Jeff D. Colgan and Robert O. Keohane, "The Liberal Order Is Rigged," *Foreign Affairs* 96, no. 3 (May/June 2017): 37, https://www.foreignaffairs.com/articles /world/2017-04-17/liberal-order-rigged. See also Michael N. Barnett, "Bringing in the New World Order: Liberalism, Legitimacy, and the United Nations," *World Politics* 49, no. 4 (1997): 526–51, http://www.jstor.org/stable/25054018.

49. Michael J. Glennon, "The Fog of Law: Self-Defense, Inherence, and Incoherence in Article 51 of the United Nations Charter," *Harvard Journal of Law and Public Policy* 25, no. 2 (2002): 540.

50. Richard Haass, *A World in Disarray: American Foreign Policy and the Crisis of the Old Order* (New York: Penguin, 2017).

51. In 2014, Human Rights Watch noted that five of the fourteen new members elected to the council—China, Russia, Saudi Arabia, Vietnam, and Algeria—have

themselves denied access to UN human rights monitors seeking to investigate alleged abuses (see "Concerns over New UN Human Rights Council Members," BBC News, November 13, 2013, http://www.bbc.com/news/world-24922058).

52. Robin Niblett, "Liberalism in Retreat: The Demise of a Dream," *Foreign Affairs* 96, no. 1 (January/February 2017): 17, https://www.foreignaffairs.com/articles/2016-12-12/liberalism-retreat.

53. Robert E. Scott, "Manufacturing Job Loss: Trade, Not Productivity, Is the Culprit," Economic Policy Institute, August 11, 2015, http://www.epi.org/publication/manufacturing-job-loss-trade-not-productivity-is-the-culprit/.

54. David Lawder, "IMF Chief Says All Members Believe in Free, Fair Trade," Reuters, April 19, 2017, http://www.reuters.com/article/us-imf-g20-lagarde-idUSKBN17L2L6?il=0.

55. Buzan and Lawson see in the fact that all great powers have embraced capitalism a decline in their ideological differences and hence improved conditions for working out disagreements (see Barry Buzan and George Lawson, "Capitalism and the Emergent World Order," *International Affairs* 90, no. 1 [2014]).

56. For a fuller treatment of reactionary thinking, see Mark Lilla, *The Shipwrecked Mind: On Political Reaction* (New York: New York Review of Books, 2016).

57. For more on border checks within the Schengen area, see "They Shall Not Pass," *Economist,* October 27, 2018, 51.

58. James Kraska, *Maritime Power and the Law of the Sea: Expeditionary Operations in World Politics* (Oxford: Oxford University Press, 2011).

59. Peter A. Dutton, "Caelum Liberum: Air Defense Identification Zones outside Sovereign Airspace," *American Journal of International Law* 103, no. 4 (2009): 691–709.

60. On this point, see Andrew Hurrell, *On Global Order* (New York: Oxford University Press, 2007); and Amitai Etzioni, *From Empire to Community: A New Approach to International Relations* (New York: Palgrave Macmillan, 2004).

II. The New Athens, a Post-Affluence Legitimacy

1. See Sarah Churchwell, *Behold, America: The Entangled History of "America First" and "the American Dream"* (New York: Basic, 2018).

2. I have been asked why a globalist or cosmopolitan movement could not be concerned with the same issues. First of all, there are very few global movements; most movements that seem global are mainly a combination of national ones. Second, the magnitude of change involved is such that they require the support of an existing community—which has yet to be formed on a global level.

3. Frank M. Andrews and Stephen Bassett Withey, *Social Indicators of Well-Being: America's Perceptions of Life Quality* (New York: Plenum, 1976).

4. Jonathan L. Freedman, *Happy People: What Happiness Is, Who Has It, and Why* (New York: Harcourt Brace Jovanovich, 1978).

5. David G. Myers and Ed Diener, "Who Is Happy," *Psychological Science* 6, no. 1 (January 1995): 12–13.

6. Ibid.

7. Ibid.

8. Richard Easterlin, "Does Economic Growth Improve the Human Lot? Some

Empirical Evidence," in *Nations and Households in Economic Growth: Essays in Honor of Moses Abramovitz*, ed. Paul A. David and Melvin W. Reder (New York: Academic, 1974).

9. Richard Easterlin, "Diminishing Marginal Utility of Income? Caveat Emptor," *Social Indicators Research* 70, no. 3 (2005).

10. Richard Easterlin, "Does Money Buy Happiness?," *Public Interest* 30 (1973).

11. David G. Myers and Ed Diener, "The Pursuit of Happiness," *Scientific American* 274, no. 5 (1996): 70–72.

12. Ruut Veenhoven and Michael Hagerty, "Rising Happiness in Nations 1946–2004," *Social Indicators Research* 79, no. 3 (2006).

13. Ibid.

14. Ruut Veenhoven and Floris Vergunst, "The Easterlin Illusion: Economic Growth *Does* Go with Greater Happiness," EHERO working paper 2013/1, January 23, 2013, http://mpra.ub.uni-muenchen.de/43983/1/ MPRA_paper_43983.pdf.

15. Betsey Stevenson and Justin Wolfers, "Economic Growth and Subjective Well-Being: Reassessing the Easterlin Paradox," Economic Studies Program, Brookings Institution, *Brookings Papers on Economic Activity* 39, no. 1 (2008).

16. Richard Easterlin, Laura Angelescu McVey, Malgorzata Switek, Onnicha Sawangfa, and Jacqueline Smith Zweig, "The Happiness-Income Paradox Revisited," *Proceedings of the National Academy of Sciences of the United States of America* 107, no. 52 (2010): 22463–68.

17. Ibid., 22467.

18. Richard Layard, *Happiness: Lessons from a New Science* (New York: Penguin, 2005), 32–35.

19. "Economic Focus: The Joyless or the Jobless," *Economist*, November 27, 2010, 84.

20. Daniel Kahneman and Angus Deaton, "High Income Improves Evaluation of Life but Not Emotional Well-Being," *Proceedings of the National Academy of Sciences of the United States of America* 107, no. 38 (2010): 16489–93.

21. Ibid., 16489.

22. The two figures ($20,000 per year and $75,000 per year) are not directly comparable. The first measures a nation's average income; the second comments on individual income.

23. Andrew T. Jebb, Louis Tay, Ed Diener, and Shigehiro Oishi, "Happiness, Income Satiation and Turning Points around the World," *Nature Human Behavior* 2 (2018), https://www.nature.com/articles/s41562-017-0277-0.

24. Fritz Strack, Norbert Schwarz, Brigitte Chassein, Dirk Wagner, and Dieter Kern, "Salience of Comparison Standards and the Activation of Social Norms: Consequences for Judgements of Happiness and Their Communication," *British Journal of Social Psychology* 29, no. 4 (1990): 303–14. Further evidence supporting that such judgments are contextual can be found in Norbert Schwarz and Fritz Strack, "Reports of Subjective Well-Being: Judgmental Processes and Their Methodological Implications," in *Well-Being: The Foundations of Hedonic Psychology*, ed. Daniel Kahneman, Edward Diener, and Norbert Schwarz (New York: Russell Sage Foundation, 1999), 61–84.

25. Jennifer Senior, "Some Dark Thoughts on Happiness," *New York Magazine,* July 17, 2006, http://nymag.com/news/features/17573/.

26. Ibid.

27. Stevenson and Wolfers, "Economic Growth and Subjective Well-Being," 69.

28. Daniel Kahneman, "Objective Happiness," in *Well-Being: The Foundations of Hedonic Psychology,* ed. Daniel Kahneman, Edward Diener, and Norbert Schwarz (New York: Russell Sage Foundation, 1999), 3–25.

29. Philip Brickman, Dan Coates, and Ronnie Janoff-Bulman, "Lottery Winners and Accident Victims: Is Happiness Relative?," *Journal of Personality and Social Psychology* 36, no. 8 (1978): 917–27. See also Senior, "Some Dark Thoughts on Happiness."

30. Ed Diener, Jeff Horwitz, and Robert A. Emmons, "Happiness of the Very Wealthy," *Social Indicators Research* 16, no. 3 (April 1985): 263–74.

31. John Knight and Ramani Gunatilaka, "Income, Aspirations and the Hedonic Treadmill in a Poor Society," *Journal of Economic Behavior & Organization* 82, no. 1 (2012): 67–81.

32. Ibid.

33. Amartya Sen, *Development as Freedom* (New York: Knopf, 1999).

34. Jeffrey D. Sachs, "Restoring Virtue Ethics in the Quest for Happiness," in *World Happiness Report 2013,* ed. John Helliwell, Richard Layard, and Jeffrey Sachs (New York: UN Sustainable Solutions Development Network, 2013), 85.

35. Matthie Ricard, *Happiness: A Guide to Developing Life's Most Important Skill* (New York: Little, Brown, 2000), 19.

36. Reinhard Bendix, *Max Weber: An Intellectual Portrait* (Berkeley: University of California Press, 1977), 124.

37. Martha Nussbaum, "Mill between Aristotle and Bentham," in *Economics and Happiness: Framing and Analysis,* ed. Luigino Bruni and Pier Luigi Porta (New York: Oxford University Press, 2005), 173. Nussbaum notes that throughout nearly the entire canon of Western philosophy, almost all schools of thought refuse to identify "happiness" with psychological "pleasure."

38. Aristotle, *Nicomachean Ethics,* trans. W. D. Ross (Oxford: Oxford University Press, 2009), 2.

39. Sachs, "Restoring Virtue Ethics in the Quest for Happiness," 84. Sachs quotes Aristotle, *The Nichomachean Ethics* (Amherst, MA: Prometheus, 1987), 54.

40. Nussbaum, "Mill between Aristotle and Bentham," 171.

41. Luigino Bruni and Pier Luigi Porta, introduction to *Economics and Happiness: Framing the Analysis,* ed. Bruni and Porta (New York: Oxford University Press, 2005), 20.

42. Stephen Wang, "Aquinas on Human Happiness and the Natural Desire for God," *New Blackfriars* 88, no. 1015 (2007): 322.

43. Ibid., 323.

44. Ibid., 326.

45. "The Shakers," National Park Service, n.d., http://www.nps.gov/nr/travel/shaker/shakers.htm.

46. See *Summer of Love: The Utopian Beginnings of Peace and Love Prevailed,*

and Ended in Chaos, Public Broadcasting Service, June 12, 2018, https://www.pbs
.org/wgbh/americanexperience/films/summer-of-love/.

47. See http://www.guardian.co.uk/culture/2011/jan/30/underground-arts-60s
-rebel-counterculture.

48. David Riesman, "Abundance for What?," in *Abundance for What?* (New
Brunswick, NJ: Transaction, 1993).

49. Ibid., 305.

50. See Stephen P. Dunn and Steven Pressman, "The Economic Contributions of
John Kenneth Galbraith," *Review of Political Economy* 17, no. 2 (2005).

51. Vance Packard, *The Status Seekers: An Exploration of Class Behavior in America and the Hidden Barriers That Affect You, Your Community, Your Future* (New
York: David McKay, 1959).

52. Adrianne Aron, "Maslow's Other Child," *Journal of Humanistic Psychology*
17, no. 2 (1977): 13, emphasis added.

53. Michael R. Hagerty, "Testing Maslow's Hierarchy of Needs: National
Quality-of-Life across Time," *Social Indicators Research* 46, no. 3 (1999): 250.

54. Mark E. Koltko-Rivera, "Recovering the Later Version of Maslow's Hierarchy of Needs: Self-Transcendence and Opportunities for Theory, Research, and
Unification," *Review of General Psychology* 10, no. 4 (2006): 303.

55. Thierry Pauchant and Collette A. Dumas, "Abraham Maslow and Heinz
Kohut: A Comparison," *Journal of Humanistic Psychology* 31, no. 2 (1991): 58.

56. Robert Sugden, "Correspondence of Sentiments: An Explanation of the
Pleasure of Social Interaction," in *Economics and Happiness: Framing the Analysis,*
ed. Luigino Bruni and Pier Luigi Porta (New York: Oxford University Press, 2005),
97–98. See also Robert E. Lane, "Does Money Buy Happiness?," *Public Interest* 37
(1993): 58; and Robert D. Putnam, "Bowling Alone: America's Declining Social Capital," *Journal of Democracy* 6, no. 1 (1995): 65–78.

57. See Gary S. Becker, "Altruism, Egoism, and Genetic Fitness: Economics and
Sociobiology," *Journal of Economic Literature* 14, no. 3 (1976): 817–26; Jeffrey Harrison, "Egoism, Altruism, and Market Illusions: The Limits of Law and Economics,"
UCLA Law Review 33 (1986); Daniel C. Batson and Adam A. Powell, "Altruism and
Prosocial Behavior," in *Handbook of Psychology,* ed. Irving B. Weiner (Hoboken, NJ:
John Wiley and Sons, 2003); and Amitai Etzioni, *The Moral Dimension: Toward a
New Economics* (New York: Free Press, 1988).

58. Derek Bok, *The Politics of Happiness: What Government Can Learn from the
New Research on Well-Being* (Princeton, NJ: Princeton University Press, 2010), 19.

59. Ibid.

60. John T. Cacioppo and Louise C. Hawkley, "Social Isolation and Health, with
an Emphasis on Underlying Mechanisms," *Perspectives in Biology and Medicine* 46,
no. 3 (2003): S44.

61. Bok, *The Politics of Happiness,* 17.

62. Ibid., 19.

63. John F. Helliwell, "Well-Being, Social Capital and Public Policy: What's
New?," *Economic Modelling* 20, no. 2 (2003): 331–60.

64. Bok, *The Politics of Happiness,* 20.

65. Ibid., 22.

66. Bruno S. Frey and Alois Stutzer, "Happiness Prospers in Democracy," *Journal of Happiness Studies* 1, no. 1 (2000): 82.

67. Ibid.

68. Zipora Magen, "Commitment Beyond the Self and Adolescence: The Issue of Happiness," *Social Indicators Research* 37, no. 3 (1996): 235–67.

69. Putnam, "Bowling Alone."

70. Pierre Bourdieu, "The Forms of Capital," in *Handbook of Theory and Research for the Sociology of Education,* ed. John G. Richardson (New York: Greenwood, 1986), 241–58.

71. See Amitai Etzioni, *The New Golden Rule: Community and Morality in a Democratic Society* (New York: Basic, 1996).

72. Amitai Etzioni, *From Empire to Community: A New Approach to International Relations* (New York: Palgrave Macmillan, 2004).

73. Layard, *Happiness,* 64.

74. Bok, *The Politics of Happiness,* 21–22.

75. Robert D. Putnam and David E. Campbell, *American Grace: How Religion Divides and Unites Us* (New York: Simon and Schuster, 2010), 490.

76. Ibid., 491.

77. Layard, *Happiness,* 72.

78. Putnam and Campbell, *American Grace,* 491–92.

79. Bok, *The Politics of Happiness,* 22. See also Kirk Warren Brown and Tim Kasser, "Are Psychological and Ecological Well-Being Compatible? The Role of Values, Mindfulness, and Lifestyle," *Social Indicators Research* 74, no. 2 (2005): 349–68.

80. Jeffrey C. Jacob and Merlin B. Brinkerhoff, "Values, Performance and Subjective Well-Being in the Sustainability Movement: An Elaboration of Multiple Discrepancy Theory," *Social Indicators Research* 42, no. 2 (1997): 171–204.

INDEX